CREATING A SUSTAINABLE WORLD

Past Experience/Future Struggle

Edited by

TRENT SCHROYER
and
TOM GOLODIK

©2006 by Trent Schroyer and Tom Golodik

Published by The Apex Press, an imprint of the
Council on International and Public Affairs
777 United Nations Plaza, Suite 3C
New York, New York 10017
Telephone/fax: 800-316-APEX (2739)
E-mail: cipany@igc.org
Web Page: www.cipa-apex.org

Library of Congress Cataloging-in-Publication Data

Creating a sustainable world : past experience/future struggle /
edited by Trent Schroyer and Tom Golodik.
 p. cm.
Collection of papers based on a lecture series organized by the
Institute for Environmental Studies at Ramapo College of New
Jersey.
Includes bibliographical references.
ISBN 1-891843-37-0 (alk. paper) -- ISBN 1-891843-36-2
 (pbk. : alk. paper)

 1. Sustainable development--Congresses. I. Schroyer, Trent. II.
Golodik, Tom. III. Ramapo College. Institute for
Environmental Studies.

HC79.E5C727 2006
338.9'27--dc22
                                    2005053036

Epilogue

Preface

WHY "WORLD" SUSTAINABILITY?

Trent Schroyer and Tom Golodik

IN THE SPRING OF 2002, the Institute for Environmental Studies at Ramapo College of New Jersey organized a Lecture Series on World Sustainability. The series' aim was to provide a forum on sustainability, involving anyone who wished to participate, and which would serve as a springboard for discourse both at the college and in local communities. Talks by a variety of speakers at that series were the starting point of an ongoing search for related materials, many of which are presented on the following pages. Overall, the rationale for this book can be said to mirror that given in the announcement for the Lecture Series:

"Since the Earth Summit in 1992, the world's nations have been committed to reconciling economic growth with environmental preservation by promoting "sustainable development." A strong program for sustainability is maintaining economic growth within the regenerative and absorptive capacities of the earth; not to do so diminishes the capacity of the planet to support living communities.

"Ultimately sustainability is a new historical insight because we need to understand how we have become trapped in ever higher levels of material consumption that correlates with a growing polarization of rich and poor. Only then will we be able to motivate people to experiment with new life-styles and act to implement the more efficient and self-reliant socio-economic forms that already exist. A strong program for sustainability means we transform our own levels of over-consumption and shrink our demands on other nation's environmental resources so that there is a just balance in international equity. . . .

"After September 11th, our lecture series has taken on a more serious mission. Our focus on "world sustainability" signals that we aspire to inform people about the sustainability option to the current "war on terrorism," which we think will only deepen world conflicts. When millions of people can use their intelligence in their own households and municipalities to wage a grassroots "war" on waste, environmental degradation, over-consumption, inefficiency, local unemployment, etc., we will all be part of the sustainability, peace and global justice movement.

This collection identifies two divergent paths that each promote a worldview based on the same root word—sustainability. When the global discourse about sustainability first began, it seemed to be a dialogue that engaged organizations and citizens from all parts of a global civil society. What soon emerged, however, was a second, very different approach—a dominant managed-market orientation. That has made the open dialogue between all concerned about sustainability more and more difficult. There remain points of agreement in that all recognize the Earth's resources are limited, the Earth's population growing and that, somehow, we have to set new rules for sustaining what has been called the 'triple bottom line' of economic, environmental and social well being.

For some, acceptance of the imperative of sustainability came from the humbling realization that we were very much a part of a fragile, intricately interconnected web. The search for new approaches to sustaining the Earth and its resources was driven by the recognition that while our ability to imagine our future might be boundless, we lived within very finite boundaries— a view best crystallized by the NASA photo of a blue-green planet against the black reach of space. That image offered the perspective necessary to distance ourselves from the intimate, but long unexamined, relationship with our home—the dawning understanding that this "spaceship" had limited resources that needed to be used wisely, considering not only the needs of those riding it today, but future "passengers."

For others, this same image—its wholeness, its finiteness—lent itself to the belief that the self regulating market, aided by satellite observations and world wide data processing would enable us to manage global complexity. In this view, what were seen as limits to Earth's resources by the first group could be overcome by science, technology and economic investments, allowing the substitution of new products for the old. In this view, we do not sustain the Earth so much as manage it for human utility. This view requires a commitment to ever improving scientific risk assessments in order to determine whether it is cost-effective to try to respond to global warming or environmental health costs.

As a result of these different agendas for the future, we must educate ourselves about the whole spectrum of sustainability actions and the impacts of each—even if some of what we learn will be disillusioning. In that spirit, Ramapo College of New Jersey has been very much a part of the discourse on sustainability, having recognized its importance more than 30 years ago when it created a major in Environmental Studies. Since undertaking this course of study, Ramapo College has graduated over 1,200 students with Environmental majors. In addition, over the last ten years, the college has sponsored a continuous series of lectures, increasingly focused on sustainability.

The planning for the lecture series was undertaken by the directors of the Institute for Environmental Studies with the help of other members of the Environmental Studies Faculty at Ramapo College. Howard Horowitz, Co-Director of the Institute, was central to the organization of lectures and workshops for the last five years. Special thanks is due Tula Tsalis who was one of the original movers of this learning process, from the Earth Summit in Rio to organizing the conferences and editing the manuscript.

Our Ramapo College colleagues whose participation made this book possible are Michael Edelstein, William Makofske, Wayne Hayes, Henry Frundt, Eric Karlin, Geoff Welch, Chuck Stead, Mitch Kahn, Eric M. Wiener, Mary Anne Carletta, Emma C. Rainforth, Daniel Somers Smith, Robert Corman, Robert A. Scott, James Quigley, Donald Wheeler, John Kenselaar, Sherrill Cox, and Carmela Federico,

We are in debt to the wisdom and support of Ward Morehouse, Wolfgang Sachs, Robert Engler, Peter Montague, Ruth Caplan, Kristin Dawkins, Gene Bazan, Diane Dillon Ridgley, Joan Gussow, Michael Shuman, Stuart Auchincloss, Catherine Keller, Miriam McGillis, Alanna Hartzok, Rob Young, Debra Harry, Dave Lewit, Glenn Scherer, Kathy Lawrence, Fred Curtis, Siddhartha, and David Dembo.

Part One

CRITIQUES OF
SUSTAINABLE DEVELOPMENT

Introduction to Part One

THE INCLUSIVE
DEMOCRACY PROMISE OF
THE EARTH SUMMIT

Trent Schroyer

THE UNITED NATIONS CONFERENCE ON ENVIRONMENT AND DEVELOPMENT (UNCED), or the Earth Summit, held in Rio in 1992, promised inclusive, democratic participation and established discourse processes that pointed forward to a 'to-be-formed' world community concerned about sustainability. This promise was seen as a particular fulfillment of the philosopher's dream of a universal community that would establish an open and impartial process of communication and discourse. This open-ended discourse would aspire to have a transparency that was free from constraints and deceptions. Institutionalization of these inclusive discourse principles in the Earth Summit was begun when processes of consultation, information sharing, and participation in decision making were articulated. These pointed forward to a unique world sustainability community that examined and acted on the principle of sustainable development, using the best available means and strategies for achieving it.

To quote from Chapter 23.2 of Agenda 21, the comprehensive plan of action to be undertaken in every area in which humans impact on the environment:

"One of the fundamental prerequisites for the achievement of sustainable development is broad public participation in decision-making. In the more specific context of environment and development, the need for new forms of participation has emerged. This includes the need of individuals, groups and organizations to participate in environmental impact assessment procedures and to know about and participate in decisions, particularly those which potentially affect the communities in which they live and work. Individuals, groups and organizations should have access to information relevant to environment and development held by national authorities, including information on products and activities that have or are likely to have a significant impact on the environment, and information on environmental protection measures."

These same symbolic principles of inclusivity and democracy were incorporated in a variety of different ways throughout Agenda 21. One was an emphasis on "cross-sectorial organizing" of all major groups. This was reinforced on so many levels to the point that it gave rise to entirely new expectations for the integration of previously excluded groups into the planning and monitoring of sustainability plans.

A deliberative process open to such a wide variety of peoples also made it essential that the U.N. have a unit that incorporated the agreements that were worked out in UNCED and provide mechanisms and procedures for carrying them out. A new institution, the U.N. Commission on Sustainable Development (CSD), emerged as the first reform of the U.N. system since its origin. The CSD would be a focus for a "politics of influence and shame" that would constantly express to the U.N. General Assembly the harmful practices that had to be eliminated. And the CSD would, for the first time, potentially have a capacity to challenge the contribution-based voting of the Bretton Woods institutions—one of the goals of UNCED.

Offsetting those hopes was the underlying fact that Agenda 21 was a voluntary agreement and not a binding treaty. The ultimate functioning of the CSD and its mechanisms and procedures was dependent on the inter-governmental process which is tied into the power politics of the international system of nation-states. When we bring the realities of the system of states into focus, the great expectations of UNCED begin to be seen in a very different frame. This analysis is covered in the following essays in Section One.

Those who participated in the Earth Summit had high hopes for realizing the promises that the Earth Summit seemed to offer. A decade later, many things had become clearer, or had surfaced from behind the scenes. These made the initial hopes for procedural democracy in the Earth Summit's process, described in the paragraphs above, seem naive. The emerging power of the corporate-state and the use of polarizing and distortive propaganda had, by this time, already hijacked the formation of a world sustainability process.

An Introduction to Part One Essays

Trent Schroyer separates "world sustainability" from "sustainable development" by showing how an ideology of sustainable development was created at the Earth Summit in 1992 and nailed down at the Rio + 10 Summit in Johannesburg in 2002.

In the interval between those two world summits, neo-liberal advocates for global market integrations, direct foreign investment, and primacy of property rights became dominant. But the victors also systematically marginalized those who were primarily concerned with social justice, equity and sustaining of local communities and ecology.

Vandana Shiva describes the corporate and government takeover of the Johannesburg Summit for commercial interests, to the detriment of the assembled polities and solidarities. Her record of this gross sell out of the second Earth Summit tells the story of the undermining of a world sustainability discourse by agents of the corporate-state.

Wolfgang Sachs et al. argue that since the mid-70s we have used more natural resources than the carrying capacity of the Earth permits. We now over shoot the Earth's carrying capacity by 30 to 50 percent. It is clear from his essay that much of the gloriously touted market efficiency and productivity is built on quicksand. For this reason the modern 'development' model is historically obsolete, and the era of copycat development as the salvation for the South is over. At the same time, though, the modern model is a dead end.

Today, Southern countries have an historic opportunity to turn 'underdevelopment' into an asset, because they are not locked into a fossil fuel production-and-consumption structure as the North is (especially the U.S.). To balance inequalities, Northern countries must take responsibility for their "environmental footprint," or the impacts of their excessive material throughput on Southern nations, and reduce their extractions of resources, food, and cheap commodities, from the Third World. This means rethinking the impacts of 'free trade' on national economies and regenerating local and regional economies with special attention to self-sufficiency in foodstuffs, and the continued role that a subsistence and social economy can play. Being "developed" by forcible market integration into the world economy is not sustainability.

Peter Montague critiques sustainable development from the point of view of the emergent field of ecological economics and has produced an essay that explicates and extrapolates Herman Daly's *Beyond Growth*. Ecological economics shows there is no way to continually expand the volume of energy used and resources consumed, no matter how efficient such processes become. To the fundamental political economic problems of efficiency and redistribution, it is now essential to recognize, as Daly argues in *Beyond Growth*, that "scale" is now a systematic policy issue that must be included in assessments of sustainability at all levels. What is at stake here is economic fairness and the viability of democratic governance itself, because national governments cannot control the destiny of their people when the independent actions of outside economic institutions and investors can so markedly influence national policy.

FROM SUSTAINABLE DEVELOPMENT TO DEVELOPING SUSTAINABILITY

Trent Schroyer

THE BRITISH JOURNAL *The Ecologist* reduced the Earth Summit's concept of "sustainable development" to a syllogism in their book *Whose Common Future?*[1] (a response to the publication in 1988 by the Bruntland Commission of *Our Common Future*[2]):

- Poverty causes environmental destruction and wealth cures it
- Development helps relieve poverty and creates wealth
- Therefore: Development helps cure environmental degradation!

The Ecologist was implying that the Commission's offering was a simplistic expression of market environmentalism that was totally incorrect. Market environmentalism is a modern version of the enclosure movements of early centuries which ignores the principle that sustaining the Earth requires sustaining the commons. Ultimately, the point was that the concept of "sustainable development" does not make sense when it confuses the spheres of economics and ecology.

Such a term is called an 'amoeboid word'[3] by the German linguist Uwe Porksen—it denotes "no-thing," has no content, and requires expert knowledge and extrapolations to show how economic advancement can result in ecological advantages. Like George Orwell's "newspeak," it is an artificial technical idealization, sanctioned by the state, but without historical reference. Orwell's characters chant 'war is peace, peace is war,' while we recite 'sustainable development, development that is sustainable.' In using the term, are we linguistically simulating a globalization laboratory that colonizes as it universalizes?

Has 'Sustainable Development' Become a Colonizing Ideology?

While preparations for the 1992 Earth Summit were going forward, so were the negotiations for the World Trade Organization (WTO). The promises of the first were soon to be overshadowed by the forces of the second. Agenda 21, the action plan that came out of the Earth Summit, was retroactively accommodated to WTO rules for extracting capital from all resources and communities of the earth. The contradictions of these two sets of global procedural rules were not entirely recognized in the early 1990s. Only gradually did we realize that sustainable development (hereafter "SD") had merged with an accelerated market environmentalism as part of economic globalization.

Voices of people directly affected by SD projects were heard at the World Sustainability Hearings, held parallel to the 2002 Summit on Sustainable Development, also known as Rio + 10. Farmers, forest dwellers, fisher folk, women and other groups from all over the world shared their first-hand experience since the 1992 Summit.[4] Their testimony, excluded from the official Johannesburg summit, portrayed a grim record of colonization:

> "Witnesses and panelists at the Hearings told stories of their battles for ecological protection and social equity at home. Speaker after speaker described how governments were failing their people nationally and internationally, talking about the damage done by globalization to the environment and human rights, and about the need for corporate accountability. . . . The general perspective . . . seemed to be that it's the fault of the usual suspects: special interests, powerful corporations, corruption in high places, and corporate-controlled media."[5]

This people's tribunal demonstrated that the basic premise of SD was incorrect, that without input and constant procedural monitoring by grassroots communities and civil society organizations, SD becomes an outright fraud. Many serious efforts by civil society are outflanked by financial and free trade arrangements which substitute corporate-state agendas for local/regional needs. Only those who are free to speak truth to power and who can network and lobby at the international and national levels can help bring about a more appropriate form of policy formation. But these voices have been increasingly pushed outside of the official decision making processes and become counter discourses trying to shape democratic spaces however they can.

There are actually two general frames for discussing SD. First are the diverse strategies of corporate SD for integrating market-guided economic growth and free trade into the world economy to eradicate poverty and to preserve the environment. Second is an affirmation of wider procedures and open discourse that insists upon strong reforms to secure the commons and elevate human and community rights over trade rights. We call this claim for wider discourse and capabilities[6] for self-determination "world sustainability" (WS).

When we talk about WS, we are concerned not only with getting our metabolism with nature right but also with maintaining an ethos that honors evidence and truthfulness, of public accountability and transparency in which legitimate democratic discourse and political action can change the rules and establish human rights.

The following is a critique of what happened to incorporate SD into the frame of corporate globalization. Reconstructing the history from the Earth Summit to the Rio + 10 conference in Johannesburg brings into focus the excluded discourse of the many local/regional voices. Only these counter discourses can restore the stakeholder dimension by asserting the increasing importance of stronger international reforms and political and cultural self-determination to the SD planning process.

Let's return to the beginning to tell this story.

World Preparations for the Earth Summit

Preparations for the United Nations Conference on Environment and Development (UNCED) between 1989 and 1992 involved a set of actors that constituted a pluralistic world. Maintaining this diversity in cultural, geopolitical and sectorial actors is essential for world sustainability.

UNCED, or the Earth Summit, was two and one-half years in the making with preparatory meetings in Kenya (August 1990), Geneva (March and April 1991) and New York (March and April 1992). One hundred and twenty national reports of the five regional economic commissions and additional reports from international and national non-governmental organizations (NGOs)[7] had been submitted to these preparatory sessions. Over 24 million pages of documentation were accumulated at Prep-Com 4, where 85 percent of the Agenda 21 text was drafted.

Other international groups gathered prior to Rio to formulate inputs, including:

- Women's Environment and Development Organizations (WEDO) at a World Congress in Miami in November 1991.
- The Eminent Persons Meeting in Tokyo at the same time.
- The Second Ministerial Conference of Developing Countries on Environment and Development met in Malaysia and produced the Kuala Lumpur Declaration calling for negotiations on financial resources.
- The member countries of the Organization for Economic Cooperation and Development (OECD) met together prior to

UNCED to co-ordinate their interests, vowing to contribute 0.7 percent of their gross national product to overseas aid.

■ A world conference of indigenous peoples took place one week before UNCED and produced the Charter of Indigenous People's that affirmed the right of self-determination.

These preparatory processes from all components of a pluralistic world fed into Rio in 1992. It was seen as the historic opportunity to influence consensus building around the previously separated issues of preservation of the environment and economic development.

Attending the world event were 114 heads of state and diplomats from 182 countries—more than were officially members of the United Nations organization itself at that time. Voices from these powerful institutions and groups celebrated it as a turning point.

The complexity of the event created furious energy, but it was ultimately as illusory as Rio Centro, where the official summit met, which was constructed on top of a drained wet land and where the newly built road from the Airport was planned to hide massive poverty areas from the official state delegates. In a similar way, the Earth Summit's final outcomes were in deep denial of ecological and social justice issues that were never confronted.

The Promises of the Earth Summit: Inter-Governmental Agreements

There were five official results of the inter-governmental process and only two of those were signed treaties—the Convention on Climate Control and the Convention on Biological Diversity. The other three—The Rio Declaration, the Statement of Forest Principles, and Agenda 21—were agreed to in principle by consensus.

The climate change agreement was a coordinated response to the growing trend of global warming attributed to the combustion of fossil fuels and large scale deforestations. However, when the process got concrete by moving beyond statements of principle and began to add regulations about timetables and targets, the opposition—especially that of the United States—blocked the attainment of this goal. This opposition has continued with the current Bush administration's rejection of the Kyoto Protocol's use of the market to reduce greenhouse emissions.[8]

The administration of Bush *père* refused to sign the bio-diversity treaty, because it gave priority to sustaining nature over intellectual property rights on one hand and it would have contradicted the international free trade dispute process on the other. The elder Bush's defense of corporate interests as "the American Way of Life" was based on claims that the science of climate control was not "sound science."[9] For those who attended the Earth Summit, Bush's statement that "the American way of life is not up for negotiation" was the nadir of the event and exposed the arrogance that is confused for virtue by recent American administrations.

Dominance of corporate interests was justified by statements about "efficiency" and economic rationality and expressed most blatantly in President Bush's opposition to the Rio Declaration on Environment and Development. In retrospect it was widely thought these 27 "ethical" norms were hopelessly weak. A follow up conference held at the U.N. in 1993 focused on "Ethics and Agenda 21" because it was recognized that there was not enough normative coherence in the Rio Declaration to guide the synthesis of facts in any implementation of policy.[10] Nonetheless President Bush's "Interpretive Statements for the Record" rejected the weak Rio Declaration and stated again the primacy of U.S. interests. These U.S. postures essentially blocked expectations of the G-77 to have the poorer countries "right to development" backed up by adequate financial resources. The final prose of the Rio Declaration did not meet expectations for a "New Earth Charter," but it drew strong criticism from the Bush administration anyway. At no point was the creation of a strong Earth Charter allowed. This was true even in 1999, when a Global Compact was presented at the World Economic Forum in Davos, Switzerland.

Debate about preservation of forests could not be finished at Rio. The resulting Declaration of Principles on Forests was presented as a "Non-Legally Binding Statement" which critics claimed was weaker than pre-existing agreements. Part of the problem were the demands of poorer countries for compensation for the conservation of their forests—as they would be unable to use them as resources for their own economic development. Rather than affirming their ecological equity as a critique on Northern over-consumption, Southern nations were sucked into the "catch up development" craze, as the Sachs *et al.* memo below explains.[11]

However, the 40 chapters of Agenda 21 were actually a laundry list of all the possible actions toward sustainability and expressed an inclusive world comprehensiveness of policy and action plans. But it too lacked normative coherence and the many contradictory proposals remain in a composite that is given direction only by the key chapters that stress "wealth creation" and "free trade and investment." It was also significant that much original opposition to the final draft of Agenda 21 was focused on Chapter 33, the chapter on financial resources. Greeted by some as an "almost revolutionary document," the comprehensive Agenda 21 proposals included recognition of the responsibility of the North to the South in terms of new financial resources. But these promises have neither been funded nor fulfilled.

Global Civil Society's UNCED:
Alternative Discourses at the Global Forum

For many individuals and organizations from civil society, the spirit of Rio was an event of incomparable solidarity that did not get expressed adequately. Like the '60s "Woodstock nation," all who participated were touched and transformed by the promises it brought to life. Those who participated in this spirit envisioned that the Earth Summit and the idea of sustainability would become a new metaphor and an emerging ethic for global cooperation and open discourse.

NGOs and citizens' organizations going to the Global Forum approached the official summit issues with diverse views. The Global Forum was held 30 kilometers away from the official event at Rio Centro and from this remote site they contested the official agreements that presented economic expansion as the principal means of achieving greater environmental protection.

The presence of thousands of people from all over the world, from every social sector, all intent on making a difference in Rio, created a unique global village. What was demonstrated by the Global Forum was that consensus building could be forged for world issues of governance via cooperative alliances within global civil society.

The Global Forum organized approximately 350 conferences and teach-ins on every conceivable topic during the two weeks in Rio. Indeed, these were constant springboards for renewed efforts at a politics of influence between the Global Forum and the official summit. The major Global Forum activity was an alternative treaty process designed to draft innovative agreements for a global governance system. These drew attention to issues that had been systematically denied by the official summit at Rio Centro—issues such as adjusting planetary equity in the interests of social justice. Alternative treaties enabled NGOs to publicize the innovative proposals, and to provide visions and programs for cross-sectorial dialogues and lobbying actions. The 46 alternative treaties that were drafted in, and after, Rio were attempts to confront the conflicts between environment and development that remained in the official documents and to critique the dominant interests that held sway at the inter-governmental event.[12]

NGOs came to Rio with position papers on women, trade, debt, sustainable agriculture, climate change, among others, and there encountered the difficult task of entering into dialogue with people who spoke different languages and did not share the same cultures. Northerners were often shocked to discover the depth of Southern skepticism, cynicism and opposition to the Northern self-interpretations of a global "we." This was most apparent in the Global Forum plenary session where a stalemate on approving a global standing committee showed resistance to any executive centralization. A hierarchy, or top down order, was not acceptable—there was more concern about constraints on local autonomy than solving problems of communication and coordination of action on a global scale.[13] Such skepticism to global centralization has continued into the World Social Forum process that began in 2000.

Another shock to Northern citizens' groups was the widely shared Southern perception that the official idea of sustainable development was a Trojan horse for Northern interests. The dominant Southern states accepted the "catch up development" that was based on the Northern model—and some NGOs mirrored that view, too. As Triq Banuri argued, the South missed the chance of pointing to historic models of local sufficiency as sustainability that predominated in many regions of the South.[14] Southern models of sufficiency could have been used to critique the unsustainability of Northern consumer lifestyles. This was a failure to distinguish the local and global in UNCED discourse and resulted in a confusion of local eco-systems being viewed from the viewpoint of global economic rationality. In this way, Southern negotiators backed into supporting the global enclosures of the local. The irony was that "catch-up" developmentalists of the South became an ally of the cynical economistic interests of the North, allowing the issue of balancing global equity to be avoided. It also implied that the Northern leadership in environmental issues was accepted without any real challenge to the North's destructive environmental footprint on the South.

Critics have pointed out many other omissions in the official UNCED documents—such as no systemic control on trans-national corporations (TNCs), no real limitation on military spending and the environmental impacts of military activities, and the failure to confront the problem of nuclear wastes. These omissions later included the huge failure between promises made at the Earth Summit and subsequent non-delivery of resources to implement Agenda 21.

Ultimately, the NGO Global Forum was an illusion that took too seriously the Agenda 21 norm for increased participation by community-based people's organizations. [15]

Inclusion of the Business Sector: The Real Trojan Horse

Another novelty of UNCED was its mobilization of the corporate sector to participate in UN affairs for the first time. Whereas this might have been a step toward an inclusive democracy, the influence that the corporations—especially the TNCs—exerted over the process was not fully documented until later. In retrospect, there is no doubt that they were able to weaken any effort to include regulation of business or financial institutions during the preparatory process for Agenda 21 and the other documents.

One story that can illustrate corporate power and long term planning acumen was the rapid reversal of the elder Bush's administration on the biodiversity treaty. While at first inclined to sign it, the Bush pulled back at the last moment saying that it "was important to protect our rights, our business rights." (William Reilly testimony before the House of Representatives' Committee on Foreign Affairs, July 28, 1992.) It turns out, as the business sector explained, that this was necessary in order not to undermine the United States—a phrase that could be read to mean American biotechnology corporate interests—at the ongoing General Agreement on Tariffs and Trade negotiations (which culminated in the formation of the WTO in 1995). At stake was the globalization of the U.S. patent laws, now in the form of intellectual property rights. No regulation of the biotechnology corporations could be tolerated. (Jonathan Plaut testimony before the House of Representatives' Committee on Foreign Affairs, July 21, 1992.)

This example is informative because it illustrates that the business sector's major interest at the Earth Summit was to ensure the elimination of any regulation of their activities. They accomplished this by promoting the Free Trade agreements that were then being negotiated and which they knew would be able to override many of the protections that the treaties were "securing" in Rio. Their aim in Rio was to limit any control of their autonomy. They secured this by becoming participants in all "learning forums"— which later became "best practice solutions." The biodiversity issue is crucial because it continued to be resisted by some states and resulted in the creation of a counter "Biosafety Protocol," which has as its premise use of the precautionary principle in complex cases. The efforts, energies, resources and public propaganda that has emerged to discredit this normative standard reveals what the real order of interests are—maximizing profit opportunities by corporations first and sustaining the planet secondly.[16] A moment's reflection reveals that the issue of sustainability is a world-scale precautionary principle. Opposition to one is also opposition to the other.

The TNCs were not only effective in blocking any proposals for their regulation, they were also able to eliminate most references to TNCs in the UNCED documents, just as they had been influential in eliminating the United Nations Center on Transnational Corporations and with it the Transnational Corporation Code of Conduct that had been worked out since the 1970s.[17] The line they pushed was that a self-regulating model of corporate responsibility must replace the command and control model of corporate accountability. But actual corporate practice was often to greenwash the corporate activities in the media while continuing extremely destructive "development" practices that they assumed would not get noticed.

For example, Monsanto proclaimed itself to be a huge supporter of "sustainable development" while pushing the genetically modified plants they developed and the specific herbicides they designed for the plants, as well as their recombinant bovine growth hormone, rBGH. They also support the Council for Biotechnology Information which is not about 'information' but about green-washing genetically modified organisms (GMOs). Of course, there were, and are today, corporations that are sincerely concerned about sustainability[18] but their voices were, and are, eclipsed by a majority who have promoted the principle that the bottom line is always first.

Critiques of "Free Trade" and Wealth Creation SD Strategies

The business "vision" at the Earth Summit derived from the claim that unless the Third World had access to global markets, sustainable development was not possible. Increasing aggregate economic growth is the only way, they claimed, to create the wealth essential to address poverty and restore the environment.

Greening economic growth meant to them that more trade and economic interdependence was better because this would force everyone to become more eco-efficient. Therefore, "trade, not aid" became the common goal for both less developed countries and transnational corporations. "Greening" meant full steam ahead for economic development because the markets themselves would eliminate destructive inefficiency.[19]

The very idea of promoting development through trade and calling it SD—as is done in Chapter One of Agenda 21—was condemned by ecologically oriented economists as promoting not "comparative advantage," as claimed, but only the interests of the more powerful trader.[20] A Global Forum alternative treaty questioned whether free trade was compatible with sustaining social communities, their natural environments, or even substantive democracy. In the Sachs memo below, developed for Rio +10, it is argued that productive eco-systems are the core assets for sustainable livelihoods and that the real barrier to sustainability is not money but community rights to protect these assets.

Other NGO treaties challenged the neo-liberal model of "free trade democracies" as internally unrealizable.[21] Instead they argued that alternative regional forms of trade would be more directly advantageous to localities. Likewise the International Federation for Alternative Trade (IFAT), a global group from all continents that included producers from developing countries and marketing and distribution organizations in consuming countries, shared this viewpoint. IFAT's objectives were to secure livelihoods in Third World countries and change unfair trading structures mainly through alternative markets for "organic foods," or "green" products.

Alternative forms of fair trade also emerged from eco-developments of indigenous resources, or organized twin trading by cooperatives and small producers of both North and South. Special relief efforts, such as Oxfam or Christian aid, created fair trading networks as part of their aid. Diffusion of information about such alternative trade networks continues to be part of all international civil society forums. Encouraging this kind of flexible evolution of trade practices is, however, systematically eliminated by the World Bank and the International Monetary Fund's so-called structural adjustment programs. After Rio + 10 these programs were called "poverty eradication" programs—a bit of cynical word magic that signals the propaganda goal.

The United Nations Development Program's (UNDP) 1992 Human Development Report, *Globalization with a Human Face*, reinforced the NGO trade critique when it stated that "world trade generally works to the benefit of the strongest" and that "in precisely those areas where developing countries have a competitive edge—in labor intensive manufacturing—the market rules are often changed to prevent free and open competition."

From the Ideology of "Sustainable Development" to Developing World Sustainability

The SD narrative does not recognize destructive "uneconomic" growth on sectors and regions.[22] Increasing economic throughput, or the volume of energy and resource used, is promoted without concern for specific uneconomic degradations. Instead, more self-regulating wealth creation is seen as primary for environmental restoration and poverty eradication—as an aggregate measure. In this view, SD is how to "eco-manage" the complexities of global ecology and economics with the appropriate technologies and techniques implicit in the "self-regulating" market system.

Ultimately, world sustainability is a learning process in which Northern countries, who have overdrawn on the bank of nature, must help create an equity balance essential to sustain poorer regions. Adjusting equity inequalities will necessitate contractions in rich countries' environmental footprints on poorer regions.[23] Creating an expanding awareness of the massive vulnerability of the world's poor majority is a first step. But only when the world sustainability movement has become a moral majority that challenges the entrenched indifference of the global middle class will it be effective. When norms such as the precautionary principle, the biosafety protocol, biodiversity, fair trade are widely affirmed it will be possible to reverse the empire building privilege that is now hidden behind a market environmentalism ideology.

In practice these world sustaining ethical principles get displaced by the massively reinforced primacy of financial investments and "free trade" as regulatory mechanisms. The real bottom line is challenging this idolatry of automatic money making as means and end. Culturally, world sustainability means that the good life has to go beyond the "goods life" because the promise of increasing affluence does not substitute for a degraded biosphere. More material affluence does not justify destruction of primal forests or biodiversity.

Although such arguments were presented at the Earth Summit, they became so marginalized by the Rio + 10 conference that the official implementation statement mentioned the WTO 46 times and the Rio summit only once. Vandana Shiva (in the next essay) describes how civil society walked out because the summit had been "hijacked" by corporate reps who wanted to impose property rights on natural resources and substitute private-public partnerships (U.N. Type II outcomes) instead of legally binding agreements. Corporate co-optation of the entire Johannesburg summit resulted in the reorientation of the main focus of poverty eradication to more economic regulations and the privatization of ecological systems.

Participatory debate was forced into separate "unofficial" channels including the meeting of the Third World Parliamentary Forum,[25] that projected a list of proposals for real world reforms that must be achieved to move toward sustainability. An abbreviated list includes:

- Stop privatizations of commons
- Affirm all international environmental agreements
- Affirm U.N. target of 0.7 percent of GDP for official development assistance
- End world debt and suppressions of financial speculation (Tobin tax on 'hot money' flows)
- Require corporate accountability in compliance with labor and environmental standards
- Shrink the WTO so that it can not override multilateral environmental agreements (MEAs)
- End military globalization and affirm resolution of conflicts under U.N.
- Stop privatization of sustainability and reform Type II U.N. proposals
- Guarantee free access to water
- Achieve gender and minority rights
- Guarantee rights to culture and language.

Most of these proposals are actually a re-ordering of the global governance norms. They are aimed at the governance transformations which will enable localities and polities to be more capable of participation in self-development and world policy inputs.

However, similar norms have been asserted in other contexts, too. For example, the counter G-8 summits, or as they were originally called in the U.K. and the U.S., The Other Economic Summits, have been taking place every year since 1985. They always brought together leaders and citizen organizations that challenge the G-8 plans.[26] In some ways, these events were actually the beginning of what has been named the anti-globalization, or alternative globalization, movement. These events are anticipations of the reforms and mechanisms that are necessary for widening discourse for world sustainability. They are manifestos of the excluded, the voice of "the other," for a change, and they represent the majority of the Earth's population and resources so much more than the club of seven rich nations.

The World Social Forums have met five times since 2000. They have picked up the mission of creating world discourse about necessary reforms and strategies for self-determination and world sustainability. At the 2005 World Social Forum in Porto Allegro, Brazil, a statement emerged, trying to express the latent consensus of this huge event, attended by 200,000 people:

- Debt cancellation
- Adoption of the Tobin tax on international financial transfers
- Dismantling of tax havens
- Promotion of equitable forms of trade
- A guarantee on the sovereignty of a country's right to produce affordable food and police its food supply
- Implementation of anti-discrimination polices for minorities and women
- Democratization of international organizations, which includes moving the United Nations headquarters far South of its current New York location.[27]

Again these proposals are naming the actions that will enable the self-development and self determination that is essential for inclusive democratic discourse.

All these currents flow into the world sustainability movement as public critiques of market regulation of political, social and natural spheres and as affirmations of non-violent discourse and resistance as a means for policy formation and cultural affirmations. That is not just a concern for sustainable ecology but also for sustaining political, social and cultural autonomy to make public discourse possible. World sustainability rests upon open procedural democracy.[28]

Why World Sustainability Is Imperative: A Philosophic Coda

Hannah Arendt's classic, *The Human Condition*, captures today's eco-managed economic globalization in her phrase the "unnatural turning loose of the natural" into the human world. This begins as the result of a two-fold alienation from the Earth; first as the directing of cosmic forces into the Earth (e.g. nuclear power) and secondly, in the unbinding of economic processes from any cultural or political restraints. Both of these "unnatural releases of the natural" result from a loss of the balance that comes from being part of nature and from having a human world which maintains normative limits by human reasoning. When this harmony is lost and the endless processes of a consumer society are used to idealize the good life—the balanced human condition as comprehended by the ancient Greeks has been undermined.

In these reflections, Arendt makes a distinction that is fundamental for a world facing a combined ecological and economic crisis. Arendt's distinction between "work" and "labor" sees the labor process imposed on us by our bodies and the recurrent cycle of all biological life.[29] In labor, the human metabolism with nature is mediated by an endless incorporation of matter and energy into the body and the body-politic, for instance, as consumption. Endless housekeeping redirects the processes of growth and decay and maintains the human world against the intrusions of nature—pollution, growth beyond carrying capacity, etc.[29] Without rational judgments that separate how, as part of nature, we are inseparably linked to the endless metabolism and waste elimination and how this differs from the unique world building of human work, we can not recognize the differences between necessity and limits of utility. Without this judging capacity we are not able to make assessments or take actions about what is sufficient for sustaining human existence. Consequently we lose our world.

By transposing both labor and work into moments of a "self-regulating" process in which the costs of material production on the one hand and the ecological limits of production do not have to be reconciled, we go beyond the human condition and aspire to be gods in our evolution with nature. On a global scale, the legitimizing of an unlimited wealth creation process creates the illusion of greater integrations of economic and technical systems—now called "sustainable development." This progress invalidates the role of culturally informed common sense and political judgment essential for self-development and self-determination. The ever widening sphere of commercialization takes a quantum jump in the current world-wide production and consumption accompanied by presumptions of global eco-management. The greatest human power—socio-political action—is increasingly overwhelmed by the "unnatural growth of the natural" and we lose the capacity to maintain our world.

This change from public mediation of wealth creation to processual economizing puts human activity on the level of all animal life and abstracts away the human institutional configurations and cultural ends that define "value" in any particular socio-cultural world. In other words, turning over regulation of the human-nature interaction to market regulation is a loss of public and social capacities. Arendt's reflections converge with Karl Polanyi's critique of formal economics as the utopian "disembedding" of socio-economic practices from human institutional regulations.[30] Arendt's reflections supplement Polanyi's substantive economics by showing how the modern economistic abstraction of work actually reduces the word "work" into what had always been separated linguistically as "labor." What was understood as work—embedded world-building activity—has been naturalistically reduced to processual life reproduction—labor—and has transformed the political and social person into a job-holding "worker." The consequences are loss of the multiple interconnections that tie human life to community and traditional culture and a reduction of human existence to economic survival which is nothing if not a loss of world.

Arendt's characterization is withering:

> "For even now, laboring is too lofty, too ambitious a word for what we are doing, or think we are doing, in the world we have come to live in. The last stage of the laboring society, the society of job holders, demands of its members a sheer automatic functioning, as though individual life had actually been submerged in the over-all process of the species and the only active decision still required of the individual was to let go . . . to abandon his individuality, the still individually sensed pain and trouble of living, and acquiesce in a dazed, "tranquilized," functional type of behavior. The trouble with modern theories of behaviorism (read 'economic rationality') is not that they are wrong but that they could become true."[31]

This evolutionary-biological image of human life functions like a collective amnesia about the human condition and constitutes a world alienation—the metabolic life-orientation of the modern survivor in the economic jungle of wage laboring and consumerism. The current corporate culture expresses this logic in unprecedented clarity. No affiliation with any social or moral community is necessary or legitimate, but this has been intrinsic to "development" since its beginnings:

> 'The smashing up of social structures in order to extract the element of labor from them' was and remains the main purpose of economic development . . . In order to achieve 'freedom of contract' all organic forms such as kinship, neighborhood, profession, and creed have to be liquidated if they claim the allegiance of the "economic individual."[32]

The modern economic individual must be economically rational and is "liberated" from any obligatory moral sense of social obligation. Only the bottom line for the property holder is primary; "shareholder" is a valid status for all. Civil liberties have been limited to protecting the private sphere and political autonomy is not necessary for the person or the republic. With neo-liberalism neither personal or civic autonomy is essential and social justice is one more choice that may or may not be made by private citizens.

Thus when we discourse "world sustainability" we are concerned not only with getting our metabolism with nature right but also with maintaining an ethos of evidence and truthfulness, of public accountability and transparency in which legitimate democratic discourse and political action can change the rules and establish human rights.

Endnotes

[1] The Ecologist, *Whose Common Future: Reclaiming the Commons* (Philadelphia, New Society Publishers, 1993).

[2] Harlem Brundtland, *Our Common Future: World Commission on Environment and Development* (New York, Oxford, 1987).

[3] Uwe Porksen, "Scientific and Mathematical Colonization of Colloquial Language," Vol. 81, No. 3, 1988, *Biology Forum.*

[4] See Earth Island Institute, *World Sustainability Hearing: Putting a Human Face on Globalization,* http://www.earthisland.org/wosh/aboutwosh.html.

[5] "World Sustainability Hearing Special Report," *Earth Island Institute Spring Journal,* 2003 Vol.18, No. 1.

[6] See Amartya Sen, *Inequality Reexamined* (Cambridge, MA, Harvard University Press,1992) pp.110-111, 150.

[7] In United Nations terminology, "NGOs" name the organizations that citizens make in the third sector of civil society. But over the years it has become clear that these organizations do participate in creating "governance" and therefore the name is misleading. Other terms such as "citizens organization" or "civil society organizations" are the alternative and thus "CSOs" are more appropriate.

[8] See Donald A. Brown, *American Heat: Ethical Problems with the United States' Response to Global Warming* (Lanham, MD, Rowland & Littlefield Publishers, 2002).

[9] See Stauber and Rampton's latest book, *Weapons of Mass Deception* (Tarcher/Putnam, 2003) and *Trust Us, We're Experts: How Industry Manipulates Science and Gambles with Your Future* (Tarcher/Penguin, 2001).

[10] The book that records some of these perspectives is Noel J. Brown & Pierre Quiblier (editors), *Ethics & Agenda 21: Moral Implications of a Global Consensus* (New York, U.N. Publishers, 1994).

[11] Tari Banuri "UNCED as a Tale of Two Cities" in Wolfgang Sachs (editor), *Global Ecology* (London, Zed Books, 1993).

[12] Robert Pollard *et al.* (editors), *Alternative Treaties: Synergistic Processes for Sustainable Communities and Global Responsibility.* See http://habitat.ic.org/treaties/index.html.

[13] See "Introduction" to Trent Schroyer (editor), *A World that Works: Building Blocks for a Just and Sustainable Society* (New York, Bootstrap Press, 1997), pp. 4-5 for an analysis of this event.

[14] Tari Banuri, "UNCED as a Tale of Two Cities' in Wolfgang Sachs (editor), *Global Ecology* (Atlantic Highlands, New Jersey, Zed Books, 1993), pp. 49-67.

[15] See Agenda 21, Chapter 23:2 (http://www.iisd.org/rio+5/agenda/agenda21.htm).

"One of the fundamental prerequisites for the achievement of sustainable development is broad public participation in decision-making. . . . This includes the need of individuals, groups and organizations to participate in environmental impact assessment procedures and to know about and participate in decisions, particularly those which potentially affect the communities in which they live and work. Individuals, groups and organizations should have access to information relevant to environment and development held by national authorities, including information on products and activities that have or are likely to have a significant impact on the environment, and information on environmental protection measures."

[16] See "The New Uncertainty Principle," *Scientific American*, January 2001.

[17] See Tom Athanasiou, *Divided Planet: The Ecology of Rich and Poor*, Boston, Little Brown, 1996, p. 199ff.

[18] See http://www.ceres.org/coalitionandcompanies/principles.php. Fifty corporations have joined the The Coalition for Environmentally Responsible Economies (C.E.R.E.S.) a coalition of investors, public pension trustees, foundations, labor unions, and environmental, religious and public interest groups and believe that globally sustainable economic activity must be environmentally responsible. CERES' mission is to encourage companies, in cooperation and collaboration with CERES, to endorse and practice the CERES Principles. Endorsing the CERES Principles represents a commitment for business to make continuous environmental improvement and to become publicly accountable for the environmental impact of all its activities.

[19] See Stephan Schmidheiny with the Business Council for Sustainable Development, *Changing Course: A Business Perspective on Development and the Environment* (Cambridge, MA, The MIT Press, 1992).

[20] The most important critique of this dogma was Herman Daly, the head of the environmental program at the World Bank who resigned and wrote *Beyond Growth* (Boston, Beacon Press, 1996) which became a seminal work for the development of the new field of ecological economics.

[21] NGO treaties such as *Trade and Sustainable Development, Debt Treaty,* and the *Treaty on the People of the Americas* were prophetic in their critiques.

[22] See Herman Daly's *Sustainable Economic Development* in Norman Wirzba (editor), *The Essential Agrarian Reader* (Washington D.C., Shoemaker & Hoard, 2003), p. 62ff. An earlier version of this essay was given to the World Bank in April of 2002 and records that Daly's efforts to ground sustainability in a new paradigm of Ecological Economics is ongoing since his resignation from the bank and publication of his *Beyond Growth: The Economics of Sustainable Development, op. cit.*

Daly comments that the expansion of the economy to include the earth's ecology is economic imperialism, or what I will simply name economism.

[23] A short definition of sustainability is to keep the volume of human extraction and emissions in balance with the regenerative and absorptive capacities of nature. But ecological balancing is only part of the meaning of sustainability. The ecology crisis has to be linked to the crisis of international economic justice where sustaining equity of the South is essential. Sustainability is a unified response to both the environmental crisis and the crisis of international justice. This perspective is developed in a major study of how an entire country can reduce its "environmental footprint" on the third world. This is presented in English as Wolfgang Sachs, Reinhard Loske, and Manfred Linz *et al., Greening the North* (New York, Zed Books, 1998).

[24] Type two partnership outcomes became essential at the Rio + 10 summit to save a summit where corporations had become central. See Kenny Bruno and Joshua Karliner, *Earthsummit: The Corporate Takeover of Sustainable Development* (Oakland, CA, Food First Books, 2002), p. 59ff.

[25] World Parliamentary Forum (http://www.forumparlamentarmundial.rs.gov.br) Declaration on the Rio + 10 Summit Johannesburg, 26 August–4 September 2002.

[26] See Trent Schroyer (editor), *A World that Works: Building Blocks for a Just and Sustainable Society* (New York, Bootstrap Press, 1997) for a record of the perspectives brought to the 1997 G-8 in Denver.

[27] "World Social Forum: The Consensus of Porto Alegre?" Inter Press News Agency, January 31, 2000 at moderator@portside.org.

[28] See Jürgen Habermas, *The Inclusion of the Other: Studies in Political Theory* (Cambridge, MA, The MIT Press, 1999).

[29] Hannah Arendt, *The Human Condition* (Garden City, N.Y., Doubleday, 1958). Hannah Arendt's claim that all European languages discriminate between "labor" and "work" indicates a dimension of the bio-social world that is totally ignored in social theory. While all modern social theories of progress project "work" as the form-giving fire and nature as the object and resource for human production, the endless recurrent necessities of sustaining biological life is lost in the modern image of "process" (of nature and economic production. We labor with our bodies and work with our hands; this fundamental difference is

documented by the universal existence of songs of labor that accompany the rhythmically ordered co-ordination of the body. (Songs of work are social and sung after work.) In the midst of labor, tools lose their instrumentality and function as means to an end; the certainty of the motion predominates. Labor constitutes the mediating inter-face of human world and nature and reflections on the meaning of this linkage for sustainable form of human survival is essential.

30 Karl Polanyi, *The Great Transformation* (Boston, Beacon Press, 1944).

31 Hannah Arendt, *The Human Condition, op. cit.,* p. 332.

32 Karl Polanji, *The Great Transformation, op. cit.,* p.163ff.

THE GREAT BETRAYAL:
WHY CIVIL SOCIETY WALKED OUT
AND WITHDREW CONSENT
FROM W$$D

Vandana Shiva

THE WORLD SUMMIT ON SUSTAINABLE DEVELOPMENT (WSSD) organized in Johannesburg from August 26 to September 4, 2002 was supposed to have been the Earth Summit II—ten years after the Earth Summit organized in Rio de Janeiro in 1992. Instead of Rio + 10, WSSD became Doha + 10. Ten months ago, the Ministerial Meeting of WTO was organized in Doha to salvage the WTO negotiations for a new enlarged round which had failed in Seattle due to citizen protest and a walkout by smaller countries who had been marginalized and excluded in the negotiations.

The implementation document of WSSD mentioned Doha and WTO 46 times at one stage and Rio only once. The draft had been introduced undemocratically by the United States and the European Union (EU), and with minor modifications was reintroduced by South Africa. There was no rebellion by governments against the surreptitious substitution of the sustainability agenda of Rio with the commercial and corporate agenda of WTO.

While the struggles of the poor in the South are related to their access and rights to natural resources—land, water and biodiversity and, hence, are intrinsically environmental and ecological struggles, WSSD was artificially presented as being about "poverty," not about the "environment." Globalization was then offered as the solution to poverty and decisions that were aimed at robbing the poor of their remaining resources and, hence, making them poorer, such as privatization of water, patenting of seeds and alienation of land, were being offered as measures for "poverty alleviation."

While the landless people and the movements against privatization marched for environmental and resource rights, globalization pundits kept repeating the mantra that the poor could not afford the "luxury" of their natural capital—they needed globalization. Globalizers do not see that globalization would rob the poor of their resources, make them the property of global corporations who would then sell water and seeds at high cost to the poor, thus pushing them deeper into poverty and over the edge of survival. During the PBS/BBC debate in which I participated, an industry spokesman clearly said that imposing private property rights on natural resources was their first priority. Globalizing the non-sustainable, unethical, iniquitous systems of ownership, control and use of natural resources was the main agenda at WSSD. The corporate hijack of the Earth Summit was the overall outcome—WSSD had mutated into W$$D.

But the implications go further than the hijack of one summit. These are dangerous trends for democracy. The substitution of multilateral legally binding agreements (Type I outcomes) by so called Type II outcomes in the form of public private partnerships are reflections of the privatization of states and privatization of the UN. The UN of "We, the People" was transformed in Johannesburg into the UN of "We, the Corporations." It appeared to be an auction house where the Earth herself was being put up for sale.

For us in civil society the Earth and one world is not for sale. That is why we withdrew our consent to the outcomes. When I had the opportunity to address the opening of the Civil Society forum with President Mbeki, I talked of how a global apartheid was being created by globalization after South Africa had fought its domestic apartheid.

President Mbeki made reference to the "global apartheid" in his draft political declaration at the end of the Summit. He had intended to say: "From the African continent, the cradle of humanity, we declare our responsibility to one another to the greater community of life, and to future generations. Meeting in the great African city of Johannesburg, which bears testimony to how industrial activity can change the environment in a matter of decades, we recall the great social and economic divides we have seen. This is a mirror of our global existence. If we do nothing, we risk the entrenchment of a form of global apartheid. Unless we act in a manner that fundamentally changes their lives, the poor of the world may lose confidence in the democratic systems to which we are committed seeing their representatives as nothing more than sounding brass or tinkling symbols."

The United States forced South Africa to change that text and remove all reference to "global apartheid." It thus contributed to the Summit being nothing more than "sounding brass or tinkling symbols." Only the governments of Norway and Ethiopia spoke up against attempts to make the multilateral environment agreements (MEAs) of Rio subservient to the trade rules of WTO and to dilute the proposals on corporate accountability that the Friends of the Earth campaign had successfully introduced in the text.

The only other "victory" was the women's alliance of ministers and the women's caucus preventing the removal of language relating to human rights in the context of health. In an age supposedly characterized by a clash of civilizations, the "clashing civilizations"—the United States, the Holy See, the Islamic countries were amazingly unified in seeing human rights in health as a threat to all shades and colours of patriarchy.

The tragedy was that all "victories" were merely success in preventing further regress—in terms of corporate accountability, multilateral environmental agreements and women's health rights. Instead of governments committing themselves to conserve water and defend and uphold water rights of all their citizens, they were selling off water in privatization deals, even though water is not the property of the state, but the commons cared for and shared by communities.

The privatization of water commons is illegal and illegitimate in common property law, natural law and moral law. This is why there were protests against water privatization throughout W$$D. That is why we withdrew our consent from the process. The police attacked one such protest on 24th August with stun bombs, injuring three people. During a TV debate, when a person displaced by a dam in Lesotho to bring water to South Africa's industry and towns called money generated by water privatization "blood money"—the head of South Africa's water supply said, "I love blood money that creates wealth."

Johannesburg made it clear that the real clash of cultures is between cultures of life and cultures of death. The anti-poverty movement, the justice movement, the sustainability movement, the ecology movement are actually one movement, the movement to defend the resources for sustenance and right to sustenance as a natural right—a right that is not given by states and cannot be taken away by greedy corporations. Corrupt deals on pieces of paper cannot extinguish that natural right. This is why in Johannesburg the movements had the moral power, not the corporations or governments. The moral degradation of the ruling elites was also evident in the privatization of life through biotechnology and patents.

Southern Africa has been made a victim of drought and famine under the joint impact of climate change and structural adjustment programs. The World Bank has forced countries to destroy and dismantle their food security systems. Faced with severe drought, lack of food security is creating conditions of famine. More than 300,000 people face starvation. Famine caused by western powers is now being used to market genetically modified organisms (GMOs) through food aid. Zambia, Zimbabwe and Mozambique have refused to accept GMOs in food aid. The WHO was mobilized to force African countries to accept GM food. The U.S. government made the force feeding of Africans with GMOs a major issue. When Colin Powell, representing President Bush, kept insisting on African countries importing GM food from the U.S. in the closing plenary of the Earth Summit, he was heckled by both NGOs and governments. African farmers had come to Johannesburg with alternatives—small scale, indigenous—based on farmers rights to land, water and seed.

The Earth Summit in Johannesburg in 2002, organized ten years after the Rio Summit which gave us the Convention on Biological Diversity and the Biosafety Protocol, was also reduced to a marketplace for pushing biotech on Africa. Hundreds of African farmers and government representatives condemned the U.S. pressure to force GM contaminated food aid. As civil society representatives from Africa stated, "We, African civil society groups, participants to the World Summit on Sustainable Development, composed of more than 45 African countries, join hands with the Zambian and Zimbabwean governments and their people in rejecting GE contaminated food for our starving brothers and sisters:

1. We refuse to be used as the dumping ground for contaminated food, rejected by the Northern countries; and we are enraged by the emotional blackmail of vulnerable people in need, being used in this way.

2. The starvation period is anticipated to begin early in 2003, so that there is enough time to source uncontaminated food.

3. There is enough food in the rest of Africa (already offered by Tanzania and Uganda) to provide food for the drought areas.

4. Our responses is to strengthen solidarity and self-reliance within Africa, in the face of this next wave of colonization, through GE technologies, which aim to control our agricultural systems, through the manipulation of seed by corporations.

5. We will stand together in preventing our continent from being contaminated by genetically engineered crops, as a responsibility to our future generation."

There were in fact not one Summit but many. There was the hijacked Summit at Sandton, the richest suburb in Johannesburg. To get to the Convention Centre we had to pass a shopping mall. It was an appropriate symbol of a summit that became a market for the Earth's resources. There was a limp official NGO gathering at NASREC. At a school, St. Stithians, was the celebration of the People's Earth Summit, and in Soweto children gathered for a Children's Earth Summit. The landless people and the small farmers had their own summits.

The alternative summits were planning a people-centered, earth-centered agenda for the future. In the midst of corruption, they were creating courage and truth. In the midst of hopelessness, they were creating hope. In the midst of violence, they were creating non-violence. When, as civil society, we walked away from the official process on September 4 and withdrew our consent, we did so in peace, in confidence and joy. We remembered Gandhi who was also assaulted on another September 11, and instead of responding to violence with violence, he shaped non-violence into the ultimate power of the weak and excluded. His *satyagraha*—the "force of truth"—was a different response from that to the events of the September 11, 2001. His *satyagraha* is our inspiration.

As we said in our statement issued from the People's Earth Summit, "We are outraged that the World Summit on Sustainable Development, instead of being an Earth Summit which reinforced the commitments made in 1992 in Rio de Janeiro to protect the Earth and strengthen the rights of the poor, has been subverted by governments and corporations for their own ends at the expense of civil society and the Earth.

"We refuse to collaborate with laws and systems of governance that deny the most fundamental birthrights of people and our responsibilities within the Earth community and future generations.

"Our collective civil society statement issued on September 4, when we disassociated ourselves with deep concern from the outcomes of the World Summit on Sustainable Development was simultaneously a declaration of our resolve and commitment.

"We celebrate our common resolve to strengthen the diversity of human cultures and the integrity of our Planet Earth. We reaffirm that 'another world is possible' and we shall make it happen."

FAIRNESS IN A FRAGILE WORLD: A MEMO ON SUSTAINABLE DEVELOPMENT

Wolfgang Sachs, et al.*

Introduction to the Memo

WHY DID WE DO A MEMORANDUM ON "Fairness in a Fragile World?" Because it is a memorandum in the literal sense of the word, meaning "speaking about what should be kept in mind, what should not be forgotten." The need for a memo implies that the official process we are going through is a process of forgetfulness. So a memorandum is needed to reflect on what tends to be forgotten, tends to get eroded, tends to fade away in the negotiations in this overall process towards Johannesburg.

Johannesburg does not promise much. I have never seen a UN conference so badly prepared as this Johannesburg Summit. I guess it is not exaggerating to say that so far nobody really knows what the agenda will be.

Why is there a Johannesburg Summit? There is only one reason. We had one in 1992—the UN Conference on Environment and Development—and now we have to have one ten years later because people ask "What is happening. What has resulted?" So there is no other choice than to have another Summit. There is no project or set of projects, which are supposed to be pursued, pushed, and brought to fruition by the time of Johannesburg.

But Johannesburg is not going to be an environment summit; it is going to be a development summit. The summit is not called "Environment and Development;" it is called "Earth Summit of Sustainable Development." In the code of international language, "sustainable development" basically means "chances of development" and of growth for Southern countries.

*The "Johhannesburg Memo" (Berlin: Heinrich Boel Foundation, 2002) is available in 16 languages at www.joburgmemo.org.

It is true that, in particular, the desires for justice and recognition of the South have been frustrated over the last ten years, so we can ask if it is justified to convene a summit on development? However, if that means that this summit forgets the new historic circumstances—that we have to learn to live within the finiteness of the biosphere—then it would be a sliding back before Rio.

It would be regression if things went in this way. We might see a summit which seems to be an environment summit, but which, on closer examination, does not show much awareness about the finiteness of the biosphere. It will be conducted as if this historic 1992 experience had not occurred! Therefore the need for a memo.

Livelihood Rights vs. Export-Led Growth

It is the challenge of Johannesburg to move beyond Rio, yet it is the danger of Johannesburg to regress behind Rio. The Rio Conference on Environment and Development strove to address two major crises: the crisis of nature and that of justice. Environmentalists—often from the North—were expected to take into account the desire of the majority of the world's citizens for a life beyond poverty and distress. By contrast, developmentalists—often from the South—were called upon to recognize the disastrous repercussions of a deteriorated nature base. Typically, environmentalists were seen to be opposing deforestation, chemical agriculture or expansion of power plants, while developmentalists were pushing for marketing timber, expanding food supplies or electrifying villages. Therefore, the Earth Summit aimed at integrating the environment and development agendas to liberate policy makers from the dilemma of either aggravating the crisis of nature by pushing for development or aggravating the crisis of justice by insisting on the protection of nature.

As it turned out, the Rio process fell short of fulfilling this ambition. How to respond to the desire for justice without upsetting the biosphere is still a puzzle for the 21st century. Of course, the fact that helping people and helping nature can go hand in hand has been demonstrated in many instances: in organic agriculture, in sustainable forestry and in resource-efficient industries as well. But on a macro-scale, the reconciliation of environment and development agendas remains light years away. Furthermore, if things are not brilliant with regard to the environment, they are worse when it comes to development. Despite the prominence of "development" in all the Rio documents, the demand of the South for recognition and equity has largely been frustrated during the past decade, reinforcing the fear of many Southern countries of falling further behind and remaining forever excluded from the blessings of the modern world.

Against this background, the South—and in particular South Africa—intend to transform Johannesburg into a development summit rather than an environment summit. While Rio was considered to be dominated by the North, it is hoped that Johannesburg will be the Summit for the South. Indeed, the conference title "World Summit for Sustainable Development" clearly reflects the intention to elevate "development" on the political agenda.

Yet, we believe that focusing on a development agenda as if the worldwide crisis of nature did not exist would signify sliding back behind Rio. It would be a regression of sorts, a rollback in the growing sensibility toward the finiteness of the natural world. And it would be a disservice to the South, since equity can no longer be separated from ecology. Instead, fulfilling the ambition of Rio requires the effective response to the demand for equity arising from the South, but in a manner which takes full account of the bio-physical limits of the Earth.

Some claim that humanity faces a choice between human misery and natural catastrophe. This choice is false. We are convinced that human misery can be eliminated without catalyzing natural catastrophes. Conversely, natural catastrophes can indeed be avoided without condemning people to a life of misery. Getting ready to meet this challenge, however, requires revisiting the technologies, the institutions and the world views that dominate the globe today.

Shrug Off Copycat Development

Partly through imposition, partly through attraction, the Northern development model has shaped Southern desires, offering tangible examples not only of a different, but of a supposedly better life. After decolonization, the newly gained political independence notwithstanding, the South set its sights on the industrial style of life and moved to catch up with the richer countries. And after the fall of communism, countries in Eastern Europe and Central Asia jumped to embrace capitalism and the glittery products of the free market. The winner takes all—including imagination. Where countries want to go, what they thrive to become, has most often not emerged naturally from their respective history and traditions, but has been forged by emulation of the Northern model. In this way, dignity has been identified with becoming modern, and international equity has been conceived as catching up with the developed countries.

The times of copycat development are over. Not because emulation of the North has not produced the desired results, but because the development model of the North is historically obsolete. Until the environmental crisis broke out, one could still attribute a certain degree of superiority to technological civilization. But it has become obvious that many of its glorious achievements are actually optical illusions. They essentially consist in transferring power from nature to man, leaving nature degraded and depleted in the process. As a consequence, natural systems, which serve as sources (water, timber, oil, minerals), sites (land for mines, settlements, infrastructure), and sinks (soils, oceans, atmosphere) for economic development are disrupted or seriously degraded.

Consider the environmental trends of the last 50 years: greenhouse-gas concentrations have surpassed tolerable levels, one-third of arable land has been degraded worldwide, just as one-third of tropical forests, one-fourth of the available freshwater, and one-fourth of the fish reserves have disappeared, not to mention the extinction of plant and animal species. Although it was just a minority of the world population which fed off nature for just a couple of generations, the feast is quickly coming to an end.

A dramatic situation has now emerged. At present, the world consumes more resources than nature can regenerate. Indeed, human activities have exceeded the biosphere's capacity since the mid-1970s. Since then, ecological overshoot has become the distinguishing mark of human history. In 1997, the overshoot amounted to 30 percent of the Earth's carrying capacity, or even to 40-50 percent if the needs of other living beings are taken into account. A large part of this overshoot is due to the extravagant use of fossil fuels, whose carbon waste would require a vast bio-productive surface area as a natural sink. Indeed, the global fossil fuel bonanza is mainly responsible for the quandary of conventional development. If, for instance, the present average carbon emissions per capita in the industrial world were extrapolated to all countries, the atmosphere would have to absorb five times more emissions than it can take—without even counting the expected increase in population. In other words, if all the countries of the globe followed the industrial model, five planets would be required to provide the carbon sinks needed by economic development. As humanity is left with just one, such an equity approach would become the mother of all disasters.

Consequently, there is no escape from the conclusion that the world's growing population cannot attain a Western standard of living by following conventional paths to development. The resources required are too vast, too expensive and too damaging to local and global ecosystems. Indeed, UNDP's 1998 Human Development Report emphasizes that "poor countries have to accelerate their consumption growth, but they must not follow the road taken by the rich and rapidly growing economies in the past half a century." While this is definitely good advice, it fails to highlight the window of opportunity which lies wide open for many countries of the Southern hemisphere.

As never before in history, there is an opportunity to transform "under-development" into a blessing. At the historical juncture where fossil-fuel dependency drives industrial societies into an impasse, economies that once were seen as lagging behind, suddenly find themselves in a favorable position. Not yet fully locked into an old-style model of industrialization, they have the prospect of leapfrogging into a post-fossil age, skipping the resource-intensive styles of production and consumption so dear to the industrial world. Thus the challenge they face is to choose a path that is both pro-environment and pro-poor. De-linking economic growth from an increase in resource use, and social progress from economic growth, can take them a long way into a sustainable future. In case of success, they could even reverse the usual master-student relationship, showing the North the way out of a self-defeating economic system. This window of opportunity, however, will close rather fast if the South continues to stick to copycat development. It will only remain open if the South musters the courage to envisage models of wealth that are different from those in the North.

Reduce the Footprint of the Rich

Without ecology there will be no equity in the world. Otherwise, the biosphere will be thrown into turbulence. The insight that the globally available environmental space is finite, albeit within flexible boundaries, has added a new dimension to justice. The quest for greater justice has always required containing the use of power in society, but now it also requires containing the use of nature. The powerful have to yield both political and environmental space to the powerless if justice is to have a chance. It is for this reason that, after the age of environmental innocence, the question of nature is inherent in the question of power, just as the question of power is inherent in the question of nature.

Power determines who occupies how much of the environmental space. Neither all nations nor all citizens use equal shares. On the contrary, the environmental space is divided in a highly unfair manner. It still holds true that about 20 percent of the world population consume 70-80 percent of the world's resources. It is those 20 percent who eat 45 percent of all the meat and fish, consume 68 percent of all electricity, 84 percent of all the paper and own 87 percent of all the automobiles. Above all, it is the industrialized countries which tap into the heritage of nature to an excessive extent; they draw on the environment far beyond their national boundaries. Their ecological footprint is larger than their own territories. In fact, the OECD countries surpass (in terms of ecology and equity) the admissible average size of such a footprint by a magnitude of about 75-85 percent. The wealthy 25 per-

cent of humanity occupy a footprint as large as the entire biologically productive surface area of the Earth.

Zombie Concepts

Especially when it comes to resource consumption, the conventional distinction between North and South is misleading. "North" and "South" are "zom-
bie categories"—concepts which clumsily survive in everyday speech despite
the fact they do not reflect political realities. The classical juxtaposition of the
G7 (plus Russia) and the G77 (plus China) still exists in international fora,
but it fails to represent the political dynamics of the real world. The collective "South" comprises the most heterogeneous situation, ranging from the
financial capital Singapore or oil-rich Saudi Arabia to poverty-stricken Mali.
As such, a common unifying interest is difficult to discern. The same is true
for the North, though to a lesser degree. "North" and "South" are therefore
mainly diplomatic artifacts.

Most importantly, though, the conventional North-South distinction
obscures the fact that the dividing line in today's world does not primarily
run between Northern and Southern societies, but right across all of these
societies. The major rift appears to be between the globalized rich and the
localized poor. It separates the global consumer class on the one side, from
the social majority outside the global circuits on the other. This global middle class is made up of the majority of citizens in the North, along with a
varying number of elites in the South, with about 80 percent of it found in
North America, Western as well as Eastern Europe, and Japan. Twenty percent of it can be found dispersed throughout the South. Its overall size equals
roughly that 20 percent of the world population which has direct access to
an automobile.

In the last decade, globalization has accelerated and intensified the integration of this class into the worldwide circuit of goods, communication and
travel, most clearly so in newly industrializing countries and Eastern
Europe/Russia. Transnational corporations largely cater to this class, just as
they provide its symbolic means of expression, such as films, fashion, music
and brand names. But entire categories of people in the North, like the
unemployed, the elderly and the competitively weak find themselves excluded, along with entire regions in the South, from the circuits of the world
economy. In all countries, an invisible border separates the fast from the slow,
the connected from the unconnected, the rich from the poor. There is a global North as there is a global South, encompassing even the area of the former
Eastern Bloc.

The consumer classes, in the North as well as in the South, have the
power to bring the bulk of the world's marketed natural resources into their

service. Due to their purchasing power, they are able to command the resource flows which fuel their commodity-intensive patterns of production and consumption. In attracting resources, their geographical reach is both global and national. On the global level, a network of resource flows, generally organized by transnational corporations, extends like a spider web across the planet, pulling energy and materials towards the high-consumption zones. On the national level, the urban-based middle classes succeed equally in capturing resources to their benefit, thanks to patterns of ownership, subsidies and superior demand. Particularly in Southern countries, market demand for resource-intensive goods and services stems mainly from that relatively small part of the population which commands purchasing power and is therefore capable of imitating the consumption patterns of the North. As a consequence, the more affluent groups in countries such as Brazil, Mexico, India, China or Russia use about as much energy and materials as their counterparts in the industrialized world—a level five to 10 times higher than the average consumption in these countries.

Reduction of the ecological footprint of the consumer classes around the world is not just a matter of ecology but also a matter of equity. Though trade in resources may help economically, it is deleterious ecologically since the excessive use of environmental space withdraws resources from the social majority in the world. Moreover, wealth on the one side is at times co-responsible for poverty on the other. Time and again, the consumer classes shield themselves against environmental harm by leaving noise, dirt and the ugliness of the industrial hinterland in front of the doorsteps of less advantaged groups. Resources are not simply out there waiting to be extracted; they often are where people reside and they are used by people to sustain their livelihoods. As the consumer class corners resources through the global reach of corporations, they contribute to the marginalization of that third of the world population which derives their livelihood directly from free access to land, water and forests. Certainly, such exports may increase a country's income, but it is not at all certain that the marginalized share in these benefits. In any case, building large dams and extracting ore, cutting trees and capitalizing agriculture for the benefit of distant consumers, often degrade the ecosystems upon which many people live. In fact, such expressions of development often do no more than deprive the poor of their resources in order for the rich to live beyond their means.

Ensure Livelihood Rights

In contrast to Rio, the Johannesburg Summit will concentrate on poverty eradication. The South may pin up the badge of poverty, demanding a greater share in the world economy. However, while the task is a noble one, its politics are ambivalent. There is certainly no doubt that the elimination of poverty calls for enormous efforts on the part of the international community. But it is questionable whether these efforts should primarily consist of higher development assistance, increased grants or increased world market integration. For what is good for government is not necessarily good for the poor. Much too often, and for quite some time now, the Southern governments, supported by their elites, have indulged in the expansion of their own consumer classes and have secured their own power base under the banner of poverty eradication. Against this background, it is clear that the struggle for poverty reduction will not be decided in controversies between Southern and Northern governments, but in conflicts between the marginalized majority and the global middle class—which includes domestic governments, corporations and multilateral institutions. After all, it has happened more than once that Southern and Northern governments have achieved consensus at the expense of the poor. While everybody agrees that poverty elimination has to have its due priority, opinions are sharply divided as soon as the key question is asked: poverty eradication, yes, but by whom?

The first answer highlights the role of investors, transnational companies and economic planners, emphasizing that the reduction of poverty will be the result of higher and broader economic growth. Since growth, in this view, is triggered by export to urban or, better, foreign markets, the most important ingredients of a poverty-reduction strategy are capital investments, factories, irrigation systems, transportation networks and marketing outlets. Moreover, greater purchasing power cannot be mobilized unless free access to Northern consumer markets is secured. In this perspective, only the integration of the most productive agricultural sectors into the world market can provide a steady flow of income and investment, which in turn may stimulate further growth. In brief, poverty would be overcome through more globalization.

Environmental issues play only a minor role in export-led poverty reduction strategies. Export-led poverty reduction is broadly the approach favored by South Africa and the recently formed New Partnership for Africa's Development (NEPAD). On the contrary, over-emphasis regarding pesticides, pollution, clear cutting, or genetically modified crops is portrayed as an obstacle to development. However, sustainable trade may rise in importance as soon as there is sufficient demand from consumers for commodities like certified timber or organic produce.

The second response—which we favor—looks to the poor themselves and recognizes them as actors who shape their lives even under conditions of hardship and destitution. In this view, poverty derives from a deficit of power rather than a lack of money. Far from being needy persons awaiting provisions, the poor must be seen as citizens who are constrained by a lack of rights, entitlements, salaries and political leverage. Any attempt, therefore, to mitigate poverty will have to be centered on a reinforcement of rights and opportunities. This is in particular true for women who are often legally marginalized. In many places, they have no access to tenure, income and influence, despite the fact that they carry most of the burden of everyday life and often have to sustain families by themselves. For women or men, a basic rights strategy, rather than a basic needs strategy, may help to overcome the constraints to self-organization. In the countryside, conflicts will often turn around rights to land, access to water, forests and undestroyed habitats, confronting land owners and state administrations. In the city, conflicts will focus on rights to housing, to unpolluted water, to running a business or to self-administration, confronting city officials, health departments, police or power cliques. Unless there are shifts in power patterns, subtle ones or sweeping ones, the poor will almost always lack the security and the resources needed for a decent existence.

Boosting economic growth is less important than securing livelihoods for the impoverished. Since economic growth often fails to trickle down, there is no point in sacrificing people's lives in the present for speculative gains in the future. Instead, it is crucial to empower them for a dignified life here and now.

However, such a livelihood-centered perspective is at odds with the export-led poverty-reduction strategies. There is convincing evidence that export-led poverty reduction may help investors, agricultural companies and wealthy farmers improve their own prosperity, yet large parts of the rural population are likely to suffer massive displacement from small farms, loss of livelihoods and forced migration to cities. Furthermore, a strategy of creating industrial jobs, which under the condition of a borderless economy would have to be competitive on the world market, is soon likely to run out of breath. Such jobs require considerable capital investment, which makes them expand at a much slower pace than the number of unemployed. Under a free trade regime, agriculture and industry in most countries of the South cannot be simultaneously competitive and job-intensive. The politics of world market integration is therefore anything but hospitable to a quickly expanding number of citizens. It renders many people redundant with respect to the official economy.

To avoid this impasse, it is important to promote sustainable livelihoods. Sustainable in both senses of the word: firstly, an activity that provides a decent income or sustenance and provides some status in society along with a meaningful life; and secondly, an activity which conserves and, if possible, regenerates the environment. Productive ecosystems are core assets for sustainable livelihoods, since grasslands, forests, fields and rivers can be valuable sources of sustenance. This is the main reason why livelihood-centered strategies of poverty removal coincide with the interest in environmental protection.

Ecology is thus essential for ensuring decent livelihoods in society. Securing community rights to natural resources is therefore a hallmark of livelihood politics. However, strengthening the rights of local communities means weakening the claims of distant income earners and consumers. Thus the direct or indirect demand of the global consumer for easily available and cheap resources will have to be checked since the interest of middle classes in expanding consumption and of corporations in profit expansion often collides with the interest of communities in securing their livelihoods. These resource conflicts will not be eased unless the economically well-off on the globe make the transition towards resource-light patterns of production and consumption.

Leapfrog into the Solar Age

At the time of Rio, sustainable development was mainly about protecting nature, but now, it is first and foremost about protecting people. For nobody can close his or her eyes in front of what can be called the 21st century challenge: how best to extend hospitality to twice the number of people on the globe in light of a rapidly deteriorating biosphere. Indeed, the historical pattern of scarcity is outdated. While in the old days the world appeared full of nature, but void of people, today the world is void of nature, but full of people. The satisfaction of needs and wants is not constrained so much by the paucity of hands and brains, but by the scarcity of resources and living systems. Nature is now more of a limiting factor than money, given that development is more and more restricted not by the number of fishing boats, but by the decreasing numbers of fish; not by the power of pumps, but by the depletion of aquifers; not by the number of chainsaws but by the disappearance of primary forests. In particular for Southern countries, the relevant question will be: How many problems can be simultaneously solved or avoided? How can both the abundance of people and the scarcity of nature be addressed by making the right initial choices?

The answer, we suggest, is to quickly move out of an industrial economy wasteful of both nature and population and head for a regenerative economy mindful of resources and in need of people. An economy that is based on the assumption that there are "free goods" in the world—pure water, clean air, hydrocarbon combustion, virgin forests—will favor large-scale, energy- and material-intensive production methods, and labor will remain marginalized. In contrast, if an economy discourages profligate resource use and privileges non-fossil resources, a decentralized and smaller-scale production pattern requiring more labor and intelligence is likely to prosper. In both North and South, the potential for higher resource productivity presents business and governments with an alternative scenario: making radical reductions in resource use, while at the same time raising rates of employment. Rather than laying off people, greater gains can come from laying off wasted kilowatt-hours, barrels of oil, and pulp from old-growth forests. People will in part have to substitute for natural resources; such an economy, evolving with a minimum input of nature, will have to rely much more on the strength, the skill and the knowledge of people. Indeed, it will be post-industrial in the true sense of the word: finding new balances among hardware, biological productivity and human intelligence.

This is even more true when it comes to changing the resource base altogether, from fossil-based to solar-based energies and materials. Apart from the obvious environmental benefits, the point here is that fossil resources usually imply long supply chains, which in turn imply long chains of value creation. Because there is usually so much geographical distance between the extraction of the resource and its final use, including a variety of intermediate steps of processing and refining, opportunities for profit and employment are spread out as well. Most countries and localities, finding themselves at the downstream end of the chain, are strangled by the high cost of fuel and resources imported from abroad. They pay, but most gains and jobs arise elsewhere. However, a change in resource base would turn this logic around. Reliance on photo-voltaic, wind, small hydro power and biomass of all sorts implies much shorter supply chains, not just for the resource, but often also for the conversion technology involved. As a result, income and jobs would largely stay at the local/regional level, recycling money in local economies. Furthermore, as sunshine and biomass are geographically diffused, they lend themselves to decentralized structures of production and use, unlike fossil resources which are concentrated in a few places, giving rise to centralized large-scale structures. The industrial pattern of squandering nature instead of cherishing people would be reversed; a solar economy holds the prospect of both including people and saving resources.

Southern countries have the opportunity to leapfrog into a solar economy, much before and much more solidly than Northern economies. In fact, it would be self-defeating for them, in terms of livelihoods and in terms of the environment, to go through the same stages of industrial evolution as the Northern countries did. For instance, Southern countries face important decisions about infrastructures such as energy, transport, sewage and communication systems, the introduction and maintenance of which, in industrial countries, have caused the Earth's resources to dwindle.

Today, many Southern countries are still in a position to avoid this unsustainable course, opting without further delay for infrastructures which would allow them to embark on a low emission and resource-light trajectory. This is equally the case for "transition" countries, where it is often preferable to build new infrastructure systems rather than upgrading the aging ones. Investment in infrastructure such as light rail systems, decentralized energy production, public transport, gray-water sewage, locally adapted housing, regionalized food systems and transport-light urban settings could set a country on the road toward cleaner, less costly and more equitable development patterns. This perspective holds true in many respects; in addition, it represents a unique chance for achieving greater economic independence decades after political independence has been accomplished.

Livelihood Rights

The politics of poverty eradication is replete with misconceptions. Popular myths include the suggestion that the (A) poor cause environmental destruction, that (B) economic growth removes poverty, and thus (C) economic growth is the recipe for the elimination of both poverty and environmental degradation. We believe that each link in this chain of arguments is flawed, making policies that are based on it counterproductive.

Admittedly, the poor environmental refugees are often pushed to deforesting and overgrazing land, but in general, they have proven to be careful guardians of resources and ecosystems. Since the poor depend on soil fertility, fish from lakes and estuaries, plants for medicine, branches from forests, and animals for subsistence and cash, they have a very down-to-earth incentive for conserving their resource base.

The argument about economic growth requires clarification as well. Only growth which increases the Gross Nature Product (to use a distinction made by the late Anil Agarwal), and not just the Gross National Product, enhances the condition of rural communities. Otherwise, growth will produce the opposite effect—loss of income and livelihood capacity. It is not monetary growth as such that is important, but the structuring of economic activities in a way that fosters the preservation of ecosystems, as well as the cohesion of communities. Economic growth for its own sake is self-defeating, unless it fully takes into account renewable energy, sustainable agriculture, water conservation, biomass-based enterprises, and the prudent use of living systems. Any degradation of the environment increases the plight of the poor, just as any improvement will reduce their vulnerability.

Biodiversity and Livelihood

Agriculture is a way of life. Local communities all over the world strive to live sustainably and meaningfully. They seek survival and livelihood, as well as joy and celebration in their surrounding nature. In fact, the lives of these communities are shaped by the fauna and flora of the specific environment in which they live. Food habits and house designs, clothing and music instruments, work patterns and feasts, all reflect the community of plants and animals that surround them. While conservation of biodiversity has been enshrined as an official objective of international politics in treaties such as the Convention on Biological Diversity (CBD), little attention has been paid to the role that biodiversity plays in the productive and cultural life of rural and coastal communities. Since these communities have been—and still are—dependent on their specific bio-diverse environment, the need for conservation has often become integral to their culture and daily practices. Villagers who are generally aware that the continuing productivity of nature sustains their lives are likely not to take more than nature can regenerate. In particular, the use of common property resources, such as fisheries or forests, is often governed by customary rules, which are designed in a way to preserve carrying capacity.

Livelihood Security and Biodiversity

There is no food security without farmer security, and that in turn is linked to the maintenance of biodiversity. Maintenance of biodiversity and enhancement of genetic resources have been carried out by farming communities, particularly women, all over the world, wherever localized food production prevails. Indeed, women play a pivotal role in both maintaining and strategically using biodiversity. Besides being managers and providers of food in the families, they are also carriers of local knowledge, skills for survival and cultural memory.

Most poor people do not own any land, but rely on common property resources—forests, lakes or even roadside areas, which are owned by the community or the state—as vital means of survival. In a study conducted in India in 1991, it was found that 80 percent of fuel and fodder that the poor use come from common property land. In terms of income, it accounts for 20 percent of their income. In Africa, rural households derive 35 percent of their energy needs from fuel wood—most of it collected from forests and common property lands. Free access to grassland, trees and water-courses is essential for the sustenance of these households. Obviously, any degradation of these ecosystems, be it through pollution, overgrazing or logging, would increase the daily workload and would eventually prove fatal.

It is particularly important in this context that the sustainable livelihoods of many rural families are dependent not just on cultivated crops, but on food harvested from uncultivated sources. For instance, in early morning hours, it is a common sight in the rural parts of Asia and Africa to see people collecting leaves, spinach, small fish or fruits from the area around the homestead. These people go to the roadsides, the paddy fields owned by others, the ponds, near the canals and other common land of the village. They also know that children who have gone for a swim in the pond, the canal or the river will come back with their hands full of uncultivated green vegetables, tubers, edible forest fruits, and most importantly, fish, which will be immediately turned into food for the family. The fish they like and eat most often are uncultivated fish, collected from water bodies. At least 40 percent of the food by weight, and most of the nutritional requirement for the rural population of Bangladesh, is met by terrestrial or aquatic sources of food that are not cultivated.

Furthermore, the livelihood of the poor, especially of women, depends on the integration of farming, livestock, poultry and fisheries. In a way, rural families comprise not only the extended human family, but also include domestic animals, such as cows, goats, sheep, chicken, ducks and pigeons. Mixed-crop fields provide much of the partner plants, which are sources of nutrition for chicken and cows. Roadside plants provide feed for goats. Children gather snails and other aquatic species for feeding the ducks raised by women. A large majority of rural poor women survive on raising cows, goats, sheep, ducks, chicken and pigs, whose feed is not purchased, but taken from surrounding fields and common property. While these animals get their feed from the diverse species available on the land, the animals and birds in turn reciprocate, sustaining the environment and enhancing biodiversity.

A single-crop mentality, which is often reflected in industrial agriculture, fails to appreciate the numerous interconnections among people, plants and animals. Adamant on optimizing the yield of one particular crop, agronomists tend to overlook the importance for people's livelihood of the wide range of subsidiary cultivated or uncultivated crops. This is one of the reasons why increased yields from monocultures do not necessarily translate into more food for peasants. On the contrary, they might have less food, as subsidiary crops are eliminated. Moreover, the side effects of chemical agriculture often affect the diversity of crops and animals. If land and water are polluted, they become like poison for people who gather food, or animals and birds that feed on them. Frequently, chemical residues contaminate freshwater springs, fish and aquatic resources or uncultivated biomass. Therefore, the claim that modern agriculture has produced more food is fallacious since it is based on the calculation of single plant harvests, for instance rice, systematically ignoring its negative effect on the entire food system.

Women and Seed Preservation

Women are the guardians of biodiversity, as they are often in charge of the selection and preservation of seeds. As they choose, save, sort out, and sow the seeds of vegetables, fruits and many other crops, they play a role, which is crucial to the enhancement of genetic resources and biodiversity. Additionally, the general practice of sharing seeds among neighbors and relatives enhances biodiversity and genetic variety. The varieties of vegetables ensure food security in terms of availability in different areas and in different seasons of the year.

In the Nayakrishi Seed Wealth Center in Bangladesh, farming women deposit their collection of seeds. The center collects local seeds with a view to adopting and improving production techniques suitable for farmers' seed. Thus, hundreds of local varieties of rice, vegetables, fruit and timber crops have been reintroduced within a short period of time. For example, farmers in the Nayakrishi area cultivate at least 1,027 varieties of rice, a number that is steadily increasing. In a country where over 15,000 rice varieties had been reduced in two decades to about 8 or 10, this represents a reversal in the trend of genetic erosion. As farmers exchange seeds among themselves, they help to increase the genetic resource base of their community.

Peasant women in Nayakrishi have started to build their "veez-sampad" or "seed-wealth." This notion is deliberately opposed to concepts like seed-banks or gene-banks. These women claim the right of control over seeds; therefore, they resent any centralization of seed wealth in the form of a "bank." Control over seeds, on the household and community level, is an important underpinning of the economic independence of farmers. It gives security, shields against money expenses and provides a heritage around which social relations are interwoven. Farmers become more vulnerable, when they lose control over seeds. For this reason, the right of farmers to their seeds, including the right to use seeds for breeding new varieties, has to be protected against the attempt of corporations to turn the vital need of sowing into a solvent demand for their products.

Land, Water and Livelihood

Land degradation, just as limited access to land, is a key factor of rural poverty. As the soil fertility declines, so does agricultural productivity, which must in turn be compensated for by costly fertilizers. This decline is often compounded by a lack of water, which then causes soil salinization or soil erosion. For these reasons, the degradation of land and water resources undermines the livelihood of small farmers. Affected farmers are often caught in a downward spiral of declining agricultural productivity, less subsistence and flight from the villages. Indeed, the rising phenomenon of environmental refugees is often closely linked to the deterioration of land. In West Africa, those children who demonstrated growth abnormalities associated with poor nutrition were most frequently found in areas of high soil degradation. It is estimated that up to one billion people are affected by soil erosion and land degradation due to deforestation, over-grazing and agriculture. Any attempt to overcome rural misery and to ensure livelihood rights, will have to focus on the restoration of soil fertility and water resources.

Soil Fertility Through Organic Agriculture

Over thousands of years of history, farming communities have learned various biological and physical methods for coping with decreasing productivity of agro-ecosystems like terracing or fallowing. Perhaps the most significant are those that make conscious use of species to counter the slow natural decline of any agro-ecological system. For example, mixed farming that combines crop and animal production, provides for manure, which makes nutrients optimally available at the start of the growing season. Moreover, it makes it possible to put nutrients exactly where they are most needed.

Deep-rooted crops are planted to bring leached nutrients up to the surface soil, in order to become available for the next generation crop. In Africa, for instance, sorghum and similar crop species are rooted deep in the earth, bringing nutrients up to the surface. They also withstand dry spells in the weather cycle, which are often exacerbated by deforesting the land. These and similar species slow down growth to survive waterlogging, while rice grows plentiful under waterlogged conditions. Such methods keep the humus content of the soil high and provide for stable fertility.

Strategies like mixed cropping, animal raising, terracing, and afforestation are widely employed to halt degradation of soils and to restore the productive power of the land. Various forms of low-input, ecological agriculture are practiced, not only because they require less capital, but because they conserve the soil—along with water, the basis of all livelihood. However, quite a number of these initiatives are not grounded in a "production" paradigm that aims to optimize the production of crop yield for economic gain. They are rather efforts by communities to generate and regenerate their ecological "relations" to plants, water and animals for food, livelihood and also spiritual connection. Such communities are not interested in competing with urban centers to acquire more cars, refrigerators, or high-rise buildings. They derive their dignity from stable livelihoods and good relations with their fellow beings in community and nature.

Water Through Ecological Restoration

Water is the essential element not only for growing crops and raising animals, but also for people's sustenance. Yet water scarcity is widespread. In many rural areas, water tables are receding, wells are contaminated and ever less runoff is kept available. Competing claims on water resources by irrigation and industry often favor the more powerful, leaving the less powerful thirsty. In addition, time-honored technologies such as village tanks or canals have been abandoned, just as community water regimes have eroded. Expanding water supplies often aggravates the problem. Therefore, water conservation and the restoration of grazing, farming and forestry to increase water collection are today the priority for livelihood politics around the globe. Initiatives for the prudent use of water abound. They range from the revival of water-harvesting techniques, to small storage dams and comprehensive watershed programs. Efforts to increase collection, however, usually imply the long-term regeneration of living systems through which the water cycle can pass. Healthy grasslands, farm lands, wetlands and woodlands are the best insurance against water scarcity. Therefore, ecological restoration for the sake of water security is essential to ensuring one of the most basic livelihood rights—the right to water.

Erosion of Livelihoods Through Industrial Agriculture

Industrial agriculture tries to produce a homogenous environment irrespective of the distinct nature of the pre-existing ecosystem. Therefore, it uses irrigation extensively. It thus creates a captive market for pumping and irrigation equipment. It also creates contracts for building dams and irrigation and drainage canals. In this way, it geographically extends the age-old problems associated with irrigation whereby water is diverted from the weaker to the stronger. Furthermore, it divorces animal production from crop production. It plants single-variety mono-cultures as a continuum over very extensive areas. Ecosystem disruption thus becomes inevitable. Increased vulnerability of crops to diseases and pests ensues. One indicator of such a disruption is the regular and quick collapse of the crop varieties, owing to emerging vulnerabilities to diseases and pests.

During the Green Revolution, for instance, fertile land was flooded with chemicals and poisons, which included insecticides, fungicides and herbicides. As a result, poisonous residues entered the environment, at both the surface and in groundwaters. Both the breeders and the suppliers of agro-chemicals are increasingly the same North-based transnational corporations. Combining both sectors facilitates the breeding of varieties which require agrochemicals. And to enable corporations to dictate how farmers use seed and agrochemicals, they patent both. By so doing, they marginalize commu-nity breeders, who maximize diversity and have thus enriched humanity with the various crops and thousands of varieties of each crop, as well as the eco-logical methods of using diversity to forestall diseases and pests. This is the way globalization affects farming community agriculture. The proven sus-tainable land use practices by local communities have to be restored and pro-moted. Local communities and in particular farmers, have to be protected from the privatization of their knowledge, technologies, practices and biodi-versity, and in particular seeds, and from the pressures to accept the use of agrochemicals.

Energy and Livelihoods

Over the last 50 years, economic policies in many Southern countries have been based on the premise that the rural economy will grow by piggyback-ing on the growth of the urban/industrial economy. In other words, it will automatically benefit from the "trickling down" effect that results from over-all national progress. The main thrust has been to invest primarily in indus-try—both heavy and light, but always big—and urban infrastructure, i.e. those sectors which are assumed to provide higher returns than investments in small, decentralized initiatives. At every step, more energy is consumed, and more entropy is created.

For creating sustainable livelihoods, massive decentralized private and non-profit sector initiatives are required instead. The objective is to produce goods and services for the local, low-purchasing power market. In small-scale sustainable enterprises, the capital cost of creating one workplace is much lower than in the industrial sector, just as returns on investment can be high-er. Such sustainable enterprises will have to be more decentralized, efficient and responsive to social and natural constraints than industry is today. Otherwise, they are not able to do what is necessary, namely to create work places at a fraction of the cost of those created in the globalized economy and to increase the productivity of energy and material resource use by at least 10 times compared to today's level.

Sustainable enterprises are decentralized. They are technology-based mini-businesses that are environmentally sound and produce for the local market. Their primary problem is their need of certain kinds of support tools such as technology, managerial skill, marketing methods and access to credit and financing to be profitable and sustainable. Availability of these is today highly facilitated by the Internet. An appropriate portal can provide rural consultancy and monitoring, an exchange service, and a range of information sources. This, of course, is not limited to enterprises. Villagers would also be able to get information about commodity prices or land records. They can shop for inputs such as seeds, machinery, spare parts and household items. Such an information network can give a boost to the dissemination of renewable energy technologies by giving a powerful tool to small enterprises and villagers alike.

Jobs and Nature Protection Through Renewables

Energy policies are usually conceptualized and designed by those who control the "modern" sector—the elites for whom commercial fuels are the only acceptable, legitimate source of energy. In their view, it is taken for granted that development means growth, that growth means rising energy use, and that rising energy use means increasing energy supplies. In this view, energy is identified with electricity, electricity with centralized grid systems, and national grids with petroleum- or coal-based energy production. Energy decisions, in the "modern" sector, are made primarily by economists and engineers who rarely take into account the needs of the marginalized majority. The installed capacity for generating electricity usually serves energy-hungry industries and towns, along with large farming interests.

The poor, however, have to be satisfied with what are euphemistically called "non-commercial" energy sources, such as wood, cow-dung, twigs and agricultural wastes. In fact, non-commercial energy in many Southern countries constitutes nearly 50 percent of the total energy used. This is a trend that has continued over the decades and, given the present growth rates of different energy sources, can be expected to continue into the future. Yet, noncommercial energy use puts heavy pressure on bushlands and forests since people who are short of cash take advantage of freely available branches and trees. The lack of commercial or affordable energy often leads to the degradation of the natural heritage. This spells gradual and silent disaster, given the fact that more than two billion people in the world are without access to electricity or basic energy services. For both social reasons—job creation and better living conditions—and environmental reasons—protection of the climate globally, protection of living systems locally—renewable energy will have to be part and parcel of any strategy to ensure long-term livelihoods.

Despite sizable investments made by governments, international agencies and even some corporations, the diffusion of commercial sources of renewable energy has a long way to go. A few isolated successes have been reported with solar photo-voltaic systems for use in pumping, lighting, community TV and other special applications, primarily in remote locations, which are too expensive to wire up to the national grid. Since many bulk applications of energy (such as cooking, water heating and space warming) need only a low-grade energy source, it makes good sense to make solar thermal devices available to households on a large scale. Some countries have had some success with improved cooking stoves, solar water heaters and similar devices, but the usual experience is that demand dries up the moment that subsidies for popularizing them are withdrawn.

Next to power production and transport, construction is the sector that consumes the highest amount of energy. A great deal of energy is embodied in building materials, such as cement, steel and bricks. Energy is also needed during operating time for lighting, heating and cooling. Since current manufacturing practices in most countries are quite inefficient, there is a lot of room for improving energy efficiency in the manufacture and delivery of building materials. For example, constructing houses in a village with unfired mud blocks instead of bricks can save several hectares of forests that would otherwise be used as fuel. In addition, major energy savings can be achieved through the use of solar passive systems for heating and cooling buildings. Apart from a few isolated architectural experiments, though, not much has been achieved in this area so far.

Biomass is another form of solar energy conversion and the most common in Southern countries. Large quantities of biomass are burnt for cooking and heating, while a small amount is converted to methane gas by an anaerobic digestion or to producer gas by pyrolysis. This area offers great benefits; it constitutes a decentralized, low-cash, but huge market, which could become an arena for small-scale sustainable enterprises. Furthermore, many countries and regions have meteorological conditions that favor the use of wind energy and mini-hydro, two technologies of great promise.

Initiating the Energy Transition

The first step in initiating the energy transition is to introduce technologies and systems that are less wasteful of energy. Many such solutions already exist and are technically and economically quite simple and straightforward to introduce. Measures to conserve energy range from technical interventions to reduce frictional losses, all the way to matching the quality of energy to the types of use to which it is put. Much of the technology needed to achieve this step is already available.

The second step is to reduce our dependence on fossil fuels and nuclear energy. These are major threats to sustainability, both because of limited resources and limited sinks for waste products. It is fairly obvious that a switch to more accessible, more benign and more sustainable forms of energy must be elevated high on the political agenda. While renewable energy is not without its environmental problems, it does offer numerous advantages over fossil fuels. But there will be no greater use of renewable energy, unless quite fundamental changes in fiscal and technological policies, pricing systems, subsidies and procurement procedures occur. More so, it will also require significant investments in R&D, marketing systems and infrastructure, involving actors in government, corporations and the research community.

The third step is to redesign production systems, transport networks, various infrastructures and houses that optimize energy savings. These measures will invariably present more significant societal impacts and will be more difficult to retrofit into existing production systems. Huge increases in energy efficiency and resource productivity are possible by transforming industrial processes, redesigning cities and transportation systems and by substituting physical movement with electronic transmission.

The fourth step, with the deepest and longest lasting impact, has to do with changes in lifestyles, in the concepts of consumption and production and in the understanding of individual and social purpose. Given the market and other forces at work, such a transition will not be easy to achieve and will involve all actors in society from the individual to the community, through the institutions of learning and faith to the machineries of global governance.

Urban Livelihoods

Nowhere is the wealth gap greater than in the cities of the world. The well-off and the destitute, the mobile jet-setter and the immobile slum dweller, the super-consumer and the zero-consumer, all reside in one and the same urban habitat of a size rarely larger than a hundred square miles. Yet they live worlds apart. Both the affluent and the dispossessed are growing in numbers, but they have little in common. Golf courses stretch out not far from factories, business districts thrive next to street markets, and affluent neighborhoods coexist with slums. Disparity reigns, and more and more urban centers exhibit the traits of a divided city. Invisible barriers separate the rich from the poor; and it is entirely possible for well-to-do residents to spend years without ever coming into visual contact with the less palatable sections of their city.

In many Southern countries, it is primarily the absence of modern agrarian reform that has led to constant migration processes from the countryside to the cities. Concentration of land tenure in rural areas is an important motive for migration to urban centers. However, urban infrastructure and settlement policies have been incapable of dealing satisfactorily with the requirements for shelter, water supply, appropriate sewage system or environmentally sound transport systems. This has been compounded by the fact that, thanks to the forces of economic globalization, corporations have gained greater freedom to choose where to locate their activities. As local governments compete with industry, socially and environmentally destructive tendencies have been enhanced in many cities, increasing urban poverty, social segregation, political violence and unequal risk distribution. Often facilities producing toxic waste have been located in areas inhabited by concentrations of poor people and ethnic minorities.

Urban poverty, however, is different from rural poverty in one important respect. Non-monetary assets, such as clean air, water, shelter or security are less available in urban than in rural areas. For over and above their poverty in money, the urban poor have to deal with contaminated water, dangerous housing, infected air, criminality and long distances. Their private poverty is thus compounded by the absence of natural (and in part social) capital.

As in rural areas, the marginalized majorities in the cities suffer from environmental deprivation. However, while the rural poor are often deprived of access to natural resources, which could serve as their livelihood means, the urban dispossessed are threatened in their physical integrity by the degradation of their living space. Water may carry pollutants, air may affect the respiratory system, body excrements may lead to infections, or land may be unstable.

Environmental problems in cities of the South derive mainly from shortage of water, from pathogens or pollutants in air, water or food and from housing at unsuitable sites. About 220 million urban dwellers, 13 percent of the world's urban population, do not have access to safe drinking water. About twice this number lack even the simplest of latrines. Sanitation for the removal of waste water is largely absent, as is the disposal of rubbish. Overcrowding in dense settlements facilitates the transmission of diseases. Air pollution is widespread in Southern cities. Water, even if available, may not be potable since contamination from human waste or from industrial sources is a frequent problem. And finally, even the land underneath one's feet is not secure. Informal settlements, often built on steep hills, are exposed to mudslides or floods. By and large, environmental problems in cities pose risks to the physical well-being of citizens. They threaten not only people's livelihoods, but people's health. Mediated through the environment, urban poverty is therefore closely linked to the wide spread of preventable diseases, such as diarrhea or infections. It goes without saying that the disabling effects of illness exacerbate the condition of poverty, most notably for women, children and infants.

To a certain degree, of course, the well-to-do are also affected by pollution. But in most urban areas of Asia, Africa and Latin America, it is low-income groups that bear most of the ill-health, injury or premature death, and other costs of degradation. They stand very little chance of obtaining healthy and legally secure living quarters with sufficient space, security of tenure, reliable services and facilities, and in areas that are not prone to flooding or landslides. More often than not, they are also forced by their tight economic situation into making sacrifices with regard to environmental quality. It is not surprising, therefore, that there is generally a strong correlation between income level and exposure to environmental risks. On the other side, however, the marginalized majority contributes little to environmental degradation. Their per capita use of fossil fuel, water, land, and their production of waste as well as of greenhouse gases is far inferior to the levels maintained by middle- and high-income groups. The causes of pollution and land scarcity are rather to be found in the consumption patterns of the well-off, along with urban-based production and distribution systems that serve them. They win out over the economically weak in the competition over shares of the limited urban environmental space. The urban poor are not only marginalized economically, but also environmentally since they claim little of the resources, but have to bear the bulk of the waste.

Against this backdrop, it is clear that a minimum of environmental health is part and parcel of urban citizenship, since the already precarious situation for citizens' rights in many cities is aggravated by the environmental handicaps they have to live with. Freedom from physical threats and safe living conditions are the foundations of a dignified existence just as much as civic and human rights. For this reason, both dimensions of the environmental struggle, the struggle to bring down the resource use of the affluent and the struggle to protect people against pollution, are essential for improving lives and livelihoods of the urban poor. Environmental policy is thus part of the larger attempt to widen the political and economic space available to marginalized citizen. Essentially, it raises the same question which is at the core of urban conflicts: Whose city is it?

Fair Wealth

Poverty is the Siamese twin of wealth. Both develop jointly and neither can be fully understood without reference to the other. Usually, the poor are conditioned by wealth, and the rich thrive on benefits drawn from the poor. Hence, no calls for poverty eradication are credible unless they are accompanied by calls for the reform of wealth. Conventional development experts implicitly define equity as a problem of the poor. They highlight a lack of income, technologies or market access and advocate remedies for raising the living standard of the poor. In short, they work at lifting the threshold—rather than lowering or modifying the roof. With the emergence of bio-physical constraints to economic growth, however, this approach turns out to be one-sided. The quest for fairness in a finite world means changing the rich in the first place, not the poor. Poverty alleviation, in other words, cannot be separated from wealth alleviation.

The concept of environmental space can help to illustrate the relationship between ecology and equity. With regard to ecology, human beings, along with other living beings, use the global heritage of nature for extracting resources, dumping wastes and domesticating living systems. This globally available environmental space, however, is not infinite; it has (flexible) boundaries. These boundaries constitute constraints for human activities, crossing beyond may provoke biospherical turbulence. Ecology, therefore, requires keeping the overall level of resource flows within the boundaries of the available environmental space.

With regard to equity, the environmental space concept reveals the enormous inequality in resource use on a global scale. Not every country occupies an equal share of the environmental space; on the contrary, the shares are of very disparate size. In the mid-1990s, for example, the average Japanese required about 45 tons of fuels, minerals, and metals annually, the average German 80 tons, and the average American 82 tons, while the average Chinese settled with 34 tons.

Clearly, the well-off on this globe occupy an excessive part of the environmental space. However, the more the boundaries of this space are put under stress, the more the distribution of the environmental space takes on a dramatic note, because a larger share on the one side implies a smaller share on the other. As a consequence, the well-off, by having cornered a disproportionately large part of the global environmental space to the advantage of just a minority of the world population, deprive the world's majority of the basis for greater prosperity. Bringing down the resource demands of the consumer world in North and South is therefore crucial in advancing both ecology and equity.

In the long run, no other principle holds for sharing the global environmental space among the world's inhabitants than the egalitarian principle. It suggests that every inhabitant of the Earth basically enjoys an equal right to the natural heritage of the Earth. May it be in accordance to the present lifestyles or in accordance to economic achievements, any other way of conceptualizing the distribution of natural resources would only codify an excessive appropriation of sources and sinks by the global North. Indeed, the affirmation of the egalitarian principle is primarily directed against the frivolous inequality which has come to dominate the relations among people with respect to nature. Although it circumscribes the presumption of the rich primarily, it still does not equally imply an entitlement to maximize the use of nature on part of the less consuming world citizens. As with any right, the right to natural resources is also limited by the rights of everybody else. Given that the right to enjoy nature's essential services is everybody else's (including future generations and non-human beings), the boundaries of the available environmental space constrain the use of this right. While the over-consumers are not entitled to excessive appropriation, the under-consumers are not entitled to catch up with the over-consumers. They may only move towards fair and ecologically harmless levels, keeping within the guardrails of bio-physical sustainability. Just as equity is a condition of sustainability, ecology is a condition of equity.

Very rough calculations suggest that the global North will need to bring down its overall use of the environmental space by a factor of 10, that is by 80-90 percent, during the coming 50 years. Otherwise it is difficult to see how global sustainability as well as fairness can be attained. From this angle, the key question of global sustainability can be rephrased: Will the consumer classes be capable and willing to live without the surplus of environmental space they occupy today?

The question also underscores the specific character of transnational environmental justice. Acting in the spirit of justice does not require dealing with the other but with oneself. Sustainability calls for fairness rather than for self-sacrifice. It is a reincarnation of the time-honored golden rule of Kantian ethics that no action and/or institution should be based on principles that cannot be shared universally. Transnational environmental justice requires transforming (post-)industrial production and consumption patterns in a way that could be universalized because overshooting the environmental space cannot be universalized across the globe. At its core, transnational environmental justice is not about redistribution but about restraint.

There will be no equity unless the consumer classes in North and South becomes capable of living well at a drastically reduced level of resource demand. Such a transformation of wealth is the central challenge of sustainability. It means bringing production and consumption patterns up to the age of ecological constraints and equity aspirations. There are several avenues for moving into this direction.

First, the search for radically increased resource productivity, the art of producing wealth with ever less resources, is the cornerstone for sustainable production and consumption patterns. Using resources more effectively has three significant benefits. It slows resource depletion at one end of the value chain, lowers pollution at the other end and provides a basis to increase worldwide employment with meaningful jobs. A mix of technological and social innovations across all sectors can render even a comfortable style of living. More resource-light solar architecture, regional food markets, hydrogen engines, low-speed cars, recyclable appliances, low-meat gastronomy are, in fact, various other cases in point.

Second, as a change in resource base is central to a transition, the material quality of things will change as well. Bio-mimicry aims at changing the material quality of processes and products by redesigning production systems on biological lines, enabling the constant reuse of materials in continuous closed cycles, and often the elimination of toxicity. Examples like bio-plastic or wind power abound.

Third, living systems can be restored. But it takes deliberate investment in forests, rivers, gardens, hill slopes, soils for restoring, sustaining and expanding the natural capital, so that the biosphere can produce more abundant ecosystem services and natural resources. River restoration, afforestation and low-input agriculture are all attempts in this direction.

Fourth, an emphasis on real wealth can diminish the importance of goods for both the producer and the consumer. By shifting business strategies from the sale of hardware to the sale of services, companies can learn to make money without adding ever more objects to the world; they will sell results rather than things, satisfaction rather than engines, fans or plastic. And last but not least, people can revalue those forms of wealth which cannot be bought with a credit card: the enjoyment of quality, friendship, beauty. In short, to cherish well-being rather than well-having.

Democratic Globalization

There is not just one way to build the world society, as there has not been just one way to build nations. National societies that have once been formed reconfiguring smaller social units, such as cities, counties or tribes, have taken the form of dictatorships, kingdoms and democracies. Likewise, the creation of the global society, which will reconfigure smaller units, such as nation states, civil society organizations and private enterprises will no doubt take different forms. However, the precise shape of the global society, its prevailing ideals, its winners and losers will evolve from innumerable debates, competing imaginations and protracted power struggles. Today, the battle is on. Names of places, such as Seattle, Port Alegre or Davos, have become symbols for the trial of strength between sections of the global society with conflicting interests, visions and backgrounds. What kind of globalization is desirable? This is the key question which has moved to center stage at the threshold of the 21st century.

The globalization process is driven by two mainsprings. The first is technology that has increased the connectivity of people across large distances. Airplanes take people to far away places, television brings home distant events, the Internet pulls people into a worldwide but distance-less space, satellites convey pictures of the Earth from outer space. For better or for worse, present generations experience the world in real time and at zero distance. This historical shift in both infrastructure and consciousness cannot be reversed. It will remain part of the human condition in the century to come.

The second mainspring is the twenty-year wave of deregulation, privatization, liberalization of capital flows and global trade, and the export-led growth policies that followed the collapse of the Bretton Woods fixed currency-exchange regime in the early 1970s. The IMF and WTO are the pivotal drivers of this process. These two phenomena must be dealt with separately. Worldwide connectivity does not necessarily imply the imperative of neo-liberal rule. Quite to the contrary, the unfolding transnational space has to be shaped by the values of justice and sustainability, which take priority over the value of economic efficiency.

Broadly speaking, there are presently two concepts of globalization, which have gained prominence in recent controversies. Corporate globalization, which aims at transforming the world into a single economic arena, allows corporations to compete freed from constraints in order to increase global wealth and welfare. This particular concept can be traced to the rise of the free trade idea in 18th century Britain and has come, after many permutations, to dominate world politics in the 21st century.

Democratic globalization, on the other hand, envisages a world that is home to a flourishing plurality of cultures and that recognizes the fundamental rights for every world citizen. The roots of this concept extend back to late ancient Greek philosophy and the European Enlightenment with their perception of the world in a cosmopolitan spirit. The cause of justice and sustainability would be caught in quicksand unless it is elaborated in the framework of democratic globalization.

A Johannesburg Deal

In light of the overall goal of sustainability, the North, the South and so-called transition countries certainly have different but not unequal points of departure. The North is most unsustainable in resource consumption, and the South is most unsustainable with regard to poverty and misery. The former must reduce its ecological footprint, while the latter must ensure livelihood rights for the marginalized majority. The first challenge implies a major restructuring of production and consumption patterns, while the second challenge implies a change in the inequality of power within and between countries. However, the South does not owe anything to the North, while the North owes something to the South. The responsibility of present Southern governments for the fate of their people notwithstanding, during the long history of colonization the North has accumulated a debt toward the South, in both ecological and economic terms. Given this debt, the North should offer reparations in the form of support to the South. This support would facilitate a transition to sustainability in both senses, by improving people's quality of life and by moving toward a resource-light economy.

Finally, the transition to sustainability requires a framework of rights and, to a lesser degree, funds and expertise. Community rights and citizen rights are essential for empowerment, while the common public values of ecology and equity must prevail over the value of individual economic efficiency in trade relations. To put it in a nutshell, restraint (in resource use and the exercise of power), reparation (from North to South) and rights (for citizens, communities and national societies) are the conceptual coordinates for framing a global deal.

SUSTAINABLE DEVELOPMENT IN SIX PARTS

Peter Montague

Sustainable Development, Part 1

THE PHRASE "SUSTAINABLE DEVELOPMENT" was coined by the World Commission on Environment and Development (the "Brundtland Commission") in 1987. The Commission defined "sustainable development" as material improvement to meet the needs of the present generation without compromising the ability of future generations to meet their own needs.[1] This definition emphasizes an important aspect of our ethical relationship to the unborn, yet it remains too vague to be truly useful as a guide for human activity because we cannot agree on the meaning of "needs." We can't really know what the "needs" of future generations will be, and we can't even agree on what we ourselves "need" vs. what we merely want.

Fortunately, more useful definitions of "sustainable development" are coming into focus. By "more useful" I mean definitions that will allow us to reach agreement, thus giving us a common basis for action. In his book, *Beyond Growth*,[2] economist Herman Daly defines "sustainable development" as "development without growth—without growth in throughput beyond environmental regenerative and absorptive capacity."[2, p. 69] This is an important definition, worth examining.

First, let's look at "throughput." Throughput is the flow of materials and energy through the human economy. It includes everything we make and do. When we speak of "growth" we are talking about growth in throughput—people making (and throwing away) more stuff and using more energy to do it. The totality of the human economy is throughput. It is calculated as the total number of people multiplied by their consumption.

The "regenerative and absorptive capacity of the environment" refers to the ability of the environment to provide (a) materials for our use, and (b) places where we can throw our wastes. This gets a little more complicated. It refers to two things, (1) the ability of the environment to provide us with the high-quality raw materials we need to make things, and (2) the ability of the environment to break down our wastes and turn them back into raw materials, an essential service.

Let's take waste first. When we throw things away, nature begins to take them apart and recycle them. For example, when we throw away wood, natural agents (called "decomposers"), such as termites, begin to eat our wood waste and break it down into raw materials—carbon, hydrogen, oxygen, nitrogen, sulfur, and so forth. Creatures such as earth worms use the termites' wastes as raw materials for soil, which provides nutrients for new trees to grow. This is called the "detritus food chain" and it is essential to life on Earth, though largely invisible from a human perspective. The detritus food chain is made up of insects, bacteria, funguses, and other creatures that most of us know little about. But without their workings, the world would become overloaded with wastes and biological processes would become clogged and stop working.[3] If you've ever visited a modern hog farm, you have an idea of what it means to exceed the capacity of the local environment to absorb waste. It is unpleasant and hazardous.

A second major benefit that nature provides for us is high-quality raw materials that we can use. Daly calls these "natural capital," of which there are two kinds. The first kind of natural capital takes the form of a stock, a fixed quantity, such as oil or coal or rich deposits of copper. We can use these stocks of natural capital at any rate we choose, but when they are used up (dispersed into the environment as wastes), they will no longer be available for our use, or for the use of future generations. (The second law of thermodynamics guarantees that we can never take highly-dispersed atoms of, say, copper and gather them back into a highly-concentrated copper deposit. The energy requirements of such an operation are simply too great. If the second law didn't hold true, as Daly says, we could make windmills out of beach sand and use them to power machines to extract gold from seawater. Unfortunately, the second law DOES hold true, and once we disperse highly-concentrated ores, we cannot afford to re-concentrate them.)

The second kind of natural capital takes the form of a flow. In general these flows are continuous (though human bungling can interrupt some of them). Examples include sunlight, the capacity of green plants to create carbohydrates by photosynthesis, rainfall, and the production of fish in the oceans. These forms of natural capital are endlessly renewable but can only be used at a certain rate—the rate at which nature provides them. Example: So long as we cut trees at a certain rate, and no faster, then nature will produce new trees fast enough to maintain a constant supply of cuttable trees. If we cut trees faster than that, nature will not be able to keep up with us and then people in the future will have fewer trees to meet their needs. The capacity of the Earth to support life will have been diminished. This is an example of exceeding the capacity of the ecosystem to regenerate itself.

Growth, then, means quantitative increase in physical size. Development, on the other hand, means qualitative change, realization of potentialities, transition to a fuller or better state. On a planet such as Earth, which is finite and not growing, there can be no such thing as "sustainable growth" because growth will inevitably hit physical limits. Because of physical limits, growth of throughput is simply not sustainable indefinitely. But development CAN continue endlessly as we seek to improve the quality of life for humans and for the other creatures with which we share the planet.

To repeat, then, sustainable development means development without growth in throughput that exceeds the regenerative and absorptive capacity of the environment. Sustainable development and the standard ideology of growth stand in contrast to each other and, in fact, are incompatible with each other.

Thus to be sustainable, the human economy (our throughput) must not exceed a certain size in relation to the global ecosystem because it will start to diminish the capacity of the planet to support humans (and other creatures). If the human economy grows too large, it begins to interfere with the natural services that support all life—services such as photosynthesis, pollination, purification of air and water, maintenance of climate, filtering of excessive ultraviolet radiation, recycling of wastes, and so forth. Growth beyond that point will produce negative consequences that exceed the benefits of increased throughput.

There is considerable evidence that the throughput of some parts of the human economy has already exceeded the regenerative and absorptive capacity of the environment. The problem of climate change and global warming is an example; it provides evidence that we have exceeded the capacity of the atmosphere to absorb our carbon dioxide, methane, and nitrogen oxide wastes. Many of the fresh water fish of the world now contain dangerously elevated levels of toxic mercury because we humans have doubled the amount of mercury normally present in the atmosphere—evidence that we have exceeded earth's capacity to absorb our mercury wastes.[4] Depletion of the ozone layer is evidence that we have exceeded the atmosphere's capacity to absorb our chlorinated fluorocarbon (CFC) wastes. This list can readily be extended.

There is also considerable evidence that we have already diminished several important stocks and flows of natural capital. The U.S. economy, for example, is now dependent upon oil imported from the Middle East because we have depleted our own stocks of oil. Most of the world's seventeen marine fisheries are badly depleted—a flow of natural capital that we have over-harvested, in some cases nearly to the point of extinction. (See *Rachel's*

Environmental and Health Weekly [REHW] #587.) This list, too, can readily be extended.

One particular limit seems worth noting at this point. In 1986, a group of biologists at Stanford University analyzed the total amount of photosynthetic activity on all the available land on Earth, and asked what proportion of it have humans now appropriated for their own use (mainly through agriculture)?[5] The answer is 40 percent. This leaves 60 percent for the use of nonhumans. But the human population is presently doubling every 35 or 40 years. After one more doubling, humans will be using 80 percent of all the products of sunlight, and shortly after that, 100 percent. Don't get me wrong—humans are important. But I don't know very many people who think it would be smart to deny every wild creature access to the basic food and habitat resources of the planet just to keep the human economy expanding. Even if we thought we had the right to use 100 percent of the green products of sunlight for our own purposes, the human population would have to stop growing at that point because there wouldn't be any more sunlight to appropriate. That time is less than one human lifetime (70 years) away.

Thus we soon will reach—or more likely have already reached—the point at which growth of the human economy does more harm than good. What is needed under these circumstances is to stabilize total consumption, total throughput.

There are two basic rationales for doing this, one based in science and one in religion. Herman Daly offers both. We have heard the scientific argument, above, which says that the capacity of the Earth to support life is being—or soon will be—diminished by growth of throughput and that sooner or later we can only hurt ourselves and our children if we persist on this path of unsustainability. The religious argument goes like this:

"I believe that God the Creator exists now, as well as in the past and future, and is the source of our obligation to Creation, including other creatures, and especially including members of our own species who are suffering. Our ability and inclination to enrich the present at the expense of the future, and of other species, is as real and as sinful as our tendency to further enrich the wealthy at the expense of the poor. To hand back to God the gift of Creation in a degraded state capable of supporting less life, less abundantly, and for a shorter future, is surely a sin. If it is a sin to kill and to steal, then surely it is a sin to destroy carrying capacity—the capacity of the earth to support life now and in the future. Sometimes we find ourselves in an impasse in which sins are unavoidable. We may sometimes have to sacrifice future life in order to preserve present life—but to sacrifice future life to protect present luxury and extravagance is a very different matter."[2, pp. 222-223]

Sustainable Development, Part 2

In his excellent short book, *Beyond Growth*,[1] economist Herman Daly says that every economy faces three problems: allocation, distribution, and scale.[2] What do these terms mean?

Allocation refers to the apportioning of resources among different products—in other words, deciding whether we should produce more corn, more cars, more bicycles, more jelly beans, or more hospitals. Because resources are limited, we can't have everything, so we must allocate our resources in some way to provide the goods that people want and can afford to pay for. The way we do this is "the market" which sets relative prices for goods.[3] Prices act as signals that cause people to put more (or fewer) resources into creating particular products that other people are willing and able to buy.

The second problem faced by every economy is distribution—apportioning goods (and the resources they embody) among different people, not among different products. Nearly everyone agrees that goods should be distributed in a way that is fair (though we may disagree on the precise meaning of "fair"). If you don't believe this statement is true, think of an extreme case. If one person received 99 percent of all the benefits provided by the U.S. economy, and all other citizens had to divvy up the remaining 1 percent, almost everyone would agree that this was an "unfair" or unsatisfactory distribution of benefits. The vast majority of people would say, "There is something wrong with this picture." This extreme example is intended to show that nearly everyone agrees that there are "fair" and "unfair" distributions of goods. What is a "fair" distribution—and how we should achieve it—are the main questions that give rise to "politics."

Unfortunately the market cannot solve the problem of fair distribution. Left alone, a market economy tends to create inequalities that grow larger as time passes. Both the economic successes and failures of individuals tend to be cumulative—the successful tend to succeed again and again while the unsuccessful tend to remain unsuccessful. Marriages tend to result in further concentration of wealth. Furthermore, as Daly says, dishonesty and exploitation are not necessary to explain inequality but they certainly contribute to it.[4] None of these statements is absolute—you can point to many individual exceptions to each of them—but the tendencies that they describe are well-recognized.

No, the market cannot solve the problem of unfair distribution. This problem must be solved by people deciding what is fair, then making public policies intended to achieve a fair distribution. After those decisions have been made, then the market can allocate resources efficiently[3] within the politically-established framework of fairness.

The third economic problem is the problem of scale—how large can an economy become before it begins to harm the ecosystem that undergirds and sustains it? Here again, the market does not—cannot—provide any answer. The market offers no mechanism for deciding what is a desirable scale or for achieving that scale. You can have an efficient allocation of resources[4] and a just distribution of benefits, yet still have an economy that grows too large and consequently damages the ecosystem. (Each of the three problems—allocation, distribution, and scale—is separate and each must be solved separately.)

The ecosystem provides us with two major services—it provides resources that we can use (such as air, trees, copper deposits) and it provides a place to discard our wastes. Within limits, the ecosystem can regenerate certain resources (air and trees, for example), and it can absorb a certain amount of wastes, recycling them via the services of the detritus food chain. (See REHW #624.) Unfortunately, it is quite possible for the economy to grow so large that it exceeds the capacity of the ecosystem to regenerate itself and/or to absorb our wastes. At that point, the economy has grown unsustainably large and further growth will diminish the carrying capacity of the planet— the capacity to support life, including human life.

As we saw in Part One, there is abundant evidence that the human economy, worldwide, has already grown so large that it has exceeded some of the ecosystem's capacity to regenerate itself, and has already grown so large that it has exceeded part of the ecosystem's capacity to absorb our wastes. These problems first appear on a local scale (the U.S. has nearly exhausted its reserves of tin, nickel, chromium, petroleum, and many other mineral resources,[5] and many U.S. cities are presently unable to provide their inhabitants with healthful air because of waste gases from automobiles). Eventually economic growth reaches a point at which local problems become global. For example, in recent years we discovered that we had inadvertently damaged the Earth's stratospheric ozone layer with our CFC wastes, and that most of the world's marine fisheries have been severely degraded by overfishing. We are now making similar unhappy discoveries at a steady (or perhaps accelerating) pace.

Economists, and business and political leaders, acknowledge only two of the three economic problems outlined above—the problems of allocation and distribution. The problem of scale—caused by growing quantities of materials and energy flowing through the economy (see REHW #624)—the problem of scale has still not been acknowledged by most economists, business people, or politicians. To them, continued growth can only be good. The vast majority of them deny that the scale of the economy must be kept comfortably within the regenerative and absorptive limits of the ecosystem (if they have thought about it at all).

There is a deep and abiding reason for their denial. For the past 400 years, growth has been the central organizing principle of all European societies, and especially of American society. Economic growth has substituted for politics, deflecting attention away from the contentious problem of fair distribution: even a small slice of the pie will grow larger each year if the total pie keeps growing larger. Thus growth has allowed us to avoid confronting difficult ethical questions about the fair distribution of income and wealth.[6] So long as the pie kept growing we could accommodate the rising demands of slaves, farmers, immigrants, industrial workers, women, and so forth.

As William Ophuls has said, "We have justified large differences in income and wealth on the grounds that they promote growth and that all would receive future advantage from current inequality as the benefits of development 'trickled down' to the poor." (On a more personal level, Ophuls says, "economic growth also ratifies the ethics of individual self-seeking: you can get on without concern for the fate of others, for they are presumably getting on too, even if not so well as you.) But if growth in production is no longer of overriding importance the rationale for differential rewards gets thinner, and with a cessation of growth it virtually disappears. . . . Since people's demands for economic betterment are not likely to disappear, once the pie stops growing fast enough to accommodate their demands, they will begin making demands for redistribution," Ophuls says.[6]

The end of growth will change American (and European) politics fundamentally, forcing us to confront basic ethical questions of economic fairness. For this reason, the environmental dangers of growth are ignored by those who think they have the most to lose—our business and political leaders (and their academic support staff, the mainstream economists).

Now stay with me as we probe a little deeper into growth. This may seem obscure, but it is important.

Growth—the central organizing principle of our society (we could also call it the main ideology of our society) has been grounded in an ethical principle developed by the English philosopher Jeremy Bentham and elaborated by John Stuart Mill in the 1830s. Bentham argued that the goal of public action was "the greatest good for the greatest number"—a goal that most people would probably embrace today without thinking about it very carefully.

Now that the end of growth is in sight (because we have begun to hit nature's limits), we can no longer pretend that we can achieve the greatest good for the greatest number.[7]

Confronting the limits of the planetary ecosystem, we are forced to ask, how much good can we achieve for how many people for how long? As Daly says, we can have "the greatest good for a sufficient number" or we can have "sufficient good for the greatest number" but the "greatest good for the greatest number" we cannot have.[8] Daly favors seeking "sufficient good for the greatest number"—meaning the greatest number of humans that can be supported year after year into the indefinite future. If your goal is to maximize human welfare, this is the formula that does it. If we live sustainably, without exceeding the planet's capacity for regeneration and the absorption of waste, billions or trillions of humans will ultimately be able to enjoy the good life on planet Earth, world without end. The alternative (which is the path we are presently on) is to load up the planet with 12 to 20 billion people in the next century until the ecosystem collapses, thus diminishing the carrying capacity of the planet and greatly reducing the total number of humans who can ever enjoy a good life on Earth. If you want to maximize human enjoyment of the good life, the choice is clear.

An essential step toward sustainable development—offering the greatest number of people a sufficiency of resources for the good life—will be policies explicitly aimed at reducing huge economic inequalities. Growth will no longer substitute for ethical public policies.

One of the main features of the modern world that creates and sustains inequality is the high human birth rate. An abundance of people provides a pool of cheap labor to do the world's work. A high birth rate creates steady pressure driving wages down. In ancient Rome the word "proletariat" meant "those with many children" and the main role of the proletariat in Roman society was to procreate to serve the patricians. Failure to help people control their own numbers—then as now—is an implicit cheap labor policy. A high birth rate tends to maintain inequality, and a reduced birth rate has the opposite effect, tending to equalize incomes and wealth.

Small wonder, then, that so many of the world's people are denied the knowledge and the means for voluntarily eliminating unwanted fertility. In too many societies (including our own) the knowledge and means for voluntarily controlling fertility are as inequitably distributed as income and wealth. The wealthy have little difficulty controlling their numbers; the technologies are readily available to them. The poor find it not so easy. There is a reason for this.

Sustainable Development, Part 3

When Adam Smith published *The Wealth of Nations* in 1776, the world was essentially empty from a human perspective, with fewer than one billion human inhabitants.[1] At that time, the planet had abundant "natural capital" of all kinds—for example, highly-concentrated metallic ores, oceans full of fish, continents covered with trees to absorb carbon dioxide from the atmosphere, and mysterious substances like petroleum oozing out of the ground spontaneously. The world of 1776 was short of *human* capital—techniques for extracting minerals from the deep earth, ships to catch fish efficiently, and machines to turn trees into lumber, for example.

Now, says economist Daly, the situation is reversed.[2] Increasingly, natural capital is scarce and human capital is abundant.

- Today there is no shortage of huge ships to sweep nets through the oceans to harvest fish—but the fish themselves are disappearing.

- Chemical factories are abundant, producing a cornucopia of useful chlorinated chemicals, but there is a shortage of natural mechanisms to detoxify and recycle such chemicals. As a result, the entire planet is experiencing a buildup of chlorinated toxicants and scientists are discovering new harmful effects in wildlife and humans each year.

- Only recently, scientists concluded that the ecosystem's capacity to remove carbon dioxide from the atmosphere has been exceeded because of human activity. As a result, they believe, CO_2 is building up in the air, pushing up the temperature of the planet. We are waiting now to learn the real consequences, but more droughts, floods, and major storms must be expected, we are told.

In sum, natural capital—both sources and sinks—are becoming scarce on a global scale for the first time ever. The Earth is no longer empty. It is full, or nearly so.

Mainstream economists do not worry about shortages of natural capital because neoclassical economic theory assumes that human capital can substitute for natural capital. To a certain limited extent, this is true. When copper becomes too expensive for making telephone wires, we substitute glass in the form of fiber optic cables (which we make by manipulating sand with large quantities of energy and accumulated know-how). However, Daly argues, traditional economists have ignored the extent to which the usefulness of human capital depends upon the availability of natural capital. Daly asks, quite sensibly, what good is a sawmill without a forest, a fishing boat without fish and an oil refinery without oil? In truth, says Daly, natural and human capital complement each other—we need them both to sustain our economy and the natural systems that support us and the other creatures. This may seem obvious to most people, but to many traditional economists it still seems like heresy.

As we have seen in Part 2, there are two kinds of natural capital—those that renew themselves (e.g., fish, trees) and those that don't, at least not on a human time scale (e.g., copper deposits and petroleum).

How do you "improve" natural capital? Renewable natural capital can be replenished by not using it and by waiting patiently. Fish stocks will replenish themselves if we refrain from overfishing. The same is true of forests. In this new economic perspective, frugality, efficiency, and patience once again become prime virtues. As Daly says, for ecological economists, *laissez faire* takes on new, deeper meaning.

Somewhere in between natural capital and human capital is "cultivated capital"—fish ponds, tree farms, and herds of cattle, for example.

Recent attempts to cultivate natural capital may provide some limited benefits. Tree plantations provide one of the services of a real forest—trees to cut—but they do not replace forest habitat or biodiversity. Fish farms do produce fish but they also require high-protein fish food, antibiotics to fend against disease, and some means of handling concentrated wastes. Clearly, cultivated capital has severe limitations, and it relies on natural capital for its limited successes.

The ultimate experiment in cultivated natural capital—or ecosystem management, as many modern engineers and scientists like to call it—took place between 1991 and 1993 in the desert 25 miles north of Tucson, Arizona. Here, a group of scientists built a complex ecosystem covering 3.15 acres under an airtight glass cover and 8 of them tried to live in it for two years. The materially-closed system—nothing was supposed to go in or out during the two years—was intended to replicate a tiny Earth, complete with ocean, desert, grasslands, and woodlands. The experiment was called Biosphere 2 (the Earth is Biosphere 1), and it was a stunning failure. From the beginning the Biospherians encountered "numerous unexpected problems and surprises."[3]

Fifty tons of oxygen disappeared mysteriously from the closed system, reducing oxygen levels to those typically encountered at an altitude of 17,500 feet—barely sufficient to maintain human consciousness. Carbon dioxide skyrocketed to levels that threatened to poison the humans as well. Levels of nitrous oxide—laughing gas—rose high enough to interfere with vitamin B12 synthesis, threatening the humans with brain damage. Finally, oxygen had to be pumped in from the outside to keep the Biospherians from suffocating.

Tropical birds disappeared after the first freeze. A native species of Arizona ant somehow found its way into the enclosure and soon killed off all other soft-bodied insects. As the ants proliferated, creatures as large as snakes had to hide from them or be eaten alive. All seven species of frogs went extinct. All together, 19 of 25 vertebrate species went extinct. Before the two years was up, all pollinators went extinct, so none of the plants could reproduce themselves. Despite unlimited energy and technology available from the outside to keep the system functioning, it was a colossal $200 million failure. The scientists concluded, "No one yet knows how to engineer systems that provide humans with the life-supporting services that natural ecosystems *pro-*

duce for free." Dismembering major biomes [ecosystems] into small pieces, a consequence of widespread human activities, must be regarded with caution . . . the initial work in Biosphere 2 has already provided insights for ecologists—and perhaps an important lesson for humanity."[4]

Thus we know that cultivated natural capital has an exceedingly limited capacity to provide the benefits that nature's own natural capital provides. We would be fools to count on replacing nature's bounty with something of our own invention. The Earth is our only home and we must protect it.

Non-renewable capital cannot be "improved"—it can only be preserved. Thus to the extent feasible, our economy should shift over to renewable resources, to be used at a rate set by nature's rate of renewal. Non-renewable resources should be left alone, or they should be liquidated thoughtfully to provide future humans with a stream of income. For example, arguably, dwindling petroleum supplies should be invested in "solar breeder" facilities—factories that make photovoltaic solar cells. The product of such a factory could be used to power the construction and operation of more factories to manufacture more photovoltaic cells, to make more factories to make more photovoltaics, and so on, providing the next generation with a legacy that allows them to tap into the endless flow of the sun's energy.

What public policies might help us make the shift to using renewable resources at sustainable rates?

First, as we saw in Part 2, stop counting the consumption of natural capital as income. Depletion should never be treated as income. It would be like burning the furniture to heat the house, congratulating ourselves on the resulting warmth. It will be short-lived. As preposterous as it may sound, most nations, including the U.S., presently treat depletion of their natural capital as if it were income, so far as national accounts are concerned—a major accounting error. Depletion is a cost, not a benefit. (The same is true of pollution—in calculating Gross Domestic Product [GDP] we count pollution, pollution illnesses, and anti-pollution expenditures as benefits, not costs. This is clearly wrong and wrongheaded but the nation's economists still endorse such a system—a sad commentary on the state of economic "science" today.)

Secondly, tax labor and income less, and tax throughput more. We will always need governments to:

- protect the weak from the strong and tyrannical;

- provide a safety net for those plagued by bad luck;

- protect the commons (such as the atmosphere) from thoughtless or predatory individuals and businesses;

- level the playing field for individuals and businesses (making sure, to the extent possible, that people start life with equal opportunity, and that the competitive environment for businesses is preserved against monopolies and oligopolies).

The present tax structure encourages businesses to substitute capital and throughput (energy and materials) for workers. Throughput depletes resources and creates pollution, so our tax structure discourages what we want (jobs and income) and encourages what we don't want (depletion and pollution). This is backwards.

After we shift over to "green taxes"—which encourage jobs and income and discourage depletion and pollution—we will still need an income tax but not primarily to provide revenue for government. We will need an income tax chiefly to reduce inequalities in income and wealth because huge inequalities undermine the main goals of a democracy: equal opportunity, a real voice in the decisions that affect your life, and a sense of shared ownership (a "stake") in the community.

Third, move away from the ideology of global economic integration by free trade, free capital mobility, and export-led growth. Instead, move toward a more nationalist orientation that seeks to develop domestic production for internal markets as the first option, embracing international trade only in those instances where it is clearly more efficient.

Daly emphasizes this point again and again: free trade as conceived by the current generation of political and economic leaders will be disastrous because it is destroying the power of national governments to control the destiny of their people. "To globalize the economy by erasure of national economic boundaries through free trade, free capital mobility, and free, or at least uncontrolled, migration is to wound fatally the major unit of community capable of carrying out any policies for the common good," Daly writes.[5]

Sustainable Development, Part 4

Sustainable development means achieving human well being without exceeding the Earth's twin capacities for regeneration (trees and water, for example) and for waste absorption (carbon dioxide, for example). As we have seen in the preceding parts, there is growing evidence that humans have already exceeded both of these capacities and that further growth in throughput (making more stuff using more energy) will only make things worse. Of course, increasing efficiency (making more useful things with fewer materials and less energy) can buy us a short reprieve. But it appears that we are approaching (or have already exceeded) the Earth's limits for handling many kinds of wastes. Sooner rather than later total throughput (measured as the total number of humans multiplied by their furnishings and the energy they require) must soon decline or we face a harsh future with (for example) more big, costly storms and more poisoned wildlife and people. Recall that hurricane Mitch killed over 10,000 people and devastated several national economies.

To bring human economic activity into line with Earth's limits, we will need to understand the forces that are pushing us in wrong directions. Chief among these is the drive toward "free trade," according to Daly.[1, 2] If there is one thing that most economists, politicians, and business leaders agree on, it is the desirability of free trade. Daly, on the other hand, says free trade undermines environmental standards, drives down wages, weakens our capacity to do better, and undermines our sense of community.

Free trade is the absence of barriers to international trade. There are three common barriers: tariffs, quotas, and restrictions on the flow of capital. A tariff is a tax on goods coming into a country—for example, a tax on Egyptian cotton imported into the U.S. A quota is a limit on imports—for example, the U.S. might accept only a certain number of Japanese automobiles. A third limit on free trade might restrict the amounts of foreign capital that could flow into a country. For example, in response to its recent (and ongoing) financial crisis, Malaysia is now severely restricting the amount of foreign capital that it will accept.

Almost all traditional (neoclassical) economists favor free trade. Among economists, free trade has taken on the character of a religious faith, its power to do good unquestioned. Among traditional economists, Daly is viewed as a heretic. He believes free trade is bad for everyone (except transnational corporations) for the following reasons:

Free trade tends to lower environmental and social standards internationally. Take the example of two nations: One nation internalizes environmental and social insurance costs to a high degree (enforcing strict environmental laws and providing benefits such as health care and social security). The second nation refuses to internalize these costs—providing no social security, and throwing toxic waste into its rivers. Products from the second country will sell for less and will tend to drive competitors in the first country out of business. Thus there is a clear conflict between a national policy of internalizing environmental and social insurance costs and a policy of free trade. The country that exploits its environment and its citizens is rewarded. The country that protects its environment and its citizens is penalized.

Of course, if we had a world government to enforce environmental rules and minimum standards for human well being, this problem would disappear. But no such government is in sight. Furthermore, the world's economists cannot even agree on how to measure the costs of environmental degradation; the vast majority of economists continue to account for depletion of natural resources as if it were income—a preposterous and wrongheaded accounting practice that is nearly universal. (Any business that treated depletion of its assets as income would be bankrupt in short order.)

One solution would be a tariff on goods imported from countries that refuse to internalize environmental and social insurance costs. Such a tariff would aim not to protect an inefficient domestic industry but to protect an efficient national policy of setting prices to reflect the full costs of maintaining community.

Wage levels are set mainly by population size and growth rates. Countries with large populations, rapidly growing, tend toward low wages. This is especially true because the laboring class tends to have a much higher birth rate than the owning class, often twice as high. Labor is the main cost in most consumer goods. Therefore, cheap labor means low prices, creating an advantage in trade. Capital therefore tends to move to low-wage countries. Daly believes that the effect of unrestricted capital mobility is the same as the effect of unrestricted labor mobility. If the U.S. had unrestricted borders, we would enjoy endless cheap labor, but wages would plummet. Unrestricted capital flow will have the same effect, Daly says. "United States capital will benefit from cheap labor abroad followed by cheap labor at home, at least until checked by a crisis of insufficient demand due to a lack of worker purchasing power resulting from low wages," Daly wrote in 1996.

Daly's words have a special resonance today when Asian economies have been devastated by overcapacity for cars, chemicals, and electronics. As Louis Uchitelle of the *New York Times* wrote recently, "In an open-border global economy nearly every car manufacturer, for example, is trying to have a presence in every market. But when all the factories crank out more cars than people can buy, down come car prices. Down go the profits of car companies. Out go the workers. And down go the number of people who can afford to buy cars. Economies can spiral downward toward recession, or worse. . . . The global economy appears, in effect, to be capable of self-destruction."[3]

The problem of uniformly low wages could be solved by maintaining low population growth everywhere, plus a fair distribution of benefits, plus policies to internalize the costs of environmental protection and social insurance. But even if all this were achieved, Daly says, free trade would still be harmful.

Free trade and free capital mobility separate the ownership and control of businesses, and force labor to become mobile—both of which undermine human community. "Community economic life can be disrupted not only by your fellow citizen who, though living in another part of your country, might at least share some tenuous bonds of community with you, but by someone on the other side of the world with whom you have no community of language, history, culture, law. These foreigners may be wonderful people—that is not the point. The point is that they are very removed from the life of the community that is affected significantly by their decisions. Your life and your community can be disrupted by decisions and events over which you have no control, no vote, no voice."[4]

Daly believes that free trade and free capital mobility have created economic instability by permitting huge imbalances in international payments and capital transfers resulting in debts that are unrepayable or excessively burdensome. Efforts to pay back loans while still meeting domestic needs have fostered government deficits and high inflation rates, furthering instability. Inflation then takes an additional toll: currency devaluations, foreign exchange speculation, repudiation of debts, and bank failures. Thailand, South Korea, Malaysia, Indonesia, the Philippines. Who is next?

Free trade appears to loosen the constraints of the ecosystem, but this is a false picture. We must all live within the absorptive and regenerative capacities of the ecosystem. Trade allows us to import environmental services (including waste absorption) from elsewhere. Within limits, this makes sense. New York City cannot grow its own food and must import it from elsewhere. But, Daly says, free trade leads to a situation in which every nation is trying to live beyond its own absorptive and regenerative capacities by importing these capacities from elsewhere.

It requires 12.6 acres of land per person (5.1 hectares) to create the flows of materials and energy needed to maintain an American lifestyle, and Europeans require nearly as much. But if you divide all the good land on Earth by the present human population, you find there are only 3.7 acres (1.5 hectares) available per person. This tells us that everyone on Earth will never be able to enjoy the hedonistic lifestyle to which we are accustomed.[5]

Secondly, if you divide all the good land in the U.S. by the current U.S. population, you find that we have only 6.9 acres (2.8 hectares) per person. This means each of us is "borrowing" 12.6-6.9=5.7 acres (2.3 hectares) of someone else's land to maintain our lifestyle.[5] (Is this one reason why we spend $250 billion each year—five times as much as any other country—maintaining our armed forces?)

Thus we in the overdeveloped North face a number of uncomfortable moral realities: with at least a billion people not getting sufficient food calories each day to maintain subsistence, they require economic growth—not merely development—to meet their needs. Yet growth is already stressing the planet's capacity to regenerate itself and absorb our wastes. It appears that the overdeveloped North will have to stop growing (and perhaps shrink) before the South can take its rightful place at the world's table.

Daly acknowledges that the roots of this problem are much deeper than free trade ideology. But, he says, "The point is that free trade makes it very hard to deal with these root causes at a national level, which is the only level at which effective social controls over the economy exist. . . . [T]he unit of community is the nation—the unit in which there are institutions and traditions of collective action, responsibility, and mutual help, the unit in which government tries to carry out policies for the good of its citizens. . . ."

Daly favors not free trade but regional trade among national communities that share similar community standards regarding wages, welfare, population control, environmental protection, and conservation. "True efficiency lies in the protection of these hard-won community standards from the degenerative competition of individualistic free trade, which comes to rest only at the lowest common denominator," he writes.[2, p. 235]

Today a growing movement of workers, environmentalists, consumers, farmers, and social activists worldwide is urging an alternative to the destructive practices called "free trade." Instead of free trade, they are promoting fair trade. Fair trade is a concept developed in the U.S. (and elsewhere) in the 1940s. Fair trade is international trade based on bedrock principles: workers are paid a fair wage—whenever possible not a minimum wage but a family-sustaining livable wage; the business unit is the cooperative or producer association; raw materials are locally derived and managed in a sustainable fashion; fair trade organizations respect the cultural identity of their trading partners; and they insist on public accountability for their business operations.[6] Different. Very different.

Sustainable Development, Part 5: Emissions Trading

As we saw in Rachel's #625, there are three problems facing every economy: resource allocation, fair distribution, and tolerable size.

Resource allocation means deciding what the economy should make— more automobiles, more nursing homes, or more chocolate truffles, for example. We can't make everything we might want, so we must make choices. In the U.S. and other "market economies," allocation is handled mainly by "the market," meaning the system of prices. Prices send signals to manufacturers to make more of this and less of that, according to what people want and can afford to pay for.

Fair distribution means just what the words say—distributing the benefits of the economy with fairness and justice. The market has no inherent ability to do this. Left alone, the market will tend to make the rich richer and the poor poorer until a small number of people ends up owning just about everything. To achieve a fair distribution, people must make political decisions about what's fair, and about how to achieve their goal of fairness. One formula for fairness, endorsed by Daly, says that high-income people should only make about 10 times as much as low-income people.[1] There are precedents for such a limit in American society. Approximately ten-to-one is the range of pay in federal civil service jobs, and in our military. A general makes about ten times as much as a private. A ten-to-one ratio allows hard-working, ambitious people to earn 10 times as much as people who prefer to take it easy and enjoy life. (And fixing the relationship between the bottom and the top would give the high-income people an incentive to favor raising the incomes of the low-income people because it would be the only way the high-income folks could increase their own income without violating the 10-to-1 rule.) The way to achieve a fair distribution (once you've decided what's fair) is conceptually simple: transfer payments. Tax the haves and transfer the money into the hands of the have-nots. Transfer payments can take various forms—you could simply write checks to the have-nots, or you could provide jobs that pay wages, for example.

The third problem—how large should the total human economy be—has never been considered a problem until very recently (although British economist John Stuart Mill did write about it in 1857). Until very recently, the world looked as if it could support an endless expansion of the human economy. But in recent decades, signs of serious trouble have emerged. In particular, it has become apparent that the world is running out of (or, more accurately, already has run out of) the capacity to absorb industrial wastes safely. The buildup of carbon dioxide and chlorofluorocarbons (CFCs) in the atmosphere, and mercury in fish, are three examples of this problem. It is now apparent that there is some optimum size for the human economy—a size that will provide a sufficient quantity of goods (sufficient to allow "the good life"[2]) for the greatest number of people, world without end. If the economy grows beyond that optimum size, it will begin to produce "bads" (such as toxic fish) faster than it produces goods, and we (and future humans) will be deprived of some of the benefits we enjoy today. There is a good chance that the total human economy has already exceeded the optimum size and that further growth in throughput will do more harm than good. ("Throughput" means materials and energy flowing through the economy— people making more stuff and using energy to do it.)

The size of the economy has never been considered a problem for two main reasons: 1) until recently, the world has always seemed nearly empty from a human viewpoint; and 2) even when the size of the economy began to cause obvious problems, people did their best to ignore the signs, to avoid facing uncomfortable choices. An end to growth is literally unthinkable for most people—especially for Americans—because growth has always been our main method for achieving a fair distribution. We have always been able to argue that poor people would be better off next year because their slim piece of the pie would grow a bit larger as the total pie expanded. Thus we have advocated more growth instead of confronting the question of a fair distribution of benefits. In other words, throughout our history we have substituted growth for politics. Once growth is removed as our all-purpose problem-solver, we will have to face squarely the problem of fair distribution. This is very likely to cause serious disagreements and perhaps even strife. It could get ugly.

As we (in the industrialized world) think about ways to make the transition from our present economy to a steady-state economy in which throughput is no longer growing, a necessary step is to become more efficient. Efficiency is politically acceptable to nearly everyone. Efficiency means cutting waste, learning to do more with less. Who could be against that? For a time, improved efficiency can give us the same benefits that we used to get from real growth.

So how do we cut waste for the least cost? Most economists favor a system called "tradeable pollution permits" also known as "emissions trading." As we will see, many (but not all) environmentalists oppose tradeable pollution permits. Most economists, including Daly, favor them.[3] However, Daly favors them for reasons that are different from the reasons given by most economists.

Tradeable pollution permits are a simple idea. First you decide how much total waste (pollution) to allow in an area. Second you create "rights to pollute" which, taken together, add up to the desired total pollution, and you establish initial ownership of those rights. The third step is where the market comes in. Some people (or corporations) can reduce pollution more cheaply than others. Those for whom reduction is cheap will proceed, thus freeing up some number of unused "rights to pollute." Those rights can then be purchased by firms for whom genuine reduction would be expensive. This scheme promises to provide society with the desired level of total waste (pollution) at the least cost. So far so good.

Daly likes this plan for one main reason: the process of issuing tradeable pollution requires society to confront each of the three economic problems separately: sensible allocation, fair distribution, tolerable size.

The problem of tolerable size must be confronted first: how much total pollution is tolerable? The market has nothing to say about this question. It is a political question. How many sick people is acceptable? How much crop damage caused by air pollution is OK? How many mercury-poisoned fish will we tolerate?

Once that question is settled, then we move to the matter of fair distribution. How should initial ownership of "rights to pollute" be distributed? What is fair? Here again, the market provides no help. This is strictly a political question that citizens must decide among themselves, based on ethics.

Should polluters automatically receive the right to pollute at their current level? This rewards polluters by freely giving them a public good (the capacity of the ecosystem to absorb wastes). Furthermore, it provides the biggest rewards to the biggest polluters. This hardly seems fair. (This is the system that Congress, with help from the Environmental Defense Fund [a mainstream environmental organization], wrote into the Clean Air Act, and this is the system that the U.S. government favors in negotiations over the Kyoto agreement on global warming.)

Another way to distribute pollution rights would be to declare them, collectively, a public good and auction them off to the highest bidder. This has the disadvantage of favoring the wealthy (many of whom made their fortunes by polluting). This doesn't seem completely fair either.

A third way to distribute pollution rights initially would be to give a small pollution right to each citizen in the affected area. Citizens could then dispose of their personal right any way they wanted—they could sell it to a polluter who could use it, or they could retire their right and thus provide a little cleanup.

After the political problems have been solved (establishing the total pollution desired, and making a fair distribution of initial pollution rights), then the market can handle the problem of allocating pollution in the most economically efficient manner (as firms and individuals buy and sell each other's rights according to their circumstances). At least that's the theory.

On paper it looks good and Daly is right: tradeable pollution permits expose three separate economic questions to public scrutiny, in the process revealing that the market has a relatively minor role to play in the overall scheme. The political questions are much larger and more difficult than the question of buying and selling pollution rights, and the market has nothing to do with them.

In actual practice, however, tradeable pollution permits have proven to be a very unfair way to allocate pollution,[4] and there is evidence that they do not always reduce pollution. In some instances, they may actually increase it.[5]

Here are some obvious problems with pollution trading schemes in actual practice:

- Emissions trading moves pollution from one location to another. In practice, this often means dumping more pollution on the poor and on people of color.

- Setting the total desired amount of pollution assumes that risk assessors can determine how much pollution is "safe" for humans and for the ecosystem. Risk assessors have a notoriously poor track record of making such estimates.

- Pollution trading requires careful monitoring and accounting of who is emitting what. Governments, including the U.S. federal government, typically rely on self-reporting by the polluters themselves, who have a large monetary incentive to issue false reports.[4] Internationally, there are no government agencies capable of accurately monitoring thousands or millions of polluters. Monitoring by citizens would appear to be the only practical solution to this problem, but no examples of such a system exist on a large scale.

- Emissions trading will complicate a permit enforcement system that already does not work. Until government can show that it can monitor and enforce limits, emissions trading should not be implemented.

- An emissions trading system has no inherent, built-in incentives to reduce pollution. Unless the system requires an annual decrease in the total pollution allowed, emissions trading will simply lock in today's pollution levels. Polluters need a constant incentive to reduce their discharges toward zero, but emissions trading inherently offers no such incentives.

- In accord with the principle that the polluter should pay, polluters should be required to absorb the costs of the entire pollution control system. Present systems give away the store to the polluters.[6]

Sustainable Development, Part 6: When Growth Stops

Here we wrap up our discussion of sustainable development, based on Daly's excellent book *Beyond Growth.*[1]

Sustainable development means, first, setting physical limits on the "throughput" of the human economy. Throughput means all the materials and energy flowing through the economy—all the things we make and use, and all the energy required to do so.

Another phrase for "throughput" is "total consumption," which is total human population multiplied by per-capita consumption.

The total throughput of the human economy must be kept small enough to avoid exceeding two physical limits of the ecosystem: its capacity to regenerate itself, and its capacity to absorb our wastes. Each year now, scientists report new evidence that the human economy has exceeded both of these ecosystem limits.

For example, nature creates (regenerates) new topsoil each year, but in much of the world (particularly in the U.S.) humans are destroying topsoil faster than nature can create it.[2] Loss of topsoil reduces our future farming capacity in a fundamental way. Topsoil destroyed today is topsoil taken from our children and grandchildren.

Pesticides provide an example of humans producing wastes faster than nature can absorb them. If nature could absorb pesticide residues as fast as humans created them, then there would be no buildup of toxic residues. But there has been a measurable buildup of pesticides at the North and South poles, at the bottom of the deepest oceans, in the drinking water of much of the Midwestern U.S., and in the breast milk of women worldwide. We have clearly exceeded nature's capacity to absorb pesticide wastes, thus denying our children their rightful share of nature's detoxification capacity.

In sum, there really are "limits to growth" and we have already exceeded some of those limits. This means that, at some point, continued economic growth (growth of throughput) will create bads faster than it creates goods (an economist would say "marginal costs will exceed marginal benefits"). Daly (p. 40) argues, for example, that the U.S. chemical industry may have already passed the point at which its toxic discharges are costing society more than the benefits provided by its products.

If this were the case, then society would receive net benefits by shrinking the chemical industry instead of promoting its growth.

Unfortunately, we have no way of measuring whether our economy has passed the point at which costs have begun to exceed benefits because, in our national accounting system (in which we measure "gross domestic product"), we count all production of goods and services as "goods." In tallying up GDP we never subtract any bads. Chemicals are counted as goods and the products they allow us to make are counted as goods. This makes sense. But when our chemical factories produce chemical waste dumps that must be cleaned up at huge public expense, those costs are counted as "goods" too, instead of being subtracted as bads. If a few hundred or a few thousand children get cancer from exposure to chemical wastes, their hospitalization, their radiation treatments, their chemotherapy, and their funeral expenses are all counted as "goods" in our total GDP. If their parents sue, all the resulting court expenses are counted as goods, not bads. In sum, the nation's brightest economists maintain our national accounting system with a calculator that has a plus key but no minus key.[3]

Therefore we have no way of knowing whether the costs of economic growth have exceeded the benefits. The nation's economists (and politicians and business leaders) simply assume that if GDP is rising, our standard of living is rising too. But, as the song goes, it ain't necessarily so. (For substantial evidence on this point, see REHW #516.)

Historically, growth is an aberration; a steady state economy is the norm. Only during the past 500 years has growth begun to seem like the normal condition for human economies. The physical limits to growth (which we are now perceiving because we have exceeded some of them) require us to return to the steady state sooner or later. If we do so by choice, we may be able to guide the process and achieve a steady-state economy with a reasonable approximation of the "good life" for most people, world without end.[4] On the other hand, if we continue to blindly accept the ideology that growth is good, then natural limits will reduce our numbers with an ecological meat axe and the suffering will be immense.

Why do we have so much trouble imagining a no-growth economy?

Daly believes there is one central reason: because a steady-state economy, one that is no longer physically growing, will force us to confront the problem of inequality, which is another name for the problem of poverty. So long as the total economic pie is growing we can say, "The poor will be lifted out of poverty by growth, so we need not take any special steps to alleviate their condition—in fact we hardly need to think about them at all because the market will take care of them."

In a steady-state economy, we will have to decide what is a fair distribution of the benefits of the economy because, in the steady state, as the rich get richer the poor must get poorer. In this situation, the only way to make sure that a fair share is available for everyone (whatever society decides "a fair share" means) is to set a limit on how much the powerful and the predatory can take for themselves. Daly says simply, "In a steady state, if the rich get richer the poor must get poorer, not only relatively but absolutely. If the total [throughput of the economy] is limited there must be a maximum limit on individual income."

Daly believes this is the key reason why we refuse to confront limits to growth: we cling to the path of unsustainable growth so that we will not have to think about limiting inequality. (p. 215) Daly argues that establishing the principle of limited inequality is a necessary (but not sufficient) condition for achieving a modern steady state. He argues that the precise range of inequality that we allow is not as important as establishing the principle that inequality should be limited.

If inequality is to be limited, this implies that there will be a maximum allowable income and a minimum income. (These standards would have to be developed within each society because needs are culturally determined.) Daly argues (p. 210) that the minimum income "would be some culturally defined amount sufficient for food, clothing, shelter, and basic health and education." The maximum income might be four times as great as the minimum (which is what Plato advocated), or it could be 10 or 20 times as great. The exact number isn't terribly important. The point is that there must be a limit on inequality—the precise limit can be worked out in practice. (The overarching goal would be to provide sufficient incentive so that all necessary jobs are filled voluntarily by qualified people.)

Daly argues that limiting inequality (in a steady-state economy) is a way to achieve three things:

- It is a way to keep the rich from leaning too heavily on the poor
- It is a way to keep the present generation from leaning too heavily on future generations
- It is a way to prevent humans from "leaning too heavily on other creatures whose habitats must disappear as we convert more and more of the finite ecosystem into a source for raw materials, a sink for waste, or living space for humans and warehouses for our artifacts."

In addition to the matter of fairness (the meaning of which each society or culture must decide for itself), in a steady-state economy we would need to limit inequality for another reason as well: to limit total human consumption, which is total population multiplied by per-capita consumption. It is total human consumption that stresses the ecosystem.

Because total consumption has two parts (human numbers and per-capita consumption), to limit total consumption, we would need to limit inequality *and* limit total human numbers. In a steady-state economy (one whose total size is established by the Earth's limits), the more people there are, the lower their average standard of living must be. Controlling growth requires us to limit both human consumption AND human population. Both limits are *essential* if we aim to control the total size (throughput) of the global economy.

In recent decades we have invented several technological fixes aimed at circumventing the natural limits of ecosystems, so that growth can continue. The "green revolution" tried to speed up the growth rates of the edible portions of wheat and rice plants[5]—but these changes were achieved at the expense of stability, resilience and resistance to disease. The latest technical fix is genetically engineered crops. The hidden costs of this latest agricultural gimmick have yet to be measured, but we can be sure that they will become apparent as time passes. Daly says, "It is for now certainly better for us to slow down our own biological growth rate than to attempt to speed up the growth rates of all the species we depend upon." (p. 85)

It seems logical that we in the northern hemisphere must confront (and achieve) the limits to growth first.

Individual countries will find it more difficult to limit their consumption as the "free trade" ideology is imposed on them by powerful traders like the U.S. "Free trade" hides the ecological costs of consumption. If Americans are doing the consuming but the related ecological limits are being exceeded in Mexico or in Indonesia, Americans can feel no incentive to reduce their consumption. Free trade even makes it difficult to keep relevant accounts because benefits are being enjoyed in one locale while costs are being created in another, thousands of miles apart.

There is considerable evidence that free trade doctrines are increasing inequalities within and between countries. As Daly says (p. 156), free trade will bring with it "a further writing off of the laboring class in this country, an increasing disdain toward uneducated and rural people by the corporate and university elite, and an increasing devotion by the former to the one thing about themselves that at least vaguely concerns the latter—their growing arsenal of guns."

Within countries, great inequality creates civil conflict. Between countries, in a full world, high rates of consumption create international conflict. To the extent that free trade makes nations less able to control their rates of consumption, to that degree it will promote war within and between countries. To promote peace, nations need to become more self-sufficient and to consume less.

Endnotes

Part One

[1]   Gro Harlem Brundtland and Others, Our Common Future (New York, Oxford University Press, 1987).

[2]   Herman E. Daly, *Beyond Growth* (Boston, Beacon Press, 1996).

[3]   See any ecology textbook; for example, G. Tyler Miller, Jr., *Living in the Environment,* Ninth Edition (Belmont, California, Wadsworth Publishing, 1996), chapter 5, "Ecosystems and How They Work."

[4]   F. Slemr and E. Langer, "Increase in Global Atmospheric Concentrations of Mercury Inferred from Measurements Over the Atlantic Ocean," *Nature,* Vol. 355 (January 30, 1992), pp. 434-437.

[5]   Peter M. Vitousek and others, "Human Appropriation of the Products of Photosynthesis," *Bioscience,* Vol. 34, No. 6 (1986), pp. 368-373.

Part Two

[1] Herman Daly, Beyond Growth (Boston, Beacon Press, 1996). Hereafter cited as Daly.

[2] Daly, p. 159.

[3] Relative prices measure marginal opportunity costs; see Daly p. 222. Efficient allocation is an allocation that corresponds to effective demand, i.e., the relative preferences of citizens as weighted by their relative incomes. An inefficient allocation is one that uses resources to produce items that people will not or cannot buy, and it fails to produce items that people want, can afford to buy, and would buy if they could find them. See Daly pp. 159-160.

[4] Daly, p. 207.

[5] U.S. Bureau of Mines, *Mineral Facts and Problems* [Bureau of Mines Bulletin 675] (Washington, D.C., U.S. Government Printing Office, 1985).

[6] William Ophuls, *Ecology and the Politics of Scarcity* (San Francisco, W.H. Freeman, 1977), chapter 6.

[7] As a matter of logic and mathematics, we never could achieve the greatest good for the greatest number because it is impossible to maximize two variables in a function.

[8] Daly, p. 220.

Part Three

[1] Herman E. Daly, *Beyond Growth* (Boston, Beacon Press, 1996).

[2] Joel E. Cohen, *How Many People Can the Earth Support?* (New York, W.W. Norton, 1995), p. 76.

[3] Joel E. Cohen and David Tilman, "Biosphere 2 and Biodiversity: The Lessons So Far," *Science* Vol. 274 (November 15, 1996), pp. 1150-1151. And see William J. Broad, "Paradise Lost; Biosphere Retooled as Atmospheric Nightmare," *New York Times*, November 19, 1996, p. C1. See also Peter Warshall, "Lessons From Biosphere 2: Ecodesign, Surprises, and the Humility of Gaian Thought," *Whole Earth Review* (Spring 1996), pp. 22-27.

[4] Ibid.

[5] Daly, cited above in note 1, p. 93.

Part Four

[1] Herman E. Daly, *Beyond Growth* (Boston, Beacon Press, 1996).

[2] Herman E. Daly and John B. Cobb, Jr., *For the Common Good* [Second Edition] (Boston, Beacon Press, 1994).

[3] Louis Uchitelle, "Global Good Times, Meet the Global Glut," *New York Times*, November 16, 1997, Section 4, p. 3. And see William Greider, "When Optimism Meets Overcapacity," *New York Times*, October 1, 1997, p. A27. And see William Greider, *One World, Ready or Not: The Manic Logic of Global Capitalism* (New York, Touchstone Books, 1998).

[4] Daly, *Beyond Growth*, cited above in note 1, p. 163.

5 Mathis Wackernagel and William Rees, *Our Ecological Footprint; Reducing Human Impact on the Earth* (Gabriola Island, British Columbia, Canada, New Society Publishers, 1996).

6 Learn about fair trade on the world wide web: http://www.fairtradefederation.com/ab_princ.html and http://www.ifat.org/fair_trade_def.html.

Part Five

1 Herman E. Daly, *Beyond Growth* (Boston, Beacon Press, 1996). See pp. 202-203.

2 Daly (cited above in note 1) never precisely defines the "good life" but on p. 14 he says, ". . . most would agree with British economist Thomas Malthus that it should be such as to permit one to have a glass of wine and a piece of meat with one's dinner. Even if one is a teetotaler or a vegetarian that level of affluence is desirable, and would serve by itself to rule out populations at or above today's level. What really must be stabilized is total consumption, which of course is population times per capita consumption. Both of the latter factors must be reduced."

3 Daly, cited above in note 1, chapter 2.

4 Michael Belliveau, "Smoke and Mirrors: Will Global Pollution Trading Save the Climate or Promote Injustice and Fraud?"available at www.corpwatch.org/trac/feature/climate/pollution/belliveau.html. And see Michael Belliveau, "Trading Places—Lethal Lessons from Los Angeles," and "Beltway Bandits—Pollution Trading as National Policy," at www.corpwatch.org/trac/feature/climate/pollution/box.html. Michael Belliveau directs Just Economics for Environmental Health, P.O. Box 806, Montara, California 84037; telephone (650) 728-5728.

5 Arjun Makhijani, "A Gamble on Global Warming," *Washington Post*, November 3, 1998, p. A17. Arjun Makijani is president of the Institute for Energy and Environmental Research, Suite 204, 6935 Laurel Avenue, Takoma Park, MD 20912; telephone (301) 270-5500. Dr. Makhijani describes a situation in India in which a pollution permit program might increase, not decrease, pollution.

6 Belliveau, *op. cit.*

7 Our thanks to David Zwick, the director of Clean Water Action, for sharing an insightful internal memo titled "Pollution Trading" that he co-authored with Paul Schwartz, in October, 1998.

Part Six

1 Herman E. Daly, *Beyond Growth* (Boston, Beacon Press, 1996).

2 Gary Hardner, "Shrinking Fields: Cropland Loss in a World of Eight Billion" (Washington, D.C., Worldwatch Institute, 1996). Worldwatch can be reached at 1776 Massachusetts Avenue, Washington, D.C. 20036-1904. Tel.: (202) 452-1992; fax: (202) 296-7365.

3 Lincoln Anderson, "Gross Domestic Product," in David R. Henderson, editor, *The Fortune Encyclopedia of Economics* (New York, Warner Books, 1993), pp. 203-207.

4 Daly (cited above in note 1) never precisely defines the "good life" but on p. 14 he says, ". . . most would agree with British economist Thomas Malthus that it should be such as

to permit one to have a glass of wine and a piece of meat with one's dinner. Even if one is a teetotaler or a vegetarian that level of affluence is desirable, and would serve by itself to rule out populations at or above today's level."

5   Vandana Shiva, *Staying Alive; Women, Ecology, and Development* (London, England, and Atlantic Highlands, New Jersey, USA, Zed Books, 1989).

Part Two

Exposing the Hidden Realities of Corporate Domination

EXPOSING THE HIDDEN REALITIES OF CORPORATE DOMINATION

Trent Schroyer

In retrospect, the dynamics of the Earth Summit, and the follow up summit ten years later, reveal that corporate globalization was always the relevant frame for the participating business sector and its allies. It has taken time to fully realize that corporate methods of securing economic power continue to undermine and distort public discourse and constitute what has been called a "war on truth."[1]

This approach is destructive of the conditions essential for a sustainable "World" as the Morehouse and Robert Engler essays below document.

But these essays require a context that most Americans do not seem to want to confront—that transnational corporations have become a growing force mostly unchecked by the rule of law. In fact, it may require recognition that corporations, the U.S. government and mainstream media have become one in many areas. Most citizens suppress or deny these possibilities. They do not want to acknowledge the bad news about what Morehouse calls an "agency relationship" between government and corporations. Or what Engler describes as a "creeping ascendancy of authoritarian practices and . . . a drift toward 'fascism lite.'"

In the current climate in this country, it is difficult to speak or write these words without being labeled an extremist who has lost academic "objectivity" at best or is giving aid to the enemy at worst! But readers are invited to consider the following before dismissing this issue and this section:

Corporate Power's Propaganda War on Truth

The evolution of the capacity of public relations (PR) for disinformation and propaganda has now reached the point of being a high art. Karl Rove's manipulation of issues for the Bush administration are only the visible part of the full "weaponization of information" that is now a U.S. government and military strategy for information dominance—truth is not relevant, but sufficient deniability is.

The Hidden Mechanisms of the Rise of Corporate Power

Corporate power has been aided by government regulations and deregulations for over a century in ways that make the American corporation the most autonomous, aggressive and amoral actor on the planet; this is an open secret today that anyone can see—if they look.

Reciprocal Violence—Economic Globalization and the War on Terrorism

The consequence of increased corporate power, corporate-state agency and the war on terrorism in the context of an accelerating economic globalization is a qualitative increase in world violence. This is the grim implication of the Engler and Morehouse essays.

A Wake-Up Call to the Sustainability Movements

Decline of truth, growing lawlessness and the increase of violence makes the more inclusive world sustainability movement imperative. The only way that the Earth can be sustained is to see SD as a corporate fraud; only a movement more critical and more focused on deliberative democracy can achieve this.

These counter intuitive realities are systematically denied by minions of whitewashers and spin doctors working in PR to manipulate and fool the public.

This essay reviews these issues as an introduction to the essays of Engler and Morehouse.

Corporate Power's Propaganda War on Truth

Ever since the mid '70s, corporate-funded think tanks and private PR firms have been developing advertising and spin techniques that enable the "engineering of consent and the "management of perceptions." They also organize "citizen's" front groups that attempt to present corporate interests as those of civil society, for example, the National Wetlands Coalition that fights to convert wetlands to building sites.[2]

These symbolic corporate green washings occupy the foreground while continued exploitation of ecosystems and communities goes on in the background. For example, Royal Dutch Shell participates in the Global Compact and claims that it is going to promote renewable energy. But its actual expenditures are less than one percent of its budget, while its hideous destruction in the Niger Delta is hidden behind sophisticated rhetoric.[3]

The capacity to manipulate news and manage behavior is illustrated by the decades-long success of the tobacco companies to discredit claims that smoking is dangerous. These disinformation techniques have become a standard commodity that public relations firms sell.[4] For example Kuwait hired 17 U.S. PR firms to justify the Gulf War to the American people. The PR included a staged "Congressional hearing" which heard "testimony" about Iraqi soldiers pulling infants from incubators. Although neither the hearing was real nor the testimony true, the event was quoted by many U.S. senators as a reason to go to war.[5]

A growing propaganda industry has demonstrated to corporations that it is easier, and much more lucrative, to deceive and create disinformation rather than to be accountable for destructive practices. The scale of this market is incredible—in 2004 corporations spent $266 billion on advertising, almost as much as the total Iraq war costs.[6]

Corporations not only use these services, they develop their own capacities to distort and create counter-factual realities. These disinformation practices are a major threat to the democratic integrity of our institutions—including science.[7] The techniques of third party testimonials and front organizations who really represent corporate interests are now used—both by corporations as well as authoritarian political regimes. These ideological constructions represent a new dimension of "governance," as a propaganda state.

The grim realities of disinformation have actually reached a new dimension as a full "system" closure. In pronouncements by the military in the U.S. and United Kingdom, "full spectrum information dominance begins with weaponizing of information." The goal is to put a positive spin on all info in order to degrade any dissent. The 314-page U.S. Army manual on information was issued November 2003. It begins with the premise that "information is an element of combat power" which goes beyond propaganda construction and distribution. What is now relevant is "mastery of the situation" and the goal is to "have our way and nothing done can make any difference." What is not understood by the public is the development of a systemic capacity to deny, degrade and destroy unfriendly information.[8] This is a partial answer to why President George W. Bush (and corporate interests) continue to deny everything that might cast official policies in a bad light. The concern is not for truth, the concern is that nothing stop the execution of their policies.

Is it any wonder that the environmental movement, assuming that science and litigation are the major tools for environmental action, has been out maneuvered? The changes in the ethos of truth adopted by governmental agencies is deeply destructive to the issues of "sustainability" and contain a profound misconception about the roots of terrorism. We live in a world where there is a crisis of truth—exacerbated by the nexus of corporate PR, the propaganda state and the weaponization of information.

The Hidden Mechanisms of the Rise of Corporate Power

The unique American path to corporate domination emerged from a wide pattern of consolidation of American corporate power, particularly during the last 25 years. From the 1886 U.S. Supreme Court decision, *Santa Clara County v. the Southern Pacific Railroad Company*, which gave corporations personhood, with the legal rights of citizens, protected by the Bill of Rights, to later privileges of limited liability charters in New Jersey and Delaware, prior governmental restraints over the corporation were all but eliminated.[9]

The "internal affairs" doctrine of Delaware charters (where 308,000 corporations are now chartered—including 60 percent of the Fortune 500) permits CEOs to pursue their fiduciary obligations in ways which have no moral limits and make it a permissible management decision to break laws when fines are less than profits. Stop and think about what it means to see that the role of corporate CEOs and CFOs is to decide how much it costs to pay fines rather than obey laws or follow moral-ethical norms, or to find ways of externalizing costs onto citizens, government and the Earth.

This has gone far beyond the point of being simply unethical and immoral—these terms do not do the job of describing major distortions of policy processes on the one hand and organized criminal interventions by corporate-state dirty tricks on the other.

Waves of deregulation have aided in the creation of a social form that is too powerful to be effectively broken up (e.g. Microsoft) and increasingly effective in its ability to find supporting government deregulations.

Engler describes the accepted governmental practice of intervention to allow oil corporations to evade both the law and the market limitations imposed by competition. His essay is a masterful accounting of the century-long collusion of oil corporations and government to control the "unclaimed wealth" of petroleum resources. Corporate-state planning for the world control of oil accompanied the formation of what Engler called the "first world government" of oil and has been a partner in financial and military actions to block development of energy systems around the world. These claims seem extreme, except that they have been independently confirmed in the recent book by John Perkins, *Confessions of an Economic Hit Man*.[10]

Perkins' book reveals the collusion of corporations and government to drive Third World countries into debt in order to give corporations access to valuable resources and to create ongoing energy market dependency in Indonesia, Columbia, Ecuador, Panama and Venezuela. Corporate names such as Bechtel, Brown and Root, and Halliburton appear again and again in these stories and continue to appear today in the Mid-East conflicts.

Perkins also documents his participation in hidden money laundering by the U.S. Treasury Department for Saudi oil revenues, used to hire American corporations to modernize the Saudi infrastructure. The assumption was made by the U.S. corporatists that it would be possible to do the same around the world, as the manipulations of Enron has shown in India and California. But failures in the attempt to extend this technique to Iran and Iraq was one reason for the Project for the New American Century, the neo-conservative plan, developed by a number of individuals now part of the Bush Administration, for the establishment of a global U.S. empire.

The fact that Perkins was recruited by the National Security Agency, and then asked to join an international energy consulting corporation, is a window into global corporatism or, as Perkins calls it, "the corptocracy," the domination by corporate interests of legislative and administrative processes. Perkins suggests that he was one of a long line of Economic Hitmen and women who "aided" the free market system in events that resulted in the demise of Prime Minister Mohammed Mossadegh (Iran 1953), President Jacobo Arbenz (Gutamala 1954), and President Salvadore Allende (Chile 1973). Perkins suggests that when Hitmen fail, "jackals" come in to do violently what could not be achieved any other way.

Ward Morehouse suggests this pattern has become a new market in itself and looks at the privatized military industry that is now literally exploding in Iraq and beyond. One example is the New Bridge Strategies Corporation which advertises its roots in the Reagan and Bush administrations and provides services in the Middle East to all comers. The new corporate warriors market is the massive growth in war profiteering which, in the age of market privatization, is another liberation of the market system. Corporate end runs around accountability are undertaken when there are attempts to bring these new "markets" under the scrutiny of old "command and control" ethical review.

Contemporary corporations' new privileged status can be seen in that corporate crime is not considered a law enforcement priority. For example the new Corporate Crime Task Force has no budget or staff, and other government regulatory agencies are starved for funds. The only agency able to bring out criminal complaints is the Environmental Protection Agency which, under the current Bush regime, has had its field agents deployed to police events like the Super Bowl, the Olympics, and others, leading to a 40 percent drop in citations.[11]

Reciprocal Violence—Economic Globalization
and the War on Terrorism

Beyond those who still expect the dominant institutions of modern society to provide security, care, and social engineering, there are other voices who assert that the dominant cultural faith in "development" is dangerously deceiving and ultimately an affirmation of structural violence.

One example of such a perspective is Emmanuel Levinas' reflections on the conflict of Western cognitive totalities and actual human experience:

> ". . . (V)iolence does not consist so much in injuring and anni-
> hilating persons as in interrupting their continuity, making them play
> roles in which they no longer recognize themselves, making them
> betray not only commitments but their own substance, making them
> carry out actions that will destroy every possibility of action. Not only
> modern war but every war employs arms that turn against those who
> wield them. It establishes an order from which no one can keep their
> distance; nothing henceforth is exterior. War . . . destroys the identity
> of the same."[12]

Today's empire building—in the form of economic globalization—is a totalizing compulsion that accepts massive destruction and dislocation as the inevitable "fall out" of the privilege to making more money. Indeed, while quantities of economic growth are measured incessantly, the counter pro-ductivities of wealth creation are not investigated, so long as they do not affect the profit making of planned commodity production.

As William Russell Easterly has noted, no one has really documented the incredible violence the global debt has bestowed on peoples all over the Earth. His book, *The Elusive Quest for Growth*, reconstructs the numerous flawed theoretical frames that guided the massive investments made by the World Bank and other international investors for decades and names it "cap-ital fundamentalism" which continues to dominate the globalist mentality of the multilateral institution.[13]

Enforced commercializations, such as Free Trade regimes that undermine subsistence livelihoods, are essentially a "third world war." In calling it that, Bernard Neitzschman points to the 120 ongoing regional wars since WWII and locates the dynamic in the imposition of development imperatives upon subsistence sectors in newly forming nation-states.[14] He defines these 3,000-plus nations as "Fourth World" peoples who constitute a third of the world's population. They are called "ethnic" groups in state system terms. Most are seeking either territorial or political self-determination and are the subsis-tence peoples that a world sustainability movement must protect.

Despite their size, these groups are invisible to many people in rich countries because they are not on the map. Their struggles for existence are against governmental and corporate resource grabs, and their resistance gets them stigmatized as terrorists, communists, or bandits. Their struggles often result in increasing the flood of international refugees. After 9/11, the repression of their movements has been re-interpreted to make it seem a fight against terrorism. But such struggles are really "low intensity warfare" and they are part of the complex consequences that spring from the economic globalization process.

Today in a world increasingly oriented toward a "war on terrorism," the anti-globalism movement itself has been stigmatized by the empire builders as a source of violence, rather than a form of radical sanity that brings attention to the roots of unnecessary violence.

How did we get to a point where the violence of creating capital and expanding development can go on without triggering a response based on traditional norms guaranteeing the right to live and to have livelihoods? How has political realism and national self-interest so massively overshadowed the spontaneous responses of caring people? Where are the "habits of the heart that derive from the thick cushion of pre-modern systems of meaning" and obligation? What has exhausted traditional public spiritedness?[15]

A Wake-Up Call to the Sustainability Movements

The American Corporation has become more than just a model for business. It is an organizing principle for society and for the global world, too. It embeds into society's institutional and cultural matrix the single-minded quest for monetary calculation and gain.

This model has been systematically objectified for the last three decades; but it is in the 18 agreements regulated by the World Trade Organization (WTO) where it has become the template for transforming all ecological and socio-cultural diversity into a universally commodified world. This corporate vision has skewed the meaning of sustainable development beyond recovery.

After the 1994 passage of North American Free Trade Agreement (NAFTA) and the WTO, transnationals became the dominant force in the world, expanding from 37,000 at the time of Rio to 62,000 by Rio + 10. As they have increased in number and economic power (51 out of 100 of the largest economies in the world are transnationals) they have been innovating new forms of co-operation and re-organizing their capacity to engineer, or "manage" consent.[16]

Thus public pronouncements that transnational corporations have started symbolically radical projects for sustainable development, or participate in learning forums, or best practice solutions, or the Global Compact, create perceptions that conceal opposite practices and realities. Of course good projects exist but the proportion of the good to the hidden massive structural violence is not seen. Most recently corporations have, with the aid of an under-funded U.N., formed "partnerships" that take the issues out of the sphere of publicly accountable actions. If the Bush administration's plans to "reform" the U.N. are successful, more corporate autonomy and more U.N. cover for corporations will result. But the constant drum beat of market fundamentalism—that only the private corporate sphere can be efficient—must be confronted. The actual truth is most often very different.[17]

Ultimately protection of the Earth will require the capacity to have open discourse that is not systematically distorted by media manipulations, spin, and outright lies. The battleground here is struggles for freedom for information and due democratic processes. It is exactly these rights that are in jeopardy and the attacks on these rights promise to get more serious.[18] To reclaim procedural democracy in policy formation will take a constant effort to create fact-checking procedures at every level. The current critique of Rupert Murdoch's Fox News practice of substituting advocacy for news is a case in point. That these distortive techniques now also shape political elections is another painful truth.

It is dubious that a world formed using a "third way" partnership strategy can be a sustainable world if it must accommodate the dominant economic development thesis.[19] The recent promise of partnerships between corporations, civil society and the United Nations must be critically examined in every case to test if it is really promoting privatizations that increase only the "liberty" of corporations. Sustainability really implies sustaining the Earth's ecological and cultural diversities as well as open procedural processes of decision making essential to a pluralistic world. Likewise the international economic institutions that now attempt to impose a wealth creation solution for all problems also have to be 'truth tested' and transformed, and their institutional histories not only recalled but used to place their present actions in proper perspective.[20]

But the wider sustainability incentive, in a still pluralistic world, is an ongoing struggle between the expanding world corporate-state system and global resistance to it and experimental alliances between civil society and diverse political units.[21] World Sustainability is ultimately the never-ending effort to regenerate the Earth, while simultaneously maintaining a dialogue between civilizations in the interest of also sustaining co-operation.[22]

The goal of sustaining the Earth and its communities can only be achieved by systematically contesting and exposing the distortions of the propaganda state. A worldwide civil society has become more active in forcing corporations to be accountable—but it is an epic struggle whose outcome is not certain.

Endnotes

1. See Derrick Jensen's "War on Truth: The Battle for the American Mind," an interview with John Stauber, published in *The Sun*, March 1999 and available at www.derrickjensen.org/stauber.

2. Mark Megalli and Andy Friedman, *Masks of Deception: Corporate Front Groups in America* (Washington D.C., Essential Information, 1991).

3. See Kenny Bruno and Joshua Karliner, *Earthsummit.biz: The Corporate Takeover of Sustainable Development* (Food First Books, Oakland Calif., 2002), pp.107ff.

4. See John Stauber *Toxic Sludge Is Good for You: Lies, Damn Lies and the Public Relations Industry;* also *Mad Cow USA*, which documents the PR cover-up of human and animal health risks from mad cow disease; *Trust Us, We're Experts: How Industry Manipulates Science and Gambles With Your Future; Weapons of Mass Deception: The Uses of Propaganda in Bush's War on Iraq.*

5. Derrick Jensen, "War on Truth," *op. cit.*

6. Lee Drutman and Charlie Gray, *The People's Business: Controlling Corporations and Restoring Democracy* (San Francisco, Berrett Koehler Pub., 2004) p. 50.

7. See Kurt Gottfried and others "On Fraud in Science," *New York Review of Books*, Vol. 52, No. 2, February 10, 2005; also see David Korten, *When Corporations Rule the World,* second edition (co-publication of Kumerian Press, Inc. and Berrett-Koehler Publisher, Inc. 2001), pp. 205 ff.

8. See David Miller *Information Dominance: The Philosophy of Total Propaganda Control?* December 29, 2003 on Spin Watch.server101.com or www,scoop.co.nz.

9. Lee Drutman and Charlie Cray, *op. cit.,* p. 35.

10. John Perkins *Confessions of an Economic Hit Man* (San Francisco, Berrett-Koehler Publishers, 2004). Also see http://www.johnperkins.org.

   The fact that Perkins has been widely read and interviewed in the alternative media and totally shut out of the main stream media is evidence of the whitewashing and scandal avoiding nature of the main stream media.

11. Lee Drutman and Charlie Gray, *op. cit.,* p. 205.

12. Emmanuel Levinas, *Totality and Infinity* (Pittsburgh, Duquesne University Press, 1969), p. 21.

13. William Easterly, *The Elusive Quest for Growth,* fifth printing (Cambridge, MA, MIT Press, 2001), p. 47.

14. Bernard Nietschmann, "Third World War: The Global Conflict Over the Rights of Indigenous Nations" in *Cultural Survival Quartely,* September 1987. Neitschmann, a contemporary cultural geographer, points out that over 3/4 of these wars are between state formations and nations trapped in these territorties.

[15] See Hans Kung, *A Global Ethics for Global Poltics and Economics* (New York, Oxford University Press, 1997), p. 132.

[16] See David Korten, *op. cit.*, pp.205 ff.

[17] Greg Palast, Jerrold Oppenheim and Theo MacGregor, *Democracy and Regulation: How the Public Can Govern Essential Services* (Sterling,Virginia, Pluto Press, 2003).

[18] Dean Ritz (editor), *Defying Corporations, Defining Democracy: A Book of History and Strategy* (New York, The Apex Press, 2001).

[19] See Trent Schroyer "On Third Ways" in Viney Lal and Ashis Nandy (editors), *The Future of Knowledge and Culture: A dictionary for the 21st century* (Penguin (India)), Fall 2004.

[20] *False Promises* collected and edited by 50 Years Is Enough Network, July 2003.

[21] The neo-liberal economic worldview does not recognize any structure between the individual and the national society (the aggregate of individuals). But communities worldwide have always had norms that regulated access to the conditions essential for life (land, water, forests, etc.) the "commons." Garrett Hardin confused this concept with an "open access regime" and this confusion has only slowly been over come in American discussions as in the *Science*, December 2003 issue devoted to "Sustainability and the Commons."

[22] For a serious encounter with maintaining a "world" see Fred Dallmayr's *Dialogue Among Civilizations* (New York, Palgrave Macmillan, 2002).

OIL BARRELS AND GUN BARRELS: THE QUEST FOR THE CONTROL OF ENERGY RESOURCES

Robert Engler

Why Study Oil?

My overall interest has been in the structure of power within the United States and its relation to the country's basic directions. Over the years this has involved examining the organization and behavior of major sectors of the society—the business system, labor, the political system, the military, the professions, the university, as well as agriculture and coal. How did such institutions relate to one another and what bearing did they have on public policies? A mid-20th century controversy over the control of offshore lands, involving the federal and state governments as well as oil corporations, suggested that the quest for petroleum—the key energy resource of industrial society—might illuminate the dynamics of power relationships. Little did I then realize the ramifications of such an inquiry.

To single out the quest for control of petroleum as the defining factor in contemporary global development and conflict could oversimplify complex historical forces. But my research throughout the United States, including considerable time in oil regions and Washington and then abroad, identified the wealth and power that flowed from a barrel of crude oil as critical components in the shaping of political economies and foreign policies. The efforts of private corporations and public governments of the northern tier industrial nations in search of "more" bear directly on issues of war and peace, development and underdevelopment. The implications of such fashionable terms as "globalization" or the older "vital national interest" come into sharp focus. And it becomes folly to continue to ignore the impact of this intensified thirst upon the lives and political awareness of indigenous people throughout the world on whose lands this "black gold" is found. It also may become disastrous for all humankind to play down the environmental consequences of the continued burning of this fossil fuel.

How did power over nature become transformed into power over people? How did the institutions that controlled much of the world's oil supply evolve into what I concluded was the first world government, the private government of oil? How has such power impinged upon this country's political practices and democratic principles? With what authority has this power been exercised? To whom has it been accountable? Are these patterns ordained, or so overwhelming as to preclude challenge? Are there energy policies which might further a more ecologically sane, economically just and peaceful society and world than what we now know? What are the political requirements for such transformation?

These are large and uncomfortable questions. But as the late Robert S. Lynd, distinguished sociologist and co-author of *Middletown* and of *Middletown in Transition*, asserted in *Knowledge for What?*, his challenge to social scientists, "No culture can be realistically and effectively analyzed by those who elect to leave its central idols untouched.

"And if fundamental change is required, it does no good simply to landscape the grounds on which these idols stand."

Sociologist C. Wright Mills (*The Power Elite, White Collar, The Sociological Imagination*) put it bluntly:

"If you don't specify and confront real issues, what you say will surely obscure them. If you do not alarm anyone morally, you yourself will remain morally asleep. If you do not embody controversy, what you say will be an acceptance of the drift to the coming human hell."

When the smoke cleared from the battlefields of the Civil War in 1865, one direction was clear. The United States was to be an industrial society, not an agrarian one, despite the lingering political power of plantations and the subsequent growth of corporate agriculture. The first oil well in the United States had come on stream in 1859, but it would be some years before the automobile and the airplane helped make it the dominant energy form.

In 1912, First Lord of the Admiralty Winston Churchill led a political fight to convert the British fleet from coal, which the nation had an abundance of, to oil, of which presumably it had none. At that time, the North Sea was not viewed as a source of oil. If the fleet shifted to oil, it was argued, it would range much further, mount greater firepower, and be able to rule an expanded empire. But he also warned that this move would launch England on a sea of troubles. There would be more borders exposed and to be defended. Britain converted to oil.

On the eve of World War I, the United States designated public lands as naval petroleum reserves for its fleet which was changing over to oil. (Two were in California, Elk Hills, the better known, and Buena Vista Hills; one in Wyoming which became the site of a major national scandal, Teapot Dome; and a substantial area in Alaska.) Increasingly, the term "vital national interest" was applied to this resource. When the United States bought Alaska from Russia in 1867 for $7 million, there was not much known about this vast northern acquisition extending through five time zones. The Russians' primary concern had been the fur trade; they never settled more than a few areas and had a limited presence beyond them. I don't think anyone asked if the Indian and Eskimo inhabitants had been consulted. It was assumed they came with the real estate. By the middle of the 20th century, native claims over land ownership became a major source of contention. International corporations found oil near Prudhoe Bay on the North Slope to the east of the reserve. They planned to drill and lay pipelines. But first a settlement had to be made with natives, some of whom viewed all of Alaska as their ancestral lands. A rejoinder to this claim by Walter J. Hickel, frontier land developer with interests in gas and oil and Secretary of the Interior under President Nixon, was "Just because somebody's grandfather chased a moose across the land doesn't mean he owns it." After extended negotiations, the aboriginal titles were surrendered and 12 newly-created native regional corporations received about 10 percent of Alaska's land area and $962 million.

From the perspective of industrial societies, much of the world was a cornucopia of unclaimed wealth—"unclaimed" meaning either held by people with limited appreciation of what was beneath the land where they lived or by those with less firepower. Indigenous people rarely thought of petroleum and minerals as commodities. And their needs were not prominent in the planning of the oil corporations, except perhaps when calculating the price of their rulers for turning over concessions and protecting installations. I recall one senior executive telling me after I had completed my testimony on the power of oil corporations in their relation to these raw material producing "colonies" before a Senate committee, "You know a great deal about oil, but you still don't understand my industry. That crude oil is worthless until we locate it, drill, transport, refine and then market it."

In the United States, private corporations generally have been accepted as the appropriate agents for providing the oil and its products basic to industrial progress and national power. The companies have drawn upon particular "oil provinces" throughout the world, which they view as reservoirs or storage tanks, depending upon where the political climate and the price of crude are most favorable at the moment. This access to inexpensive, abundant and relatively secure oil has been pivotal in their accumulation of tremendous capital. The 800-mile Alaska pipeline, for example, completed in 1977, was built by a consortium of the majors dominated by British

Petroleum, Atlantic Richfield and Exxon, at a cost of $8 billion. More recently, an Afghanistan pipeline planned by western oil companies and the United States government was to cost $4 billion.

At one point in the '80s, 40 percent of all industrial profits in the United States were garnered by the oil industry. The economic power of the major companies grew out of their integrated character. Each controlled wells and fields, pipelines, refineries, transportation and marketing, in addition to significant areas of research. Any customer or competitor seeking to challenge prices received an education in the workings of "the system" and of the arrangements and understandings among the majors. American farmers, heavily dependent upon petroleum, repeatedly attempted to organize against oil industry command over pricing. But they discovered that their co-operatives were at a disadvantage for the companies could always shift the battleground. If at the marketing end the prices of the co-op gasoline stations were undercutting those of the industry, the latter would raise the prices of the refineries from which the co-ops obtained their petroleum products. If the competition persisted, in part because the co-ops built some refineries, the price of crude oil would be raised at the wellhead. Farm co-ops have remained active but they have not defeated big oil.

In recent years there have been mergers of some of the largest of the integrated corporations, for example, ExxonMobil and ChevronTexaco. Notwithstanding their wealth and economic power, the usual explanation is the increasingly high cost of finding and producing oil for expanding markets and also the need to compete aggressively with Russian, Chinese and Indian enterprises. "Orderly marketing procedure," that is, effective control of price, remains of sufficient concern, despite a currently favorable market, for the corporations to continue their vigilance about available supply, anticipated demand and targeted profits. At those times when they have been able to set desired prices at the pump, they were charging the replacement value of the oil. The consumer, in effect, became an investor, one without any rights as such.

Abundance and competition have been twin bogeys of the giant oil corporations since 1929. On the eve of the Great Depression, east Texas witnessed the largest discovery in the United States until that time. Oil was soon selling for ten cents a barrel. The challenge became how to keep supply in balance with demand so as to protect profits. Responding to the industry's concern about "oversupply," commissions in each oil-producing state were encouraged by the federal government to regulate output. The Texas Railroad Commission monitored the largest volume and owners of every well in that state had to file with the Commission monthly figures for production and existing stock. The United States Bureau of Mines then collated the statistics on a national scale and also prepared forecasts of likely demand, based on information supplied by the industry. The Interstate Oil Compact Commission to Conserve Oil and Gas then coordinated the allocation by each state of its quotas for its wells. For example, just before the so-called energy crisis of the 1970s, oil wells were allowed to produce on the average eight days a month. If a well produced oil in excess of this rate, it would be in violation of state law. If it was transported across state lines this "hot oil" would be in violation of federal law (the Connally Act). By gathering and distributing all the facts of production, reserves and expected demand in order to help shape desired prices, the Bureau of Mines, a federal agency, did what the industry could not do without running afoul of anti-trust regulations. To oil corporations which in their public declarations were ardent champions of "free private enterprise," action to check "the nightmare of competition" was acceptable governmental intervention.

Government has also intervened sympathetically on behalf of the oil industry in the area of taxes. For a long time the so-called depletion allowance was the most glaring example of oil privilege. Originally justified as protection for small producers and wildcatters in their search for oil and gas, it was designed to help extractive ventures recoup capital investments before calculating income taxes. The depletion allowance had been limited to the actual cost of investment. Then, under oil industry pressure, it was raised to 27.5 percent of gross income. This meant that oil producers were rewarded as if oil was an asset they had placed in the ground. Over the producing lifetime of a well, corporations, especially the giants, received deductions in their taxes up to sixty times their investment costs. Challenging this depletion allowance became a major career risk in the Congress. Defenders of the privilege sought to widen its political support by extending the allowance to other minerals. Even the gravel industry managed to get a five percent depletion allowance, although no one has ever claimed that the nation was running out of gravel.

The oil industry and sympathetic politicians succeeded in shielding profits from overseas oil operations through special tax reductions. For example, when the rulers of Saudi Arabia, which has the world's largest known reserve of oil, realized that Venezuela, a very large producer and a founder of the Organization of Petroleum Exporting Countries (OPEC), was getting more in royalties than their own country, they sought to raise the price of crude oil they were selling to Aramco, in which Standard of California, Texaco, Jersey Standard and Socony Mobil were partners. But the companies and the American government persuaded Saudi Arabia to achieve the level of payment it sought by raising its taxes on the oil rather than by increased royalties. This enabled the companies to write off the Saudi taxes against income taxes owed to the United States. The companies ended up paying almost no taxes to their own government when the corporate income tax rate was about 30 percent. Once again cost had been shifted to the United States Treasury. Republican Senator Owen Brewster, who chaired an investigation which included oil profits and tax arrangements, concluded that his committee's findings about such cases "provided a liberal education in corporate tax evasion."

The American government has shouldered much of the risk for oil corporations. It has provided research aid and subsidies, especially in frontier areas of technological development. Internationally, the State Department often serves as the industry's law firm, clearing obstacles to concessions, contracts and markets. The diplomatic corps, and, at times, the military, run interference in the race for leases and reserves. In Latin America and elsewhere the U.S. military is called upon to protect privately-owned pipelines and installations from dissidents opposed to the draining of their nation's resources by U.S. corporations. Government and corporate intelligence services regularly exchange information, especially in oil regions, in the name of anti-terrorism.

An energy message to the nation in 1973, heralded as the first ever given by a president of the United States, drew extensively upon industry sources for data and recommendations. How had this come about? Some 30 heads of leading energy corporations, who constituted the National Petroleum Council which advised the Secretary of the Interior, had their economists pull together industry-generated figures on reserves and needs. A report on the Council's findings and recommendations was submitted to the Secretary of the Interior who, in turn, forwarded it to the White House where it became the basis of President Nixon's address.[1]

This case is not unique. Advisory committees composed of corporate executives are found in the Interior, Energy and other federal agencies. They keep watch on personnel appointments and budget allocations. There is a permeation of oil interests at every level of government. In the administration of George W. Bush, it starts at the top. The President had been an oilman, albeit unsuccessful, in a small company. Vice-President Dick Cheney had headed Halliburton, a major oil field service corporation. National Security Advisor Condoleezza Rice had been on the board of Chevron. They assume that reliance upon private oil corporations is the American way of doing things. Enron, though not a major energy corporation, was one of their consultants in reviewing government appointments in the energy area. The *Guardian Weekly*, a British publication, recently had a story about

Robert Wilson, a scientist who has headed the Intergovernmental Panel on Climate Change. Wilson traced the history of the growth of dependence upon fossil fuels and with the backing of several thousand fellow scientists has warned of the increasing dangers of global warming. Exxon and Mobil took the lead in challenging his findings and there followed an announcement that he would not be reappointed.

In 2001, the National Energy Policy Development Group, chaired by Cheney, issued a report, "National Energy Policy," which relied heavily upon closed meetings with energy industry representatives. There was little if any consultation with environmentalists, industry critics or independent scholars. The report projected that in the next 20 years energy supply would have to increase from 19.5 million barrels of oil per day to 25.8 million barrels. New refineries would have to be built. Low profitability was the explanation offered as to why the industry had not anticipated this need and expanded capacity in the previous decades. The improved performance of existing plants along with new technological and regulatory developments concerning safety were seen as justifying the stepping up of nuclear power generation. "Improving the climate" for overseas investment and exploration through diplomacy, economic policy and military strategy would be intensified to secure access to all fields and pipeline routes throughout the world. No mention was made of military costs or of how much of the present $350 billion published military budget and the $35 billion published intelligence budget relates to energy objectives.

Solicitude was expressed for protecting the air, water, land and the health of humans and wildlife. Each has suffered heavily from oil operations and use. But no serious program was suggested for dealing with these social costs. Technological efficiency which would reduce energy consumption was recommended. And "sustained development," a mantra of ecologists now co-opted by corporate public relations, was readily invoked. There was limited reference, however, to reducing demand or trying seriously to get more from less. "Conservation may be a sign of personal virtue," Cheney declared on the eve of the report's release, "but it is not a sufficient basis for a sound, comprehensive energy policy." There was no ambiguity about the report's underlying premise: the development of *more*, enlarging the supply—the distinctive American response to a range of problems, including economic deprivation and inequality. Private enterprise, motivated by profit (with the unacknowledged support of public subsidies) remained the best instrument for attaining this goal.

The report favored the further opening of public lands within the United States for energy development. The Bush administration had lost a round in its corporate-endorsed battle to permit drilling in the Arctic National Wildlife Refuge, a true wilderness and spectacular sanctuary for many species of animals and birds. Nevertheless it has been projected that the refuge's development, while not expected to yield a vast quantity of petroleum, will pave the way for corporate access to other heretofore protected but less well known public lands. The present installations at Prudhoe Bay in the Arctic are impressive technological feats and appear well-maintained and land-scaped. But the scarred earth, the roads, pipelines and periodic spills offer a somewhat different story, one not reported to visitors flown into the area or to the general public.

It is important to remember that roughly 30 percent of the land area of the United States is publicly owned and that one-fourth to one-third, excluding public lands, has been under lease to energy corporations. A farmer or other landowner who leases his property grants exclusive rights to a corporation for exploration. If petroleum is found or the prospect is very favorable a "standard" contract is offered with a one-eighth royalty. This cash nexus helps explain the identification often shown by farmers, even in states such as North Dakota, with strong populist traditions with positions of the oil industry.

Renewable and alternative energy and related technologies were accepted as having a modest place in the nation's energy portfolio. There were restrained discussions on the virtues of solar, wind, geothermal, hydropower and biomass sources, as well as the long run potential of hydrogen and fusion. Mention was made of the reduced harm to the earth and the environment from adoption of these renewable and cleaner fuels. But no sense of urgency was reflected in their development or federal investment recommendations, in contrast to the emphasis on the increase of coal, natural gas, oil and nuclear power, massive construction of new power plants, the expansion of refinery capacity and upgrading of pipelines, the electricity transmission grid and other segments of the nation's energy delivery system. The report suggested public education stressing the benefits of alternative fuels, implying that the lack of consumer interest has been a major deterrent to such change.

Advertisements by British Petroleum and Royal Dutch/Shell invite the conclusion that they have pioneered environmental sensitivity. BP seeks to be identified as Beyond Petroleum. They are more enlightened than Exxon Mobil which remains active in coalitions which dismiss the fears of scientists about global warming. But the industry is vigilant lest alternative and renewable fuels weaken its influence over traditional markets and pricing. It exerts its considerable economic power to monitor the pace of transition to more benign energy and technology. Those seeking a more fundamental and rapid change in the nation's energy base may have to challenge the assumption that the oil corporations know best, that through the marketplace they remain the most experienced in meeting consumer needs and the public interest. They will have to mobilize politically to confront not just big oil, but also its allies in the automobile and related industries, as well as in the Congress, the White House, state legislatures and the mass media.

The National Energy Policy report concludes with great concern that United States dependence on imports—16 percent of its natural gas, mostly from Canada, and 52 percent of its oil—continues to increase. It urges the government to negotiate treaties and alliances in Latin America, the Middle East, Africa and Asia which will open up energy-rich lands to private enterprise. More oil and gas should be sought from such relatively reliable places as Canada and Mexico. (The U.S. now draws 15 percent of its imported oil from Canada, 14 percent each from Venezuela and Saudi Arabia, and 12 percent from Mexico.) It views it as imperative that the nation diversify its sources and put into place adequate defenses for the far flung installations and pipelines.

There were few surprises in the report. It reflects the oil industry's ability to function within the offices of public government and have its views presented to the American people through public documents as products of disinterested research and deliberation. It illustrates the by now familiar convergence of the interests of the industry and the Bush administration on critical points of public policy. Why then the fierce stonewalling to conceal the identity of private participants and the full contents of the agenda?

There is strong suspicion that there was also discussion by government and energy officials of strategies for gaining more effective access to the vast oil and gas reserves in Iraq and Iran and about the desirability of privatization. Undoubtedly there was related appraisal of the continued reliability of Saudi Arabia as "swing" producer and of the likely impact of the new vigor of OPEC as champion of the producer states. Obscuring the origins and implications of presumably public policy for oil are not unfamiliar tactics. Certainly it is in keeping with President Bush's style of obfuscation in which terms such as freedom and terror are employed, ripped out from any meaningful political or social context, and the focus is kept on evil rather than oil. Was the formulation of energy policy, so interlaced with issues of war and peace as well as the health of the economy, none of the public's business?

When did oil become so central to economic vitality and national security? Why the increased overseas involvement for a nation possessing so plentiful and varied an energy base?

Superior access to oil had been critical to the Allied victory over Germany in World War I. In the 1920s, the accelerated industrial shift to oil along with the growing importance of the automobile and the airplane heightened the demand appreciably. European nations and their oil corporations had hastened to acquire and divide drilling rights to former German concessions and to oil-rich regions of what had been the Turkish Empire. In the United States interest was mixed. Wildcatters and individual entrepreneurs were more eager to locate foreign fields than some of the large oil companies who were involved in developing their productive domestic holdings. But the U.S. State Department was sensitive to the exclusion of its nationals from such prospects and became a vigorous advocate of an "open door" policy. It ultimately succeeded in gaining for American corporations a foothold in the Persian Gulf area. These principled calls then subsided and the door was shut tight against other claimants. Among the less reverent, such endeavors in the Middle East and Latin America earned Secretary of State Charles E. Hughes the title Secretary for Oil.

At the end of World War I, it had been widely predicted that the next global war would be fought over oil. Assured access to oil had become essential and certainly was a critical factor behind such conflict. The United States remained able to draw upon abundant and varied sources, but the geopolitical ambitions of Japan and Germany pushed them to reach beyond their borders. There is evidence to support the interpretation that Japan, having almost no domestic supply, planned to gain control of the oil fields of the Dutch East Indies. Anticipating a military response by the United States, Japan attacked its fleet at Pearl Harbor. Germany, deprived of its colonies at the conclusion of World War I, sought unsuccessfully to compensate for the loss of resources by cutting through the Soviet Union to gain control of the oil fields in the Caucasus.

At the request of Standard of California and Texaco, the original partners in Aramco, Saudi Arabia became a major recipient of the U.S. lend-lease program, which funded embattled democracies during World War II. No one had ever hinted that Saudi Arabia was a democracy, let alone an embattled one. But the fear of possible replacement by British oil interests was persuasive for the Roosevelt administration. The United States was assured access to one-fourth of the world's known reserves and the ruling monarchy acquired a strong military guardian. When the war ended, the Middle East was a dollar area, no longer under the dominion of the pound sterling. One significant goal of the Marshall Plan was to further the conversion of Europe from coal to oil, crude coming from the Middle East, with Saudi Arabian oil flowing through a new pipeline terminating on the Mediterranean in

Lebanon. The Mediterranean became an American sea, its tankers protected by the Sixth Fleet. Refining took place in Europe, largely in American-owned plants.

Immediately after World War II there were comparable prophecies about a third world war. Given the growing demands of the older industrial societies and the thirst of newer ones such as India and China, petroleum emerged as a pivotal component of national rivalries and conflicts. On a not-too-distant horizon was a projected specter of consumption of oil outstripping discoveries.

The imperial reach of the United States and its corporations has extended to wherever crude oil and natural gas might be available. For example, in 1951 under its popular nationalist premier Mohammed Mossadegh, Iraq nationalized the holdings of Anglo-Iran, now British Petroleum. Iran was the site of the world's largest refinery and believed to possess one of the biggest reserves in the Middle East. The grievances included the failure to provide the technical training which would enable the Iranian people to operate the oil installations, instead of being offered only menial tasks. Such obstacles as the high prices charged in selling oil back to local businesses made it difficult to develop local industries. And the familiar pattern prevailed that the British government was receiving more in taxes from its oil company than the Iranian government gained in royalties from its own crude oil.

The Iranian action was perceived as a dangerous and possibly contagious threat to established colonial relationships. There was also the possibility that Iran's vast reserves might begin to enter the global market outside of the corporate control system. A blockade was established against Iran, markets for its crude oil were shut and no purchasers were to be found. The United States refused economic aid to the beleaguered country. Under the orchestration of the U.S. Central Intelligence Agency, the offending Mossadegh regime was overthrown. (Richard Helms, the deputy director of the CIA who was in charge of dirty tricks, later became United States Ambassador to Iran.) A new corporate consortium was created for developing the oil fields. Anglo-Iranian retained a 40 percent interest and the five largest American oil corporations shared a similar percentage. After considerable protest, smaller corporations received five percent of the allocated American share. The full details of how production was to be divided among the multinational corporations and how their U.S. taxes were to be determined were not made public. The increasingly familiar explanation for this secret government-corporation collaboration was "national security."

In 1956 Egypt nationalized the Suez Canal and the international oil companies were worried. Not about passage through the canal—they were building supertankers which wouldn't fit and were designed to sail around the Cape of Good Hope off South Africa. Their fear was of the precedent. If a canal could be nationalized, might not a pipeline be next? Pipelines were vulnerable and going through regions that were or could readily become unstable in the Middle East, Latin America and elsewhere. Sabotage was always a possibility. People were increasingly questioning the decisions of their rulers who had been signing away to northern tier industrial companies what was often their nations' most valuable resource. The notes of a Mobil Oil official summarized the remarks of then Secretary of State John Foster Dulles to an assemblage of concerned oil executives. It is the right of a nation to nationalize, he reminded them. But he then reassured them somewhat by explaining that facilities such as pipelines are affected with a larger international public interest and cannot be at the disposal of any one country to nationalize. Since adequate compensation is never paid, nationalization is in effect confiscation, Dulles concluded. The American government would not abandon its corporate citizens.

A year later there was a revolution in Iraq against a pro-western dictatorship. The threat was to rich fields, where the oil was inexpensive to lift, and pipelines seemed imminent. In response, the United States landed marines in Lebanon and the British dropped paratroops in Jordan. A world war might have ensued, given the Soviet Union's concern over such moves, had not the United Nations and intensive diplomacy arranged the withdrawal of these forces. The United States subsequently announced that so long as Iraq didn't interfere with Western oil installations and planning it would not take further military action.

In the 1960s OPEC was created. Led by Venezuela and the major Middle Eastern producers, OPEC was an attempt to counter the arbitrary setting of crude prices by the corporations and their allocation of output quotas for each country which would fit into corporate targets of supply and demand. The companies' objective, as always, was to protect prices and profits. But for the producing countries, crude oil was their principal source of income. Without information and participation in price determination, it had been impossible to meaningfully plan national budgets.

Initially, the oil companies voiced indignation and labeled OPEC a conspiracy. Its actions could upset the multinationals' carefully constructed price systems. It undermined the industry's efforts to convince the consuming public that, heretofore, oil was traded in a free market governed by the laws of supply and demand. A sympathetic western press had no trouble in identifying OPEC as a cartel, a term rarely applied to corporate collaboration, because of its increased involvement in the collective setting of outputs and prices. But gradually the oil giants came to appreciate the part that the new organization could play as a moderating force in restraining the more militant producing countries and in sharing the overall objective of keeping supply and price in harmony with profit goals. But OPEC was not always successful in preventing countries such as Nigeria and Venezuela from "cheating;" that is, selling beyond their allocations. Subsequently, OPEC was to chart a more independent course less to the liking of the western corporations.

In 1971, the American Petroleum Institute, the industry's leading trade association, proclaimed in full page advertisements across the country that "the U.S.A. and its 205 million people use all we can get." The nation then had six percent of the world's population and accounted for about one-third of the daily fossil fuel consumption. Where once the international companies had found it relatively easy to deal with dictatorships and corrupt ruling classes in gaining control of much of Middle Eastern oil, the emergence of popular movements critical of this acquiescence and the creation of national oil companies forced a reappraisal of Western strategy and the increased involvement of the U.S. government. Former Secretary of State Henry Kissinger (more recently a consultant for companies planning pipelines across Afghanistan) in the mid-70s justified intervention, including militarily, anywhere to fend off economic "strangulation" of the United States and other nations brought on by disruption of this oil supply. Strategic planning to lock in supplies from Saudi Arabia and elsewhere in the Middle East, as well as from Africa and Latin America, had high priority. In 1980, President Jimmy Carter warned that an attempt by any outside force to gain control of the Persian Gulf region would be repelled by any means necessary, including military force.

When Iraq invaded Kuwait in 1990, the United States quickly sent troops while claiming that Saudi Arabia was next on Saddam Hussein's timetable (and would give him control of 45 percent of Middle Eastern reserves). The dictator responded that challenging Western imperialism was carrying out "Allah's will" and embodied the aspirations of all Arab people. President George H.W. Bush in turn insisted that "our cause could not be more noble" and that the United States, "on the side of God," would do "what has to be done" to bring about a new world order.

In 1997, a core of neo-conservatives created a Project for the New American Century to lay out a long-sought course for a dominant and permanent global presence by the United States. The Middle East was of special concern, and unfriendly Iraq and its vast oil reserves were targeted as a major threat to the vital interests of the United States. Scant attention was paid to Iraq's many grievances against western oil companies and governments, not the least of which was the holding down of its production allowances. Many of the think tank participants, including Richard Perle, Paul Wolfowitz, Donald Rumsfeld and Dick Cheney, were soon to emerge as advisers and policy makers for the present Bush administration. They were now in position to implement their plans for mobilizing against Iraq, and ultimately integrating its reserves into a corporate world order controlled from the United States. This wedding of national and corporate interests would give the United States leverage in dealing with an increasingly uncooperative OPEC. Privatization remained an attractive but more difficult goal for these planners.

Firm relations with stable governments in energy-rich regions and where there was movement of oil and natural gas to refineries and markets were essential for an industrial nation's security. The senior vice president for international affairs of Unocal (formerly Union Oil of California) was testifying before the U.S. House of Representative's Foreign Affairs Committee in 1998. He was discussing the political problems in constructing pipelines through Afghanistan and the needs of his company which was seeking to become a major presence in South Asia. Iran was to be avoided, as was Russia, and putting a pipeline through Turkey would hazard the hostility of the Kurds who were less than in love with Turkey or the West. With the assistance of the C.I.A. and Unocal, at one point the United States negotiated with the Taliban as probably the most amenable host.

The attack upon the World Trade Center in 2001, presumably provoked by such experiences as the resentment over the lingering presence of U.S. troops in Saudi Arabia after Iraq had been forced back from Kuwait, prompted speedy American movement to develop military bases in the former Soviet republics in the Caspian Sea area. Geologists believe that this basin may be one of the largest remaining sources of oil and increasingly valuable natural gas. The encirclement of Iran by American bases and military installations has attracted much less public attention.

When I first began to assemble my research on the place of oil in the global political economy, I thought that figures such as those cited earlier on American energy consumption—now 5 percent of the world's people, we consume 25 percent of the world's daily fossil fuel energy—might make a difference in citizen awareness of the inefficiency, vulnerability and perhaps immorality of the modern industrial society. My innocence was revealed as two presidents of the United States, Lyndon Johnson (Democrat) and Richard Nixon (Republican), cited such percentages as evidence of how great and strong we were, how envious the rest of the world must be, and as Nixon concluded, "May it always be that way." Meanwhile, the American economy continues to create new wants and then bombards the consumer to convert such wants into needs. For many of its citizens, their identification is now best found on credit cards. And what is called the national security budget sustains a permanent war economy to help ensure that we get ours while also controlling the flow of energy to other nations.

What about the people who live in the raw material producing colonies, as well as those whose homelands increasingly rely upon petroleum products but do not possess such resources? In past years, the major oil companies have lobbied international public agencies against loaning money to any country which sought to develop its own energy base. The argument was plausible but self-serving: Look, they need investment capital so badly, why should they waste scarce capital on oil drilling and installations? We will be glad to develop these. That is our business. The international lending agencies responded to this pressure by refusing to advance funds to nations seeking to gain a measure of independence by harnessing their own resources. Then when there was an international oil crisis and prices spiraled, these people discovered how heavily they were paying by not having autonomous sources and local refineries.[2]

In recent years global resistance has strengthened among those whose lands have served primarily as energy reservoirs for 20 percent of the world's population. The latter, primarily the northern tier industrial nations including the United States, now have 85 percent of the income and consume about 80 percent of the world's goods. The World Bank reports that the poorest 1.3 billion live on less than a dollar a day. Yet, even among these people, there is desire for a greater voice in control and more use of petroleum products to power newly acquired technological equipment at home and work. Developing nations such as China and India, each with a population of over a billion, encourage expectations for a more modern life. They are actively seeking to enhance domestic production of energy and also compete in the world, including in Southeast Asia, Africa and Latin America, for substantial and reliable supplies of oil and natural gas which are becoming more expensive to find. Meanwhile, over two billion of the world's population still lives essentially pre-industrial lives, their use of fossil fuels limited or nonexistent. It should also be noted that possessing and gaining wealth from petroleum are not guarantees of just distribution. Venezuela is a classic example, one among too many, where tremendous profits fail to reach the great bulk of its people and there are glaring gaps between rich and poor.

Alternative Directions

The well-being of the United States need not be threatened by these patterns. But the challenge is urgent to create and implement a national energy policy which is economically just and environmentally sane. And this should not come from the corporate councils of the energy industry, even when not meeting in secret sessions. Perhaps most importantly, it should not follow that the only or best way to attain energy security is through global relationships which assume our privileged need and right to dominate the world through control of energy resources and superior gun power. From this imperial perspective petroleum is the linchpin, assuring the continued and unbridled usage for ourselves while strategically regulating the flow for others.

One productive measure would be to reappraise our present technologies, asking how we might design and apply more energy-efficient processes for our homes, factories, offices, public spaces, and transportation systems, including our highways, than those we presently accept. There are engineers and scientists who believe that present energy usages could be reduced as much as 50 percent without appreciably changing the ways we live. For the time being this would not involve challenging the purposes of such use, including the many obvious areas of waste.

If we are genuinely committed to protecting and improving the best of "the American way," the search for alternative technologies should encourage craftsmanship and socially useful work. We must learn to be skeptical of technologies premised on the assumption that bigness is always better and fail to address concerns for a human-scale society, one whose decisions are accountable to the citizenry. The pervasive mythology that holds technology to be the ultimate determinant of an inevitable course is one of the most crippling barriers to the formulation of responsible public policy. We then do things because they can be done—and are profitable. The pattern in military procurement is a conspicuous example. Weapons and processes are funded because experts believe they can be produced. That they are likely to become obsolete and replaced by newer instruments and techniques is often an added incentive. Herman Melville expressed this vividly in *Moby Dick* when, in a moment of lucidity in Ahab's mad, vindictive pursuit of the White Whale through the oceans, the Captain reflects that "all my means are sane, my motives and objectives mad."

Energy

There is tremendous energy waste in the present military system, probably the nation's single largest user. When we calculate the energy spent in its worldwide activities to protect fields, installations, pipelines, tanker routes and the countries that supply us, we gain a more inclusive account of the cost of overseas petroleum. How much of our foreign policy is based on the assumption that such dependence is in the national interest, indeed is our only possible course? Aren't there alternative energies? Aren't there more peaceful and just approaches to vulnerable people throughout the world?

In agriculture, another major consumer of petroleum, there are what are called advances—such as hybrid seeds, artificial fertilizers and pesticides—generally with increasing yields and profits. All are petroleum-based. They transform farming into a stage in the industrial system. They also hasten the elimination of small farmers here and throughout the world who cannot meet the substantial financial requirements. For many, it was the only way of life they knew. For some, producing food has been an occupation they loved and felt was a real contribution to community well-being. We have only the most proximate way of measuring the loss of skill, pride and independence.

There has been a growing awareness of the pollution of the soil, water and air from such transformations. And the ever-increasing burning of fossil fuels has evoked concern about carbon dioxide emissions, global warming and rising sea levels. Concerted political action to counter this man-made climate change has to be prepared to take on the coal, oil and automobile industries and electric utilities. Some of the corporations, including Exxon, played an active part in the withdrawal of the United States from the Kyoto Protocol of 1997 in which the nations of the world agreed to a modest start to reduce such emissions. Perhaps a more difficult challenge is to persuade American consumers that there are energy alternatives which, if developed, would enable them to keep driving and enjoy other conveniences and comforts which they have come to view as their rights.

If things go dramatically wrong in the application of technology, one conventional explanation is that these "accidents" are rooted in human failing. When the supertanker Exxon Valdez ran aground on a submerged reef in 1989, spilling perhaps half of its cargo of crude oil that had come down the 800-mile Alaska Pipeline from the Arctic Slope, the veteran captain was blamed for drunken driving, or more accurately, for turning over the helm to a subordinate and going below because he had been drinking before reboarding his ship. As the lead witness in the government investigation at the site of the spill, I testified for some three and a half hours, answering an array of questions as to what factors the government should be looking into to understand what happened and hopefully to prevent similar disasters in the future. I cited such factors as the pressures by giant oil on the state legislature for cutbacks in environmental controls and appropriations, including those dealing with tanker traffic; the lobbying in Washington, again by the industry, against a requirement of double-hull tankers and more stringent supervision of tanker movements; and the insistence by Exxon that oil spills could not happen in Prince William Sound, but if one did, the involved corporations would be ready with the necessary equipment and manpower. A major spill ("the big one") did occur and the corporations were not ready. It was local fishermen and women in their small boats who were mobilized and ready to act. Of course, the captain was culpable for not being on the bridge. Subsequent investigations also disclosed the absence of a good radar system at Bligh Reef where the tanker was grounded and of ice reports from the Coast Guard which, if available, might have helped to keep the ship in its lane.

All during the hearing, my eyes kept surveying Prince William Sound from the deck of our small ship. It was the most beautiful body of water I had ever seen. I thought of our ship's captain who, with tears in his eyes, described the already observable harm to the rich marine life, including otters, orcas, fish and birds. And earlier, on an island beach near Bligh Reef, I watched a hastily recruited crew of workers rake the oil-soaked shore and skim the water. What will happen next, I asked a veteran spill chief from a construction company serving Exxon. "Oh, more crude will surface in a few weeks." The spill ultimately affected several thousand miles of coastline and harm to wildlife, fish and the fishing industry as well as to the humans who worked on the cleanup has continued to this day. Was the cleanup just public relations, ultimately paid for by the taxpayers?

At the close of the hearing, the chairman, a dedicated and highly respected public servant, asked me if I had any last question that I recommended that his commission pursue. "Yes," I replied, "I think you ought to raise the question as to why the United States wants all this oil." (At the time the country was drawing up to 25 percent of its domestic oil from Alaska.) There was a silence. Then the chairman signaled for the microphone to be cut off and the stenotypist to stop so that this portion of our dialogue would not be on record. No one, he then said, in the state legislature, in the Governor's office, in the Congress or in the White House wants to hear that question.

While the multinationals are merging to strengthen their capital, presumably for an intensive search for more oil and gas, it is myopic to dwell on the dependence and vulnerability of this country. The United States has substantial energy resources to tap, including natural gas and coal. We also have experienced scientists in advanced laboratories who are focusing on modifying these energy forms to meet environmental standards. Such efforts should be encouraged and expanded. Having learned how to liquify natural gas, we can now ship, creating an increasingly usable and cleaner fuel. Cleaner coal need not be an impossible challenge.

There is now considerable research and a growing number of pilot projects tapping renewable energies. These could replace some of the uses of nonrenewable fuels. Solar is extraordinarily attractive energy for an array of purposes, its use neither draining the resource nor ravaging the environment. Hydropower, geothermal, biofuels and hybrid energy—combining electric power and gasoline or natural gas—are all feasible for dealing with portions of the nation's energy needs. Wind power is in use in a number of communities throughout the United States and experiments continue to improve its performance. For many scientists hydrogen-powered fuel cells are the most promising alternative for petroleum. Although hydrogen is found almost everywhere, there are significant problems in converting and harnessing this element as a convenient and efficient energy. The dream of a hydrogen economy remains very alive, and there are exciting projects by automobile and oil companies and by the government. But much of the practical application still seems to be in the future.

Alternative and renewable energy and mass transit are among the productive areas for federal funding and setting loose at our universities imaginative and dedicated young engineers, scientists and planners. This might do much to diminish the influence of the petroleum corporations in shaping national energy policies. Their public relations now portray their role in society as that of enlightened environmentalists. But they still view petroleum as a commodity and they retain a tremendous capital investment in the going petroleum-based economy from which they draw sizable profits. Given their proclaimed commitment to the benefits of free enterprise, how could they possibly object to a little competition?

We should be wary of corporate activities concerning public policy where technological change is involved. The backing of parties, politicians and public issues in support of the oil industry's interests and agenda tells you much about its priorities. The "dancing attendance" by oil representatives upon the bureaucracies and legislatures of the federal, state and local governments is less visible, but the impact is often formidable. One recalls how the electric trolley car was driven off the streets of the United States by a campaign of segments of the oil and automobile industries which claimed that they were inefficient and disrupted traffic. Their real objective was to protect the market for gasoline and diesel-powered buses. (The trolley car has returned to some communities with the support of federal grants, now bearing the more high-toned name "mass light rail transit.")

The relations of Standard Oil of New Jersey, the nation's largest oil company, and I.G. Farbenindustrie, the industrial arm of Hitler's war machine, offer a sobering picture of the impact of corporate power on the political economy and the national security of the United States. The two giants had a series of agreements in the late '20s and '30s, some of which concerned synthetic rubber. The German industrial combine came into its own after World

War I when Germany lost its colonies and its source for raw materials. It created chemical and other scientific laboratories. One major concern was rubber. There were a number of synthetic processes for rubber which the American oil and rubber companies knew about. But what was believed to be the most promising was a particular process held by I.G. Farben with Jersey Standard. By 1940, the U.S. government, including its military, had become very interested in this synthetic rubber. On the eve of our entry into World War II, we had been cut off from natural rubber in Southeast Asia because of our declining relations with Japan. Jersey Standard (Exxon) repeatedly reassured the American government that it was working on the best possible process for synthetic rubber at its Linden, New Jersey, research headquarters. All the while its German partner was refusing to release the patents which would allow production to begin. Meanwhile, Jersey Standard was building refineries for high octane gasoline for the German air force.

As all of this damaging information became public through the Assistant Attorney General in charge of anti-trust, the late Thurman Arnold, the board of directors of Jersey Standard feared that citizen outrage might lead to nationalization. But this never happened. The nation mobilized for war, Jersey Standard settled with the government, and the desired synthetic rubber went into production. Subsequently, synthetic rubber production was allocated to the nation's four major rubber companies in proportion to the share of the market each had held.

Once the war ended, the oil industry launched a major public relations drive to reassure the public that oil corporations were responsible citizens. It portrayed itself as being on the frontiers of progress and its advertisements featured men in white peering through microscopes. Jersey Standard sponsored a television series with Pablo Casals, the world's greatest cellist and a leading symbol of anti-fascism. Casals had refused to return to his native Spain as long as Franco ruled and he lived out his life in Puerto Rico. Jersey Standard also developed a program for supporting education, and to further its image as a friend of intellectual life and the arts as well as education, it judiciously distributed its funding across the nation.

The energy problems of this country are not going to be addressed successfully either by public relations or technological fixes. The nation must begin to shift away from misguided production and consumption patterns which are destructive of the natural environment. At its heart this is a political challenge—one with a moral dimension in that so many people throughout the world are adversely affected by our fossil fuel dependency and aggression, as are the futures of our children. There is an imperative need for broad public discourse concerning the requirements for living peacefully with our fellow human beings and with nature—an agenda now almost totally absent from our present national politics which does little beyond calling for "more" of the same. Hopefully, from such discussions in our communities and in democratic political processes there will emerge a genuine national interest and commitment to alternative and renewable energy. One positive consequence would be the nation's moving away from policies shaped by private interests in public garb and toward democratic accountability for fundamental technological changes and energy decisions.

Treating natural resources such as energy as commodities becomes increasingly inappropriate. Yet there is no automatic magic in public ownership. Created with great hope and pride in 1938, Pemex, Mexico's national oil company and the world's fourth largest oil producer, has often been corrupt, careless with the waters and lands of the oil regions, and indifferent to the lives of fishermen and peasants who have been adversely affected by the company's oil operations. There is much to be learned about maintaining institutions in harmony with our historic belief in democratic control and accountability. But further centralization of power, either private or public, can only undermine such commitment.

I am told that at a demonstration in Washington some people were wearing sweatshirts which read "Justice, Not Just Us"—a pithy summary of the Declaration of Human Rights which defends the right of all people to live fully and to develop and share resources.

The late Gunnar Myrdal, one of the ablest economists I have ever known, used to warn us not to try to run the world as a company town. In contrast, the Bush administration has embarked on a selected global crusade against "evil" wherever it may be found—which somehow is usually near oil fields and installations. The nation is moved toward a permanent mobilization for pre-emptive wars, with no end in sight and without the consent of the American people. All this is defended in the name of anti-terrorism and freedom. Meanwhile, the embedding of corporate representatives in public government and private mercenaries in our overseas military forces further the distortion of responsible government. The creeping ascendancy of authoritarian practices, notably the serious inroads upon civil liberties, suggest a drift toward a brand of "fascism lite," cloaked by the banner of 100 percent Americanism and the untrammeled right to own a Hummer.

The late E.F. Schumacher, author of *Small Is Beautiful*, deplored the plundering and extinction of natural resources in support of giant, technocratic society which he viewed as obsolete. He proposed an intermediate technology which serves rather than enslaves and destroys. Mankind is too clever to survive without wisdom, he wrote.

Henry Geiger, a printer and longtime editor of the humanist journal *Manas* once wrote "Only the virtue of not yet disillusioned men holds present day civilization together. And faith, not what they have faith in, is the glue. . . . Science which leaves out man turned out to be anti-human in practice. Theories which explain intelligence in terms of blind forces are impotent to solve the problems of intelligent beings. Education which has no view of man except as passive clay to be modeled by experts produces little but rebels and zombies. What is happening in the world today is not evidence of the potentialities of human behavior, but of the distortions under the influence of dehumanizing beliefs. . . ."

And for a last word, this from the poet Dylan Thomas, "Do not go gentle into that good night. Rage, rage against the dying of the light."

Endnotes

[1] Several years later Democratic Senators Lee Metcalf (Montana) and Edmund Muskie (Maine) asked if I would accept nomination as public-consumer representative on the Council. This was part of their legislative effort to require more balanced membership on all such committees. After some hesitation, I accepted, adding that I had as much a sense of humor as anyone. A few months later I was informed by Senator Metcalf that the NPC had reviewed and rejected the proposal, explaining that there already was such a spokesperson on the Council—from the Consolidated Edison Company of New York.

[2] For a careful analysis of theses relationships, see Michael Tanzer's *The Political Economy of International Oil and the Undeveloped Countries*, Beacon, 1969.

CORPORATE POWER, POPULAR RESISTANCE, AND SUSTAINABLE DEVELOPMENT IN AN IMPERIAL AGE*

Ward Morehouse

The U.S. Presidential election in 1933 occurred during the Great Depression. Franklin D. Roosevelt was elected president with a strong mandate to deal with burgeoning unemployment and increasingly widespread financial dislocation. Roosevelt's effort to cope with this crisis resulted in a series of measures in the first 100 days of his presidency that sought to provide relief in one form or another for the economic distress of the time. This package of actions was perceived by corporate officials and other owners of great wealth as profoundly threatening to their position of dominance in society. They responded with the kind of action that had served their interest well in other parts of the world during the early decades of the 20th century—they sought the services of a senior military official to lead a military takeover of the United States.[1]

However, they misjudged their man. General Smedley Butler, a retired commandant of the U.S. Marine Corps, refused and went public with word about their plot. On his retirement, Smedley Butler published a memoir summing up his military experience and its relationship to U.S. corporate interest in the Third World in these words:

"I wouldn't go to war again as I have done to protect some lousy investment of the bankers. There are only two things we should fight for. One is the defense of our homes and the Bill of Rights. War for any other reason is simply a racket.

"I spent thirty-three years and four months in active military service as a member of this country's most agile military force, the Marine Corps. And during that period, I spent most of my time being a high-

*Adapted from "On Being a Gangster for Capitalism," *Ecologist Asia,* October-December 2003.

class muscle man for Big Business, for Wall Street and for the Bankers. In short, I was a racketeer, a gangster for capitalism.

"I helped make Mexico, especially Tampico, safe for American oil interests in 1914. I helped make Haiti and Cuba a decent place for the National City Bank boys to collect revenues in. I helped purify Nicaragua for the international banking house of Brown Brothers in 1909-1912. In China, I helped to see to it that Standard Oil went on its way unmolested.

"During those years, I had, as the boys in the back room would say, a swell racket. Looking back on it, I feel that I could have given Al Capone a few hints. The best he could do was to operate his racket in three districts. I operated on three continents."[2]

That pattern of using military force to protect or expand U.S. corporate interests elsewhere in the world has been reaffirmed many times in succeeding decades. Thomas Friedman, the foreign affairs columnist for the *New York Times*, illustrates this well:

"The hidden hand of the market will never work without a hidden fist—McDonald's cannot flourish without McDonnell Douglas, the building of the F-15. And the hidden fist that keeps the world safe for Silicon Valley's technologies is called the United States Army, Air Force, Navy and Marine Corps." [3]

The Post 9/11 Scene

The relationship between U.S. military power and corporate interests has been thrown into sharp relief by the September 11, 2001 terrorist attack and the Bush administration's response. Bush has used the disaster as a foil to attack Afghanistan and Iraq to advance U.S. corporate interests. That has spawned a massive outpouring of U.S. commercial interests jockeying for position in these newly conquered countries. Take, for instance, the newly created corporation, New Bridge Strategies, described in its own words in the box on the following page.

The box sets forth the purposes and method of operation as it seeks to facilitate the penetration of U.S. corporations in the wake of U.S. military operations in Iraq. It also illustrates interlocking relationships of the government of the United States and U.S.-based corporations and underscores the agency relationship between government and corporation and the revolving door linking former officials in current and previous administrations and corporate entities like New Bridge Strategies. A striking characteristic of these former government officials is that they have all served in prior Republican Party administrations generally considered to be more friendly to corporate

New Bridge Strategies: Who We Are and What We Do

New Bridge Strategies, LLC is a unique company that was created specifically with the aim of assisting clients to evaluate and take advantage of business opportunities in the Middle East following the conclusion of the US-led war in Iraq. Its activities will seek to expedite the creation of free and fair markets and new economic growth in Iraq, consistent with the policies of the Bush Administration. The opportunities evolving in Iraq today are of such an unprecedented nature and scope that no other existing firm has the necessary skills and experience to be effective both in Washington, DC and on the ground in Iraq. It is for this reason that we have created New Bridge Strategies and brought together the knowledge of American business professionals with over 25 years of experience in Iraq and throughout the Middle East and the political experience of some of the most successful governmental political professionals in Washington, DC, and London to provide a complete package of business services offering:

    a. Assistance to companies engaging in US Government process to develop post-war opportunities

    b. Identification of market opportunities and potential partners

    c. On-the-ground support in Iraq

    d. Legal, technical, cultural and potentially financial support for ventures.

New Bridge Strategies maintains a physical presence with staff on the ground in Beirut, Damascus, Geneva, Houston and Washington, DC, and it has plans to expand into Iraq as soon as possible.

New Bridge Strategies principals have years of public policy experience, have held positions in the Reagan Administration and both Bush Administrations and are particularly well suited to working with international agencies in the Executive Branch, Department of Defense and the US Agency for International Development, the American rebuilding apparatus and establishing early links to Congress. Also, because of their long history of work in the Middle East and Iraq, they possess Arabic language skills and business expertise in fields such as: telecommunications; real estate; food and beverage; energy; oil and gas; manufacturing; high-technology and distribution.

Editor's Note: This information is quoted directly from the words of New Bridge Strategies.

Source: http://newbridgestrategies.com/whoweare.asp

interests. The reality, though, is that there is little difference between Republican and Democratic administrations in the U.S. government; both seek to serve and be served by major corporations, both in the United States and internationally.

But corporate penetration of government runs much deeper in the U.S. A major new study, *Corporate Warriors* by P.W. Singer, documents how corporations have broken out of the guns-for-hire mold of traditional mercenaries and now sell skills and services that until recently only state militaries possessed. Their "products" range from trained commando teams to strategic advice to military commanders.[4]

This new "Privatized Military Industry" involves hundreds of companies, thousands of employees, and billions of dollars in revenue. Whether as proxies or suppliers, these corporations have participated in wars in Africa, Asia, and the Balkans and Latin America.

These trends and other evidence of large corporations, primarily U.S.-based, gouging the public treasury have led some human rights organizations to launch a campaign against corporate profiteering from the U.S. war in the Middle East. Initiated by the Meiklejohn Civil Liberties Institute in Berkeley, California, this campaign has been joined by the Council on International and Public Affairs in New York. Thus far, efforts to get Congresspersons to introduce a bill attacking war profiteering have been unsuccessful. But support at the grassroots is growing and a number of labor unions, local municipalities, and other civil society organizations have adopted resolutions against profiteering from war.

Exposing Instruments of Corporate Rule

The harsh reality of the American Empire which has emerged from the 9/11 tragedy and subsequent preemptive use of military force by the U.S. is reflected in a major new study of instruments of corporate rule and how they undermine the principle of self-governance on which the United States was founded. The book entitled, *The Elite Consensus: When Corporations Wield the Constitution*, examines "instruments which support corporate power." These instruments include the World Bank, the International Monetary Fund and the World Trade Organization, the Council on Foreign Relations, the Cato Institute, NATO and the United Nations, to name a few. It includes public relations and advertising corporations into which elites pour hundreds of billions of tax-deductible dollars, along with corporate propagandists posing as journalists and pundits.

The book shows how few people shape ideas, policies, values, news, information and language when writing laws and rewriting histories. It makes it clear that by the time "issues" or even honest candidates appear before the voters, they have been sterilized, sanitized, disinfected and fumigated to order by the elite consensus.[5]

By that time intellectuals at corporate think tanks have done their trashy-but-footnoted studies and reports. By that time, journalists, TV news writers, public officials and community leaders have been "properly educated." People's energies have been channeled to Potemkin Villages propped up by corporate fairy tales and democratic myths.

Organizations like the CATO Institute, the Chamber of Commerce, the Business Roundtable and the Heritage Foundation have spent years and billions of dollars fabricating "idea deconstruction systems" constantly spewing cockamamie that frames and reframes the country's agenda. Their managing of the nation's discussions can be seen in the ways Social Security, fast track legislation, global rights agreements like NAFTA, war in the Middle East, energy and health care policies, revelations of corporate usurpations and other issues in the news are mass-produced from coast to coast.

The book examines the iron fist inside the PR-camouflaged corporate glove, and helps us remember that when huge groups of people challenged governance by corporations, public officials have responded with violence.[6]

Post 9/11 Repression and Resistance

Arrayed against this expose of how corporations rule is the Bush administration's bold initiative to use the 9/11 tragedy as a cover for repression of U.S. civil liberties and strengthening corporate domination of civil society. This repression, while concentrated on the U.S., is having a ripple effect around the world. Expression of democratic principles and free thought as set forth in the Universal Declaration of Human Rights and other international conventions is taking a hit in many countries, not just the U.S.

The impact on the United States is more visible because of the immediacy of 9/11 to Americans, the sheer size of the U.S. economy, and the prior existence of political space—now sharply diminished—for new ideas and challenges to transparent manifestations of political power.

Lewis Lapham, editor of one of the leading periodicals for political debate in the U.S., offered his biting critique of the U.S. government responses to the 9/11 tragedy in an essay entitled "American Jihad": "We have more to fear from the fatwas issued in Washington than from those drifting across the deserts of Central Asia. The agents of al Qaeda might wreck our buildings and disrupt our commerce, maybe even manage to kill a number of our fellow citizens, but we do ourselves far greater harm if we pawn our civil rights and consign the safekeeping or our liberties to 'Mullah' John Ashcroft and the mujahedeen in the hospitality tents of the American crusade.[7]

Almost three years later, Lapham's gloomy assessment seems, sadly, to reflect what is happening on the ground. The Patriot Act, a large and complex piece of legislation that attacks many fundamental rights long enjoyed by Americans, was adopted in the wake of the 9/11 tragedy without serious discussion by members of Congress, few of whom had even read the Act. It was followed by the Homeland Security Act, and more recently, the even more odious draft legislation known informally as "The Patriot Act II," recently approved by the House of Representatives.

The brazen behavior of 'Mullah' Ashcroft, the U.S. Attorney General at the time, has had one encouraging consequence. His actions sparked widespread resistance at the local and state level across the U.S. Over 298 (on website: http://www.capital.net/~force/bordcres.htmlwww.capital.net/~force/bordcres.html) municipalities were moved to adopt resolutions opposing Bush-Ashcroft legislation and executive orders along related lines. Alaska, Hawaii, and New Mexico have taken state-level positions of resistance.

But a giant step forward in resisting anti-terrorist actions by Ashcroft and his minions was taken with the adoption by Arcata, California, of a local ordinance which prohibits municipal employees from providing information to the federal government under Bush-Ashcroft anti-terrorism laws and regulations. Thus, the stage is set for a direct challenge between local governments asserting their right to free speech, self-governance and other civil rights on the one hand, and the federal government (and, in all probability the Department of Justice) on the other. This kind of local or state resistance to unjust actions by the federal government has a long history in U.S. political life, going back to the very beginning of its history as an independent nation.

But even if Clinton and Bush-Ashcroft anti-terrorist legislation were repealed tomorrow, serious limitations would remain in the defense of basic human rights under the Bill of Rights. Perhaps the most egregious is the usurpations of the constitutional rights of natural persons by corporations, largely through judicial decisions over the last century and more.

Political mobilization around critical local initiatives is essential in bringing about change in a society that aspires to be democratic and has many of the attributes of a democratic society even as it struggles to deal with the growing inequality that makes it a plutocracy.[8]

U.S. activists engaged in resistance to the Bush-Ashcroft-Clinton assault on civil liberties are essentially on the defense. Their adversaries have been defining the agendas for resistance as executive orders are issued and repressive legislation is submitted to Congress in the name of fighting terrorism.

Even if we were to reverse time and go back to the status quo before President Clinton proposed his anti-terrorism legislation, followed by that of

Bush-Ashcroft, we would find a Constitution with a seriously flawed Bill of Rights and a body of legislation and judicial opinion that challenged, if it did not violate, many of the international standards for human rights set forth in the Universal Declaration and other international human rights conventions and agreements and that protect and enhance corporate power.[9]

Global Penetration by the U.S. Corporate Empire

Why does repression of civil liberties and enhancement of corporate rule in the U.S. matter to environmental and political activists in the rest of the world?

One reason is the enormous size of the U.S. economy—by far the largest in the world today. Another is the dominance of the global political economy by U.S.-based corporations, which are increasingly overtaking nation states in the scale of their operations and the concentration of productive assets in their hands.

The annual revenues of the 500 largest corporations in the world—the "Global 500"—are some $10 trillion, around twice the size of the gross domestic product of the United States. In a single year, 1994, the Global 500 revenues increased by 9 percent, and profits soared by a colossal 62 percent. The Global 500 in that same year eliminated 262,000 jobs. Even more striking is the startling capital accumulation among the top 200 global corporations.

Frederic Clairmont writes: "The velocity of transnationalization of capital as measured as a share of world GDP is stunning: from 17 percent in the mid-1960s to 24 percent in 1982 and over 32 percent in 1995."[10]

Yet there are encouraging signs emerging as the disempowered learn new tricks in resisting authority and asserting peoples' rights.

The emergence of corporate-driven globalization in recent decades has also galvanized opposition through the emergence of grassroots globalization that links popular resistance against corporate power worldwide. While we are far from declaring victory, there are occasional breakthroughs such as occurred at the World Trade Organization session in Cancun, Mexico, in September 2003.[11]

The emergence of the World Social Forum, initially in Brazil and, in January 2004, in India, represents a step forward in building a global forum for disempowered voices.

Another important task in the struggle against corporate hegemony is revitalizing people's tribunals, sanctioned by countries individually or collectively through the World Court and the newly established International

Criminal Court. These are important for those otherwise denied their day in court in current judicial systems.

The work of the Permanent People's Tribunal, headquartered in Rome, needs to be revisited as an important mechanism for the examination of rights violations. A legacy of the Bertrand Russell war crimes trials of the 1970s, it has undertaken notable work in examining the human rights impacts of the World Bank and International Monetary Fund and corporate violations of human rights.[12] Other international tribunals include the International People's Tribunal to judge the G-7 held in Tokyo in 1993 and the Global People's Tribunal on Corporate Crimes against Humanity, which took place in Seattle at the time of the World Trade Organization meeting in 1999.[13]

Particularly noteworthy in setting the stage for a new round of people's tribunals in the current decade are the series of four tribunals on Industrial and Environmental Hazards and Human Rights, which took place at the Yale Law School in the U.S., in Bangkok, and in Bhopal, India, and which finally culminated in a session in London to mark the tenth anniversary of the Bhopal disaster.

Out of these tribunals emerged the Charter on Industrial Hazards and Human Rights in 1996. That instrument sought to reflect a process of empowerment from below rather than dictation from above, thus constituting a building block in constructing a people's jurisprudence for the future. The critical distinction in the mode of its articulation is captured in this excerpt from the introduction to the Charter:

> "The Charter on Industrial Hazards and Human Rights does not bestow rights from above as a gift from the state. It is a set of demands from below, to be seized by individuals and groups acting in the context of particular struggles. The way in which it is interpreted and used will necessarily vary from one situation to the next, but it nevertheless articulates a universal vision of a world in which people are able to lead their lives without industrial hazards."[14]

Corporate Hegemony and Sustainable Development

What have the foregoing stories of resistance to corporate domination have to do with sustainable development? Much depends, of course, on how "sustainable development" is defined. One of the best known definitions is that of the World Commission on Environment and Development—"development is sustainable when it meets the needs of the present without compromising the ability of future generations to meet their own needs . . . it is linked to concepts like economic, social and environmental equity within and between generations."[15]

If we look at the social, political, and environmental consequences of corporatization worldwide, we are driven to a melancholy conclusion. This conclusion has been expressed nowhere in more compelling language than by Joel Bakan in his work, *The Corporation: The Pathological Pursuit of Profit and Power*. Bakan asserts four propositions to support his assertion that the corporation is an agent of social pathology:

- The corporation's legally defined mandate is to pursue relentlessly and without exception its own economic self-interest, regardless of the harmful consequences it might cause to others—a concept endorsed by no less illuminary than the Nobel Prize-winning economist Milton Freidman.

- The corporation's unbridled self-interest victimizes individuals, society, and, when it goes awry, even shareholders and can cause corporations to self destruct as recent Wall Street scandals reveal.

- While corporate social responsibility in some instances does much good, it is often merely a token gesture, serving to mask the corporation's true character.

- Governments have abdicated much of their control over the corporation, despite its flawed character, by freeing it from legal constraints through deregulation and by granting it ever greater authority over society through privatization.[16]

In short, if one gives credence to Bakan's analysis and conclusion, it is difficult for me to see how the global community or any significant portion thereof will be able to achieve "sustainable development" as defined above without radically altering the character of these legal fictions which have come to dominate the entire planet Earth.[17]

Hope for the Future

It is not always easy to project a future of hope and possibility in the face of domination and exploitation by rapidly growing and seemingly invincible corporate power. Yet there is hope. At least that is how it seems to Satinath Sarangi, a key figure in the long and dark struggle for justice for survivors of the world's worst industrial disaster in Bhopal. When asked recently how this struggle, in which he has been engaged for almost 20 years, affected him, he responded with these words: "It has made me more hopeful, which is weird. Even under these circumstances, things are possible. You have the government, the corporations, the legal system against you. The scientific bodies are apathetic. Medical institutions don't care. And yet things have been done and victories have been won."[18]

The major lessons of 20th century history also tell us that we should not lose hope. As Howard Zinn, the author of *A People's History of the United States*, reminds us:

> "The struggle for justice should never be abandoned because of the apparent overwhelming power of those who have the guns and the money and who seem invincible in their determination to hold on to it. That apparent power has, again and again, proved vulnerable to human qualities less measurable than bombs and dollars: moral fervor, ingenuity, courage, patience—whether by blacks in Alabama and South Africa, peasants in El Salvador, Nicaragua, and Vietnam, or workers and intellectuals in Poland, Hungary, and the Soviet Union itself. No cold calculation of the balance of power need deter people who are persuaded that their cause is just."[19]

References

[1]   Arjun Makhijani, *Manifesto for a Global Democracy*, New York, The Apex Press, 2004, p. 26.

[2]   Smedley Butler as quoted by Makhijani, ibid, p. 26. See also Smedley Butler, "War is a Racket," 1935 (reprinted 1995 by Crisis Press, Gainesville) as cited in Mike Ferner, *War and Peace and Democracy*, Toledo, Ohio, Program on Corporations, Law & Democracy, 2002.

[3]   Thomas Freidman, "A Manifesto for the Fast World," *New York Times Magazine*, March 28, 1999, as cited in Makhijani, ibid, p. 25.

4.   PW Singer, *Corporate Warriors: The Rise of the Privatized Military Industry*, Ithaca and London, Cornell University Press, 2003

[5]   George Draffan, *The Elite Consensus: When Corporations Wield the Constitution*, New York, The Apex Press for Program on Corporations, Law & Democracy, 2003.

[6]   This section has been adapted from Richard L. Grossman and Ward Morehouse, the Foreword to Draffan, ibid, pp. xvii - xix.

[7]   Lewis Lapham, "American Jihad," *Harper's Magazine*, January 2002, as quoted in Ward Morehouse and David Dembo, "September 11 and the Rule of Law: And the Council's Response," New York, Council on International and Public Affairs Summary Report for 2001.

[8]   Adapted from Ward Morehouse and David Dembo, "Dissent is Patriotic: Resisting the Assault on Our Civil Rights," New York, Council on International and Public Affairs Summary Report for 2002.

[9]   Ward Morehouse, "Taking the Offensive: How Do We Make Democracy Work?," *Dissent Is Patriotic Newsletter*, Northampton, Bill of Rights Defense Committee, September 2003.

[10] Frederic F. Clairmont, *The Rise and Fall of Economic Liberalism: The making of the Economic Gulag*, Revised edition, Penang, Southbound Books, Mapusa, Goa, The Other India Press, 1996 as cited in Ward Morehouse, "Consumption, Civil Action, and Corporate Power: Lessons from the Past, Strategies for the Future," in Dean Ritz, ed., *Defying Corporations, Defining Democracy: A Book of History and Strategy*, New York, The Apex Press for Program on Corporations, Law & Democracy, 2001, p. 35.

[11] Frederic F. Clairmont, "Transnational Gulag: Reflections on Power, Inc.," *Economic and Political Weekly*, 1-8 March 1997, p. 450.

[12] See Ward Morehouse, "Technological Autonomy and Delinking in the Third World" in Dieter Ernst, ed., *Confronting the Unholy Alliance of Power, Privilege and Technology in Rich and Poor Countries. The New International Division of Labor, Technology, and Underdevelopment—Consequences for the Third World*, Frankfurt, 1980.

[13] For a report of the International People's Tribunal to judge the G-7, see the *People v. Global Capital—the G-7, TNCs, SAPs and Human Rights* (Tokyo, July 1993), New York, The Apex Press and Mapusa, Goa, The Other India Press, 1994.

[14] Introduction to the Charter on Industrial Hazards and Human Rights (1996), New York, Council on International and Public Affairs see also Permanent Peoples' Tribunal on Industrial Hazards and Human Rights, Findings and Judgment: (4th and Final Session, London, 28 November - 2 December 1994), Rome, Permanent People's Tribunal and London, Pesticide Action Network, UK; and Permanent People's Tribunal, Findings and Judgments (3rd Session on Industrial and Environmental Hazards and Human Rights, 19-24 October, Bhopal-Bombay).

[15] SustainAbility *et al.*, *The Changing Landscape of Liability*, London and Washington, SustainAbility Ltd., n.d. (?-2004).

[16] Joel Bakan, *The Corporation: The Pathological Pursuit of Profit and Power*, New York, Free Press, 2004, jacket copy.

[17] While legal instruments such as corporations are used in many countries around the world as instruments for organizing economic activity and defining relationships of those engaged in such activity, in the abuse of power that results from the kind of social pathology which Bakan analyzes, size is a critical variable. By and large, with inevitable exceptions because of the huge universe of such entities worldwide, the problems addressed by Bakan in his book are a function of size. At least not to the same degree, do small "mom and pop" corporations follow the kind of pathological behavior which Bakan examines in his book. Corporations that are social psychopaths are giant corporations which have now become larger than most nation states.

[18] Satinath Sarangi, Interview, *Corporate Crime Reporter*, July 28, 2003, p. 15.

[19] Howard Zinn, *Failure to Quit: Reflections of an Optimistic Historian*, Monroe, Maine, Common Courage Press, 1993, p. 27.

Part Three

Sustainability as Regenerating Knowledge Systems

Introduction to Part Three

SUSTAINABILITY AS REGENERATING KNOWLEDGE SYSTEMS

Trent Schroyer

DESPITE QUANTIFIABLE GAINS IN GDP, integration into the world economy of marginalized people[1] has been an overwhelming failure and results in an endless struggle for survival for those who seek a resting place this side of material salvation from necessity.

Within the essays in this chapter we learn to aspire, instead, for a world where economics would be only one part of the larger context of human life, and not idealized as the ultimate measurement of human activity and social progress.

Classical Political Economics as a System of Knowledge

Stephen Marglin, in an essay "What Do Bosses Do,"[2] contended that the choice of technology within the workplace was, in many cases, for purposes of control and legitimizing the authority of the boss, rather than for purposes of efficiency. What started with that seminal piece and culminates in his essay "Sustainable Development: A Systems of Knowledge Approach," below, is essential for the sustainability movement today. An introduction to this essay will provide it with contemporary relevance.

Justification of the division of labor within the particular shop is not a matter of technical efficiency, as Karl Marx, following Adam Smith, assumed. Successful devaluing of workers' autonomy in the conceiving and executing of work found its justification in a system of knowledge, political economics, that became central to the transition from mercantilism to capitalism. Classical political economics imagined an efficiency-producing market whose self-regulating mechanisms appeared to justify dis-embedding workers' control over their work situation. What this dis-embedding actually achieved was something quite different: it eliminated all the holistic norms that secured any contextual meaning for work.

This ideological function of reducing the importance of workers in the classical political economics knowledge system during the transition to capitalism was premature. The technical competence of craftsmen to competitively conceive and execute their tasks is in no way transcended by the necessities of technical learning.[3] The movement to industrial systems can not be conceived of as an automatic technical learning process—other socio-cultural mediating factors are involved.

From this perspective, cultural alternatives have, both in the past and today, been fused to situations where craft production or other micro-industry combinations can be supported by socio-political arrangements that facilitate the optimal integrations of local-regional, national, and even wider markets.[4]

Culture Systems of Knowledge and Sustainable Development

Marglin's argument in the essay below is a generalization of this thesis. Culture systems of knowledge have different epistemologies, forms of transmission, and innovation, as well as differing power relationships in all these dimensions. Each culture combines forms of knowledge in different ways that change over time. On this account all cultures are combinations of episteme (E-knowledge), systemic disembedded cerebral knowledge, and techne, (T-knowledge), contextual intuitive practical knowledge. Whereas systems of E-knowledge present themselves as universal forms of knowing—science, logic, theology; T-knowledge is implicit, personal and contextually dependent—craft, art, practical common sense.

A comparative approach to different socio-cultural contexts would, in the framework of a knowledge theory of culture, describe different ways of mixing episteme and techne; dis-embedded universalisms and practical body-centered intuitive competences. Whereas Marx could express disdain for all artisans and subsistence "workers" who resisted integration into factories or the market economy, labeling them the petty bourgeois, this can now be seen as an evolutionary prejudice.

One account of the origin of these types of knowledge distinguishes between the human capability for integrating contextual judgments (being able to assemble parts into a whole) and the separate ability to deconstruct operations into detailed parts—an analytic ordering that is not contextually bound. Citing the book by Oliver Sacks, *The Man Who Mistook His Wife for a Hat*, Marglin defines[5] contextually embedded knowledge as an intuitive and yet practical way of creating or making as techne; episteme is defined as logical deduction from self-evident invariant axioms or principles that are independent of contexts. These distinctions do not favor the epistemic but try to indicate that non-epistemic, non-analytic, ways of knowing are essential and are ultimately embedded in the human body's capabilities "to put the puzzles together," not in two different types of cognitive analysis.

Today we are reminded again and again that body-based competences are relevant and cannot be dismissed by theories of the evolutionary superiority of Western cognitive knowledge. What has been dis-valued as reactionary craft sensibilities or ethno-sciences of healing and horticulture are rooted in traditional forms of cultural practice. They remain as relevant to the sustainable practice of social life as more cognitively universal forms of knowledge.

Situating Knowledge in the Andres

Frederique Appfel-Marglin and Kathryn Pyne Addelson's essay on "Situated Knowledge" is an application of a feminist epistemology of knowledge that extends these perspectives. They point to PRATEC (Andean Project for Peasant Technologies), a small organization in Peru that began with the recognition that the green revolution was not as fruitful as regenerating traditional Andean horticulture. By affirming a peasant techne domain, rather than modern epistemic agronomy, they came to understand the Andean world not primarily as one to "know" but, rather, one to live in, to participate in, and to collectively create. They came to see that the introduction of hybrid seeds and the technical packages of the green revolution not only interrupted the regenerative cycles of the local cultivars, but of the local cultures, as well.

This was true despite the fact that, with irrigation, hybrid seeds, chemical fertilizers and pesticides, more crops could be raised in a year than using traditional horticultural practices. This artificial "greening" was destructive—it destroyed the cycle of rituals and it destroyed the reciprocities called for in the joint regeneration of the biological and cultural worlds. The green revolution transforms peasants into individuals dependent on the market, on external commodities, rather than on each other, nature, and their deities, or *huacas*. The penetration of the green revolution broke down the natural regeneration of the peasant communities, losing the holistic meaning of traditional practices and social and cultural identity, too.

The members of PRATEC stepped away from their professional episteme and began learning how to act and write from within the Andean collectivities. As a result, they came to understand with clarity the impossibility of comprehending the local Andean techne from within their professions.[6]

This story is again generalized in Marglin's essay below where the advocacy is for development economists to recognize that local stocks of knowledge about horticulture, healing, work and socio-political organization are the basis of a lived world. Interventions of E-knowledge have to be done in ways that supplement, not disrupt, these successful modes of subsistence. Of course, in some situations, the disruptions and loss of the natural world have gone so far that some forms of economic growth and the introduction of commercial exchanges must proceed, but even then it can be done in ways that are sustaining of systems of techne.

Mutual learning, then, is the model recommended by both essays and initiatives have begun to establish mutual learning centers for horticulture and healing in South America and India. But it involves a conscious stepping away from the over professionalized mind-set as essential for participation in other cultural contexts.

De-colonization is not to preserve traditional culture but to allow a space for organic growth of indigenous cultures—not to stop essential economic growth or the consumption of material goods. In the absence of demonstrable redistribution of wealth in the poorer nations, its goal is to decouple the introduction of technologies, including social technologies, from their cultural and political consequences. This requires investigations of the activities and spheres in which such decoupling can occur—such as agriculture, health, local-regional economics, ecological practices for sustainability of the Earth and communities, and others. However, all of these investigations begin with a general questioning of the episteme of economic development.

India as Model for World Sustainability

Siddhartha's story of India's struggle for independence shows that the modernizing brought on by Nehru's five-year development plans complicated traditional India while, at the same time, providing for institutional changes that realized some forms of democratization in India. This has liberated some of the poor in India but, ironically, trapped others.

The May 2004, Indian election has relieved a fear that India would continue to promote Hindu nationalism and push more neo-liberal market and privatization reforms. The election signaled an astonishing rejection of the sinister communalism and all-out affirmation of neo-liberal economic policy. Instead, the success of the new progressive alliance endorsed a more pluralistic polity and at least a half step back from wholesale privatization.

But the overall realities of India are, despite recent excitement about increased economic growth, continued grim poverty for, and oppressive domination of, the vast majority of the people.

Huge numbers of people are still in the "informal sector" in India. Barbara Harriss-White claims that 88 percent of Indians are still struggling—squashed by land owners, money lenders corrupt civil servants.[7] Of those, 74 percent still live in rural areas and 14 percent in small municipalities. Yet the remaining few who are powerful and wealthy still have the ability to neutralize most legislation that would disrupt their advantage in the accumulation of wealth or undo the restraints imposed by traditional caste or economic status

The intermediate classes in the rural and small towns seal the poor, struggling workers and subsistence peoples in a prison of debt, dependence, caste hierarchy and patriarchal prejudice. As Arundhati Roy so elegantly put it, India doesn't live in the villages, Indians die there. Siddhartha surveys the social movements that are trying to represent the social justice interests of the majority of the poor.

But it is the life-centeredness of community and religious practice that led to a gradual recognition that the right to life and livelihoods, articulated by members of the National Alliance of Peoples Movements (NAPM), provides a culturally-shaped alternative. Reduction of poverty by aggregate economic wealth and export-led development helps some, but enforcing a basic right to land, and access to water, forests, or fishing stocks helps the many. It is not growth in income that is essential, but securing the indigenous life— resources and commons—that provides subsistence wealth. Reconstruction of the economy must be done around the central principle of sustaining life. As Anil Agarwal suggests, the Gross National Product needs to be replaced with a Gross Natural Product.[8]

Free trade that undermines the local production of fish, coconuts, coffee, wheat through the importation of agricultural commodities is counter-productive for subsistence and village sectors. A "right to life and livelihoods" principle expresses the politics most appropriate for subsistence worlds, and the principle can be extrapolated to other worlds, too. Thus NAPM's advocacy of "first livelihoods" expresses the common sense that indigenous resources, or commons, are essential to maintain the reciprocity of life-centered communities.

Reciprocity of living ecology and subsistence livelihoods is ultimately a moral principle, as embodied in Gandhi's *satyagraha* or truth-force, that can be used to guide actions for every community and municipality the world over. Subsistence expresses the wisdom that all human existence must be bounded by the limits of need rather than want, in order to realize true freedom and happiness.[9] To constantly aspire to transcend one's current level of consumption, the mythology of "development," ultimately undermines this moral ecology.

Exclusive focus on economic growth is destructive to subsistence communities, in fact, all communities, unless it fully takes into account renewable energy, sustainable agriculture, water conservation, biomass-based enterprises, and the prudent use of living systems. Any degradation of access to ecological resources increases the plight of the impoverished, just as any improvement of these indigenous resources will reduce their vulnerability.

In this situation, the calm and gentle practices of the Fireflies Ashram, founded by Siddharta, seem to be a way forward that combines the logic of regeneration of indigenous cultural knowledge with a subtle guidance toward a convergence with secular human rights. Fireflies Ashram and Pipal Tree, an Indian trust cooperating with Fireflies, are experimenting with a new paradigm for social transformation that is inspired by Gandhian ideals and the cultural and social practices of local communities. This involves seeing the Earth as mother, re-interpreting festivals and religious practice to incorporate the dimensions of personal growth, compassionate action and connectedness with nature.

The communities concerned are often subsistence-based, and there is an attempt to create appropriate conditions for their empowerment and putting them in touch with other processes of learning. In practical terms, this means shifting from chemical to organic farming, restoring lakes and instituting water conservation methods, developing women's self-help groups, building peace-committees in areas prone to inter-religious conflict, promoting education to prevent HIV/AIDS and developing programs for health and sanitation.

Fireflies Ashram is also trying to influence intellectuals, journalists, students, teachers, police, bureaucrats, political leaders with its eco-social-spiritual approach, projecting an alternative kind of globalization that is more just and fulfilling. This program has two dimensions. The first has to do with re-interpreting the cultural practices and traditions of the people, especially the festivals. The second has to do with initiating sacred song movements, as well as music and film festivals, where the values of the Charter of Human Responsibilities are sung and participated in by the village communities.

Re-Situating Economics for Sustainability

Wayne Hayes takes on the task of showing how economics emerged and how it can be reconstructed as an aid for world sustainability, not its demise. Is it possible to regenerate economics with a sensitivity to the Earth and living communities? No other task is as important since economics is the major source of destructive interventions into traditional subsistence worlds.

Hayes begins by reconstructing the meaning of economics and shows that its original mission was the management of the human household. Thereafter he surveys the major thinkers and forms of economics to see how these might be utilized without destroying the earth. Discussing the evolution of economic thinking from Adam Smith and David Ricardo to Joseph Schumpeter, he shows that the goal of growth and free trade was reinforced in ways that made the business model of capitalism seem inevitable.

Hayes shows how it was Karl Polanyi's distinction between formal and substantive economics that created a place for sustainability in the modern world. This interactive provisioning with nature, in the context of ever changing co-operative practices, was later expressed more ecologically by Herman Daly, who brought externalities back into the object domain of economics. This makes the throughput of energy and materials a fundamental frame for economic analysis and brings the dimension of scale into any economic analysis. From this point, Haynes assesses the possibility of ecological economics, as well as Lester R. Brown's eco-economics, as new ways of making economics compatible with sustainability.

But Hayes also goes on to show how neo-liberal economics arose and how the contemporary regime of economic globalization came to be. Reconstructing the origins and transformations of the institutions that came out of the Conference at Bretton Woods—the World Bank and International Monetary Fund, he shows how they changed their orientation as neo-liberal economics became the operating policy frame. In this context, the World Trade Organization further complicates the situation of sustainability.

There is no middle ground between neo-liberalism and sustainability. The essay's conclusion is worth repeating here: "The alternatives, based on rethinking the eco-economy, cannot be dictated by ideology or by centralized authority, but rather built piece by piece, from the ground up."

Endnotes

[1]   See Jerry Mander and Victoria Tauli-Corpuz (editors), *Paradigm Wars: Indigenous people's resistance to economic globalization* (San Francisco, International Forum on Globalization, 2005).

[2]   Stephen Marglin, "What Do Bosses Do?" *Review of Radical Political Economics*, No. 6, Summer 1974.

[3]   Frederique Apffel Marglin and Stephen A. Marglin (editors), *Dominating Knowledge* (New York, Oxford Clarendon Press, 1991)

[4]   See Michael J.Piore and Charles F. Sabel, *The Second Industrial Divide* (New York, Basic Books, 1984), Chapter 2, and Karl Polanyi, *The Great Transformation* (Boston, Beacon, 1944), Chapter 14.

[5]   Marglin and Marglin, *op. cit.* p. 237.

[6]   This story is continued in a follow up book edited by Frederique Apffel-Marglin and the PRATEC entitled *The Spirit of Regeneration: Andean Culture Confronting Western Notions of Development*, (New York, Zed Books, 1998).

[7]   Barbara Harriss-White, *India Working: Essays in Society and Economy* (New York, Cambridge University Press, 2003), pp. 4 ff.

[8]   Cited in Gabriele Dietrich and Nalini Nayak, *Transition or Transformation* (Chennai, India, Tamilnadu Theological Seminary, 2002).

9   Ivan Illich asserts that the last 500 years has been a war against subsistence. This insight has
    influenced more people to see this counter intuitive view point than any other 20th cen-
    tury philosopher. See Ivan Illich, *Shadow Work* (Boston, Marion Boyers, 1981) chapter 3;
    also see *The Future of Knowledge and Culture: A Dictionary for the 21st century* (edited by
    Vinay Lal and Ashis Nandy) (New York: Penguin, 2005) that shows the continuation of
    this viewpoint.

SUSTAINABLE DEVELOPMENT: A SYSTEMS OF KNOWLEDGE APPROACH

Stephen A. Marglin

THIS PAPER TAKES AS ITS POINT OF DEPARTURE TWO PREMISES—the first premise is that growth in the availability of goods and services is necessary, specifically for the bottom 40 percent of the people of the Third World whose conditions of material life are inadequate by any human standard. These conditions are all the more inadequate in light of the affluence enjoyed by the elites of Third World countries, not to mention ordinary people in the First World and much of the Second World as well. The second premise is that the Western experience of development provides a poor model for achieving this growth.

The first premise commands wide assent. There is considerable disagreement about the tactics and even about strategies, but little about the moral and practical necessity of growth. The second premise is more controversial because the attractions of the Western model are so obvious: the elevated levels of gross national product that have been achieved in the West permit broad masses of the population to enjoy levels of physical comfort to which only elites aspire in most of the world. But the Western model remains less than compelling. Environmental destruction, meaningless work, spiritual desolation, decay of the family and the community. These are some of the characteristics of the Western model that make it a dubious example for the rest of the world to follow.

These problems are compounded when the Western model is transplanted to culturally alien soil. In many Third World countries, the uncritical pursuit of the Western model has exacerbated, perhaps even caused, urban violence, political instability and repression, social and economic polarization, and, last but hardly least from our perspective, the destruction of valuable stores of local knowledge—knowledge of agriculture, of the body, health, and illness, and knowledge of political accommodation, knowledge acquired and developed over centuries and even millennia.

Sustainable Development and Systems of Knowledge

The importance of alternative models is highlighted by the fact that the issue of sustainable development, once marginal to the development debate, has now claimed center stage, and in a very real sense has come to set the terms of the debate as we prepare to enter into the 21st century. Sustainability has focused on two issues: First, the adequacy of the resource base for continued growth at rates achieved in the half century since World War II, or for that matter, even the sustainability of current rates of resource use. Second, the despoliation of the environment that has accompanied postwar growth. To this list we propose to add a third issue, the sustainability of the dominant cultural model of development. In fact, we believe these are not separate issues at all. Rather, we believe that the depletion of resources, the despoliation of the environment, and the decay of the society are linked through the dominant system of knowledge. The ideological dominance of a single knowledge system justifies particular forms of acting in and on the world that threaten the sustainability of both material and social processes.

Knowledge disembodied and disembedded, knowledge based on the separation of mind and body and taken out of the context of time, place and persons; knowledge instrumental and rational, knowledge based on the separation of ends and means and speaking only to means by logical deduction in the manner of a computer program—there is a place for such knowledge in any culture as the world enters the third millennium of the Christian era. The problem comes when such knowledge refuses subordination to a cosmology, but pretends itself to be a cosmology, a theory of reality. As a cosmology, it leaves no room, at least on the ideological level, for other, equally necessary, systems of knowledge. As a cosmology, such knowledge gives us scientific management, which turns the worker into an appendage of the rule book and the machine, for whom work has no meaning other than the paycheck at the end of the week. It gives us scientific forestry and scientific agriculture, which threaten to degrade the environment and exhaust the world's resources. It gives us scientific medicine, which transforms the person into a set of laboratory readings and poisons our bodies with chemicals as it prolongs life empty of meaning. It gives us scientific politics and administration, which transfers disembedded forms of instrumental and rational politics to the Third World, aiding and abetting the creation and maintenance of authoritarian and repressive regimes. In short, we see the dominance of a particular knowledge system as the thread that connects apparently disparate practices and beliefs about the self, work, the environment, and the body politic—practices and beliefs that threaten the sustainability of the present course of world development.

Every knowledge system has its own theory of knowledge, its own rules for acquiring and sharing knowledge, its own distinctive ways for changing the content of what counts as knowledge, and, finally, its own rules of governance, both among insiders and between insiders and outsiders.

Thus a knowledge system does not refer to a specific domain of knowledge. It refers rather to a way of understanding, perceiving, apprehending, and experiencing reality. Economists and physicists, chemical engineers and personnel managers, all deal with different domains of knowledge. But this in no way prevents them from sharing a common system of knowledge.

It might help if we formalize these ideas by distinguishing two kinds of knowledge system, which we call episteme and techne.[1] For episteme, the theory is that knowledge is obtained by logical deduction from (self-) evident first principles. Knowledge is held to be purely cerebral, disembedded from the body, and indeed from particular contexts; episteme produces universal knowledge. Episteme is instrumental, having nothing to say about the good and the beautiful and indeed eliminating these concepts from the realm of knowledge altogether. Its logic easily becomes the logic of calculation and maximization.

Epistemic rules for transmission and innovation are highly individualistic; in principle epistemic knowledge is an open book which anyone can read, and changes—either in the first principles, or more rarely, in the rules of logic—can be proposed by anyone. Under episteme, governance is (also in principle) a mixture of egalitarianism within the knowledge community and hierarchical superiority *vis a vis* outsiders. Techne has a very different epistemology, emphasizing a variety of sources which range from intuition to authority. It is knowledge embedded in practice, often implicit in nature, indeed often tacit knowledge literally embedded in the body, as the knowledge of a wheelwright, surgeon, or pianist is embedded in the hands as well as in the mind. It is, in a word, non-dualistic. Techne obscures the distinction between ends and means; the medium and the message may not be one, but neither are they perfectly distinct as they are in the epistemic conception.

Technic transmission and innovation are non-individualistic; transmission is explicitly embedded in a social process, often a hierarchical one like the relationship between master and apprentice, teacher and student, parent and child. Innovation is generally respectful of, if not reverential towards, authority. Commentary and emendation, rather than outright criticism and denial, and are the primary methods of changing a techne. The authority of the fathers is interpreted rather than denied. The knowledge community is hierarchical internally (as in the relationship between master and apprentice), but if not egalitarian in its relationship with other knowledge communities, is at least pluralistic—"live and let live" might be the emblem of technic power relations with outsiders.

From the point of view of the modern West, techne is at best an inferior sort of knowledge. In some readings it is little better than mere belief, superstition, and habit, an obstacle to "real" knowledge. By contrast, episteme is considered not merely one kind of knowledge, but knowledge pure and simple.

Our view is quite different. We believe that knowledge in all cultures is a combination, sometimes a tension, between episteme and techne. We would argue, indeed, that techne is essential to all understanding, not to mention action; pure episteme is a fantasy world in which human beings become computers. This fantasy is not a mere daydream: let run amok in the real world, it produces bizarre and even horrible consequences. This notwithstanding, the Western construction of reality has, at the ideological level if not at the functional level, elevated episteme to the point that techne is at best considered inferior knowledge. From a knowledge-systems perspective, the central problem of the Western cultural model with respect to sustainability is the imbalance between episteme and techne; the marginalization of techne puts to one side our best hope for softening the destructive effects of episteme on our selves, our work, our land, and our body politic.

The Environment

Our reliance on episteme has propelled us to manage, or rather to mismanage, our forests and fields, our air and water, to the point that fear for the future of the environment is no longer the preserve of a marginal fringe, but the concern of the solid and sober-minded as well. But despite the growing recognition of the results, the discussion continues to revolve around issues of management, with hardly a sidelong glance to the possibility that our entire approach, based on episteme, is misconceived.

We propose to make that sidelong glance a forthright gaze. Our point of departure is the hypothesis that an uncontained episteme exacerbates environmental problems (which doubtless have a multiplicity of causes) and that progress towards models of development which do not make unsustainable demands on the environment requires the subordination of an episteme of calculation and maximization to a techne of prudence and judgment. This in turn, requires us to replace the instrumental attitude in which nature is a resource for the production of goods and services with a sense of humankind embedded in and part of nature.

It is the disembedding of human beings from the environment—some even object to the word "environment" on the grounds that it puts human beings too much at the center and conceptualizes nature as our surroundings. That makes possible an instrumental attitude in which nature becomes the object of calculation and maximization and a "resource" for the production of goods and services. But the omni-presence of uncertainty—overwhelming and non-quantifiable—makes a mockery of such calculation.

As Keynes understood investment decisions to be beyond the scope of epistemic calculation and maximization and therefore properly belonging to the realm of techne, so we understand ecology. And for the same reason: the overwhelming uncertainty and ignorance in which we must act. Of course we differ from Keynes in one important respect. Where he saw the needs of his day as requiring entrepreneurs whose "animal spirits" would make them willing to take chances and damn the consequences, we see the present environmental situation as requiring caution and prudence, a disposition not to take chances where there are safer alternatives available. This, we emphasize, is not because we know with certainty that ozone depletion, the greenhouse effect, acid rain, and so forth will be calamitous, but precisely because we do not know one way or the other.

This perspective leads us to a critical examination of the ideology of knowledge underlying developmental policies that threaten the environment. A case in point is high-tech agriculture, with its reliance on hybrid or "synthetic" seeds, chemical fertilizers, herbicides and pesticides, large scale irrigation, and heavy equipment. There is little question that this package has increased output enormously over this century, but there is considerable uncertainty over its sustainability into the next century. But is there an alternative? Our hypothesis is that there well may be alternatives, but that these have been marginalized by the dominance of agronomic episteme, and by those whose economic interests lie in promoting high-tech agriculture.

Take the matter of seeds. There is some evidence that a satisfactory alternative to hybrid and synthetic seeds is to select and propagate the better indigenous varieties. According to some reports, "mass selection," as this technique is called, leads to yield increases comparable to those achieved by hybridizing and synthesizing new varieties, particularly under the actual field conditions that cultivators face.[2]

With mass selection farmers are able to carry over seed from one year to the next. But the offspring of hybrids are practically sterile (as many a farmer who thought he could avoid the high cost of hybrid seed by saving his own learned to his dismay), so the farmer has no choice but to turn to commercial seedsmen. With hybrids, therefore, cultivators become absolutely dependent on the seed company. In the case of synthetic seeds, farmers can carry over seeds from one year to the next, so in principle the situation is better. In practice, synthetics, like hybrids, fall prey to pest and disease within a matter of a few years, so new varieties must be continuously produced, keeping the farmer dependent on commercial seeds.

What is a disadvantage to the farmer (and, we believe, to the community as a whole) is an advantage to the seed companies. It has even been suggested that the profitability for the seed companies rather than the superiority of the strategy of hybridization is the reason for the adoption of this strategy in the case of the first and greatest success of high-tech agriculture, the invention and diffusion of hybrid corn in the United States in the first half of this century.[3] In this view hybrid corn was the fruit of a grand collusive effort between the government-funded research establishment and the seed companies.

We do not doubt the importance of profitability in shaping development strategies. But we would question whether this is the whole story in the case of the development of hybrid seed, or indeed even the most important part of the story. Equally important, in our view, is the ideology of knowledge which exalts episteme and, therefore, strategies which can claim the mantle of science. Alternatives, especially alternatives which build on the technai of farmers and others, lack the cachet of the epistemic approach.

In the Third World, the problem is compounded by the association of episteme with the West and the "modern," and the association of techne with the traditional and the "backward." By the time the lessons of high-tech agriculture in the United States were packaged for export, first to Mexico and then to Asia and now to Africa, the obvious success of agronomic episteme, and the prestige and power of episteme as a more general system of knowledge, combined to marginalize research efforts aimed at what would now be called sustainable, low-tech, agriculture. There are no apparent alternatives to the Green Revolution not, we hypothesize, because of technical or economic infeasibility, but because the ideology of knowledge has starved research along paths other than the path of episteme.

A central objection to the proliferation of agronomic episteme is precisely that it gradually eliminates and marginalizes the farmer's techne. Of course some farmers, particularly in the United States, become masters of this episteme themselves, either directly, or as managers of enterprises that engage technicians and scientists as servants of the enterprise. But most farmers, particularly in the Third World, become appendages of the machine and the rule book, not to mention the bank and the extension agent. This is harmful not only to the individual whom it deprives of an important basis for investing work with meaning, but also for its social and political consequences. The knowledge lost is lost for good, irrespective of new conditions which might require agricultural techne. The farmer who becomes a factor of production, the object of the agro-industrial complex, becomes more easily manageable as a political object as well.

The issue of the effects on the farmer of the elimination of his agricultural techne by agronomic episteme has gone generally unnoticed in all the discussion of sustainable agriculture. Agriculture, once embedded in a ritual cycle and deriving "holistic" meaning from that cycle (and this within living memory in much of the Third World), has over large parts of the world become wholly instrumental, as the production of industrial commodities has become.[4] At the same time farmers have become increasingly dependent upon an agro-industrial complex that includes not only the manufacturers of equipment, chemicals, and seeds, and the banks who provide the credit necessary to purchase these inputs, but also the research establishment that has transformed techne into episteme. Deprived of control, the agriculturalist is no more able to invest his work with an individually constructed meaning than is the industrial worker; he or she is sustained only by poverty and the promise of the new system to "deliver the goods" that will alleviate that poverty. But can such a system survive in an era of abundance? Can a plethora of goods, even a relative plethora, substitute for the barrenness of purely instrumental work?

Meaningful Work

Without doubt, work has become more productive in terms of the output of goods and services over the last two hundred years, but it is by no means clear that the organization of work is sustainable. To be sustainable in an era in which limits to growth are recognized, work must be intrinsically meaningful. But work in the West is largely disembedded (the Lutheran notion of a "calling" is exceptional in this view), so that any meaning attached to work must be an individual construction, an act of creativity difficult if not impossible to achieve when others—be they capitalists or commissars—control one's work.[5]

The ideological dominance of episteme has played a crucial role in the success of the project of capitalists and commissars to take control of the production process. Michel Foucault has argued that from very early in the industrial era factory supervision and control were part of a larger "scientific" conception, typified by Jeremy Bentham's all-purpose "panopticon," a structure deemed by the father of utilitarianism to be equally serviceable as factory, prison, or school.[6] More recently, "scientific management" provides an example of a technique of top-down control, equally serviceable to capitalist or commissar (as Lenin well understood), which is facilitated by the ideological hegemony of episteme. Scientific management not only allows the boss to appropriate the workers' knowledge of production, but it transforms this knowledge from a techne that was the basis of workers' control of production to an episteme that becomes the boss's control: recast in epistemic form, knowledge of production becomes accessible only to the boss and his agents. Scientific management has not only empowered managers directly, it has at the same time done so indirectly, by legitimizing the transformation of knowledge from techne to episteme as "progressive," thus inhibiting resistance by allowing it to be labeled as "anti-progress." Workers and trade unions, sharing the Western belief in episteme as a superior world view, are put in the position of fighting limited rearguard actions as they accommodate to a form of "progress" in the workplace that increases the dominance of the machine and the rule book—and those who set the pace of the machines and write the rules.

The dominant model of work organization has distorted the creativity of both bosses and workers: bosses' preoccupation with issues of supervision and control operates to the actual detriment of efficiency, and at the same time, the initiative and creativity of workers is expressed in figuring and acting out ways to circumvent this control.

Outside the West, work is based on different cultural foundations. Research on a handloom weavers' village in eastern India, for example, reveals work embedded in life and sustained by a very different balance of techne and episteme. It is not the case that a necessary condition for the sustainability of non-Western forms of work organization is poverty and the lack of alternatives, for hyper-prosperous Japan provides another example of an alternative model of work organization, and arguably Japanese economic success rests in no small part on this model. According to Masahiko Aoki, the superior flexibility of Japanese firms, the ability to respond to shocks, is attributable to the larger scope for workers to exercise initiative.[7] We would hypothesize that this results from a better balance between episteme and techne within Japanese culture, which leads to a greater respect for workers' techne and the possibility of enlisting their techne in the quest for quality and quantity, in sharp contrast with the West, where workers' techne is dissipated in a defensive struggle against their bosses.

It is questionable whether a sustainable society can be achieved on the basis of the repression of the vast majority of the citizenry, in an age where creativity will be in ever greater demand to meet the myriad challenges and problems that the present model of development has thrown up. The Soviet Union used stridently to claim that she was showing humankind the way of the future. And, with the irony in which Clio delights, well she might be:

underlying *perestroika* and *glasnost* may be the recognition that Soviet society is unable to cope because it has repressed the creativity of the greater part of its citizenry.

The Self

The dualism of work and life compounds with the ideological dualism of mind and body to focus medical research and action on individualized therapies, involving generous doses of drugs, to treat problems of the economy and society as if they could be reduced to problems of biology. The same episteme which transforms the worker into a factor of production also transforms health and sickness into a set of laboratory readings. It may well be asked whether one practice is any more sustainable than the other, whether there is not an intimate connection between understanding the self in terms of episteme alone and the growing epidemics of drug abuse, street violence, child abuse, and similar ills of modernity.

The Body Politic

Dysfunction and even disaster have followed from transplanting Western episteme stripped of a local techne. These problems are complicated by the concentration of epistemic institutions in the upper layers of the polity, particularly at the national level. Because of the ideological subordination of the more complex, participatory, relational, consensual, technic institutions which operate at the local level, not only have participatory institutions been omitted from the package transplanted to the Third World, but this package has actually destroyed the legitimacy of traditional participatory institutions in the recipient societies.

About half a century has elapsed since Nobel Laureate Kenneth Arrow demonstrated the impossibility of deriving a society's ranking of policies from the rankings of the individual members of the society by any sort of democratic or vote counting procedures, unless there are mechanisms for adjusting the individual rankings themselves, mechanisms such as socialization to ensure a basic uniformity of preferences; adjustments through cognitive and affirmative interaction; and finally, when all else fails, adjustment through brute force.[8] Unfortunately, the wrong lessons have been drawn from Arrow's results: subsequent research has been largely directed toward studying alternative mechanisms of aggregating preferences rather than towards understanding how these mechanisms of adjustment operate either to facilitate or to replace vote counting. Arrow, in effect, begins by denying culture in assuming unbounded preference domains only to end up by implicitly asserting the necessity of culture; for it is culture that assures the requisite uniformity of preferences.

Viewed in a larger social sense, an "impossibility theorem" exists for each of the different methods of collective decision making. If all issues are dealt with by force, the society will be brutalized. Excessive reliance on authoritarian expertise will lead to dissatisfaction, unrest, and social polarization. Participatory methods of decision making, however desirable intrinsically, cannot be used in every conceivable instance.

The blend of participatory, representative, conventional, managerial, and coercive arrangements which are appropriate for a particular society can only emerge through its own experience; no simple blueprint will suffice for this purpose. Moreover, systems are dynamic in nature, and cannot be determined for all time to come; their very flexibility in responding to new problems is the sign of health, and a prerequisite for longevity. The delicate blend appropriate to each society is the techne of its political system. The elements of this system are often tacit and unarticulated; and a too explicit articulation could actually be harmful, in that it might hamper adjustment to new realities.

The problem faced by many Third World countries is that they have taken the achievement of the Western political system to be their goal, and for that purpose they imported an epistemized version of this system. The universality of episteme makes this an obvious course of action. In this epistemic version, the entire emphasis has been placed upon the national level representative institutions and bureaucratic machinery, and almost none on the underlying participatory basis of these institutions. Thus, not only has the imported political system been truncated in form, the import has led to the eventual elimination even of indigenous participatory institutions. As a result, the people of many of these societies have lost the ability to communicate with each other or to live with each other.

The epistemization of Western political and social institutions has also had negative effects on the First World. Local participatory institutions, which have been an integral part of the political techne of Western societies, are disappearing gradually, producing a slow but inevitable erosion of political participation and an increasing epistemization of politics. As in the case of scientific management, the domination of epistemic thinking has facilitated the project of "scientific politics:" in the guise of depoliticizing administration, democracy has been reduced to mere vote counting.

The Case for Cultural Pluralism

From the point of view of the West, alternative models, particularly models which draw on the value and knowledge systems of non-Western cultures, are regarded with a great deal of skepticism—when they are regarded at all. Indigenous cultures are widely regarded as obstacles to growth. Although we have no intention of romanticizing tradition, we do see indigenous cultures in a more positive light. Our earlier work has explored a variety of indigenous practices which appear as backward, irrational, superstitious, obscurantist, or just plain absurd when viewed against modern Western norms. These practices turn out much more positively in a critical comparative perspective which does not presuppose the superiority of Western theory and practice.[9] This is so even in terms of economistic criteria which give no weight whatsoever to the role these practices play in the maintenance of the indigenous cultural fabric, and even more the case when a "holistic" attitude is adopted. Moreover, many of these practices reveal indigenous cultures to be kinder and gentler to the poor, to women, and the environment than modern, Western practices.

Our overarching purpose is to create space for alternative models by undermining the hegemony of the dominant model, based as it is on what we understand to be very possibly an unsustainable, and in any case a destructive, ideology of knowledge. We see the problem with the Western model as systemic, as a whole greater than the sum of its parts. The problem is not the workplace, the domestic sphere, the environment, and the polity, but the underlying system of thought, of organizing reality—the knowledge system that produces the pathologies that appear in these various domains.

Precisely the attraction of alternative models is that they might provide a better way of integrating various aspects of our lives than does the dominant Western model. It is not, of course, a question of going back to some earlier set of practices and beliefs, but of reasserting and in some cases even recapturing the rationale, the techne, that underlies other ways of being in the world, of making our modern episteme the handmaiden of this techne, rather than its destroyer.

Endnotes

1   Fredrique Apffel Marglin and Stephen A. Marglin (eds.), *Dominating Knowledge*, (Oxford, Clarendon Press, 1990).

2   See C.O. Gardner, "Population Improvement in Maize," in David B. Walden (ed.), *Maize Breeding and Genetics* (New York, Wiley, 1978); N.W. Simonds, "Plant Breeding: The State

of the Art," in T. Kosuge, *et al.* (eds), *Genetic Engineering of Plants: an Agricultural Perspective* (New York, Plenum Press, 1982).

3   Jean-Pierre Berlan and Richard Lewontin, "The Political Economy of Hybrid Corn," *Monthly Review*, July-August, 1986.

4   Arjun Appadurai, "Technology and the Reproduction of Values in Rural Western India," in F. Apffel Marglin and S. Marglin, *op. cit.*

5   S. Marglin, "Losing Touch: The Cultural Conditions of Worker Accommodation and Resistance," in F. Apffel Marglin and S. Marglin, *op. cit.*

6   Michel Foucault, *Discipline and Punish* (Harmondsworth, Penguin, 1979).

7   M. Aoki, "A New Paradigm of Work Organization and Coordination? Lessons from the Japanese Experience," in S. Marglin and Juliet B. Schor (eds.), *The Golden Age of Capitalism* (Oxford, Clarendon Press, 1990).

8   Kenneth Arrow, *Social Choice and Individual Values* (New York, Wiley, 1951).

9   F. Apffel Marglin and S. Marglin, *op. cit.*

SITUATING OURSELVES

Frederique Appfel-Marglin
and
Kathryn Pyne Addelson

IN THIS CENTURY, MOVEMENTS OF LIBERATION have struggled against a system of dominating knowledge that has enabled oppression of women, minorities, and the lower classes in the West and supported political and economic imperialism globally. (Apffel-Marglin, 1996) The dominating knowledge has been embodied in the modern sciences that fuel development. Western science was said to be rational and its knowledge objective, a universal knowledge to be used by all peoples. Other ways of knowing were dismissed as superstition, mere opinion, traditional beliefs, all of which needed to be corrected by Western education. In the capitalist democracies of the West, the dominant place of science was legitimated by philosophical theories on what objective knowledge of reality had to be. The object of knowledge was the real world, the knower was "anyman" who abided by the criteria of scientific method.

For years, feminist theorists criticized the abstract epistemology that legitimates the dominating knowledge. They persisted in asking, "Who are the knowers?" They insisted that the so-called "objective knowledge" was, in fact, produced by knowers with a politically skewed perspective—that of dominating males. The pretense of the patriarchal epistemology was that knowers were "disembodied' whereas they were actually embodied as white, higher class, Western educated men.

Socialist-feminist standpoint theory was an early, contested "epistemology," a creative development of Marxist analyses on the special, revolutionary location of labor. With the standpoint epistemology, these feminists opposed the account of objective scientific knowledge by insisting that women, as a dominated class, were in a position to offer a truer account of the human and natural world—and in a position to change the world in which the dominating knowledge exercised its power. According to these theorists, what is known is the dynamic of a system of capitalist patriarchy that conceals its own oppressive nature under the labels of rationality and objectivity.[1]

Standpoint theories have been criticized on the grounds that they homogenize women's experience, speaking as they do of the oppression of "all women." They are made from the perspective of white, higher class women of the (dominating) West and show disrespect for the knowledge, experience, and needs of women of color globally—or so the argument goes. In our terms, the criticism is that these standpoint theories share the faults of the epistemology of science: they are not properly embodied. The knower is "anywoman." (see Harding, 1986, Haraway, 1991, 1988)

A question came to haunt the feminist theorists: what sort of theory could possibly deal with these embodied knowers, with all their differences of experience, politics, and perspective?

One answer that has received a good deal of attention is Donna Haraway's epistemology of "situated knowledges." Like other feminist theorists, Haraway takes "communities" as the significant knowers—not individuals, as the epistemologies of modern science do.[2] She indicates that members of the communities are situated in terms of their class, race, gender, and other such variables that enter into power differences, and so their knowledge is always partial, not total and universal. Communities come to knowledge through "conversations." Knowers are heterogeneous, not homogeneous. Haraway wishes to change modern science, not to abandon it in some romantic flight back to what is "natural." She is no epistemological Luddite but rather a feminist embracing a post-modern world. From her new position, she offers an account of objectivity that is an alternative to the old epistemology of modern science and the newer, socialist-feminist standpoint theory.

We believe that Haraway's sketch of an epistemology contains many fruitful ideas, and we would like to develop some of them. We also believe it has very serious flaws that, unless corrected, facilitate the dominating knowledge rather than transform it. We do believe, with Haraway, that knowers must be situated—radically situated—but we have a number of questions about her proposal. Who are the knowers? What sorts of situations are in question, and what sorts of "communities"? What is "the known"? Or rather, what sort of knowledge is in question here? One of the most pressing of our questions is why Haraway seems to take the point of her epistemology to be giving an alternative account of objectivity. Who is it that cares about objectivity and why? Most important of all, how are we to situate Haraway herself as a knower—that privileged knower who presents us with an alternative epistemology? Is she "anywoman," as in the standpoint theories? If not, what are the salient features of her situation?

We believe that the significant situation of theorists like Haraway (and ourselves) is our situation as trained, employed professionals. One of the great flaws of the old epistemology of science was that it hid the fact that scientists are embodied first and foremost in their professions and disciplines (and their job sites). Like the epistemology of modern science, Haraway's "situated knowledge" does not take a special account of her own position as a professional with cognitive authority. The "dominating knowledge" of development globally and in the West itself is defined and administered by professionals and paraprofessionals, and any alternative must take that into account not by ironic asides in journal articles, but in practice. Being of good will and engaging in postmodern theorizing does not mean we do not contribute to the domination we criticize (and we believe Haraway would agree to this).

Feminist criticism of the old epistemology of science was that it pretended to be disembodied. The feminist counter-theory to the epistemology of the dominating knowledge must be embodied in feminist practice. This is particularly important if feminist theorizing is supposed to be relevant to political action. We believe this requires a change in the way feminist epistemologies are conceived, and the locations in which they are tested, and most of all, a change in the understanding of who is to be served, and how the service is to be made.

In this paper, we agree that knowers must be situated, but more radically and more specifically than Haraway's proposal seems to require. We offer a different account of knowledge-making by arguing that notions of objective knowledge central to the abstract epistemology of modern science are, in fact, those needed to legitimize the position of power, influence, and authority that professionals hold. Alternatives must deal with that political fact. We believe this means that a challenge to the dominating knowledge should primarily take the form of a change in the situated practice of professionals, with theory following to explain the practice.

Professionals (whether feminists or more traditional scientists) are embodied in institutions and practices of domination. We will discuss this in terms of the "double participation" of professionals in their disciplines and in political situations outside the work of their disciplines. In the old epistemology, it was the situation of professionals that set the terms for making (and applying) knowledge. In our view, the terms for making knowledge are far more complex and they must be uncovered in particular situations of community life.[3] Because of this, our account cannot be given in the abstract way that philosophers often give their theories. We require a different method of presentation, and so a good part of this paper is taken up by discussing a case in which professionals did indeed take account of their situations and change them. The case we will discuss is that of PRATEC, an organization in Peru that works with peasant communities of Andean peoples.

Part One
Issues in the Epistemologies of the Professions

Feminist epistemologies have, for the most part, been presented both as criticisms of the standard epistemology of modern, Western science and, building on that criticism, as alternatives to it. The science of modernity (so called) has several planks in its epistemological platform which have been denied in the new feminist epistemologies—the abstract individualism and the notion of objectivity are among them. In any debate, opponents tend to focus on the same issues as a way of managing effective criticism and defense. The issues important to the epistemology of modern science have framed the feminist debate, influenced the methods, and helped set a boundary on what counts as epistemology. Knowledge is a relation between knower and known, and a normative epistemology sets conditions on that relation and describes the character of knower and known.[4] According to Lorraine Code, the dominant epistemologies of modern science are defined around the ideals of objectivity and value neutrality. Objectivity (in this sense) requires a detached, neutral, distanced, disinterested approach in a publicly observable space. (Code, 1995) Donna Haraway calls it the "god trick" of escaping constraints that location imposes. The distance is between the knowing subject and the object of knowledge, and so the distinction between knower and known is central—there is a knower, an object known, and objectivity characterizes the relationship. In this sense, knowledge is not a reciprocal relationship, something that is important to the possibility of a dominating knowledge. The knower knows and defines the object, the object at best gives feedback through test or observation devised by the knower. Defining the point of the knowledge belongs to the knower.

Equally important is the universality claimed for this knowledge. Although there are many objects of knowledge, there is one knowledge about those objects, a knowledge that (in Sandra Harding's words) must be consistent and coherent because it is one knowledge. Thus the subject of knowledge, the knower, must be unitary and coherent, not heterogeneous, multiple, and conflicted. (Harding 1993). The knower required by this objective knowledge is stripped of social, political, historical, and even biological features. As Aristotle said millennia ago, so far as nature goes, all rational beings know the same truths—thus the "god trick."

The Socialist-feminist standpoint epistemologies were developed by using Marxist criticisms of the old analysis of objective knowledge by transforming them in a direction suited for a feminist movement. Haraway offers her alternative as a radical transformation of standpoint theories (perhaps a postmodern transformation) that also counters the traditional epistemology of modern science. Haraway does not look for objectivity in the god trick, in the positionless position of the archimedean point, where one has removed the clothing of culture, society, and individual talent and stands naked as Barbie's Ken, without penis or breast. Rather, Haraway proposes that we need the knowers to be fully embodied, located in the extreme. Rather than views from nowhere she wants "Views from somewhere." And if the knowers are uniquely located, so is their knowledge.

In the demand for full location, Haraway also rejects the universalizing standpoint theories of the Socialist-feminists. Her "somewhere" isn't the standpoint of all women of all classes, races, ages, and cultures. There is no "truest" knowledge for all women. Rather, every view from somewhere gives only a partial knowledge—not the eternally true, whole knowledge of the epistemology of modern science nor the historically located truth of the feminist standpoint. The knowing subject is heterogeneous, multiple, and conflicted. (Harding 1993) This is the counter to the claim of modern science that the subject of knowledge must be unitary and coherent, and to the feminist standpoint claims based on the unity of women's position. In Haraway's terms, knowledge depends on a power charged social relation of "conversation." Objectivity becomes "positioned rationality"—presumably the community outcome of the "conversations." (Haraway, 1988)

It seems fair enough to ask how Haraway (and we ourselves) are situated, and what power-charged conversation she is taking part in, and with what community. We know certain things—for example, the epistemology of modern science that she and other feminists criticize was devised, for the most part, by professionals trained in science, humanities or the social sciences. Many of the feminist critics (including ourselves) have reframed the abstract epistemologies in order to criticize them. In making these criticisms, we are situated within the work of our professional disciplines, and the point of the criticism is set within that work—including classroom work and writing articles and books that may have readers outside the usual, professional circles. The "conversation" seems to take place among members of a relatively narrow community of knowers, with a much larger "community" of listeners to our lectures or readers of our writing. In fact, the point of finding an alternative notion of objectivity seems to be of interest to that narrow, professional community.

Because of the way these feminist theorists are situated in their disciplines, the alternative epistemologies run the danger of being as abstract and universal as the old epistemology of science, concealing rather than revealing the sources of dominating knowledge. Those sources lie at least in part in the professions. It is worth criticizing the old theories epistemologies in their role as norm-givers for the knowledge professions rather than as abstract theories about who knows and what is known and knowable.

It seems to us that in the old epistemology of science, objectivity is less a condition on knowledge than a code of ethics and politics for the professions and disciplines of the sciences. The embodiment of these purveyors of objective knowledge is indeed in science—not science the ideal body of knowledge but science the real body of professions, disciplines, research institutes, careers, departments, funding agencies, and the like. Even the insistence on standards concerning objective and universal knowledge of reality seem to us a justification for the powerful status of professions in modern society, and of course, the authority of the knowledge makers. Even the abstract criteria of the epistemology are translations of conditions on the professions. For example, one main criterion for an occupation being designated as a profession is detachment, in the sense of having in a particular case no personal interest such as would influence one's action or advice, while being deeply interested in all cases of the kind. (Hughes, 1984) This is the distance required between knower and known that translates into objectivity. It yields the asymmetry in the relationship between knower and known that is essential for the dominating knowledge. Feminist theorists, of course, claim that "special interests" are endemic. But this norm of professional detachment is at the foundation of disciplinary methods, and it has been the basis for criticisms feminists make of traditional theorists and of each other, including the demands for embodying the knowers.

If we see the epistemology of modern science as an explanation of the cognitive authority and social power of professionals, then the scope of criticism widens to include the dissenting theorists themselves. Haraway and other feminist theorists offer their epistemologies as proposals on the nature of political and social life, even on the nature of nature. This is something that professionals regularly do. Everett Hughes, a forefather in the sociology of the professions, wrote that, "every profession considers itself the proper body to set the terms in which some aspect of society, life or nature is to be thought of and to define the general lines or even details of public policy concerning it." This authority is justified on "the professional claim that the practice rests upon some branch of knowledge to which the professionals are privy by virtue of long study and by apprenticeship under masters already members of the profession." (Hughes, 1984:375, 376)

In her proposal on situated knowledges, Haraway denies these claims of the professions. At the same time, she (and we) derive authority, audiences, publication outlets, skills, and salaries in institutions and through activities that are justified by professional claims like this. Most feminist theorists participate in the institutions, deeply, and the institutions even allow a place for feminist dissent. After all, self-criticism taking no theory to be above challenge, is supposed to be one mark of the rationality and goodness of Western science.

So let us suppose that one crucial way in which both scientists and feminist theorists are situated is in their disciplines and professions and the organizations and institutions within which and through which they labor. Those labors include producing knowledge and training others so that the knowledge (dissenting or not) is spread and used—perhaps globally. Now suppose that the professionals are also situated in communities outside the primary professional locations—as they would be in spreading knowledge to others, for example in offering feminist theories to social change groups, or in educating women about contraception and other reproductive topics. They then have a double participation in the outside communities, as professionals and as members of the community group.

In situations of double participation, the professional might be impressed with the implications of her place as a professional. The tension between her disciplinary knowledge (and its point and style) and the knowledge of others situated in the community might be extreme. The point of the situated "conversation" might be very different from the point she is accustomed to in writing books or teaching classes or serving as an outside, expert advisor. She might begin to make new and radical criticisms of the knowledge and training her profession took as its territory—far more radical than she made as practicing professional. She might see the nature of the dominating knowledge and the avenues it uses to dominate. She might glimpse the outcome of the collective work of professionals. This, in fact, is what happened in Peru, with a trio of professionals working in development. We will tell their story as an example of how both criticism and positive "theory" look when the knower is genuinely situated and has taken his or her situatedness in the professions seriously enough to change it.

The story will also lead us to asking about responsibility as professionals and theorists.

Part Two
The Case of PRATEC

PRATEC (Andean Project for Peasant Technologies) is a small organization in Peru. It was founded in 1987 by Grimaldo Rengifo, who invited two other men to join him, Eduardo Grillo and Julio Valladolid. In the late 1950s and the 1960s, the universities opened their doors to a more popular strata— a response to the government's perceived need for more trained technicians and engineers to man the development effort. Until that time, the universities were elite preserves. These three men are among the first generation of Peruvians from non-elite peasant background to have access to university training. They had spent their professional lives working for development. Rengifo was the director of a large Peruvian-Dutch development project, Grillo was the director general of the National Bureau of Agricultural Statistics and Research in the Ministry of Agriculture and Valladolid was teaching plant genetics at the Agrarian Faculty of the National University of Huamanga in Ayacucho. Through its extension program as well as through its research and teaching, that faculty was deeply involved in bringing the green revolution to the Peruvian countryside.

The three had devoted themselves to development in the belief that this was the way to help their people. They lived through many phases and fashions in development: community development, participatory development, appropriate technology, sustainable development. They tried everything available, always striving to capture the reality of Andean peasant agriculture and of peasant life in general. At long last they came to the conclusion that the problem lay in the very idea of development through the green revolution.

The green revolution was born in Iowa in the 1930s with the development of hybrid corn, and it promoted a "revolution" in agricultural practices. The emphasis was on using the rational and objective knowledge of science and technology to increase productivity—to get the most from the land through the use of irrigation, fertilizers and pesticides, machinery, and particularly, through hybrid seed that gives greater yield and consistency in the product and which is often developed to be resistant to certain pests and diseases. The knowledge was embodied in professionals and paraprofessionals based in universities, extension programs, and corporations, and it was to be passed on to peasants and other farmers along with the seed and fertilizers. The objective knowledge required a radical transformation in peasant ways of life and a dependency on the professionals and the corporations, not simply for pesticides and fertilizers but for the seed itself. Plants naturally regenerate themselves by producing the seed for next season's growth of natural progeny—plants like themselves. Hybrid plants do not produce seeds that breed true, so seeds must be bought anew every year, integrating the peasants into the market economy. Use of the methods also led to a monoculture that was alien to the peasant way of life.[5]

The efforts at development failed among these peasants. Evidence for the failure lay scattered throughout the Peruvian landscape in what some have called "the archaeology of development:" deteriorating infrastructures, abandoned to the elements after the project officials had left, uncared for by the peasants for whom they were intended. In an effort to understand themselves and the peasant reality, the members of PRATEC began to study other disciplines. They devoted themselves to reading all they could about peasant life in studies from sociology, anthropology, history and other fields. They emerged from that experience feeling that in all those studies, peasant reality was being described from a position outside that reality.

Once they began to understand peasant reality from the inside, they realized that development consisted of a package of practices, ideas, epistemologies and ontologies that came from the modern West and were profoundly alien to the native peasantry. Traveling throughout the country, they became convinced that native agriculture and culture were not only adequate to the native environment but were alive and vibrant—despite the efforts of development, education and before that of a long history in which native culture was the target of "extirpation of idolatry." Native agriculture and culture embodied a different mode of being in the world, of being a person, of relating to others both humans and non-humans, and of notions of time, space and nature. They realized that it is only from the perspective of development, which makes one wear modern Western lenses, that peasant agriculture and culture looked backward, stagnant and altogether lacking. From their new perspective, quite the opposite was the case.[6]

They came to realize that agriculture and culture were inseparable. The green revolution is the spawn of the objective rationality of scientific knowledge, for it is supposed to be universally applicable, as if knowledge of growing foodstuffs and other plants were separable from the local way of life. But in the Andes, rituals, festivals, ways of organizing labor and kin groups were intertwined with the nurturance and regeneration of the natural and cultural worlds. The three saw that the introduction of hybrid seed and the package of the green revolution not only interrupted the regenerative cycles of the local cultivars but of the culture as well. With irrigation, hybrid seed, chemical fertilizers and pesticides, two or three crops could be raised in a year, where only one or two were raised before. But this destroyed the cycle of rituals. It destroyed the ability to regenerate the biological and cultural world, transforming these peasants into individuals dependent on the market rather than on each other, nature, and the *huacas* (deities). For the penetration of the green revolution, the natural generativity of the seed had to be broken down as well.

As they came to understand this, PRATEC members realized that as trained professionals, the knowledge imparted to them at the university was implicated in bringing about the commodification of the peasant world, and that it was inimical to peasant autonomy and life. They felt they had to change themselves and discover radically different ways to do their work. The question was, how to do it?

Increasingly since the 1950s, the peasantry has been engaged in what Peruvian anthropologist Enrique Mayuer has called a "silent movement" (personal communication). They have taken over the lands of the larger landed properties, the haciendas in direct action without forming political parties or syndicates.[7] With the agrarian reform of 1969 (which simply made official what had been going on for a long time), peasant reappropriation accelerated. The government tried to replace the hacienda system with government cooperative schemes. It took only 25 years to reveal the total debacle of that state scheme. Andean peasants are reappropriating these lands as well as organizing themselves in their own way. This was their resistance.[8]

The members of PRATEC wanted to facilitate or accompany that movement not to theorize or lead the movement. Such a posture would in their eyes betray the communitarian ethos of Andean peasants. Being intellectuals and not farmers they found their own way of participating in the resistance by passing on to others like themselves what they had learned. In 1990, they offered a post-graduate year long course in Andean agriculture and culture for technicians of rural development of Andean backgrounds. In that course they present the Andean world on its own terms as well as deconstruct modern Western knowledge. The course is autonomous but accredited in one of the provincial universities. This "passing on knowledge" was particularly important because, in the agrarian faculties of Peruvian universities, Andean agriculture is nowhere taught. What is taught is temperate zone industrial agriculture. But they also helped other technicians and intellectuals come to a realization of the implications of professionalization and of development grounded in modern Western epistemologies.

The members of PRATEC began deprofessionalizing themselves and learning how to act and write from within the Andean collectivities—an action that one of us has called a "moral passage." (Addelson, 1994) In this way, they came to know with clarity the impossibility of participating in the Andean collective actions from within their professions. Their action brought with it an understanding of the nature of the knowledge they were taught in school and at the university, and a new and clearer vision of the Andean world. They speak of this double realization as a process of decolonization of the mind, which has allowed them to see and thus participate in the Andean world. They share this double realization with others like them in the context of the course they started teaching in 1990.[9]

By "deprofessionalizing" themselves, the members of PRATEC rejected a location in the professions and the constraints of academic disciplines. They devote themselves to the task of writing of peasant agriculture and culture from an Andean point of view. In order to do this they locate themselves alongside the peasants who have retaken lands and have established there their own way of tilling the soil and of organizing themselves. The knowledge that they make is born from sustained and intimate interactions with Andean peasants over a lifetime. It is a collective way of making knowledge. That process has required of them a simultaneous and thorough deconstruction of modern Western epistemologies and ontologies—a process that is always ongoing, since the realization that the words, concepts and categories they had been using turn out to distort or blind them to some aspect of peasants' lives always arises.

The deprofessionalization meant not only that the members of PRATEC abandoned the right to know the Andean world in terms of their disciplinary concepts and methods, and thus abandoned the cognitive authority of their professions, it meant a total change in their lives. Their writing emerges from their own passionate bonding with Andean peasants and the Andean landscape. Their deprofessionalization meant that there was no longer a double participation for them, namely a participation in their professions and one in "the field." (Addelson, 1994:161) They have left behind the "conversation" in the community of their professional peers. The world of which they write is the world they are making alongside the peasants, one to which they are bonded through a multitude of particular relations. They quit their jobs because they realized that willy-nilly in their professions they were agents of governance, particularly the state's goal of imposing development on the country. They joined the collective action of the Andean peasants engaged in retaking possession of lands and re-establishing their own forms of organization and practices. They speak of the Andean world not as judging outsiders but as ones bonded to that world. They write books and articles as intellectuals not with the intent of adding to the fund of knowledge and of creating an objective account but as their chosen field of action.

Part Three
What Do We Learn from PRATEC?

Haraway claims that feminists do not need a totality to work well, and we certainly agree—a feminist standpoint is a political construction that depends on the possibilities of the historical situation, and up to this point in time, it has always been partial. Haraway also says that professionals must take responsibilities for the social relations of science and technology. We certainly agree with her on that, and on her opposition to anti-scientific metaphysics and a demonology of technology. A thorough commitment to situated knowledge operates against a totalizing demonology and against a totalizing, nostalgic return to "nature." In fact there are two sides to our understanding of situated knowledge.

First, all knowledge is in fact situated, including scientific knowledge and the knowledge in technology, whatever the professional or political pretense that it is not. So resisting the dominating knowledge of science and technology is a matter for situated knowers—who may, at appropriate historical moments, join together in much broader coalitions.

Second, knowledge produced by feminists ought to be situated not in the academy alone but in the communities. Any professional who claims to offer a theory to guide feminist action or to do her political work through her teaching alone ought to be fully self-conscious about her situation as a knowledge maker and be certain that she is embodied as well in a community situated outside the academy, one that can set the point and purpose of the knowledge and offer criticism in the flesh. Such communities are very hard to come by these days and the best route for many theorists to take may be to step out of the role of theory maker to "the" women's movement. If one is lucky enough to be part of such a community, it will be clear that she should not be there as leader—as it was clear to the members of PRATEC.

Despite all these caveats, we must say that feminist professionals have made a beginning on some good work within the academy. One of the barriers to that the PRATEC members had to break through was the division of the universities (and so of the professional knowledge) into departments, schools, divisions of science, humanities, and social sciences. These divisions mark out territories of knowledge, authority, and employment—divisions which have become embodied in modern, Western world of markets and nations.

When the PRATEC members turned to reading in history, sociology, anthropology, and other specialties, they discovered not only was peasant reality explained from a position outside (what we would describe as the objective knowledge or the detachment of the professional), they discovered that academic studies divided peasant reality into an agricultural domain that was the specialty of agronomists, and a cultural domain where anthropology, sociology, history and a few other disciplines did their work. Within this organization of knowledge, they could not understand a world in which nature and culture were inseparable. This division into domains is a very deep source of the domination of the organization of modern, Western knowledge, and a major reason that the idea of the objectivity and universality of scientific knowledge has even a shred of plausibility. And of course the pretense of objectivity, neutrality, and detachment legitimates the domination. One outcome of the organization of the knowledge work is to support the domination. The PRATEC members came to see this because of their engagement in the Andean peasant communities.

Theorists need to look at their disciplines with an eye for significant outcomes of the collective, professional work. This is part of our responsibility, to see how the way we work, and the way we understand our work, promotes the dominating knowledge. (see Addelson, 1994: ch.7) Taking the responsibility seriously requires a radical change not only in our theories but in our disciplinary practices.

Feminist professionals in the academy have made some significant changes, particularly in eroding the Balkanization of knowledge into disciplinary bailiwicks. Women's studies is an interdisciplinary field that has affected teaching and research in many academic departments. This does not remove the clear and present danger that feminist professionals may act as instruments of the dominating knowledge. For example, scholarly and activist work on reproduction often simply accepts the worldview of individual women's rights and choices, equal opportunity for individuals, and the freedom to make a lifeplan or chose a lifestyle. This, of course, is the political face of the old epistemology of science. The outcome has often been disastrous. In the abortion controversy in the United States, many women have been silenced and some have been driven into the anti-abortion ranks. In some African nations, the individualistic, Western-democratic "rights" stance has divided women over the issue of female circumcision.

The complaint that the women's movement is white and middle class is a complaint against the dominating knowledge—and against the domination of those whom it supports. The domination is real, of course, and it must sometimes be dealt with in its own terms—through using the instruments of rights, individuals, and life plans. The trick is to understand that these are instruments designed to open up a space for resistance. Pretending that winning battles in those terms counts as victory means losing the war.

Aihwa Ong writes that the non-Western woman is inscribed within the concerns of Western feminist scholars. Non-Western women "may not seek our secular goal of individual autonomy nor renounce the bonds of family and community. . . . We begin a dialogue when we recognize other forms of gender- and culture-based subjectivities and accept that others often choose to conduct their lives separate from our particular vision of the future." (Ong, 1994:379) This cautionary statement needs to be taken seriously, not only about non-Western women or women of color, but about white women in the United States as well, for example those opposing feminists on issues feminists define as their own.

Trained professionals and paraprofessionals do their work in many situations outside the academy, of course. Those in development, the bureaucracies and governments, and in the market place have a more immediate place in implementing the dominating knowledge. In this paper, our focus has been on professionals within the academy, particularly those who "make theory" in order to see what happens when we press the notion that knowers are situated and knowledge is partial. We believe that taking this notion seriously requires radical revision in the disciplinary understanding of what it is to know, and what are the objects of knowledge, and what is the point of the knowledge. Donna Haraway's suggestion on situated knowledge may be a move in the right direction—if professionals take it seriously enough to situate themselves.

In closing, we want to use the PRATEC case to flesh out the idea of "conversation." The notion of conversation is used widely by academic philosophers in the United States, often with a kind of democratic "town meeting" or "elected representative" model lurking under the surface. (see Rorty, 1979,1991) Those are hidden images that oil the machinery of domination by science, the market, and Western democratic nations. We don't know what Haraway intended by "conversation," but the PRATEC understanding is radically situated. It is in harmony with the idea of knowledge as embodied in collective action. Conversation is embedded and its nature is radically situated.

Part Four
Andean Conversations

The members of PRATEC write of the Andean world not primarily as a world to know but as a world to live in, to participate in, to be a part of and to collectively make. It is in this way that the knowledge is embodied, and it is a very different embodiment from the work they knew in their professions and their work on development. The Andean world and the peasant methods of agriculture are not the object of their knowledge, as they would be for professionals in anthropology, say. Nor is it an objective knowledge that comes out of "conversation" in any usual sense of "talk." Rather, it is a knowledge in which the unit is the act, and knowledge is released from a narrow connection with thought and language. (Addelson, 1994:146) This knowledge is based on collective action, and so knowledge emerges out of particular encounters and relationships in particular localities, for particular purposes.

In the collective way of making knowledge, emotional bonding with particular persons or actors generates new insights and knowledge. Furthermore these persons or actors need not only be humans but can be any aspect of the environment that becomes part of the collective action.[10] The members of PRATEC also speak of conversations with an active sentient world. This is how Grimaldo Rengifo formulates it:

> In a world like the Andean one . . . the focus is on mutual attunement,
> . . . for inasmuch as mutual conversation flowers, nurturing flows.
> Dialogue here does not end in an action that befalls someone, but in
> reciprocal nurturing. . . . One dialogues with the mouth, the hands,
> the sense of smell, vision, hearing, gestures, flowerings, the colors of
> the skin, the taste of the rain, the color of the wind, etc. Since all are
> persons, all speak. The potatoes, the llamas, the human community,
> the mountains, the rain, the hail, the huacas [deities] speak. (Rengifo,
> 1993)

When he says that Andean peasants converse with the stars, the moon, the plants, the rocks, etc., Rengifo is not speaking metaphorically. Understanding such conversations as metaphorical or symbolic comes accepting, in thought and action, a dualism between organism and environment. This Andean conversation is a way of living together and acting collectively.

Andean peasants grow plants, raise cattle, llamas and alpacas. They speak of these activities as *criar* a word which has no exact equivalent in English but could be rendered by the word "nurture." They say that as they nurture a plant, soil, animal, water, whatever, they are at the same time nurtured by that plant, soil, etc.; they nurture each other. Organism and environment are one. These conversations are actions of mutual nurturance in which the world is regenerated. The Western dualism between organism and environment is not there.

The conversation between peasants, the soil, the water, the clouds, the sky, the stars, the sun, the moon, the plants and all the beings of their world is not a conversation engaged in for the purposes of achieving a more objective knowledge garnered from all the situated knowledges of these various agents. It is engaged in for regenerative and procreative purposes, procreation being the raising and nurturing of the next generation which in a peasant context means also the regenerating of the world through mutual nurturance.

The emphasis is on the lived body that experiences and nurtures rather than merely records phenomena. The body is in constant contact with its environs through touch, breathing, ingesting, smelling, etc. The environment is not external, a distanced object of observation, rather it flows through the body. As Grillo writes: "conversation cannot be reduced to dialogue, to the word . . . here conversation engages us vitally: one converses with the whole body. To converse is to show each other reciprocally, it is to share, to commune, to dance to the rhythms which in every moment corresponds to the annual cycle of life." (Grillo, 1993)

The Andean peasant does not experience her gazing at the rising of a constellation in a particular region of the horizon as a unidirectional act on her part. Rather it is experienced as the constellation and the gazer being united in a conversation. Grillo continues: "that conversation is inseparable from nurturing and letting oneself be nurtured." Conversation is a reciprocal act of nurturance. The word "nurture" connotes a caring relationship that lets the nurtured one come forth freely, emerge from the dark, invisible earth or womb and unfold according to its own rhythm. In the word "nurturance," there is no sharp distinction between the internal bringing forth of nature and the external human actions of making or helping. In nurturing we bring forth through the one being nurtured. In nurturing one attends to the nurtured one's rhythm of growth. In so doing the nurturer is not unaffected. The very act of nurturing nurtures oneself allowing one to participate in the unfolding and the growth. The conversations that make this happen do it through the openness one has toward the beings nurtured and toward the world. It is that openness that implicates one in the processes that one attends to.

The Andean conversation is very different from a conversation based in the image of democratic politics that are argued out in the artificially lit chambers of legislatures in the Western democracies or negotiated in the shabby halls of New England town meetings. They are very different from the "discussion periods" scheduled at the end of scholarly panel sessions in the meeting rooms of atrium hotels. Those democratic and scholarly images and practices themselves embody the dualisms of mind and body, organism and environment.[11]

We are not recommending that the Andean conversation be imported into urbanized, industrialized nations. Conversation is a way of life, embodied in our selves, our ways of being in the world and our ways of knowing. Ways of living and knowing aren't like cuisines that can be transformed by importing tasty ingredients from exotic lands to sell in supermarkets and serve up in restaurants. Ways of living are like the natural seed of plants regenerating themselves even as they change themselves and their worlds. We are saying that if professionals begin to see the importance of their own situations, then they will begin to see how it influences their definitions of knowledge and "conversation." That would be one step on the way to intellectual and moral responsibility. Every great journey has begun with one step.

References

Addelson, Kathryn Pyne. 1997. "The Birth of the Fetus." in Lynn Morgan and Meredith Michaels (eds.) *Fetal Positions/ Feminist Practices*. University of Pennsylvania Press.

——.1994. *Moral Passages*, NY; Routledge.

Alcoff, Linda and Elizabeth Potter (eds.)1992. *Feminist Epistemologies*. NY; Routledge.

Apffel Marglin, Frédérique and S.A. Marglin, eds. 1996. *Decolonizing Knowledge: From Development to Dialogue*, Oxford; Oxford University Press, Clarendon.

——. 1996. *Dominating Knowledge: Development, Culture and Resistance*, Oxford; Oxford University Press, Clarendon.

Burt, Sandra and Lorraine Code, eds. 1995. *Changing Methods: Feminists Transforming Practice*. Broadview Press Peterborough, Ontario, Canada.

Code, Lorraine. 1995. "How Do We Know? Questions of method in feminist practice." pp. 13-44. in Burt and Code.

Grillo, Eduardo. 1993. "La Cosmovision Andina de Siempre y la Cosmologia Occidental Moderna" Desarrollo o Descolonizacion en los Andes? Lima, PRATEC.

Haraway, Donna. 1991. *Simians, Cyborgs, and Women*. New York: Routledge.

——. 1988. "Situated Knowledges: the science question in feminism and the privilege of partial perspective" *Feminist Studies* v.14 no. 3. 575-99.

Harding, Sandra and Merrill Hintikka. 1983. *Discovering Reality*. Dordrecht, Holland: D. Reidel.

Harding, Sandra. 1986. *The Science Question in Feminism*. Princeton, NJ: Princeton University Press.

——. 1993. "Rethinking Standpoint Epistemologies" in Linda Alcoff and Elizabeth Potter, eds. *Feminist Epistemologies*, New York: Routledge.

Herrmann, Ann and Abigail Steward. 1994. *Theorizing Feminism*. San Francisco: Westview Press.

Hughes, Everett C. 1984. *The Sociological Eye*. New Brunswick, NJ: Transaction Books.

Jaggar, Alison. 1983. *Feminist Politics and Human Nature*. Totowa, NJ: Rowman and Allanheld.

Keller, Evelyn Fox and Helen Longino. 1996. *Feminism and Science*. NY: Oxford University Press.

Kloppenburg, Jack Jr. *First the Seed.* Cambridge University Press, 1988.

Latour, Bruno. "Mixing Humans and Non Humans Together: The Sociology of a Door Closer." in Leigh Starr (ed.) *Ecologies of Knowledge.* Albany, NY; SUNY Press.

Nelson, Lynn Hankinson. 1990. *Who Knows: From Quine to a Feminist Empiricism.* Philadelphia: Temple University Press.

——. 1993. "Epistemological Communities," in L. Alcoff and E. Potter, eds. *Feminist Epistemologies.* NY: Routledge.

Ong, Aihua. 1994. "Colonization and Modernity: Feminist Re-presentations of Women in Non Western Societies." in Anne Hermann and Abigail Stewart (eds.), *Theorizing Feminism.* San Francisco; Westview Press.

Rengifo, Grimaldo."La Educacion en los Andes y en el Occidente Moderno" in ibid.

Rorty, Richard. 1991. *Philosophical Papers.* 2 vols. New York: Cambridge University Press.

——.1979. *Philosophy and the Mirror of Nature.* Princeton, NJ: Princeton University Press.

Stich, Stephen. 1990. *The Fragmentation of Reason: Preface to a Pragmatic Theory of Cognitive Evaluation.* Cambridge, MA: MIT Press.

Endnotes

[1]   Jaggar, 1983 gives an overall account, and Hartsock, 1983 gives an original presentation that is often used as a target by critics.

[2]   Haraway's proposal on situated knowledges is in Haraway, 198. For communities rather than individuals being the subjects of knowledge, see essays in Alcoff and Potter, 1992, and references given there.

[3]   Feminist theorists of course feel that the terms for knowledge making lie in women's experience, and that they serve women and the women's movement. Once feminism made a place for itself in the academy and the Washington-based interest groups, and after the women's movement in the United States lost its mass character, the claims of feminist theorists became abstract and embodied not in efforts of the women's movement but in the disciplines and professions and interest groups. There are significant exceptions to this— feminist professionals who have continued to do political work as a basis of their theorizing, but for the most part, theory has become disembodied.

[4]   Feminist epistemologies are for the most part normative. There are efforts at "naturalized epistemology" which claim to be descriptive rather than normative, but they take for granted the cognitive authority of science. The origin is with W.V. Quine back in the 1960s. Nelson, 1993 discusses the issues from a feminist point of view, and the idea has taken hold in more traditional parts of the discipline. See Stich, 1990 for a discussion of normative and descriptive.

[5]   On the development of hybrid corn in the U.S. and the precursor to the Green Revolution, see especially Jack Kloppenburg Jr. *First the Seed,* Cambridge University Press, 1988.

6 PRATEC members had become aware of the richness and diversity of cultivars that are grown in this ecologically variable environment. The Andes are one of the 8 world centers where agriculture first emerged 10,000 years ago. The peasants continue to grow an astounding variety of plants. Valladolid mentions 3,500 varieties of potatoes, over a thousand of maize, many varieties of other tubers and grains.

7 Two leftist Marxist parties, the Confederacion Campesina del Peru (CCP) and the Confederacion Nacional Agraria (CNA), arrogated to themselves the leadership of a peasant movement with the intention to establish communal land holding. The silent movement Mayer and PRATEC speak about refers to the direct action of Andean peasants inspired by their native culture and mode of relating to the land. According to Danish anthropologist Sren Hvalkoff (personal communication), the CCP and CNA never succeeded in their aims.

8 Shining Path and MRTA (Movivniento Revolucionerio Tupac Amaru) are neo-Marxist revolutionary movements. PRATEC rejects the path of confrontation and violence.

9 Since 1994, Frédérique Apffel Marglin has been collaborating with PRATEC, lecturing in their course, participating in workshops, organizing workshops with PRATEC in the U.S., translating their work, and undertaking collaborative research.

10 Haraway seems to agree with this, though once again we need a fuller discussion from her to be sure of her position. See Haraway 1988. Addelson discusses non-human actors in Addelson, 1997 and see also Latour, 1995.

11 In her postmodern turn, Haraway slyly suggests that the coyote (from Native American religion) be imported into United States imagery. She more usually and continually offers up information age images—the cyborg being one. Because we really believe in situated knowledge, we have a hard time understanding why she does this and what the community is that is supposed to pick up these ways of talking, or even what the ways of talking have to do with the ways of life in the world. It is not that we feel that images are not important, it is that we feel that they are so important that they need to be situated in the communities which will take them to heart and action. Haraway's proposals are clever but unsituated.

CULTURAL ALTERNATIVES TO DEVELOPMENT IN SOUTH INDIA

Siddhartha

"Developing" India

THE IDEA OF DEVELOPMENT HAS HAD A MAJOR INFLUENCE on the formation of economic and political institutions in modern India. Nineteenth century conceptions of development in Europe sorted societies on a temporal scale and considered agrarian societies to be backward and industrial-capitalist societies to be the final point on an historical evolutionary line. These ideas exercised a powerful influence on the imagination of the Indian intellectuals in nineteenth century colonial India. In visualizing a future for India, many of these intellectuals understood industrialization as a necessary transformatory process and saw the state as the agent for ushering in social progress. These ideas were to prove important even in the aftermath of British colonial rule.

In independent India, the idea of development was institutionalized through centralized planning apparatuses. State planning came to be seen as the main instrument through which India could develop. The Indian state initiated large scale programs to increase agrarian and industrial production. In addition, it also attempted to regulate population growth, increase literacy levels, achieve self-sufficiency in energy requirements, uplift the socially weaker groups, to name a few. In what was termed as the "mixed economy" approach, the Indian state carved for itself an important place in the economy alongside the private sector. In the first couple of decades, these ideas of development acquired widespread social legitimacy. In the 70s and the 80s, we witness the emergence and growth of social activism that is increasingly skeptical and critical of the dominant paradigms of state-led development. This is the period which witnessed the rise of the non-governmental sector in India. Activism related to environmental issues, sustainable technologies, women's rights, empowerment of the socially exploited castes became visible in different parts of the country. Large state initiated development projects (dams, for example) were severely criticized for violating human rights and causing ecological destruction.

Social Movements for Peace and Justice

In the 1990s, the Indian state introduced major structural reforms to "liberalize" its economy. These reforms were initiated to reduce the state's presence in the market and allow for greater private initiative. This is also the phase where the Indian economy is integrating into the global economic structures at a faster pace than before. In the emerging model of development, the state has a diminished role to play in regulating economic growth and it is also withdrawing from its social welfarist obligations. These new reforms combined with increased investment by multinational companies are transforming India in significant ways. New forms of disempowerment have appeared calling for new kinds of social activism.

Independent India has seen the emergence of many powerful and creative social movements, which have sought to extend and deepen democratic processes in the country. Indian democracy, with all its shortcomings, has been agile in allowing space for the social movements, each with its own demands and ideological perspective (although, it must be added that increasingly ideology is giving way to the requirements of practical political achievement, except in the case of some cultural-nationalist or religious movements). Without democracy, it would be impossible for the pulls and pressures of a complex society with numerous castes, tribes, linguistic regions, and religious affiliations to find at least partial expression. The constitution of India and the judicial system have also helped to defend the rights of aggrieved communities.

Even in these days of neo-liberal economic reforms and the associated structural readjustments, social movements aid India's experiments with democracy and continue to energize the processes of democratization in the country. They have thrown up a number of charismatic leaders like Medha Patkar (the anti-dam Narmada movement), Vandana Shiva (bio-diversity protection, the struggle against the patent laws, etc.), Thomas Kocherry (the fishworkers' movement), P.V. Rajagopal (the Ekta-Parishad movement of adivasis and small farmers/ landless laborers) and Aruna Roy (the right to information movement). Social movements in India act as a check on the state and try to ensure that the empowerment of the marginal and weaker sections is not sacrificed at the altar of neo-liberal globalization.

The Adivasi (tribal) population has suffered much displacement due to mining, the building of large dams, the development of national parks by the forest departments, and the occupation of traditional tribal lands by settlers. The best known case is that of the tribes who have been displaced as a result of the construction of a series of large dams on the Narmada River (Medha Patkar, the leader of the anti-dam movement, has won considerable support both within and outside the country for her campaign against large dams). Tribes are also being evicted from the Nagarhole forest, near Mysore, because it has been declared a national park. In several of these cases, the World Bank had initially stepped in to back these state programs, but as a result of mass movements opposing these undemocratic initiatives, the Bank has become more cautious.

In the case of the Dalit movements (the former untouchable castes), their rise to political prominence has been nothing short of dramatic. Up to a few decades ago they could be beaten, humiliated, even killed. Today, the Chief Minister of Uttar Pradesh, the most populous state in India, and part of the traditional Hindu heartland, is a Dalit woman. The Dalit movement is firmly against upper caste Brahminical ideology, which is believed to have systematically oppressed and humiliated Dalits through the centuries. The Dalits are among the poorest and most exploited sections of Indian society and the Dalit movement is sure to increase in importance in the decades ahead.

Recent times have seen the rise of a conservative movement upholding Hindu cultural nationalism in India, sparking fears about whether the country can retain its secular social fabric for long. While scholars like K.N. Pannikar feel that the country is likely to experience a spell of religious fascism, others like Ashis Nandy feel that India is too complex a society for this to happen and that cultural nationalism cannot become a unified phenomenon due to the many conflicting tendencies within. India is the second largest Muslim country in the world with a population of about 150 million Muslims. Liberal Islamic thinkers like Asghar Ali Engineer believe that Indian Islam should also undergo radical reform in order to be part of a pluralistic society. At the moment Indian Islam, like Islam elsewhere, is going through a crisis. If a liberal Islam emerges as a strong force in the world, India is the most likely place for this to begin from.

Cultural Seeds for the Transformation of Indian Life

India has been home to many diverse social philosophies and cultural practices; major religions like Buddhism, Hinduism and Jainism emerged in India and today it has the second largest Muslim population. This old and complex society has stepped into the twenty-first century retaining cultural institutions from the pre-colonial, colonial and postcolonial eras: alongside sophisticated software industries and nuclear power plants one finds caste struggles, dowry deaths and religious figures teaching meditation and yoga.

Indian society has witnessed immense religious, ethnic, linguistic and regional diversities throughout history. Important religions like Buddhism, Hinduism and Jainism established centuries ago remain potent living religions even now. For example classic Hindu philosophy such as Ramana Maharishi, a great Indian spiritual teacher in the Advaita tradition and the more contemporary philosophy of Jiddu Krishnmurthi continue to attract world wide interest.

The hierarchical social institution of caste that has remained resilient continues to exist in a constantly transforming state. All of these religious and social institutions have had to respond to intellectual-political challenges posed by contending philosophies and practices. In medieval times, there were strong Bhakti (devotion) movements all across India which sought to dissolve the institution of caste and as we will see below continue to have relevance. Another great challenge to the caste system came from the widespread support for British ideas of individual liberty and freedom among Indians in the 19th and 20th centuries.

The nationalist leaders of the Indian independence movement also remain sources for social transformation, namely, Mahatma Gandhi and Jawaharlal Nehru, and the leader of the Untouchable castes, B.R. Ambedkar. Gandhi was a critic of modernity and advocated policies where development would start at the village level and then move outwards. His ideas represent the anti-thesis of present day consumer ideology. For him there were enough goods being produced "to fulfill every man's need but not every man's greed." On the other hand, Nehru, the first Prime Minister of India, was the great modernizer. He saw the big public sector factories and the dams as "the temples of modern India." Political debates even today reflect the tensions between the Gandhian and Nehruvian perspectives.

Ambedkar, the chairman of the Indian constituent assembly, the body that was authorized to frame the Indian constitution, believed that only Western political institutions grounded in conceptions of individual freedom could emancipate the Untouchable castes from the inegalitarian caste system. Eventually he converted to Buddhism and made a call for all Untouchables to do likewise. He believed that if the Untouchables remained within the Hindu fold there would be no emancipation for them. The Untouchable castes today represent about 20 percent of the population and the vast cultural changes taking place among them have had a major impact on the evolution of contemporary India.

In the past few decades the best of social action had taken a secular approach. This was partly understandable, given the complexity of dealing with the complex cultural traditions of India, which were sometimes also exploitative of the poor and the excluded. The emphasis on secular action was also part of the modernizing influence of Nehru, India's first prime-minister. This was a departure from Gandhi's idea of village republics where development was seen as emerging from below, rooted in the re-interpreted cultures of the people.

In today's India, which has succumbed to the pressures of the global neo-liberal economy, the poor are rapidly being marginalized and even eliminated, if we note the hunger deaths, malnutrition and suicide of farmers reported daily in the national media. In addition, we find that the total neglect of the traditional cultural arena by the secular and progressive forces has led to various degrees of fundamentalism creeping into Indian religious life, creating murderous conflict between communities.

One of the big problems in countries like India is that the secular activists have moved so far from the cultural and religious beliefs of the people, leaving them helpless when communalism (religious fundamentalism) begins to take root. In an age of globalization, many people, including the poor, are being manipulated by opportunistic political parties to see religions and ethnic identity in exclusive terms, thus dividing people and promoting violence. In the past years, all the countries of South Asia have witnessed violent cultural conflicts.

An innovative program for renewal of a better balance of cultural traditions has been promoted by Fireflies Ashram.[1]

Promoting Peace and Regeneration Through Cultural Renewal

Fireflies, an inter-religious, secular ashram of Pipal Tree is in the process of creating social and political transformations in the villages and urban communities in south India through social practices that includes re-interpreting India's cultural and religious traditions.

Fireflies encourages the view that all great religious traditions are the collective heritage of humankind. However, we also respect those who feel the need to deepen their understanding and practice of any one single spiritual tradition.

Fireflies acknowledges and learns from the wisdom of seers and sages such as Gautama Buddha, Kabir, Christ, Basava, Vivekananda, Mahatma Gandhi, Ramana Maharishi, and J. Krishnamurthi. We also strongly believe in the contribution that secular thinking has made to the advancement of human freedoms. In this light, we consider it important to integrate modern secular thinking with those intuitive insights that give deeper meaning to our daily lives. The sacred and the secular have to converge and fuse if we are to solve the grim personal, social and environmental problems facing humanity today.

Fireflies Ashram and Pipal Tree are experimenting with a new paradigm for social transformation that is inspired by Gandhi and the cultural and social practices of local communities. This involves seeing the Earth as mother, re-interpreting festivals and religious practice to incorporate the dimensions of personal growth, compassionate action and connectedness with nature. The communities concerned are often subsistence communities, and there is an attempt to create appropriate conditions for their empowerment and put them in touch with other processes of learning. In practical terms, this means shifting from chemical to organic farming, restoring lakes and evolving water conservation methods, developing women's self-help groups, building peace-committees in areas prone to inter-religious conflict, promoting education to prevent HIV/AIDS and developing programs for health and sanitation. In addition, Fireflies Ashram is also trying to influence intellectuals, journalists, students, teachers, police, bureaucrats, political leaders, etc. with its eco-social-spiritual approach, projecting an alternative kind of globalization that is more just and fulfilling.

This program has two dimensions. The first has to do with re-interpreting the cultural practices and traditions of the people, especially the festivals. The second has to do with initiating sacred song movements as well as music and film festivals, where the values of the Charter of Human Responsibilities are sung and participated in by the village communities.

Here are the assumptions that lead to the re-interpretation and celebration of cultural renewal:

- We are of the opinion that in South Asia the best and the brightest thinkers have moved into the "secular" arena as a result of scientific and rational thought.

- As a result of globalization, traditional ties of caste and community have weakened. Millions of people have become socially and psychologically insecure and are taking to religion in an ardent way.

- While we view religion in a positive light, we are worried about the rise of intolerance and fundamentalism in the guise of religion.

- Those who are interpreting religion/culture for the masses have their own narrow vested interests or are too sectarian/fundamentalist in their interpretation.

One of the major causes of inter-religious conflict and unsustainable development (which obviously includes environmental degradation) is our inability to give the right or appropriate interpretation to our deepest beliefs, whether these are religious or secular. In India, most of these beliefs are integrated in religion and therefore it is necessary to re-interpret religion and culture on a continuous basis to give direction to people's lives. Only then can notions like democracy, participation, pluralism and compassion begin to come alive on a day to day basis.

Renewal of Festivals via a Hermeneutics of Hope[2]

It is in this context that we celebrate festivals with the rural and urban poor people in our project areas. Fireflies is an ashram that emphasizes both celebration and renunciation. Celebration that does not degenerate into self-indulgence, and renunciation that does not negate, but rather, steps back to better appreciate life on Earth. Once a year, in an outpouring of gratitude for the richness and diversity of our planet, artists and musicians from various faiths and traditions come together at Fireflies for the Earth Music Festival.

Fireflies celebrates all major religious and harvest festivals with farmers, students, teachers, and spiritual and community leaders. We use these occasions to initiate dialogue and introspection on issues linked with the festival. Our purpose becomes clearer if we describe one such festival celebration. We celebrated the festival of Ganesh, the elephant-headed God, in August 2004, along with thousands of people in the project area of Uthiri. Our experience with local communities in celebrating the Ganesh festival has been edifying and has given us the hope that, without being complacent, we are on the right track.

A discussion was held with the animators and some of the peace committee members on the meaning of the Ganesh festival. It was found that the God Ganesh was the God of Knowledge and the remover of obstacles. After considerable discussion it was decided that the following three sets of questions would be discussed with people before and during the festival:

- If Ganesh is the God of Knowledge, what is our own understanding of Knowledge? What is our vision of society? How do we see religious tolerance and pluralism?

- If Ganesh is the remover of obstacles, what are the social obstacles that are dividing us and preventing meaningful development? What can we do about it?

- If Ganesh is partly from the natural world (the elephant head) and half from the human world (the lower half), does he not represent the bond between Nature and Human beings? If so, then what are we doing for the environment?

The discussion among the people was really alive. Many different opinions were advanced. The re-interpretation of Ganesh became a democratic people's process. People realized that they would have to respect all human beings regardless of which religion they belonged to. They felt that development could take place only in the context of a vibrant civil society, where the local democratic institutions and development efforts were respected. This was the message of the Ganesh festival.

It was also felt that one could not honor Ganesh without protecting the environment. People also decided that in the future they should buy unpainted Ganesh statues. People immerse literally millions of painted clay statues in the ocean, river or pond at the end of the festival. Since the paints contain lead, water bodies turn toxic. To prevent this harmful practice from continuing, we educated local villagers on the ecological implications of this unsafe custom. We explained that being half-animal and half-human, Lord Ganesh would quite possibly view this practice as dishonoring Nature. As a result of our dialogue, many villagers have agreed to immerse unpainted clay Ganesh statues for the next festival.

Transformations of Other Religious Festivals

Ramzan—This very important Muslim festival was celebrated on a large scale with over 2,000 people participating in it and secular and religious leaders from different dispensations elucidating, from their perspectives, social values, peace and harmony for the edification of the audience. This was followed by a community dinner.

Christmas—On 25th evening, we celebrated Christmas with a cross section of people, including urban visitors. The highlight of it was a stylized, masked dance that drove home the need for harmony with nature through the symbols of the five elements—water, earth, air, fire and ether.

Male Raaya means the rain deity in Kannada. He is considered to be the bestower of rain. Until a few years ago his appeasement was thought to be essential to fend off drought. For nearly three years, there was no rain in many parts of the state. After several discussions with local leaders, youth, farmers and women, we asked whether mere obeisance to Male Raaya is enough or do we have a co-responsibility with him to care for our living and breathing environment?

At the end of these discussions, we arrived at a consensus to hold a *puja* for the god in which more than a thousand people participated with fervor. To show our responsibility to the God, a large number of the families collectively took the oath to plant two saplings each on the dry lake bed where the *puja* was performed and they proceeded to do so. And to every one's surprise and joy, this year—after the long spell of aridity—there was rain aplenty and the lake, which was parched and cracked, was filled.

Call it coincidence or what you will, the people drew a moral from this re-interpreted revival—of being co-responsible with our environment to make it habitable.

At communally volatile places, Fireflies has set up Peace Committees that keep a constant vigil to diffuse any inter-religious conflict. Those on the peace committees include the local police, religious leaders, school teachers, petty shop owners and youth. They have been able to successfully ward off many instances of conflict and bring in amity and peace. They also encourage celebration of festivals in common, irrespective of their religions.

Sacred Song, Movement and Music and Film Festivals

Fireflies has initiated a sacred song movement to encompass a wide spectrum of people. The purpose of the movement is to use one of the hoary traditions, sanctified by its unifying ability, to reach as large a section of people as possible, especially among the less privileged. The songs are culled from the ancient and the modern but the common burden of them is in carrying the message of the Gandhian tenet: "Every living being is thy neighbor." The songs were written, composed and sung by groups in a collective manner.

Theatre and music festivals are held regularly at Fireflies. The most well known music festival is an all night one that brings together about 2,000 people each year. The first year this festival was dedicated to peace in Iraq. The second year to "Water." In 2005 the theme was "Trees." In the midst of the music there are brief discourses and films on the themes.

Another monthly program involves leading film personalities like directors, cinematographers, script writers, and film critics who would interact with the audience after screening a film or two and discuss it.

Traditional Sources for Sustainable Agriculture, Medicinal Plants and Bio-diversity

Fireflies is situated amid five villages of Kaggalipura Panchayat where water scarcity and the high input costs of chemical farming have discouraged the expansion of farming as a livelihood. Fireflies is enabling an expansion of agricultural livelihoods through field training and empowerment programs and one of the paths to this end is again the traditional cultural sources.

In March, we celebrate Ugadi, New Year's Day, with the village folk. A large group of men, women and children gathered in Fireflies to participate in the traditional practice of sowing seeds in a sacred bowl. On the ninth day, the seeds germinate. Good germination, according to local belief, signifies good crops in the following season.

We spoke to the village men and women about the contemporary relevance of Ugadi. The farmers have been dialoguing with us about the increasing dependence of their entire agricultural ecosystem on hybrid seeds and massive amounts of chemical fertilizers. This has led to serious degradation in land and nutritional quality. They are also concerned about the acute shortage of rain and groundwater. We explained to them the interconnectivity of the many harms we have perpetrated on Mother Earth—how short-sighted measures such as cutting trees, burning grass in summer and digging more and more bore wells is making the land more arid than in the past; how using chemical fertilizers and pesticides drastically reduces soil fertility over time, and most of all, how our disrespect and ignorance is leading us farther and farther away from our land, our rivers and lakes, our very life support system.

Fireflies appreciate the urgent need for agriculture to progress from chemical dependence to organic interdependence. Organic farming employs human intervention, as distinct from natural "do-nothing" farming; organic farming is labour intensive (in contrast with chemical farming which is capital-intensive). Both the earth, as well as farmers in countries like India, are suffering due to widespread chemical pesticide and fertiliser use, which may fetch short term gains, but in the long term leads to capital loss and damage to the earth and its dependents. Nature offers her own intrinsic and interconnected system that ensures the growth and survival of all living things. Reliance on chemicals is a radical shift from this system, and a shift towards a system based on individualist and capitalist values.

At Fireflies, organic farming methods, which encourage Nature's system to flourish, are practiced and are introduced to the farmers of neighbouring villages. With the aid of an agricultural scientist, and using traditional methods, the farmers act as contributors to Nature's system as opposed to being controllers, employing methods which increase soil fertility and result in healthy and successful crops. Emphasis is placed on mono-cropping for increased soil fertility. By using natural fertilizers such as cow manure, compost and wormi-compost, soil fertility is increased while providing a means for recycling waste, thus illuminating the fact that life forms are interdependent on each other and are not self-contained unrelated entities. Natural pesticides such as neem, tobacco, cow urine and garlic are also used on a trial and error basis. The contribution of plants and animals is integral to organic farming, again highlighting the need for all of Nature's involvement in the processes of growth.

Biodiversity Restorations and Livelihood Creations

Fireflies is attempting to develop a medicinal plants nursery on its campus and hopes to develop a community health program based on medicinal plants. Workshops and empowerment projects that seek to increase local bio-diversity as well as to foster new livelihoods related to biodiversity that include agro biodiversity and cultivated species, medicinal plants cultivation, aromatic plant cultivation and spice cultivation.

Women's groups also take part in a number of training sessions organized by Fireflies. The sessions give women the tools to produce and sell cottage products like soaps and agarbathi to the local community. This provides them a stable source of livelihood for those who cannot find work everyday, and a supplemental income to the daily wages they may already receive. They are able to produce these products with locally available materials and the market for their goods is usually within the local community.

At the ashram, the resident sculptor, Caroline MacKenzie, is working with local stone carvers to sculpt traditional themes in more innovative ways. These innovative sculptures, depicting and questioning images from the local culture, can be found throughout the ashram grounds. The local artisans are currently working directly under Caroline's supervision. In the months to come, they will be able to use their new skills to get commissions for sculp-tures and generate income for their community.

Empowerment Programs for Local Development

A series of leadership training workshops were initiated since September 2004 for illiterate and literate women from both the rural and urban sectors belonging to disparate castes, religions and languages. Till now 300 women have benefited from these training programs. The training includes areas related to local democracy and governance, micro-credit, ending wife-batter-ing and domestic violence, women and child health, income generating skill formation, etc.

Self-help groups (SHGs) for women have been organized in a slum of Bangalore. They provide a social outlet for women to gather away from the pressures of home and family to discuss issues and work toward community solutions. These SHGs are also a platform for the delivery of savings and micro-credit. Women gather in small groups, between 10-15 members, and save on a monthly basis. With the funds they save, they can give members of the group loans for micro-enterprise purposes. After some time, they can also receive loans from mainstream banks at competitive interest rates to fund their projects.

HIV/AIDS Awareness and
Prevention Programs in Bangalore Slums

In Ullalu village, on the outskirts of Bangalore, which is a settlement of displaced persons, in tandem with Grameena Swaraj Samiti headed by Sudha S. Reddy (one of the main movers of Fireflies), volunteers have been active in educating the people on healthy sexual practices. Women of the village have taken up the activity of spreading the new-found knowledge and inducing people to adopt new practices.

Sanitation has always been an issue in slums where many families are living in close quarters and without sufficient latrines. The slum is located on the southeastern outskirts of the Bangalore city, and is even more prone to these problems as the residents are living in makeshift housing after being forcibly removed from their previous homes. Reddy, through Grameena Swaraj Samiti, has built toilet and bathing facilities for the community. The facilities use solid waste material from the toilets in biogas plants to generate gas to heat water for bathing in the cold seasons. There are also plans to distribute the excess gas to homes in the vicinity for cooking purposes. The facilities are maintained by a local community, and maintenance costs are funded by a token fee that members pay to use the facilities. The facilities have proven to be popular with the slum communities, and there are plans to construct similar structures in other parts of Bangalore.

Fireflies has established a medical center for residents of neighboring villages. Fireflies opened the medical center in 2000 to address a shortage. Dr P.F. Thejesh, a doctor from nearby Bangalore, sees patients three days a week. Approximately a hundred patients visit the center each week.

Along with the renowned Dr. Agarwal's Eye Clinic in the city, Fireflies conducts regular eye-camps for the villages and urban poor communities. Fireflies has helped scores of poor people have successful cataract operations. Hundreds of free spectacles have also been distributed for the poor.

Computers in Rural School Education

As part of advancing the cause of education, a computer unit was set up in the local village school and the teachers trained in their use. Fireflies got a renowned computer-education outfit called Schoolnet to train the teachers on how to create new and interesting programs that could be read by the students. Not only have they been able to make use of the computers as an efficient tool in education, now the students too have been learning their use to increase their knowledge-content.

Fireflies has just set up a new information technology unit where farmers will learn about seeds, water and soil conservation, marketing and prices. A facilitator downloads material from the web and leads regular discussions with local farmers on relevant issues.

Fireflies Ashram and Earth Spirituality

Earth Spirituality deals with the interconnectedness of human beings with each other and the Earth. Whether we acknowledge it or not, we are all intimately connected with trees, birds, animals and all other human beings. We have co-evolved with the rocks and the waters. We are not merely beings, we are inter-beings. Each step that we take on Earth is sacred and is connected to everything else. This awareness enhances our joy.

In the last century or so, a radical and alarming divide has emerged between human beings and the Earth. For the first time in human history, we have separated ourselves from nature and confined ourselves within impersonal concrete cities, many of which are reeling beneath the impact of industrial and noise pollution. Despite enormous wealth and more resources than ever before, we have managed to create large pockets of exclusion and poverty. These and other related factors, we feel, have led to our present civilization crisis. Despite the fruits of science and technology, many human beings today suffer from loneliness and anxiety and are increasingly out of touch with their true nature.

Earth stands for a larger Reality that is both transcendent and immanent. Tragically, for many people in the world today, she has been reduced to nothing more than real estate, wealth, mineral or resource. We seem to have forgotten that the Earth is the source of all life, and that we have evolved from her. We are children of the Earth, and if we treat her with respect, she will continue to nourish us physically, psychologically and spiritually.

Sacred Tulsi at Fireflies

Fireflies has chosen as its symbol the tulsi plant (basil), considered sacred in the Indian subcontinent for centuries. Tulsi symbolises the bond between the spiritual, the personal, the social and the ecological. The roots of the tulsi mingle with all the healing waters of our planet. Our gods and sacred scriptures live in the branches of the tulsi. In the leaves are found all the diverse human communities. The flowers of the tulsi represent compassionate sages and prophets. Its seeds represent visions waiting to be born. Each day we meditate around the tulsi, planted in a circular enclosure by diverse religious and cultural communities from all over the world.

Endnotes

1   Fireflies Ashram is part of Pipal Tree, a registered non-profit trust, and closely connected with an international movement called The Alliance for a Responsible, Plural and United World. It is also a founder member of the Tokyo-based Global Forum for Cultures and Development (ECUDEV). As a living and learning community, Fireflies is a vital and integral part of the Global Eco-village Network (GEN). http://www.fire-flies.net.

2   Our program to give personal and social meaning to our festivals and religious practices is called "The Hermeneutics of Hope." We believe that all our scriptures, festivals and cultural practices must be meaningfully and compassionately interpreted to give sense to our times. This is a participatory process where each interpretation is respected, whether it comes from an illiterate village woman or an information-technology specialist.

ECONOMIC STRATEGIES FOR SUSTAINABILITY

Wayne Hayes

Introduction

HOW CAN THE ECONOMY BE HARNESSED to serve sustainability? What makes this question so ironic is that the growth in the physical scale of the economy under the prevailing regime of economic globalization has depleted resources, destroyed ecosystems, overwhelmed natural waste disposal sinks, waged war on subsistence cultures, and produced shocking maldistribution of wealth and income. How, then, can the economy be turned around to reinforce sustainable development rather than to destroy ecosystems, resource endowments, and indigenous cultures? This alchemy must be resolved to promote sustainability.

The now familiar definition of sustainable development from the Bruntland Commission Report (World Commission on Environment and Development) defines sustainable development as: "development that meets the needs of the present without compromising the ability of future generations to meet their own needs." How operational is this definition? What economic strategies can promote sustainability? Can the precept adequately define guidelines for policy prescription and ethical principles? Does it ensure justice? Will democracy be nurtured?

Ecological economics takes up the challenge of working out a functional analysis from which to base public policy and normative legitimacy. The global economy, a robust engine of change, must generate sustainable development rather than amplify entropy. The U.S., the single most powerful economy in history, must be given foremost consideration. With only 4.5 percent of the world's people, the U.S. consumes about 25 percent of global resources and produces the same proportion of greenhouse gases. The U.S. dominates the Bretton Woods institutions—the International Monetary Fund (IMF), the World Bank, and the World Trade Organization (WTO)—which shape the global economy, enforcing its ideology of neo-liberalism.

The purpose of this essay is to provide sustainers an overview of how economics might appropriately relate to sustainability. The reader will find aspects of the intersection of economics and sustainability throughout this anthology. Two chapters, in particular, complement this essay:

- "Fairness in a Fragile World: A Memo on Sustainable Development," by Wolfgang Sachs

- "Ecological Economics and Sustainable Development," by Peter Montague

Sachs has contributed a sobering explanation of the current status of sustainable development without resorting to orthodox economic analysis. Montague provides a succinct overview of the seminal book in ecological economics, *Beyond Growth: The Economics of Sustainable Development*, by Herman Daly.

Part One
Situating Economics I: Ecology and Economics

What is an economy? The national economy is measured as the monetized market value of the total amount of goods and services produced in a nation. Probe the language and we discover that the term "economy" derives from the Greek *oikonomia*, household management, based on *oikos*, "house," and *nemein*, "manage." Now consider the etymologically related term, "ecology," which is defined as "the branch of biology concerned with the relations of organisms to one another and to their physical surroundings." Ecology also derives from the ancient Greek term *oikos*, but instead of management, focuses on logos, "reason" (*Oxford English Dictionary*).

We must unravel these critical terms, ecology and economy. Confusing them will fog our analysis. Consider two aspects of the relationship between economics and ecology.

1. Which should precede the other? Surely, we must understand the home of humanity before we muster the audacity to manage it. The sheer complexity should daunt us and make us prudent. However, this is not the case. In the last century and more, economy has obviously trumped ecology, to the detriment of the earth. This imbalance cannot be sustained. This implies that at some time in the future a threshold will be crossed and the economy/ecology will crash. We do not know when. We also recognize that many humans, particularly those living in the industrialized temperate climatic zones, have greatly, but unevenly, benefited from economic growth, enshrining economic growth as a prize worthy of emulation by others. Six billion people driving SUVs cannot happen; the earth cannot support such recklessness. The

hubris of economics cannot endure. Hence, we must explore more deeply the nexus between the management of the human house, economy, and our understanding of its internal relations, ecology. Harmonizing this essential distinction must ground any approach to the economy that supports sustainability, even if that strategy originates from outside economics per se.

2. Scrutinize ends and means. Management of the human house, economics, implies the administration of means, a service function. The purpose of the economy is to serve humanity and the expanded human "house,"—our planet—not the obverse. Ends must come before means. Means must be subordinate to ends. Ecology should precede economics.

In both these instances, the prevailing hierarchy of economy and ecology must be inverted: Means define ends and reason restrains the will to control. This brings us back to our initial question: How can the economy be harnessed to serve sustainability? How economics can be made congruent with ecology is the challenge that the Brundtland Commission posed when it defined the mission of sustainable development. Economics, like technology, must serve sustainability, and ends must be defined in terms of culture and nature through open, participatory, ethical discourse, reinforcing democracy and transparency.

Sustainability should not reinforce the privileged position of economics, but should spark an inclusive conversation. The emerging field of eco-economics does attempt to reconcile ecology with economics, building an intelligible and critical bridge between science and social thought. Further, eco-economics lends itself to both normative considerations and prescriptive analysis, enlarging the scope of sustainability analysis to include ethics and public policy. The emerging field of eco-economy drives the discourse of sustainability further away from the dominance of economics.

The extended essay in this collection by Wolfgang Sachs exemplifies the truth inherent in inverting economics and ecology and in listening to other voices and stories. For example, Sachs realizes that copycat development, the replication of the economic development practices of the global rich, will surely lead to global ruin: more poverty within vast ecological catastrophe. Orthodox western economics can neither be extended to the majority of the Earth's human inhabitants nor can it be sustained indefinitely by the 20 percent or so who enjoy its cornucopia. Sachs reveals the parasitical political character of global capitalism masquerading as shared economic development.

Situating Economics II: Economic Globalization

This entire volume examines economic globalization, the backdrop to the story of sustainability. Prominent economists who have provided insight to validate economic globalization include Joseph Schumpeter, the Austrian champion of exuberant capitalism, and David Ricardo, the neoclassical economist who authored the principle of comparative advantage, the cornerstone of the neoclassical theory of trade.

Joseph Schumpeter coined a fateful term to capture the dynamics of capitalism: "the perennial gale of creative destruction." Indeed, Thomas Friedman calls this elusive doctrine "the business model of globalization capitalism." Schumpeter recognized the turmoil endemic to capitalist expansion, as did Karl Polanyi (in *The Great Transformation*), but Schumpeter disregarded the concurrent misery and devastation, instead envisioning an often hidden generative capacity. Yet, the doctrine of creative destruction has become a fixation, a dogma embraced by the faithful on a crusade for triumphant global capitalism.

Growth remains the engine of economic globalization without which the system as constituted would crash—although with runaway material growth Earth's ecosystems will surely crash. Schumpeter put it this way: "Capitalism, then, is by nature a form of economic change and not only never is but never can be stationary." Schumpeter derided the "textbook picture" that depicted economic progress as the result of market-based competition. Rather, he pointed to innovation in products, sources of supply, organization, and technology that created a new context "which strikes not at the margins of the profits and the outputs of the existing firms but at their foundations and their very lives." Indeed, Schumpeter foresaw that capitalism itself would fall victim to the turbulent task environment of its own making:

> The capitalist process not only destroys its own institutional framework but it also creates the conditions for another. Destruction may not be the right word after all. Perhaps I should have spoken of transformation.

David Ricardo's theory of comparative advantage, superficially examined, claims that benefits derive to all who trade at long distances. Ricardo recognized that local specialization in the production of goods that can be produced inexpensively can result in mutual economic gains when traded for goods produced more cheaply in other areas. Both parties to the transaction benefit. However, Ricardo was also formalizing the common sense insights of Adam Smith into a broad theory of economic society based on the institutionalization and rationalization of trade through totalizing markets—a notion fundamentally antithetical to sustainability (Polanyi, *Economy* 131-132).

Ricardo assumed that neither labor nor capital were mobile, that externalities were absent, and that prices changed little with trade, conditions contravened by economic globalization (Daly 152-153; Ekins 307-308). Comparative advantage is the creed of the WTO, the IMF, and the World Bank, providing the basic tenet underlying neo-liberalism.

The international experience, however, demonstrates that the gains from trade are exaggerated, are unequally shared among and within nations, and that the ensuing burden of debt service often leads to the dreaded, now staunchly resisted, structural adjustment programs imposed by the IMF. Other consequences of comparative advantage undermine sustainable development:

1. As poor countries compete in commodity markets, prices drop. The terms of international trade depend greatly on market structure. Industrial nations enjoy decisive advantages in maintaining prices through oligopolistic practices and from policies protecting home markets, despite the preaching of free trade doctrine to the weaker trade partners.

2. Subsistence production is not accounted as global trade, but when resources and people are shifted, often through coercion, into the monetized economy, these activities do show up in the market economy, exaggerating the gains and disguising the losses from trade.

3. Intensive specialization can lead to dependence and the permanent loss of diversity, economically and ecologically. Specialization can morph into runaway monoculture that destroys natural systems and the livelihood nature supports—although to the advantage of land owners and agribusinesses peddling seeds and chemical elixirs.

4. Export trade is highly subsidized, including its distribution and transportation functions. Removal of these subsidies encourages local production and consumption and averts the high energy costs and resulting pollution of long-distance transport. Export-oriented growth policy, propped up by coalitions of vested interests, deters domestically oriented policies—all in the name of free trade.

Despite the historical record, as reported by Sachs in this anthology, and the limits within their own theories, the doctrines of comparative advantage and creative destruction continue unabated as the main economic principles underlying the neo-liberal agenda. Sustainers should recognize this reality when contemplating the role of economics in promoting sustainability—and look elsewhere for economic strategy.

What Brand of Economics Supports Sustainability?

All this does not signal the end of economics for sustainability, but promotes the invention and application of a more humble version of and scope for what Polanyi calls substantive economics, as distinct from the formal economic analysis practiced by academically certified economists (The Economy). This inversion of economics is the foundation of a strategy of sustainability and a preoccupation of this essay. Simply put, economics has a place, and economics must be put in its place. So, what is that place? How can we properly situate economics for sustainability?

To guide us through the labyrinth of economics, consider three schools of thought, each with implications for sustainability:

1. Classical economics originated with Adam Smith's landmark book, *The Wealth of Nations*, published in 1776, and has been steadily augmented by (British) political economists such as David Ricardo (comparative advantage), Alfred Marshall (price theory, or microeconomics), and John Maynard Keynes (macroeconomics). We will discuss below aspects of microeconomics and macroeconomics in relation to sustainability. But neoclassical economics will not support sustainability, even in the guise of "environmental economics," which acknowledges, but trivializes as "side effects," the social costs of markets.

2. A big leap forward comes with the advent of ecological economics. The seminal work in ecological economics belongs to Herman Daly, *Beyond Growth: The Economics of Sustainable Development*. Daly, an academic economist who also worked for the World Bank, provides a critical analysis of how orthodox microeconomics and macroeconomics comes up short for sustainability. Peter Montague provides a succinct overview of Daly in another chapter within this collection— I will refrain from repeating his excellent summary. But note, Daly uses the tools of economics to critique economics—still thinking in the language of economics. Two major advances of ecological economics are the decoupling of qualitative development from quantitative growth and the embedding of the economy within nature.

3. In contrast, eco-economics takes a step away from the profession of economics. A principal contributor, Lester R. Brown, founded the WorldWatch Institute. Eco-economy uses economics as a practical tool to shape situations for the purpose of promoting sustainability but embeds its diagnosis and prescription in cultural and natural

contexts. For eco-economy, economic analysis, like technological innovation, remains a means, not the ultimate objective.

Those who are not economists should realize that as we move through this typology, the dominance of neo-classical economics, including its virulent current manifestation as neo-liberalism, ceases (George). The concrete realities of culture, ecology, and ethics displace the primacy of abstract economics, ceding territory to a discourse based on pragmatism and common sense, thus providing access to economic practice for sustainers.

Finally, note that this discussion of economic globalization and the contributions of ecological economics and eco-economy contain no mention of any significant contribution by Karl Marx, a major figure in economic thought. While Marx contributes to the discussion of class, distribution, and justice, his version of material progress differed only in kind from the modernist economic project (Schroyer 65). John Stuart Mill glimpsed a "steady state" in which a stationary condition of economic equilibrium could be achieved without the dread of stagnation. Rather, qualitative development would emanate from creative leisure (Daly 3), thus recognizing the limits of material satiation, essential to Gandhian "enoughness" (Riwan). No champion for the environment or for the principles of sustainable development emerged within neoclassical economic thought.

We turn to a critical examination of those economic categories that speak to sustainable development, distinguishing among neoclassical economics, ecological economics, and eco-economics. Then, we will close with some remarks on substantive economics and on coping with global capitalism.

Neoclassical Economics
The neoclassical school of economics yields two major theoretical divisions: microeconomics, the behavior of the basic economic units, and macroeconomics, the dynamics of the aggregate economy. Neither is satisfactory for sustainability, but should nonetheless be critically understood, as they are in ecological economics.

Microeconomics
Microeconomics deals with the behavior of the fundamental economic units, such as the firm and the consumer. Its flawed assumptions about perfect competition among small firms defy the reality of mammoth transnational corporations as the principal agency of economic globalization. Instead of recognizing such market distortions as externalities, discussed below, neoclassical economists claim to catch sight of Adam Smith's "Invisible Hand" of the unfettered market. Neoclassical economics is not only blind to environ-

mental degradation and social disintegration but is enthralled in a mystical séance of market perfection, a reification exceeded only by neo-liberalism.

Microeconomic theory projects that human behavior is motivated by an intense utilitarian urge to "maximize satisfaction" and is totally preoccupied with unsustainable, self-centered materialism. This cultural premise, happily, is not widely shared, but still assumed for the construction of theory, little of which has been historically informed or empirically confirmed. Market distortions, such as externalities, create theoretical problems, which, too, can be swept away as inconsequential aberrations. The founder of microeconomics is Adam Smith, refined greatly by Alfred Marshall into formal price theory.

Macroeconomics

Macroeconomics attempts to explain economic aggregates, categories such as consumption, unemployment, savings, investment, money, finance, and the rates of interest. The founder of macroeconomics is Lord John Maynard Keynes, a dissenting architect of the Bretton Woods accords that ground economic globalization to this day.

Put mildly, macroeconomics has been obsessed with economic growth. In the world of the macroeconomist, more is always better. No consideration is given to what is produced, so long as it enhances the total flow of goods and services. Prisons, bloated health care costs, responses to toxic spills, the repair of the damage caused by climate change all are "goods" that add to economic output—not "bads" which should be prevented. The depletion of natural capital and the stress induced on waste sinks are not considered within this methodology. Growth is good, period.

But not every observer concurs. Note how a shift away from the context of industrial society and toward nature and subsistence alters the story of growth as seen by Vandana Shiva, below:

> Instead of living up to its promise to alleviate poverty, economic growth actually undermined ecological stability, thereby destroying people's livelihoods and causing further poverty. Moreover, development strategies have been based on the growth of the market economy, even when large numbers of people operate outside of this network. The emphasis on the market economy has resulted in the destruction of the other economies of nature's processes and of people's survival, but this destruction is seen as nothing more than the "hidden negative externalities" of the development process. (87)

The article in this collection by Wolfgang Sachs also tells the other story of economic growth, within which ecological systems are sacrificed and patterns of human livelihood demolished, not as accidents or externalities, but as government enforced policies of neo-liberalism reinforced by powerful, but undemocratic and opaque, international agencies: the World Bank, the IMF, and the WTO.

A half-century ago, the industrialized nations, haunted by the Great Depression, had installed economic growth as public policy (Shonfield). In the U.S., the national government assumed the role of growth underwriter in the New Deal of President Franklin Delano Roosevelt, an obligation codified into U.S. law with the Employment Act of 1945. Woe to the political leader whose term in office is marred by declining Gross National Product, recession. Since globalization, however, the role of central banks in macroeconomic policy has been gradually eroded, constrained by the forces of global finance—an erosion of sovereignty.

We next turn toward economic categories and strategies that reject the neoclassical heritage of economics: ecological economics and eco-economics. You will find them accessible, even welcoming, to non-economists.

Ecological Economics
Fortunately, ecological economists recognize the blinders their neoclassical colleagues bring to sustainability. Externalities are not trivial side effects. Growth has been decoupled from human well-being and not to be considered as outside of natural limits of resource endowments and carrying capacities. In his overview of Herman Daly's seminal treatment of ecological economics, Peter Montague points out the three functions within which economics claims a legitimate standing and the proper role of economics in each:

Allocation: the efficient allocation of resources toward competing ends. Efficiency has long been the principal concern of economics. Competitive markets—not corporate-dominated oligopolies—can perform well here so long as side-effects, such as externalities, are incorporated into prices. Ecological economists recognize a legitimate role of the market in society based on the efficiency of allocation of resources—"all other things being equal," as economists typically condition their conclusions.

An externality is a consequence, positive or negative, of an economic activity that affects other parties without this affect being incorporated into market prices. Thus, market price deviates from the "true" social cost, sending the wrong signal. Note also the subtle linguistic trivialization. Interestingly, the economics profession has long neglected to assess the size or significance of externalities or to calculate the damages perpetrated on its victims, who by definition had these harms inflicted upon them without their participation—despite the obvious dysfunctions of industrialization and urbanization. Indeed, the bias of public policy in the U.S. has been to protect the producers, not the public at large. Daly comments on the trivialization of externalities by neoclassical economics:

> When increasingly vital facts, including the very capacity of the earth to support life, have to be treated as "externalities," then it is past time to change the basic framework of our thinking so that we can treat these critical issues internally and centrally. (45)

A related topic, rarely brought into view, is the plethora of perverse, often hidden, subsidies, including externalities, enjoyed by corporations in such established industries as energy, agriculture, and transportation. Not only do these gifts typically promote older, dirtier, less efficient industries, but they also stymie the development of innovative, cleaner alternatives—depressing prospects for sustainability. For example, subsidies to cotton farmers in the U.S. disadvantage cotton cultivators in Africa and subsidies to nuclear power generators present an unfair advantage to start-up wind power producers. These often hidden subsidies undermine economic efficiency and promote environmental damage, but go largely neglected in the economic literature. A study released in 2001 by Norman Myers and Jennifer Kent estimates the global cost of perverse subsidies at two billion dollars, about 5.6 percent of the $35 trillion global economy (187-188). The subsidy-rich, environmentally poor Bush-Cheney energy policy was formulated behind closed doors with input from energy giants like Enron but with no public disclosure. Eliminating perverse subsidies must be a first step toward building a sustainable economy.

Distribution: the socially acceptable distribution of the goods and the bads produced by the economy. This issue lies outside the domain of technical economic analysis, incorporates values and ethical choices, and is properly resolved by democratic political institutions. Hence, the term political economics—as if there were any other kind.

Left to itself, a market society will produce large maldistributions in wealth and income. In practice, the market-driven returns to capital, as profits and capital gains, accrue to the wealthy few, the capitalist class, while the returns to labor, wages and salaries, go to a multitude, the working class. This dynamic produces a class-based inequality of both wealth and income, which translates into differential political power. In the past, the inequalities were mitigated by redistributive tax policies—anathema to neo-liberalism, as exhibited by the recent Bush tax cuts. In the era of economic globalization, inequality has grown sharply within nations, including the U.S., and on the global scene. Yet, economists regard this normative concern as outside the ken of "scientific economics." Therefore, when issues of social justice are openly discussed in the context of sustainable development, do not turn to economics for insight.

Worse, the laissez faire policies of neo-liberalism preclude all attempts to either share wealth or income, or to prevent or compensate for externalities. Should any remnant of the welfare state threaten to redistribute goods or avert bads, the hammer of global competition will punish those who misbehave. International investors will withdraw confidence, undermine the currency, and demolish the economy—with the blessing of the IMF (Stiglitz 201-213). Without unions, wages decline further as the weak collectively race to the global bottom—all in the name of progress.

Scale: the appropriate size of the material economy relative to nature's carrying capacity. This aspect of macroeconomics has been altogether disregarded by the dominant neoclassical school of economic thought. In sharp contrast, ecological economists such as Herman Daly have emphasized the importance of scale, which is central to sustainability (48-52). Neoclassical economics regards nature as outside the economy, not situating the economy within nature—abdicating concern for the planet. Natural capital, the stock of resources and ecological services basic to all life, has therefore been denied economic value. When Adam Smith wrote, the scarcity of labor and capital constrained production, not nature's resources and services. That condition has largely been reversed, but natural capital depletion is yet not recognized by neoclassical economics.

The distinction between development and growth is fundamental to ecological economics and central to sustainable development. Daly writes:

> Since physical growth is limited by physical laws, while qualitative development is not, or at least not in the same way, it is imperative to separate these two very different things. Failure to make this distinction is what has made "sustainable development" so hard to define. With the distinction, it is easy to define sustainable development as "development without growth—without growth in throughput beyond environmental regenerative and absorptive capacities." (69)

This insight buttresses the discussion of sustainability and provides an operational definition to promote a strategy of sustainable development.

This entire discussion of economic functions situates the boundaries of professional economics, a vital contribution of ecological economics to sustainability. Ecological economics initiates the synthesis of ecology with economics, building an intelligible and critical bridge between natural science and social thought that can support sustainability. Further, ecological economics lends itself to both normative considerations and prescriptive analysis, enlarging the scope of sustainability to include public policy and ethics.

Yet, sustainable development requires much that is outside the range of ecological economics, expanding the discourse further. Which is why ecological economics should be extended to encompass the eco-economy, to which we now turn.

Eco-Economy

The argument so far has been to abandon, even resist, formal economics as usual, especially the virulent, dominant strain of neo-liberalism, the underlying ideology of contemporary economic globalization. Environmental economics extends neoclassical economics toward rudimentary environmental impacts, but trivializes, even disguises, very real "external" effects of economic activity and decision-making, resulting in faulty market signals. Ecological economics has contributed significant insights to support sustainability, such as the essential distinction between growth and development and the identification of eco-taxation devices. These are necessary to support economic strategies for sustainability, but not sufficient. Where next?

Karl Polanyi has pointed the way by his distinction between the formal economy analyzed deductively by the economics profession and the substantive economy that Polanyi identified through history and anthropology (*The Economy* 142-148). The meaning of this shift for sustainability is that the primacy of economics surrenders to the concrete analysis embedded within culture and nature. Non-economists who recognize the centrality of the economy to sustainability are working out the vision of an eco-economy. Lester R. Brown writes: "we need a vision of what an environmentally sustainable economy—an eco-economy—would look like" (*Eco-Economy* xv) and "The preeminent challenge for our generation is to design an eco-economy, one that respects the principles of ecology" (*Eco-Economy* 21).

An example Brown cites is the application of wind energy to turbines, thus replacing coal mining in Europe and opening up economic opportunity on marginal lands in Kansas. Brown rightly examines specific practices with an eye toward the material basis of these practices, a triumph of common sense over formal, deductive economic rhetoric. Schumpeter's innovation wears a different color: Paul Hawken, Amory Lovins, and L. Hunter Lovins delineate a form of industrialism built on living systems (310-313). This grounding in innovation and common sense emerges from the thoughtful integration of ecology, economics, and technology. Markets that tell the true price and development decoupled from physical growth, as prescribed by ecological economics, provide sympathetic preconditions reinforcing an eco-economy.

Note well how the eco-economy embodies the practice of sustainability as vernacular, common sense, virtuous, ecologically and economically durable practices that remain accessible to all of us within our households, our communities, and our regions. The vision of eco-economics harkens back to the innovation that Schumpeter envisaged as the real engine of progress. Old habits of mind, institutional inertia, and vested interests hinder the progressive tendency inherent in the eco-economy.

Eco-economics, not neo-liberalism, takes up Schumpeter's challenge. The process of creative destruction envisioned by an innovative eco-economy requires the dismantling of an ossified economic order and its high-priests, the economists, who defend it. This is the ultimate economic strategy promoting authentic sustainability.

The concluding section of this essay examines how economic globalization has been absorbed by neo-classical economics to form the dominant ideology guiding contemporary global transformation. The theory and practice of neo-liberalism subverts sustainable development and frustrates the actualization of both ecological economics and eco-economics, as explained above.

Part Two
Economic Globalization: Neo-liberalism and the Prospects for Sustainability

How did the contemporary regime of economic globalization come to be? The story begins at Bretton Woods as an arrangement among nation-states under the auspices of the United Nations to provide order to the international economy, to promote post-World War II economic growth, and to forestall relapse into a global economic depression similar to the 1930s. The original mission of the Bretton Woods institutions was subverted into the ongoing catalyst of economic globalization under the ideology of neo-liberalism beginning in the 1980s.

The story spells out the implications of neo-liberalism in theory and in practice, noting how the altered character of the Bretton Woods institutions has stimulated a world-wide backlash to the prevailing form of economic globalization. Finally, this section speculates on the significance of neo-liberalism for the prospects for sustainability and suggests alternatives. This segment builds on the essay above, unraveling the economic aspects of sustainable development.

Bretton Woods

The story of neo-liberalism emerged in an idyllic setting within the White Mountains of New Hampshire, at the palatial Bretton Woods retreat in July 1944. The official title of the gathering from 44 nations was the United

Nations Monetary and Financial Conference. There, the presumed victors of World War II gathered to anticipate the post-war state of the economy of the North Atlantic community. The specter of relapse into the Great Depression, the global economic slump which the war economy had remedied, haunted Bretton Woods. Progressive reform rooted in nationalism comprised the Bretton Woods agenda.

Two leaders set the stage for post-war economic planning: Lord John Maynard Keynes, the august British economist, and Harry Dexter White, an intimate adviser to President Franklin Delano Roosevelt of the United States. No one at Bretton Woods imagined a transcendence of the nation-states whose interests they represented and promoted. The global economic institutions they envisioned, based on the acumen of Keynes, rested on the accepted cornerstone of national economic policy making, the welfare states constructed throughout the 1930s. Reconstruction of the war-ravaged industrial nations was foremost, with little thought to what were then the colonies of Asia, Central and South America, and Africa.

The UN Monetary and Financial Conference at Bretton Woods founded two principal agencies, technically specialized operations of the United Nations, the World Bank and the International Monetary Fund (IMF). Both are headquarted in Washington, DC.

Keynes himself soon abandoned support for the Bretton Woods accords after the U.S. blackmailed the British delegation with threats of withdrawal of desperately needed post-war loans if the dominance of the IMF and World Bank by financial and trade interests was challenged. The developing nations were held hostage by a regime of strict financial austerity (Monbiot 2).

That was then. The original mission of Bretton Woods promoted economic integration within the international order, particularly among the industrial nations. Contemporary economic globalization advances quite another cause, not Adam Smith's mythical "invisible hand," but the tangible helping hand extended to the true beneficiaries of globalization, transnational corporations. Herman Daly, the seminal ecological economist puts the case this way:

> Globalization refers to global economic integration of many formerly national economies into one global economy, by free trade, especially by free capital mobility, and also, as a distant but increasingly important third, by easy or uncontrolled migration. Globalization is the effective erasure of national boundaries for economic purposes ("Globalization" 1).

Ironically, economic globalization dismantles the authority of the international order by undermining national sovereignty. This analysis provides the working definition of economic globalization used here: the dismantling of national and sub-national restraints on economic activity. Daly, again:

> Since there can be only one whole, only one unity with reference to which parts are integrated, it follows that global economic integration logically implies national economic disintegration—parts are torn out of their national context (disintegrated), in order to be re-integrated into the new whole, the globalized economy ("Globalization" 1).

Renato Ruggiero, former Director-General of the World Trade Organization (WTO) unabashedly stated as much: "We are no longer writing the rules of interaction among separate national economies. We are writing the constitution of a single global economy" (qtd. in Daly, "Globalization" 2).

Margaret Thatcher, however, proclaimed the ultimate catchphrase of economic globalization: "There is no alternative," abbreviated to simply TINA. The triumphalism of neo-liberalism has proved to be premature.

The protest of the WTO summit in Seattle in November 1999, and subsequent, but often suppressed demonstrations, have modulated such arrogance as that exhibited by Thatcher and Ruggiero. Other scenarios have been put forward. One is based on a reform of the original Bretton Woods accords, reverting to traditional nationalism. Another, voiced at the World Social Forum at Porto Alegre, Brazil, in 2001 and 2002, claims "Another world is possible," founded on federated but decentralized global networks (Cavanagh and Mander, *et al.* 3). The former is compatible with environmental economics and perhaps with elements of ecological economics, as defined above, while the latter provides fertile soil within which eco-economies might thrive, the best hope for sustainability.

The proponents of economic globalization make the universal claim that export-driven economic growth will diminish poverty and, by raising income, elevate environmental protection standards. Neo-liberals also postulate that specialization promotes trade and efficiency, as we have seen in the economic thought survey, above. As in other matters of economic theory such as the scale of externalities and the efficacy of comparative advantage, such claims reflect faith but are not based on empirical research. Winners presumably greatly outnumber temporary losers.

Of course, the added material and energy demands of physical growth also diminish resources, create pollution, and exacerbate the waste disposal load. Such illusory economic policies, presupposing an "invisible hand," cannot incidentally promote sustainability, but must be intentionally designed to achieve such goals, directly and not as a side effect or a trickle-down.

No one disputes that poverty reduction and the integrity of the Earth stand as high priorities. Neo-liberalism and economic globalization advocates openly proclaim that these ends are outcomes automatically produced by their policies. Should these proponents therefore be held accountable for the outcomes? Should the terms of the debate focus on results, not on predictions or promises? Sustainability rests on what Schroyer dubs *A World That Works*, on achieving specific desirable and intended outcomes tied to human needs, social justice, and earth-vitality. Does the World Bank or the IMF ever openly state that, say, its policies, below, are installed to enrich corporate clients? As Deep Throat admonished: "Follow the money." Reckon the results.

The Bretton Woods Trio

The logic built into the economic planning of Bretton Woods rested firmly on Keynesian macro-economic theory, predominant through the 1930s and entrenched in the national welfare states. This economic order extended to the Marshall Plan that continued well after World War II in the war-torn nations of Europe. Keynesianism, in practice, promoted the expansion of the role of the state, management of national currencies, and redistribution through progressive taxation, functions anathema to contemporary neo-liberalism. The economic planners at Bretton Woods devised an international system based on the cooperation of interdependent nation-states. No one foresaw a seamless globalization that transgressed the sovereignty of the same nation-states that founded the Bretton Woods institutions.

Three powerful, ostensibly independent but interlocking branches now constitute the bulwark of the transglobal economic order originally devised at Bretton Woods. Only since 1980 have they been inverted into the core institutions engineering economic globalization from above.

International Monetary Fund

The lead institution of the Bretton Woods accords, the International Monetary Fund (IMF) was envisaged by Lord Keynes to provide the liquidity to underwrite national deficit spending to expand national economies, to forestall competitive devaluation in currencies, and to correct failures and distortions in financial markets. The IMF, with scant resources in its early years, fell short of becoming the central bank to the world but had the latent capacity to prevent a relapse of global depression due to inadequate aggregate demand (Dillard 701; Stiglitz 196).

The fierce criticism of the IMF by Nobel Laureate and former chief economist of the World Bank, Joseph E. Stiglitz, highlights the shift in paradigm of the IMF from its original Keynesian mission to neo-liberalism:

> The Keynesian orientation of the IMF, which emphasized market failures and the role for government in job creation, was replaced by the

free market mantra of the 1980s, part of a new 'Washington Consensus'—a consensus between the IMF, the World Bank, and the U.S. Treasury about the 'right' policies for developing countries—that signaled a radically different approach to economic development and stabilization (16).

The most infamous current policy of the IMF is the Structural Adjustment Program (SAP), a set of conditions imposed in return for IMF loans, so desperately needed by poor, heavily indebted countries. The SAPs institutionalize the neo-liberal proclivities of the IMF. The debtor nation must rapidly expand the sale of exports by devaluing the currency, thus lowering price to foreign customers, and by promoting resource extraction, often through liquidation, forced sales of assets to transnational corporations. Government-funded services, such as health and education, must be sharply curtailed. Subsidies to consumers for food or energy must also be slashed while direct and indirect subsidies to export industries are encouraged. Wages are also cut and unions busted, even while purchasing power shrinks. Environmental regulations must be relaxed, increasing pollution and destroying natural environmental services. Restrictions on financial markets must also be eliminated, opening up the national currency to financial speculation, increasing the rate of interest, and contributing to the bankruptcy of native firms. Tariffs, of course, must be eliminated, even if this demolishes local industries and opens up the floodgates of imports, adding to external debt service (Cavanagh and Mander, *et al.* 37-52).

The Structural Adjustment Program of the IMF is the antithesis of sustainable development, crystallizing the antagonism of neo-liberal orthodoxy and sustainability. Satisfying IMF conditionality is typically a mandate for assistance by the World Bank and other international agencies. The control over the national economy by Bretton Woods is virtually complete. The devastating and infamous SAPs are now vigorously resisted.

World Bank

Bretton Woods laid the foundation for the International Bank for Reconstruction and Finance, soon called simply the World Bank, but as a companion to the IMF centerpiece (Stiglitz 11). The original mission of the World Bank was to finance the reconstruction of war-ravaged Europe and to forestall lapsing into another global depression. Later, by 1965, the role of the World Bank expanded to provide seed money for infrastructure projects, mostly electric power and transportation, that would stimulate economic development and reduce poverty in the "developing nations" (Dillard 704-705). The official motto of the World Bank is: "Our dream is a world without poverty" (Stiglitz 23). The World Bank has recently incorporated sustainable development into its mission.

In the 1980s, the World Bank joined the IMF in adopting a missionary zeal in pursuing neo-liberal policies, purging heretics from its staff, and installing a free market ideology that blamed world poverty on failures of governments (Stiglitz 13). The World Bank integrated its operations with the IMF, but as a junior partner. Joseph Stiglitz comments:

> Although the mission of the two institutions remained distinct, it was at this time that their activities became increasingly intertwined. In the 1980s, the Bank went beyond just lending for projects (like roads and dams) to providing broad-based support, in the forms of structural adjustment loans; but it did this only when the IMF gave its approval—and with that approval came IMF-imposed conditions on the country (13-14).

The World Bank provides loans to infrastructure projects. As natural assets and resources are privatized as a pre-condition, the beneficiaries of these loans become transnational corporations who gain control of assets and resources, not the local populations who forfeit ownership. Cavanagh and Mander, *et al.*, write:

> In recent years, the World Bank has provided hundreds of billions of dollars in low-interest loans to subsidize the efforts of global corporations to establish control over the natural resources and markets of assisted countries. Corporations in the energy and agricultural sectors have been among the main beneficiaries (39).

In fact, the Institute for Policy Studies names the World Bank as "the major contributor to global greenhouse gas emissions through fossil fuel projects that primarily benefit global corporations." Regional development banks tend to follow the lead of the World Bank, exacerbating the problem (Cavanagh and Mander, *et al.* 39).

Thus, the World Bank has also been captured by the neo-liberal agenda, partnering with the IMF in a joint effort to promote economic globalization, to advance the interests of transnational corporations, and to destroy prospects for sustainable development.

World Trade Organization

The lowering of tariffs became a point of contention at Bretton Woods, with no firm agreement. In 1948, a charter forged in Havana for the International Trade Organization was proposed, but Congress balked at ratification rather than compromise national sovereignty. Soon afterwards, trade negotiations commenced in Geneva, founding the General Agreement on Tariffs and Trade (GATT). Under President John F. Kennedy, the scope of GATT increased and tariffs dropped sharply, but disputes over agricultural subsidies undermined general agreement (Dillard 702-705). In 1986, trade negotiations resumed in Punte del Estay, Uruguay, concluding in Marrakech in 1993. In 1994, President William Clinton signed the master agreement that included 117 nations. On January 1, 1995, the World Trade Organization (WTO) was created, converting GATT and concluding the Bretton Woods trio (Stiglitz 7).

The WTO, founded as a treaty among sovereign nations, is perhaps the most controversial of the core institutions of economic globalization. WTO prevents governments from regulating international trade and investment, thus favoring the interests of transnational corporations over nations. The WTO can levy permanent sanctions against nations it deems as transgressors of its trade rules. Import substitution policies, seen by many as crucial to incipient sustainable development, are not permitted under WTO rules. "The Battle of Seattle" in 1999 has focused attention and ire on the WTO more than on the IMF or the World Bank—and the WTO disdains notoriety.

The WTO decides its cases surrounded by secrecy, delegating anonymous trade specialists for its tribunals. It promulgates not only in matters of tariffs, but also in what it deems to be non-tariff barriers to trade, such as India's national constitution which permits generic pharmaceuticals, Canada's cultural policy that restricts magazines from the U.S., and the European Union's preference for bananas produced by cooperatives and not agribusinesses Dole and Chiquita (Cavanagh and Mander, *et al.* 45). Thus, unlike the IMF and World Bank, the WTO intrudes on the domestic affairs of rich and powerful nations, including the U.S.

Tariffs have shrunk persistently since Bretton Woods, but agricultural subsidies chronically divide nations and work to the disadvantage of developing countries. Trade-Related Intellectual Property Rights (TRIPs) have divided poor and rich nations, with the U.S. siding with patent-holders such as giant pharmaceutical and agribusiness firms. At stake are patent claims over agricultural seeds and medicinal plants and the future of biodiversity itself.

The WTO appears to recognize its deficit of accountability and its excess of controversy. Despite its small budget and staff and its hesitation to leap into disputes, the WTO mission and methods contribute to the legitimation crisis of economic globalization (Nye 107-108). The controversies surrounding the WTO even divide political conservatives who decry the erosion of sovereignty. The WTO appears to tread gingerly, at least for now. However,

WTO critics sound an ominous note, claiming, "the WTO is a blueprint for the hegemony of the largest corporations based in the rich countries" (Cavanagh and Mander, *et al.* 46).

Consequences of Bretton Woods
Under the Regime of Neo-Liberalism

The WTO occupies a strategic niche in the march of neo-liberalism and economic globalization. Fundamental to neo-liberalism is the aggressive abolition of impediments to unfettered trade among nations, facilitating the unhindered movement of goods, resources, currency, and investment, but not enabling migration. Neo-liberalism champions the rights of corporations to seek cheap resources, maximum profits, fluid investment opportunity, and expanded markets—all in the name of efficiency and the eventual gains accruing to all stakeholders. Anathema to neo-liberalism are tariffs; regulations of all kinds, such as labor and environmental standards; and restrictions on flows of currency, capital, and investment, even for unproductive speculation. Freedom in the context of neo-liberalism means abolition of all governmental oversight, even if popular and democratic. So, for some, the WTO represents liberty while for others it stands for domination by transnational corporations.

The revamped Bretton Woods accords set in motion what economic historian Karl Polanyi calls a double-movement. From above, the proponents of economic globalization maneuver to set the stage for transnational corporations to enjoy privileges denied sovereign peoples and to literally control the fate of the Earth. The myriad dialectical reverberations from below, now dubbed the anti-globalization movement, collide with the centralized movement from above. The resolution of the double-movement will determine the prospects for sustainability (Polanyi, *The Great Transformation*). Proponents of neo-liberalism are heavily outnumbered, but hold predominant political and economic power. The situation remains fluid.

Neo-Liberalism and Sustainability

Neo-liberalism cannot be reconciled with sustainability; there exists no middle ground. The principles underlying each and the dynamics they drive are thoroughly incompatible. If neo-liberalism triumphs, sustainability cannot be achieved, with drastic implications for future generations of humans and for the hospitality of the Earth for life. The stakes are high and the prospects grim.

Consider what neo-liberalism means in practice. The neo-liberal program of economic globalization makes the world safe for transnational corporations to roam the Earth at will. Neo-liberalism shifts power from the nation-state and sub-national governments toward transnational corporations. The consequences are stunning: the capacity of popular resistance is undermined; the protections afforded labor and the environment are curtailed; publicly held assets, including natural resources, are liquidated, a license for exploitation; internal national financial management is supplanted by global financial circuits, including rampant currency speculation; indigenous economies built on internal trade, public goods, and subsistence livelihood are demolished; and welfare state provisions providing economic security, public health, and education are eliminated. This is what "free trade" means in practice and why the neo-liberal agenda has met with increasingly stiff but spontaneous opposition, the diverse amalgam of anti-globalization advocates.

Note the transformation of the role of the state in the globalization process. Rather than expressing the will of its citizenry, the state is displaced by the remote agents of globalization, the Bretton Woods trio. This convoluted process, ironically, is obfuscated by neo-liberalism as the spread of democracy. The void thus created becomes the terrain of the nascent civil society movement, loosely termed NGOs, non-governmental organizations. Sustainability thrives on democracy and demands that national and sub-national political forms be recaptured and invigorated.

Neo-liberalism projects that its policies will provide widely shared prosperity by inducing accelerated economic growth. The record says otherwise: global economic expansion was far higher, 3.2 percent, from 1961-1980, before neo-liberalism, than since the Thatcher- and Reagan-led initiatives were installed, 0.7 percent from 1981-1999 (Pollin 131). Further, global ecological deterioration has intensified and inequalities in income and wealth have sharpened. Half of humanity, three billion people, subsists on under $2 per day and the richest 20 percent consume 86 percent of the earth's resources (Shah 7). The number of people living in poverty actually increased in the 1990s (Stiglitz 5). The East Asian financial collapse of 1997-1998 shook faith in the international monetary regime. South America has rejected structural adjustment programs. Africa has been largely excluded from economic globalization, contributing only about 4 percent to world trade, and poses special problems of AIDS, a colonial legacy, and race. The Islamic world resists the materialist trappings of westernization. Oil, the foundational resource of modernization, exhibits chronic and irreversible scarcity.

Despite the contradictions of theory and practice, proponents of neo-liberalism and economic globalization claim hegemony over globalist discourse, caricaturing dissent as narrow and parochial. However, the terms of debate cannot be so glibly simplified. The rich communal texture of sustainability engenders more diverse worlds than the homogeneity implicit in market-ruled globalization.

Sustainability must not to be confounded with parochialism, isolationism, or xenophobia. Sustainability demands a cosmopolitan outlook, negotiating and integrating levels of social organization ranging from the local through the regional and the national into the global order of things. Sustainability, like ecology, thrives on diversity. Indeed, sustainability presents a daunting conceptual challenge that must be worked out in practice, not given to pre-ordained or ideologically driven preconceptions. The practice of sustainability presumes an illuminating public discourse built on a vibrant civic culture, from your neighborhood to the global village we all share. The level of human development evoked by sustainability poses an imposing challenge of societal evolution that can only be conceived in inter-generational context—although we don't know how much time we have available until catastrophe.

Prospects

An international economic order, such as one consistent with the original design of Bretton Woods, could arguably be compatible with sustainable development, although this is now a contestable assertion. The post-war obsession with physical growth in the scale of economic activity collides with the limits imposed by nature as raw material resource and as sink for waste disposal. Ecological economics and eco-economics claim that development can be decoupled from the scale of material and energy consumption. Cultural innovation and enhanced technology can offer flexible and ethical complements for lightened material burdens imposed on the Earth, enhancing life opportunities that can be sustained indefinitely.

An eco-economic outlook provides a prerequisite for the transition to sustainability, offering an alternative to neo-liberalism. As stated above, economics must be relegated to a service role concerned with appropriate means, not a dominant epistemology that presumes to define ends. These ends must be cast in terms of human needs and nature, harmonized so that the provision of livelihood can persist universally and sustainably from generation to generation.

As this essay is written, neo-liberalism enjoys the advantage. The ascendancy of neo-liberalism, however, has been challenged, as the diverse authors in this anthology illustrate. As the global South and many sectors, regions, and citizens of the industrialized world attest, the relatively short era of incipient economic globalization has met with stiff resistance. Should conditions deteriorate, such as indicated by global warming and by widespread social and ecological dislocation, struggles against neo-liberalism will intensify. The outcome of this struggle is unresolved, but day-by-day the damage to nature and to humanity becomes more conspicuous, despite the official denial perpetrated by neo-liberal orthodoxy.

The alternatives, based on rethinking the eco-economy, cannot be dictated by ideology or by centralized authority but rather built piece by piece, from the ground up. The cosmopolitan outlook and the decentralized public discourse so required indicate that there is much work to be done. Time is short but opportunities for sustainers abound and expand. There is an alternative.

Works Cited

Brown, Lester R., *Eco-Economy: Building an Economy for the Earth*, New York, W.W. Norton, 2001.

Brown, Lester R. "Eco-Economy Offers Alternative to Middle East Oil" appeared in an unpublished collection edited by Trent Schroyer and Tula Quast.

Cavanagh, John, Jerry Mander, *et al.*, *Alternatives to Economic Globalization: A Better World Is Possible* (San Francisco, Berrett-Koehler, 2002).

Daly, Herman E., *Beyond Growth: The Economics of Sustainable Development* (Boston, Beacon Press, 1996).

Daly, Herman, "Globalization and Its Discontents," Minnesotans For Sustainability. August 2000. Viewed on April 25, 2005. http://www.mnforsustain.org/daly_herman_globalism _and_its_discontents.htm.

Dillard, Dudley, *Economic Development of the North Atlantic Community: Historical Introduction to Modern Economics* (Englewood Cliffs, New Jersey, Prentice-Hall, 1967).

Diwan, Romesh, "Gandhian Economics," (Ed. Trent Schroyer) *A World That Works: Building Blocks for a Just and Sustainable Society* (New York, Bootstrap Press, 1997), pp. 86-91.

Ekins, Paul, "Trading Off the Future: Making World Trade Environmentally Sustainable" (Ed. Rajaram Krishnan, Jonathon M. Harris, and Neva R. Goodwin), *A Survey of Ecological Economics* (Washington, DC, Island Press, 1995), pp. 306-311.

Friedman, Thomas L, *The Lexus and the Olive Tree* (New York, Anchor Books, 2000).

George, Susan, "A Short History of Neoliberalism" appeared in an unpublished collection edited by Trent Schroyer and Tula Quast.

Hawken, Paul, Amory Lovins, and L. Hunter Lovins, *Natural Capitalism: Creating the Next Industrial Revolution* (New York, Little, Brown and Company, 1999).

Monbiot, George, "Making Generosity Redundant." Monbiot.com. December 20, 2001. Viewed on April 25, 2005. http://www.monbiot.com/archives/2001/11/20/ making-generosity-redundant/.

Myers, Norman, and Jennifer Kent, *Perverse Subsidies: How Tax Dollars Can Undercut the Environment and the Economy* (Washington, DC, Island Press, 2001).

Nye, Joseph S, Jr., *The Paradox of American Power: Why the World's Only Superpower Can't Go It Alone* (New York, Oxford University Press, 2002).

Polanyi, Karl, *The Great Transformation: The Political and Economic Origins of Our Time* (Boston, Beacon Press, 1944).

Polanyi, Karl, "The Economy as Instituted Process" in (Ed. George Dalton) *Primitive, Archaic, and Modern Economies: Essays of Karl Polanyi* (Boston, Beacon Press, 1968).

Pollin, Robert, *Contours of Descent: U.S. Economic Fractures and the Landscape of Global Austerity* (New York, Verso, 2003).

Schroyer, Trent, "What Is Real Wealth?" in (Ed. Trent Schroyer) *A World That Works: Building Blocks for a Just and Sustainable Society* (New York, Bootstrap Press, 1997), pp. 65-68.

Schumpeter, Joseph, *Capitalism, Socialism and Democracy* (New York, Harper & Row, 1950).

Shah, Anu, "Free Trade and Globalization: A Primer on Neoliberalism," *Global Issues*. February 9, 2004. Viewed on April 25, 2005. http://www.globalissues.org/TradeRelated/FreeTrade/Neoliberalism.asp?p=1.

Shiva, Vandana, "Recovering the Real Meaning of Sustainability" in (Ed. Rajaram Krishnan, Jonathon M. Harris, and Neva R. Goodwin) *A Survey of Ecological Economics* (Washington, DC, Island Press, 1995), pp. 86-88.

Shonfield, Andrew, *Modern Capitalism: The Changing Balance of Public and Private Power* (New York, Oxford University Press, 1965).

Smith, Adam, *The Wealth of Nations* (New York, Random House, 1937).

Stiglitz, Joseph E., *Globalization and Its Discontents* (New York, W.W. Norton, 2002).

World Commission on Environment and Development, *Our Common Future* (Oxford, Oxford University Press, 1987).

Part Four

Smaller Footprints:
Sustainability as
Capacity Building
and Democratization
of Wealth

Introduction to Part Four

SUSTAINABILITY
AS CAPACITY BUILDING
AND DEMOCRATIZATION
OF WEALTH

Trent Schroyer

THINKING ABOUT "WORLD SUSTAINABILITY" ULTIMATELY MEANS identifying the socio-economic forms that people need to sustain their personal socio-economic existence. The perspective of Amartya Sen is helpful because he defines "freedom" in ways that go beyond the "lack of restraints," or the negative freedom of neo-liberalism. Freedom for Sen means having the "capabilities (and) outcomes" needed to make freedom happen. "Capability is . . . the substantive freedom to achieve alternative functioning combinations (or, less formally put, the freedom to achieve various lifestyles)."[1]

When local/regional peoples have capacity to acquire and maintain their food, water, health, housing, security, etc., they can act effectively in their own interests and they can move toward sustainability. If they are forced into situations that degrade these capacities, they cannot do this. Indeed, the capacity to protect their equity in land, water, soils, local organizations and financial arrangements was the means by which the "Asian tigers," Japan, South Korea and Taiwan became the only nation-states to "develop" since WW II. How they achieved this is of great historical importance, particularly because all other struggling "underdeveloped" countries have failed to duplicate their success.

David Korten claims that "equity-led sustainable growth" was actually the secret of Japan, South Korea and Taiwan's successful Asian capitalist revolution, not neo-liberal "export-led industrial development." Comprehensive land reforms, securing of small rural agriculture, affirmation of member-managed and multi-tiered local organizations including co-ops, irrigation societies, farmer associations, women's and youth organizations were among the capacity building means that enabled these countries to achieve "development."[2] Korten argues what actually made the difference was the protection and extension of these local-regional economies and habitation tools. National economic improvement of the countryside's local economies were the sufficient historical conditions for development, at least until the late 1980s. After that, although their entry into wider trade is portrayed by neo-liberals as a free market driven strategy, it was actually a capacity building, import-substitution mercantile strategy. The Asia capitalist revolution cannot be used to justify the neo-liberal development model as the means for creating sustainable modern societies. Sustaining and building rural local economies and regional capacities was the key then, and now, too, in the midst of contemporary economic globalization.

Every project in the sustainable development tool-kit is dominated by neo-liberal planning assumptions deriving from international "free investment" and "free trade" rules. However, perspectives in this book have shown that, rather than operating to enable eradication of poverty, greater redistribution of income, protection of health and ecology, these rules often do precisely the reverse, ensuring only the profits of corporations. Financial investment practices, particularly, diminish public institutions' capacity to meet citizen needs, while substituting privatized services and governance. This goes along with jettisoning the precautionary principle—founded on normative principles—and its replacement with risk assessment, based on mathematical and economic formulations.

Taking one case—the World Trade Organization's General Agreement on Trade in Services (GATS)—these rules do not improve self-development "capabilities" in Sen's sense, only corporate profit potentials. GATS actually functions to undermine the commons protections for spheres that are not commercial.[3] That GATS rules are now being "improved" for the next WTO meeting—despite wide-world opposition, tells us who is doing the planning and that the process is insulated from critical discourse.

Are there other ways of providing institutional and structural supports in lieu of the free investment functions of the corporate system? Can community conditions be nurtured to sustain civil society organizations? Most importantly, is there another approach to financial arrangements? The answer to each of those questions is "yes." They are already present but need to be separated from the corporate ideology that seeps into every "development" planning scenario.

The Democratization of Wealth

The democratization of wealth, in a variety of ways, enables communities, municipalities and states to have the capacity to create freedom for its citizens.

Michael Shuman argues that the only way a community can get control over its wealth is to rebuild it from the ground up. He begins his "Going Local" strategy with the usual Agenda 21 "visioning" approach oriented to an accounting of sustainability indicators, but he goes on to argue that this is not sufficient. Communities should create a local bill of rights based on a community survey of what constitutes basic needs and existing assets.[4] This means taking inventory of local assets and defining unused resources; current problems can be turned into new opportunities.

Communities can create community corporations linked to community needs. These can include non-profits, or co-operatives, but most important are for-profits with residential restrictions on stock ownership (the Green Bay Packers model). Regionally defined stock holders do not skip town and these local community corporations provide commodities and services for local necessities. For example, environmental initiatives can be reframed as contracts for community reinvestments.

Communities have set up local businesses that take care of their needs for energy, food, water, housing, clothing, materials recycling industries, etc. As they expand, they function as economic multipliers that keep money in the region. By focusing on local import substitutions, new businesses can be fostered. Especially new services can become a large portion of the local economy because local knowledge and technology can now replace imported materials. New livelihoods and wealth generation can emerge.

An enabling step toward this democratization of wealth is to create community financial structures that learn how to set up and inter-relate the many community financial services now existing. Looking around, it is clear that community development financial institutions (CDFIs) exist everywhere and, as Shuman is fond of saying, "anything that exists is possible." For example, the early form of the South Shore Bank, or the Self-Help Credit Union in Durham, the Women's Self-Employment Project in Chicago, or Working Capital in Cambridge.

A strategy for leveraging financial capacity more regionally is to integrate local financial institutions. Hence, unions in Holland set up a financial institution, ASN Bank, and convinced the Postbank to administer a special fund run by ASN for investing in local needs industries. The Triodos Bank in the United Kingdom looks for community projects first and depositors second. But, ultimately, it is going to take political innovations like pushing for pension fund investments to be channeled into socially responsible investing and green purchasing.

Perhaps the most fundamental issue is to recognize that financial services have moved from banks to mutual funds and pension funds and that this asset securing practice may be the key. For example, the California Public Employees' Retirement System (CalPERS) pension fund performs the crucial role of corporate accountability and is helping organize a nation-wide coalition for state treasurers to do the same. Many other proposals and initiatives exist to require community obligations for all private financial institutions, obligations that could be transformed into seed capital for new CDFIs.

Documentation of the democratization of wealth has been extensively researched in Gar Alperovitz's *America Beyond Capitalism*.[5] He breaks down asset securing mechanisms into sectors. For example, worker owned firms, or employee stock ownership plans, of which there are now 11,000, or enterprising cities, neighborhoods and nonprofits, or state and national innovations. The number and depth of these models for shifting ownership of assets to institutions and securing the economic situations of participants establishes a major strategy for building self-development and self-determination capacity.

Both Shuman and Alperovitz indicate that there is a middle ground between right and left that can be discovered in the actual economic experiments for self-reliance, and citizen asset-based wealth maintaining solutions to poverty and inequality. But these examples of democratic capacity building are often obscured by negative liberty arguments of the anti-public right and the anti-privatization prejudices of the left. But if the issue of democratization of ownership and enabled access to capital for the economically insecure is kept central, it may be possible for many already existing solutions to be supported by both persuasions. Ultimately, it is in everyone's interest to admit that the public and the private are mutually supportive and social cooperation is the secret of stability despite the extreme polarizations of the current Bush regime. As Alperovitz asserts, the founding ideal of America was "equal liberty," not just liberty for the super rich.

Alanna Hartzok provides another example of how to enhance the democratization of asset wealth. She brings the issue of democratization of land assets to our attention as a primary sustainability goal. Documenting the inequality of land ownership and the large proportion of wealth that is generated by land rents, she restates the principle that comes from Tom Paine and Henry George:

"Men did not make the earth. . . . It is the value of the improvement only, and not the earth itself, that is individual property. . . . Every proprietor owes to the community a ground rent for the land which he holds." (Paine)

These rights were originally protected by commons arrangements that were part of all traditional worlds, but in the money system era new accounting procedures are essential to retain this right. If we put a dollar value on the services that the Earth provides, it has been calculated that over 50 percent of the GDP derives from this source. Therefore, it is everyone's Earth birthright to share in this community asset.

This principle underlies Alaska's Permanent Fund as a model that has a resource use tax that is invested with dividends shared with the entire population. The fact that Alaska is the only state that has not had an income drop in the last decade shows that asset sharing of wealth works to lessen poverty.

Twenty cities in Pennsylvania, with Harrisburg as the best case, are applying the same split system for taxing land, while allowing improvements on sites in ways that promote the efficient and optimal use of the best urban locations. Sprawl and land speculation is stopped and accumulation of revenues for municipal investment increased. Application of this principle world-wide has the potential of resolving resource wars and eradicating poverty while enabling public and private asset creation. This is a sustainability tool that is especially effective against corporate globalization and can be extended to other aspects of the Earth's services such as water, forests, minerals, the atmosphere, electro-magnetic frequencies, and even satellite orbits

David Lewit documents the participatory budgeting process that has emerged in Porto Alegre, Brazil, the site of three world social forums in the last five years. Describing both the world social forum process and the unique budgeting process in Porto Alegre, Lewit shows how the slogan "another world is possible" can actually work.

He describes critical discourse at the World Social Forum about NAFTA. Its planned extension to wider areas of Central and South America is described, as well as the UN Millennium Forum of Civil Society, and the common agreement on investment and society. Lewit points to the open ended processes of world sustainability discourse that will be widened each year from now on.

In Porto Alegre, Lewit studied the budgeting process which begins at the local levels and goes forward as a participatory planning procedure. This is a model for fair and equitable investment for capacity building. With 50,000 citizens actively involved, over $200 million is invested in projects that are essential for local infrastructure improvements, such as water and sewage, housing, education, day care, medical services, etc. They bring expertise into the planning process as a public phase of planning, and not as top down decision making. Details of this planning process are an impressive story of how to mobilize the most marginalized and poorest sectors into expressing their needs in public. Participatory budgeting is also a means of achieving participatory democracy. That it takes place in the context of public asset allocation is significant.

This procedure has now spread to 100 cities in Brazil and to other South American countries and has the fantastic consequence of eliminating corruption due to the open and transparent process of planning. Lewit is working to see this process adopted in New England where town meetings are still able to influence local decision-making.

Joan Gussow shows why local food production is a capacity that all localities should secure. This is essential in order to retain local agricultural land capacity and to ensure food safety by letting consumers know where and how food is grown. But most of all, we have to secure our local farmers, their farm lands, and their stock of knowledge about how to grow food. These assets are rapidly dwindling as farmers over 70 are now the most rapidly growing group of farmers, and farm lands are being scooped up by real estate speculators. If we let these disappear, we become dependent on remote, unaccountable food monopolies that aim for profit first and health second. Having local food capacity is the best way to protect a region from the dangers of food terrorism, too, given that our food inspection systems are thin. We have no option but to become more involved.

Re-localization of food production and consumption is essential to resist corporate agribusiness globalizations that displace farmers in every part of the world. Gussow's reflections are an honest effort to get consumers to face the costs of their lack of attention to the food supply system and a record of her own history of learning how to be largely food self-sufficient.

William Makofske's essay reminds us that for all the solace we may derive from the legions of PR flacks and lobbyists in the pay of Big Oil who tell us all is well with the world—we may find ourselves facing a stripped down future sooner than later if we don't make some intelligent choices, as individuals, as communities, as a society, right now.

Despite a certain inevitability about the "end of oil" played out in charts and graphs in which production competes with consumption and goes home the loser, we in the industrialized West continue to hope for some *deus ex machina*, some intervening salvation which will allow us to continue our old ways without the need to confront the coming future and the change that that future will most certainly entail. We see deliberate resistance to change in this country displayed in larger cars, bigger homes, accelerating consumption.

No mere theorist, Makofske practices the brand of sustainability that he preaches, having reduced fossil fuel energy consumption in his own home by 90 percent, compared to the average home's use. This was achieved using proven construction and conservation techniques that are affordable and available today and do not require changes in lifestyle that are either startlingly severe or unappealingly ascetic. They do require that we confront not only the essential wastefulness of many of our choices, but the unpleasant impact that these choices are having, and will certainly continue to have, on ourselves.

Makofske argues that the dream of unlimited resources—the "electric too cheap to meter" mantra that the nuclear industry once murmured in our ears—has come and gone or, perhaps, never was. Our insistent reliance on petroleum has left us to confront growing geo-political troubles that affect our national security and put us into a competitive brawl for energy with the rest of the world, who only want to mimic our over-consumptive lifestyles. Although realization has begun to dawn at personal and local levels—the recent unanimous Climate Protection Agreement of the U.S. Conference of Mayors is only one example—national policy is still largely blind to the sea change. It is on the national level that we must now intelligently and pragmatically acknowledge the impact our energy craving is having on the environment if we are to avoid, as Makofske puts it, "environmental degradation, damage to health, economic risk from importing oil supplies from unstable regions, the cost of war and conflict, and climate change," all of them pipers we are paying in one form or another.

The new paradigm must be sun-based to a large degree, whether in the form of wind, solar water heating, or photovoltaic, to name some, because of solar availability, accessibility and, most importantly, renewability. The sun, after all, has provided energy for about 4.5 billion years and is considered to be at the mid-point of its useful life. The laws of science and the marketplace have aligned, Makofske says, and the underlying calculus of consumption leaves us little room but to seek more efficient ways of producing and using energy and to seek the information we need as consumers and citizens to create sustainable decisions.

Endnotes

1 Amartya Sen, *Development as Freedom* (New York, Knopf,1999), p.75.

2 David Korten, *Getting to the 21st Century: Voluntary Action and the Global Agenda* (West Hartford, CT, Kumerian Press, 1990), p. 73ff.

3 Lori Wallach and Patrick Woodall, *Whose Trade Organization: A comprehensive guide to the WTO* (New York, The New Press, 2004), Chapter 4 which is subtitled "Perpetual Servitude." Citizen study groups on the unintended consequences of WTO rules and their ideological nature would be a useful exercise for citizens groups who would soon see the incredible corporate interest embedded in these rules.

4 Details about process are found in Michael Shuman, *Going Local: Creating self-reliant communities in a global age* (New York, Free Press, 1998).

5 Gar Alperovitz, *America Beyond Capitalism: Reclaiming our wealth, our liberty and our democracy* (Hoboken, New Jersey, Wiley, 2005).

GOING LOCAL:
HOW CAN WE CREATE VIABLE
LOCAL ECONOMIES?

Michael Shuman

There is a prevailing view in the world right now that "bigger" is cheaper. Several thousand protesters are going to be descending upon Washington, D.C. soon to protest world economy diplomats associated with the IMF and the World Bank. What's interesting is both the proponents and the opponents of globalization actually agree on one point, and that is that big corporations are the wave of the future. I happen to believe that both of them are wrong on that point, that big corporations are not the wave of the future.

Indeed we have big fish eating smaller fish, but ultimately the piranha will prevail. And the piranha are the small businesses that I think are the wave of our financial and community future. The world right now is really facing a wrestling battle between two women—TINA and LOIS. TINA represents the viewpoint of Maggie Thatcher: "There is no alternative to the global economy!" she has proclaimed, and I would say that 99.9 percent of planners, mayors, and economic development people pretty much have embraced the same philosophy of implementing TINA at the local level. This can be reduced to two mantras. The first is "Get Toyota to locate in your back yard," and the second is prioritize export-led development—"get your goods and services as far and wide in the world economy as possible." Both of these mantras, I am going to argue, are fundamentally dead ends. There is an alternative, and the alternative is LOIS, "Locally Owned Import Substituting development." And the picture I have here is of Jane Jacobs. Those of you who have had the opportunity to read some of her works over the last generation will find a lot of resonance in what I am about to say from her work.

I would like to talk about three major points. The first is why LOIS is a better catch than TINA. The second, why LOIS is more available than we think. And the third is how LOIS can be courted at the local level, so we can make sure she is a part of our lives. So, let's start by examining why LOIS is a better catch than TINA and talk first about local ownership, and then talk about import substituting development.

Everyone these days talks about sustainable development, sustainable communities, sustainable business. What do we mean by this? If you think about it just from first principles, in my view you have to answer at least three questions about sustainable development; that is, the WHAT, HOW, and WHO of production. The WHAT of production is, are you producing goods and services that genuinely serve the needs of the local community, or are you producing tobacco and Gatling guns? The HOW of production is, are you producing with labor and environmental standards that are high? The WHO of production is, who owns this particular factory, bank, farm, whatever? What's interesting about the sustainability discourse is that there is a lot of discussion about the WHAT, a lot of discussion about the HOW, and almost no discussion at all about the WHO! And if you don't talk about the WHO, you can make almost no progress on the HOW or the WHAT. It's a fundamental flaw in sustainability movement and analysis. And the reason is this: Every community in every country today is in a competition for a diminishing number of ever-larger companies, and those companies are playing a little game with communities. The game is "We will move into your area, we will set up a plan, we will set up a factory, we will set up an office, if you pay us some money."

So, to pull just one of many examples you could look at over the last 10 years, BMW came to the United States and said "We are going to build a plant with 2,000 jobs—what can you give us?" Well, the state of Nebraska said, "Hmmm . . . we can give you $100 million of tax abatements and capital improvements and bond issues." Now, $100 million for 2,000 jobs, that's pretty good! But then the state of South Carolina steps forward and says, "No, we can do better than that—$150 million! And not only that, we are a low-wage, no-union state." Well, that did the trick. BMW said off we go to South Carolina, and as my chart shows here—eyebrow-popping numbers!— things like $20,000 a job that Illinois was paying in the 1980s, $50,000 a job that Indiana was paying. Now Alabama comes in with Mercedes Benz at $200,000 a job. Kentucky brought in Tabasco and Co-Steel from Canada for nearly $400,000 a job. There is nearly no end in sight, and if these numbers get larger and larger, it raises serious questions about what does it really mean to win this competition. What are we really winning? I mean, are you really losing if you are paying out all this money per job?

Now, another phenomenon has happened too, which is that many companies have realized, "Hmm . . . this is a very, very lucrative game. Maybe we can get into the act too." And so you have companies that once were part of a community thinking "We're going to threaten to leave, and extort some money that way." So what happens is a company like Walt Disney Corporation—the Magic Kingdom in Anaheim—threatens to leave unless the state of California invests $1 billion in improving the highways around Anaheim. Or you have the New York Stock Exchange threatening to leave New York for Connecticut or New Jersey, unless $1 billion is given to it.

The extortion game is being practiced by anyone who has even slight global ambitions. And at one level, all of us are losers in this competition, and the reason is that there are 700 million people in the world who are un- or under-employed, and their numbers are going to double in the next 10 years. They are more than delighted to work for a buck or two a day, and it makes sense for any firm that is willing to move to go take advantage of that cheaper labor force and just move the best technology overseas. There is not a single piece of labor or environmental legislation that comes before your county, your state legislature, Congress, the World Trade Organization, without the argument coming forward: If you do this, if you pass a living wage, if you ramp up your anti-pollution standards, we are going to hurt the business quantity. We are going to scare businesses out of here, and we are not going to be able to attract new businesses to come here. And you know something, it's absolutely true! It's absolutely true that everything you do to ramp up the quality of life is a deterrent to business. It's a terrible dilemma we are in.

And what is the way out of it? Well, in my view, there is only one way out, and that one way out is local ownership. Local ownership of business has four distinct advantages. The first is they are long-term generators of wealth for the community, often for many generations. The second is that a local business is not interested usually in moving to Mexico or Malaysia, they are not going to suddenly depart and punch a blow in the economy. When a business deserts a community that it's been affiliated with for a long time, what happens? Well, suddenly people are thrown out of work, suddenly people are thrown on the welfare rolls, suddenly the tax base goes way down. Suddenly the schools and the fire and the police can no longer be paid for, and the community goes into a death spiral. A community that is largely made up of local young businesses will never go into a death spiral like that.

The third advantage of local ownership is that a community can raise its labor and environmental standards with absolute confidence that the local young businesses will adapt rather than flee, because fleeing isn't in their vocabulary.

The last advantage of local ownership of business is that they have a lot more room to succeed. You may have heard a statistic (the SBA puts this out) that something like 70-80 percent of all new businesses fail within five years.

There are many complicated reasons for that. But the kinds of businesses that actually succeed with a greater probability are local young ones. Why is this? Because a non-local, young business is looking for the absolute highest rate of return. When this is not achieved, it is shut down.

Sperry Rand Company, about 20 years ago, commanded all of its subsidiaries to achieve a 22 percent rate of return per year on investment—22 percent! The Library Bureau in Herkimer, New York, was not doing that well, and Sperry Rand said "We're shutting it down." Well, that was the biggest business in the community, and it would have destroyed Herkimer. Instead, what they did there was very smart. A group of workers, the city council people, and some bankers got together and they basically bought out the company, and the Library Bureau operated as an independent company for another 10 years—not achieving a 22 percent rate of return, but achieving a 17 percent rate of return. But frankly, they could have achieved a zero rate of return—you know, just breaking even—and it would have made sense to keep the plant open.

Now this is very interesting, isn't it? To a private owner of a plant that can move anywhere in the world, they are looking for the highest rate of return. To a community owner, to a local owner, they are just looking for a positive rate of return. So all of this is "wiggle room"—it's room to succeed if you are a local young business.

Now I don't want to be overly ideological about what I mean by local ownership. It comes in many, many different flavors. According to the small business administration, half the U.S. economy is small business and locally owned. Non-profits tend not to have global ambitions. They're 6 percent of the U.S. economy. There are 47,000 successful cooperatives in the U.S. There are 6,300 municipally-owned enterprises. Many of these are oriented—like New Jersey Transit—to transportation or solid waste management, but then you have some oddball cases like in North Dakota with state-wide savings banks. There are worker-owned enterprises that tend not to want to flee and desert their own work forces. Some 2,500 employee stock ownership plans actually hold a majority of the ownership of the companies they are in. There are public-private partnerships, like Burlington Telecommunications. The fact that you have a big public partner means that the company is not going to leave. And then you have my favorite example of local ownership, which is the stock that actually requires that for you to purchase it—whether privately or as part of a public market—you have to be a resident of a given area. When the first issue of Ben and Jerry's stock came out, you had to be a resident of Vermont to buy the stock. Unfortunately, subsequent issues didn't have that restriction on it, and now Ben and Jerry's is owned by Unilever. So, you have got to hold on to that "place" orientation.

An example of a company that has held on to that place orientation is the Green Bay Packers. Green Bay Packers is the only team in the National Football League that is not 100 percent owned by a single individual. As a result, Green Bay is the only team that is not practicing extortion. You have instances like Art Modell, head of the Cleveland Browns, saying "Build me a big stadium, give me a lot of money or I'm out of here." They didn't do it, and he brought the team to Baltimore. Well, this is going on all over the place, but it's not happening to Green Bay because Green Bay is 60 percent owned by the people of Wisconsin. They will never let it become the Baltimore Packers. Now, if this works, if local ownership works for shaping the business behavior of a football team, surely it can work for factories or for banks or for parks. And that is why, again, the summary . . . the bumper sticker I would give you is "Ownership Matters." Local ownership is key to sustainability.

Let me move now to the import substitution piece of LOIS. Import substitution is really a fancy way of saying we want to become self-reliant. We want to gradually get rid of a lot of our outside dependencies on imports and be able to meet as many of our own needs as possible. Why would you want to do that? Well, every time you choose not to buy the local good and service—that is, a good and service that you might be able to do for yourself—three nasty things happen. The first is you become vulnerable to lots of nasty surprises that you have no control over. For example, the fact that we are very dependent on foreign oil means that we have a very strange and problematic foreign policy. The fact that we are dependent on outside imports of beef means that we are now suddenly vulnerable to mad cow disease. There was a wonderful and a scary statistic that the U.S. Department of Agriculture put out about a month ago, saying that last year 6,000 Americans died from *E.coli* and other kinds of contamination in meat. Of that, 80 percent came from imports. That means more people died from imported meat than died at the World Trade Center. So, vulnerability is a very significant problem the more we depend on outside goods and services.

The second problem has to do with a concept called the economic multiplier. To give you an example of what a healthy economic multiplier is: You are all students here at Ramapo, and you spend your dollars on tuition at the college. If you had a healthy multiplier here, the college purchasing agents would say, "We should be spending our money on New Jersey goods and services." So they decide they are going to buy food for the commissary from New Jersey farmers, and those farmers in turn pay tax dollars, and the New Jersey government supports Ramapo. This circle of money is the key to local economic health. The more dollars that circulate, the faster those dollars circulate in a given geographical area, the stronger the economic multiplier, the stronger the job base, the stronger the income, the stronger the wealth.

Now, what would an unhealthy multiplier look like? Same thing we started with—you spend your money with the college, the college goes out and buys food—but instead of buying food from New Jersey, they decide "We're going to buy it from Seattle." So, suddenly Washington State farmers are enjoying all the benefits, and that means the multiplier suddenly starts to go from New Jersey to Washington . . . and whether or not it comes back, no one knows. Where it really goes, ultimately, is to Washington State. So you give a nice tax boost to Washington State!

To put this in a more positive way, the advantages of import substituting development are three-fold: The first is, you minimize your dependency and nasty surprises. The second is, you maximize the economic multiplier. And the third is, you maximize the tax receipts that can support everything that the public sector does, from a university like Ramapo College, to public assistance and health programs.

To give you a sense of the power of this kind of analysis, I have examined some numbers from Vermont. Vermont has done a wonderful import dependency study a few years ago, and what did they find? They found that about $2 billion a year in food expenditure was going to buy food from out of state, which is nutty because Vermont is this great agricultural wonderland! In insurance investments also, nearly $2 billion. Energy, mortgage interest . . . the most interesting number to me is the smallest one: credit card interest. Because there are very few local banks in Vermont, and none of them issue credit cards, people hold credit cards from out of state. The interest payments alone on those credit cards outside of Vermont are $250 million a year. That is $250 million in lost multiplier, and $250 million in lost tax benefits. So, you can see that these are very big and significant numbers here, and that is why import replacement is so critically important for a healthy economy.

Now I want to point out one little caveat here, because a lot of people think that import replacing development means that we are going to become like a feudal kingdom, we are going to build big walls and we are going to pull up the drawbridge, and we are going to be an economy that never touches the rest of the world. That is not what we are talking about here. In fact, an import replacing economy may well experience an increase in imports. I want to explain why that is true.

Let's talk about North Dakota. North Dakota is a state that is pretty dependent on a lot of things. One thing it's dependent on is sources of electricity from outside utilities. So supposing North Dakota says, "We want to be self-reliant in energy." They decide, "We are going to build some wind machines." And lo and behold, the wind machines leave them self-reliant when it comes to electricity. But now they have a new dependency. They had to import wind machines. So North Dakota says, "Hmmm, let's try a substitute for that import. We are going to build our own wind industry." So they build the wind industry, they build their own machine parts, but then they are dependent on outside parts and metal manufacture.

The point is that this process never, ever ends. You will always be dependent on something. But an economy that systematically tries to substitute for imports is continually becoming more diversified, continually getting a larger and larger multiplier and having a healthier and healthier public economy that can't be threatened by the departure of one business or the loss of one kind of good and service. It's totally the opposite strategy of "Hmm, let's figure out the one niche in the world that New Jersey is good at and put all of our eggs in that basket." That is what's going on right now, and it's lunatic because it makes no sense from an economic standpoint.

The only argument that economists raise to this kind of analysis is a question of scale. They say, "Alright, Shuman, it makes sense if we could do everything locally—with local ownership and import substituting development—it would be great to do. The problem is that not every community can build its own automobiles. Not every community can build planes or air conditioners. Therefore, it's impossible for us to conceive of becoming self-reliant because the optimal scale of production is so big for so many goods and services. There is no way any community can become self-reliant." Well, this brings me to the next part of my talk, which is really the essence of the next book I am writing, tentatively titled *Small is Profitable*. What I want to argue in this book is: In fact, economies of scale around the world are shrinking, and whatever data we have from even two or three years ago about economies of scale being very large—they are obsolete, throw them out, because the trends that are occurring right now in the global economy are pushing towards "small" faster than most people understand. And just to pull a couple of examples to give you a sense of what I am talking about here: We used to think that big banks were the most cost-effective financial institutions. We now know from studies by everyone, from the Federal Reserve to the Consumers Union, that regional banks and local banks actually have lower default rates, lower administrative costs, they pay more on savings accounts, they charge less on checking accounts. Sooner or later the consumer is going to wake up to that.

What about energy? We used to get our energy from gigawatt-scale nuclear and coal plants. I guarantee you that in the next 25 years, most of your electricity is going to come from regional wind plants and rooftop floatable voltaics.

Food. We are moving increasingly from Safeway-oriented food delivery to community supported agriculture. I will have more to say about that in a second.

Materials. The way we used to get big materials like metals was a company like Anaconda would go to Africa or Latin America and they would dig big holes and bring that material up north, overthrow a few governments along the way, and then they would process those materials, and *voila!* . . . steel. Well, that is not the way it's done now. The way it's done now is through recycling, through re-use, through value-added activity. That is the way that we are producing cost-effective materials now. And these are fundamentally local and regional industries. Now, these examples may seem like I am pulling some rabbits out of thin air, so let me give you at least ten reasons why economies of scale are shrinking, and why LOIS is a better and better gal to do business with.

The first one is that global distribution of goods and services is really very expensive. It turns out that global production often is cheap, but the distribution is very costly. And food is a great example of that. In the year 1900, when you spent a dollar on food, 40 cents went to the farmer. The rest went to inputs and to distribution. Today when you spend a dollar on food at the Safeway, 9 cents winds up going to the farmer, and 67 cents goes to distribution. By distribution I mean marketing, advertising, packaging, refrigeration, transportation, middle people—stuff that has nothing to do with food. And what you realize is that "You know, if we set up a local food system where a small farmer does business directly with a small buyer, you get rid of all that crap." Even if it's more expensive to make the food, if you get rid of most of that 67 cents of waste right now on a dollar of food, you are delivering cheaper food, and that is why we are seeing around the country, and indeed around the world, a proliferation of community supported agriculture structure, urban farming and farmers' markets. This stuff isn't being driven by people trying to be politically correct, it is being driven by economics. And it's happening in many other fields as well.

Telecommunications, for example. Last year, AT&T decided to split into four companies, because they decided big was bad. British Telecom split into three companies. If you think the distribution costs are expensive now, just wait a couple of years, because the price of oil is pointing up, and as the price of oil goes up, transportation gets more expensive, and global shipment of goods and services gets to be less and less of a bargain.

Cheap oil was the linchpin of the global economy, and that is disappearing. The stock price of West Coast Crude Oil in 1998 was about $12 a barrel; it was $30 a barrel in 2000. It came down after 9/11. The Saudi's gave us a break for a while, but now it's back up again. So roughly, it's not quite tripled over the last four years, but you are getting a sense that the price is definitely moving in that direction. And scarcity is going to, of course, necessarily shrink the supply and raise the price. And this is actually good news for the local economy, not only for the reason that I mentioned—but as oil prices get higher, people are going to conserve more, and conservation is an inherently local activity.

Another thing that is going to happen is people are going to start subsituting for petrochemicals and replace them with biochemicals. Petrochemicals are the biggest pollutants in the world—they are almost everything that we consider a toxic waste! A PCB or some other kind of nasty stuff is somehow related to petrochemicals; that is, the use of oil for plastics or for medicines or for dyes. Well, it turns out that you can actually systematically replace all of that nastily-produced stuff with very environmentally benign kinds of plastics and dyes and so forth by basically converting agriculture and forestry waste into these other biochemical kinds of substances. Already, most newspapers in this country are using soy ink. A large part of the detergent market is using bio materials.

When Henry Ford was thinking about building a new car in the 1930s, he thought he would build the whole thing with vegetable matter. He was going to use ethanol for the fuel, and he was going to make the plastic for the body out of these kind of biologically derived plastics, and then he was going to use goldenrod in the wheels. It never happened because the price of oil plummeted after World War II. But if the price of oil goes up, we are going to see a shift in the economy toward the biochemicals, and the fact is that agricultural and forestry waste is too heavy to drag around. You have to process it near the forest, near the farm where it came from. That means every rural county in this country is going to have an industrial renaissance as they become the new producers of these biochemicals that are the alternative for the petrochemical economy.

A third reason why we are going to experience diminished economy is the scale. Environmentalism is spreading like wildfire. Greens—whether or not you believe in the politics of green, even slightly green people favor local business. They favor it in general, they favor recycling, they favor waste reduction—which are usually local activities. They also favor putting taxes on use of oil, which we are going to call "green taxes," and I will have more to say about that in a little bit. But if we put taxes on various kinds of pollutants and various kinds of energy, it's going to mean that everything I have just been talking about—about the expensive distribution of local goods and services—it is going to get even worse. And as things get more expensive to ship internationally, the advantages to local producers who ship over very small distances are going to get larger and larger.

A fourth phenomenon: niche marketing. Local business that is serving local markets can do better at intuiting, designing, manufacturing flexibly and delivering "just on time" goods and services. There will never be a niche General Mills. General Mills will never deliver fresh bagels to New York, because New Yorkers know what good bagels taste like, and they come from the local bagel producers. The same thing about beer—once you start tasting micro-brews, you stop buying Coors and Bud . . . and micro-breweries are flourishing all around the country.

Financial services. Once the bank realizes, "Gee, it's a lot better if we actually know the people we are making the loans to," we are going to have a better business. That is going to begin to take over the financial services sector. Even automobiles—we are learning how to make automobiles increasingly at a regional level. I think we are going to see the beginning of regional kinds of companies, so there will be a "California Car," there will be a "Northwest" kind of car, there will be an "East Coast" kind of car, and you may well be driving those in the next few years. And this is going to revive industry around the country in very surprising places.

A fifth trend. We know that around the world, that as countries get richer, people spend more of their money on services and less on goods. You know, after you have your 500th refrigerator, you decide "Hmm, maybe I want to do something different with my money." And so we are getting to a saturation point with many kinds of goods that people are buying right now. Don't take my word for this—Paul Krugman, in *Popular Internationalism*, says a steadily rising share of the workforce produces services that are sold only within that same metropolitan area, and that is why most people in Los Angeles produce services for local consumption, and therefore do pretty much the same things as most people in metro New York, or for that matter, London, Paris, and Chicago. Most production, most goods and services, are inherently local. Now people say maybe the Internet is going to change all of that. It will change a little bit of that. I don't know how many of you get your massages over the Internet—there may be one or two in the audience—but most of us like to get our massages from real people in the same room. The same thing about health care or lawyers or accountants. The relationship matters. And because of that, services are always going to be mostly personal, and personal means they are going to be mostly local.

A sixth trend. What matters in the economy these days is not brawn, but brains in several respects. The wealthiest communities in the U.S. are not the biggest ones, they are the smartest ones—Silicon Valley or Redmond, Washington. The smartest companies are not the biggest companies, they are companies that wisely use machines. The little computer I use is my publications business. And I fit on this publications business. I have an administrative division, known as an Excel spreadsheet and QuickBooks; I have a design division in my company which is one of those newsletter design programs; I have a secretarial force in my computer known as a word processing program; I've got a whole data management division known as Access. And my point is that you can fit what used to be several dozen staff on your own computer and work from home. That means that many companies that used to be very big and require a lot of people now can be very small if you use technology wisely.

Another thing that is happening is that we used to think that wealth was associated with the use of a lot of materials, and because of that you had to build near the mine. Because if you were, say, in the Pacific northwest and there were a lot of aluminum smelters, then all the aluminum industries like Aerospace had to be built near these factories. Well, now products depend less and less on materials, or less and less at least on bulk materials.

Let me show you some interesting patterns here. Starting from the 1800s and going to the present, the amount of any material that we are using per unit of gross national product (GNP) has decreased. You can see we became peak steel users around 1910—the year of Andrew Carnegie—and then we have been using successively less and less steel since then. Cement peaked around the year of Joe Stalin, in the early 1930s, and we have chlorine peaking in the 1970s. Then we kind of woke up to the environmental problems with that. Ammonia peaked a little after that. Aluminum peaked also in the 1970s. And this is true—you could look at any given bulk material here and it's the same pattern. We are learning how to use fewer and fewer materials in order to produce more and more wealth. That is environmentally a very good and smart thing to do, but it also means that any company, anywhere in the world, can produce a whole range of things that they weren't able to before.

Trend number seven. People are shrinking subsidies. Now there are maybe some people in here that like subsidies, that think it's good to support business with government money; but if you believe as I do that small is important for well being, then you hate nearly all subsidies, because virtually all subsidies go for big business. Every year there's a report of a group called the "Green Scissors," which is a coalition of Friends of the Earth and other environmentalists on the left, and the National Taxpayers Union and other right-wingers, and basically they try to identify what are all the subsidies that are bad for the environment and bad for efficiency. And they find tens of billions of dollars a year. One of their recent studies found $21 billion going to big oil, gas and nuclear. Big money and timber, $5 billion a year. Big water projects, $8 billion a year. Big agribusiness, $5 billion a year. (We mostly got rid of that subsidy in the last Farm Bill.) Big highways, $13 billion a year. You wipe out those subsidies like both the left and right want to do—small business will have a revolution! I think it's going to happen relatively soon. I think the days of these subsidies are numbered, and it's good news for community development.

Trend number eight. It turns out that when people are given a choice between buying local and buying global, they actually usually buy local—all other things being equal. Maybe they are kind of wising up to that stuff about the local multiplier and the local tax base. But to give you an example of this, a couple of years back in Pennsylvania they were trying to evaluate what would be the impact of our giving consumers the option to buy green power. Green power would come from local windmills or other environmentally benign sources, and it would cost more than conventional power. They projected that in the first year, only 3,000 Pennsylvanians would power-switch from regular electricity to the more expensive local "green" electricity. In fact, 100,000 people power-switched, and around the country every time there has been this kind of shift, the officials have been surprised at how many people want to go local. We're seeing this in the spread of local money systems that encourage people to buy local; we are seeing this in the spread of community reinvestment institutions, which I will say more about in a couple of minutes.

Trend number nine. Large businesses are dreadful places to work, and that is one reason why more and more people, myself included, are working out of a home. There are 20 million people who are working at home these days. That is double the number from 10 years ago. You know, if a community wants to take seriously creating an industrial park, the way to create an industrial park is not to create a huge zone where Toyota locates. An industrial park is changing all the zoning laws that get in the way of home businesses, and then the whole city becomes an industrial park consistent with the way people live.

Trend number ten. Terrorism. Community self-reliance is a wonderful antidote to terrorism in two ways. The first is that small is not only beautiful, but small is not a very likely target for a terrorist attack. The second thing is that if you don't have a lot of long supply lines that you are depending on for goods and services, then there's nothing that you can be hurt by if there's an act of sabotage or there's a war that goes on. You become invulnerable by becoming more self-reliant. Now, it's interesting that *The Wall Street Journal* about a month after 9/11, on the front page in a column called

"Capital" which comes out once a week, had the following quote. It said "Even before terrorists leveled the World Trade Center, economic and technological forces were combining to decentralize the economy. September 11th will only reinforce these centrifugal forces." So all these things together are pushing to decentralize the economy. The horizon of small business opportunities is expanding every single day, and that is why I think we need to think seriously about how we get on the lowest train—the locally-owned, import substituting train—to take advantage of it as soon as possible to help our own communities.

That leads me to the last part of what I want to talk about, which is how LOIS can be courted—five easy pieces, five strategies that we can use in order to promote LOIS—and they have to do with local planning, local skill-building, local purchasing, local investing and local policymaking.

Local planning. The goal of local planning needs to be to identify and seize all LOIS business opportunities. There are a lot of different ways we can do that. The first way, I think, is every community needs to define its own "Bill of Rights." Remeber those questions I mentioned earlier? The what, the how, the who of production? Now, if you, as "Mahwah," were to get together and try to answer these questions, your answers would be a lot different than Lovett, Texas. That is a good thing. You need to figure out what your answers to those questions are, and then I would suggest start evaluating all the businesses in the area, and those that rose to the standards that you defined as being high would get a "Good Community-keeping Seal of Approval," and that would help to target people's purchases and people's investments.

The second kind of activity related to planning—why not evaluate all of the assets in your community that are potentially usable for small business. Assets are, of course, labor, capital and land—and it's not just the positives, because abandoned land is potentially usable land. Shut down factories, obsolete equipment is potentially reusable equipment if you refurbish it properly. Unemployed people are potentially employable people. So one needs to look at the full range of assets out there that are deployable for new small business.

The third kind of thing we need to do is find those import dependencies. Here is an example of a study that Oakland did in 1979. They, like Vermont, tried to take a look: "Well, what are the leaks in our economy?" They found three interesting leaks. Outside landlords were getting $43 million a year from local tenants. Outside banks were getting $40 million a year from local mortgage holders. And $150 million a year was going from consumers to outside retailers. So they learned something very important from this study. If we are serious about improving the economy of Oakland, we need more locally-owned retail. We need more locally-owned homes, and more locally-owned banks, actually, to help people buy those homes.

Now, what's interesting is that only three cities in one state have performed this analysis. There are 36,000 municipalities in the United States. That means almost no one has done this, and if you don't do this there is no way you can possibly know whether or not anything you are doing in terms of economic development makes any sense. That is what's so crazy in economic development right now. I mean, people are saying "Let's throw some money over here on a stadium, throw money over here on a factory," and *voila*, there is some economic activity which you have no idea whether if you used that same money for something else, you could do even more with that. The only way you can judge that is by looking at what all the local alternatives are for that expenditure of money.

The fourth kind of planning exercise for a community is to assess subsidies. There is a prevailing view right now that communities have no money; states have no money. This is wrong! They have a lot of money that they are spending on business development right now. They are just spending it on all the wrong things: stadiums, football teams, convention centers, Wal-Mart sites, industrial parks, big highways . . . and the most recent favorite, casinos. None of these things make any sense, because none of them are locally owned and none of them are related to import substituting development. We need to systematically screen subsidies for LOIS. Every grant, every loan, every loan guarantee, every capital improvement, every tax abatement, every bond issue, should only go to those businesses that are locally owned and import substituting. And even then . . . even then, I would open up every subsidy to a public bidding process to make absolutely sure that the best local businesses got subsidies.

The second kind of activity we should be doing is local skill-building. Here the goal is to mobilize and nurture entrepreneurs to focus on LOIS business opportunities. A couple of thoughts about how we might do that: The first is to set up an inventory of experts in the community. I visited my parents in Florida a couple of weeks ago, and every time I go there it's such a depressing experience to see thousands of elderly people doing nothing but watching television and going to the beach. I mean, these are wasted lives! Retirement should be the point when the expertise that you have is linked to those who are just getting started in society. We should be linking young and old together to give more value to elderly and to give all of that information, all of that knowledge and wisdom, renewed life in young people. One place where they did this is, believe it or not, Kerala, India. They have a program called "Life Begins at 55," and basically the program creates a comprehensive inventory of retirees and links them, profession by profession, field by field, with young business people getting started. No reason why you can't be doing that here in New Jersey!

Another thing that we need is business schools with attitude, business schools that take LOIS seriously. There was a study done in Cornell a few years back looking at the relative charitability of business and economic students, and they found that the first year's donations on average equalled all of the other graduate students put together. Now, people were surprised by that result, so they went back and did another study. This time they looked at all the graduate students, and what they found is after the first year the charitability of business and economic students declined, scraping bottom when they became full professors. Something is fundamentally wrong with these fields when they are promoting that kind of anti-charitability attitude. So I suggest we need to build business schools from scratch—new, community-friendly business schools.

To give you an example where it was done, Mondragon, Spain—late 40s, early 50s—six unemployed steel workers got together and set up a community school. They taught one another from scratch how to build businesses, how to manage people, how to deal with finances. Today Mondragon is 160 interlinked cooperatives with an annual product of $8 billion a year. That all grew out of a smart community business school. It could happen here.

The next idea is incubators. Incubators are basically places where you can do focused mentorship. As you know, food industries require big pieces of equipment, they require special kinds of licenses, so it's hard for small food businesses to get up and running. But an incubator provides those businesses with all of the equipment, for free or for cheap. There are also non-profit incubators, like the Tides Center in San Francisco.

A fourth idea is trying to get rid of the drain brain. I think that it would be interesting if a community created a scholarship fund that basically said, "Look, we understand that you may not want to go to college here inside the community, but we are going to give you this great scholarship, or great low-interest (or no-interest) loan, on one condition. You've got to come back here after you graduate and work here for five to ten years and pay taxes here." To me that seems like a really good idea, or a really good deal, and yet there are no place restrictions these days on any scholarship. It doesn't make any sense.

Another item. Local purchasing. And here the goal is, we want to encourage and help residents and businesses alike to buy local. There are lots of ways we can do this. One simple way is to create a directory. Here's a directory that the state of Massachusetts produces of all local food producers in Massachusetts. They basically market Massachusetts-grown. I am now in the middle of preparing a "Buy Annapolis" directory for the state capital of Maryland. We have just dropped a 5,000-piece mailing that goes to all businesses in Annapolis, and we are just asking them one question: "Are you a majority-owned company whose owners live within Annapolis or live within the surrounding county?" And by asking that question, we are going to then create a booklet that will give people an idea of where they can buy food or hardware or anything else in order to honor locally-owned business.

The second idea is creating relationships between businesses—"B2B Brokering." There is a group of businesses in Switzerland called "Wir." It involves 60,000 businesses, and these businesses all, when they join Wir, get a list of the other businesses inside. They get a special currency, a special set of discounts, and it basically is a system that encourages businesses, all geographically defined, to buy and sell from one another. The state of Oregon did this in the early 1980s. It was something called the Marketplace. They basically said, "Hmm . . . we want to promote import replacement by businesses in the state. How do we do that?" We are going to go to this business here that is manufacturing flags. "Oh, it turns out you're importing cloth. What if we can find you a producer of cloth inside Oregon—same price, same quality—would you do it?" Always, the answer is "yes." So they would make the deal, and then the cloth producer in Oregon would pay a finder's fee to Oregon Marketplace. It's a very clever arrangement. At its peak in the early 1990s, it was doing $40 million of import replacement contract work a year. That is certainly something you can be doing in New Jersey as well.

Another great way of encouraging people to buy local is through local money. Local money comes in many ways. It can come through computer debits and credits, that's the LETS system. It can come through printed money like the Ithaca Hours. (Ithaca thought that its boat had really come in when a crook went to the local credit union which deals in local currency and said "Your money or your life, and I only want local currency!") And it also comes in the form of time dollars. Time dollars is a way of getting people to exchange voluntary hours with one another.

What's interesting about local currency is one important fact. Wal-Mart will never take it, because the purpose of Wal-Mart is to systematically take dollars from our community and send those dollars to Arkansas, to the Walton family. Local currency has exactly the opposite purpose. When that money goes to a local vendor, it's then re-spent in the local economy, because it only has value within the local economy. So as a kind of a crude screen about what business is locally friendly and what business isn't—if they take the local currency, they are a friendly business.

A fourth way of promoting local buying is through the selective use of state and county and local government contracts. Government contracting is a business that is greater than $1 trillion a year—it's huge! And if you just take a piece of that purchasing behavior and say "Alright, we're going to try to get all public institutions in New Jersey to buy New Jersey," you are going to make a huge difference for the local economy. Mayor Harold Washington, whose picture I have here, was Mayor in Chicago in the mid-1980s, tried to do "Buy Chicago" for the local purchasing and was able, I think, to get a big boost in the local economy by channeling more and more of the city's purchasing to local goods and services providers.

The fourth kind of activity—local investing. Here the goal is to encourage and help residents and businesses to save and invest locally. And there are a lot of ways that this can be done. As many of you know, there is an Act, a Federal Act called the Community Reinvestment Act, that requires banks to disclose certain amounts of information each year that can help us determine whether or not they are reinvesting in the community. Well, this information is good, but it's not great—you can do better than that. The city of Burlington, Vermont, actually required a lot more information out of their local banks, a lot more disclosure to determine just which ones were community friendly. You can build local banks. You can either do that directly by building a credit union that only reinvests locally, or a commercial bank like the Southshore Bank, that primarily reinvests locally. Or you can do what, say, the state of Pennsylvania does. The State of Pennsylvania took $100 million of state pension money and put it into certificates of deposit in small community-friendly banks around the state, so basically they were able to support the strengthening and the expansion of community banks in the state this way.

Now it turns out that banking is only a tiny fraction of savings in this country. Five out of six dollars that are saved are in the form of stocks, bonds, insurance funds, mutual funds, so we have to find a way to get those things to reinvest locally. And here we are really in kindergarten—there aren't many good examples of this. There are a few state funds—Michigan has a strategic fund where they allocated $21 million of state money and basically were able to attract $70 million of private money, all to invest in Michigan-oriented businesses. The better example is in Canada. There are four provinces in Canada that have what are called Lever-sponsored investment funds. These were started by the unions in these provinces that hold the pension funds up as unions, but you don't have to be just a union member in order to be reinvesting your pension monies. An outsider like me could put my money in this labor-sponsored fund. And here's the real kicker—they reinvest all of their money in labor and environmentally-friendly businesses owned within the provinces. The other kicker is that you get a little tax credit when you put your money into those funds. If New Jersey was able to give a tax credit for a labor-sponsored investment fund, you would do an incredible service in encouraging people to reinvest locally.

Then, of course, there are public pension funds. I have Nelson Mandela's picture here, because this man became free because of creative use of public pension monies. I don't know how many of you remember, but in the mid-1980s basically half the states, 100 cities, determined that their public pension funds would no longer go to businesses that were doing business in South Africa. That shift in policy created a revolution in South Africa, and ultimately the end of apartheid. If we can now not just put a negative screen on investment—we hate apartheid, we hate the bigger power—and start putting positive screens, we will favor locally-owned businesses. It can have a tremendous impact on community development.

The last thing I want to talk just briefly about is local policymaking. I could give you several hundred examples of where local government can mobilize the government to steer community economies from TINA to LOIS, but I just want to give you a couple of things that I think are most interesting.

One is the living wage. You know we have a minimum wage in this country. If you work 40 hours a week and you earn minimum wage, you are declared to be in poverty! So we have a lot of poor people in this country who are working. We've got to increase the minimum wage to above the poverty line! So many people are talking a living wage of about $10 a hour. One argument against the living wage is that it's inflationary, it will raise prices, that small businesses can't afford it. Well, in Vermont they did a nice study of what would be the cost, what would happen to prices if we insisted that everyone in the state got $10 a hour. They found that in every sector of the economy but one, the price rise would be under 1 percent . . . and the one exception was fast food! There, at McDonald's, you would have a 4 percent rise in prices. So here's a question: Would you be willing to pay less than 1 percent for all goods and services except your Big Mac, and there you would spend 4 percent more to eliminate working poverty in your state? To me this is a "no brainer," because the situation we have right now is a bunch of bad businesses that are getting subsidized by good businesses that are paying dirt cheap wages. We've got to stop that, and a living wage is a good way to do that.

Green taxes. I believe these are the waves of the future. You know, now the tax system is really crazy. We tax labor in the form of wage taxes, we tax capital in a variety of ways, but capital and labor are the things we want to encourage! How about taxing things we don't want? We don't want pollution, we don't want people to use a lot of energy and other things that are scarce resources, so why not put taxes on those things? Well, that is what green taxes are all about.

An example of green taxes at work is bottle bills, and these are great examples of green taxes. But we need to put green taxes on pesticides and fertilizers, we need to put green taxes on all kinds of energy use, on tobacco use. That will be a real revolutionary shift in the way that we structure the public sector.

Zoning reform. Many of you are probably familiar with the new urbanesque movement. Their tenets are simple. We will make better use of our communities if we don't keep tearing up forests to build subdivisions, and instead have denser communities and have more diversity in the community. So, actually I can walk to my store, or walk to school, or walk to a stadium. Right now the way that we do zoning, you have to drive absolutely everywhere, and it's terrible for the environment. And it means you have under-used kinds of communities. You have residential areas that are like Death Valley by day and busy at night; you have commercial areas that are busy by day, Death Valley by night. We need to bring these things together.

Last, lobbying. I believe that we have to push the federal government in a lot of the directions that I have just talked about. There's a reason why communities and states have gotten creamed over the last 20 years—creamed versus businesses, that is—and that is they don't have any lobbyists! I did a survey a few years ago of how many registered lobbyists local and state governments have—they had 116. Remember, 36,000 municipalities, 50 states . . . you know, several thousand counties . . . and we have 116 registered lobbyists representing all of them? Boeing has more than that! You know, it's easy to see why we are losing at the lobbying day right now.

Well, let me bring this all to a conclusion here and basically make three final points. The first is that everything on my "to do" list that I just shared with you can be done by groups—by campus groups! They don't require big-time expense, big-time government action. You can do all the studies and planning initiatives I was talking about. You could do all the skill-building initiatives I was mentioning, you could start your own local currency and promote local purchasing, you could start your own reinvestment institutions. Or you can even push for a variety of policy changes. Government participation is helpful—it brings money, it brings legitimacy, it brings speed—but if government's not playing ball, you should carry the ball down the field yourselves!

The second point I would make is that, as Kenneth Boulding once said, "Anything that exists is possible." I have not given you anything in this talk that is a hypothetical. Every example that I have given you is real and is occurring somewhere. The problem is that these things aren't taking place together in one city or one state, and that is what really needs to shift. You know, it's easy to take a local currency experiment or a community bank and say, "You know, this 'Ithaca Hours' isn't going to change very much," or "This community credit union isn't going to make a difference in the global economy," and it's true. But you have to start putting these things together. Local ownership, side by side with local purchasing, local investing, local business training, local policy that is supportive of all this stuff . . . just start putting all these things together and then you have a powerful alternative to the global economy.

I believe that you have an important first step in all of this. Most of you sitting in this audience are students. Most of you have to write papers, you have to do research projects. Why not just take one project over the next year and make it relevant to this agenda? Try to pick one piece of the local economy that you want to study and that you want to put together, because you folks can make it happen!

There are some great historic epics that we've had in the last couple of hundred years. In the 18th century, many people challenged the rights of kings with democracy. In the 19th century, we overthrew the institution of slavery. In the 20th century, human rights came to the fore, both for women and people of color. The 21st century is going to be a monumental struggle between the advocates of cheap goods and those who believe in place—and by place I mean favoring families, communities, and ecosystems. Right now those who favor cheap goods run both political parties—they are in power— and they have convinced us that our happiness can be found in the next sale at a shopping mall. Now, I find a little bit of happiness at a sale in a shopping mall, but the family and the community and the ecology come first, and what we need to do is we need to transform today's dissidents into tomorrow's leaders. There is no better place to start than here! As Gandhi said, "Every step is insignificant, but it's still very important that you take it."

LAND ETHICS AND
PUBLIC FINANCE POLICY
AS IF PEOPLE AND PLANET
MATTERED

Alanna Hartzok *

Evaggelos Vallianatos, reflecting in an article for *Progressive Populist* called "Why Small Farmers Are Essential to Democracy," said, "When democracy thrived in Greece, so did farming. The two were inseparable." He noted that it was not the philosophers who laid the foundations for ancient Greek democracy but those who worked very small plots of land. To Vallilanatos, "Democracy was the Greek smallholders' answer to tyranny" and the "genius of Greek civilization." He well remembers the joys and pleasures of childhood on the small Greek farm where he grew up. But he also remembers, "My father's farming was wrecked when the Americans converted Greece to agribusiness."[1]

Unlike Vallianatos, most of us are born landless, without any real place to be or any memories of the land as sustainer. For most of us, our parents were renting or making mortgage payments while we were growing up. They did the best they could, then we were launched into the world of labor. While some of us never made it to the first rung of the ladder, others found employment as highly skilled laborers. Usually, the more highly skilled a laborer is, the further removed he or she is from the land. Yet that which all laborers need to survive comes, ultimately, from the earth itself.

By some estimates, at least 60 percent of the land value in western countries is in the hands of one percent of the population. In 1990, the value of all land in the United States was put at $3.7 trillion.[2] By now that number is likely to be more than $6 trillion, although the federal government no longer tracks land ownership and values. Apparently such numbers are too politi-

*Adapted from a Presentation at the Richard Alsina Fulton Conference on Sustainability and the Environment, March 26–27, 2004, Wilson College, Chambersburg, PA.

cally sensitive. In Florida, one percent of the population owns 77 percent of the land. Other states where the top one percent own over two-thirds of the land are Maine, Arizona, California, Nevada, New Mexico, and Oregon.[3]

Calculations by the Urban Land Institute show that more than half of all corporate earnings are generated by real estate and real estate-related activities.[4] Control of 22 percent of our private land, an area the size of Spain, is held by 568 companies. Those same companies' land interests worldwide comprise a total area larger than that of Europe—almost two billion acres.

John Mohawk fully grasped the problem of our land tenure system. He said, "When land became a 'commodity' and lost its status as provider and sustainer of life, Western civilization began its history of subjugation and exploitation of the earth and earth based cultures.[5] Today, this subjugation and exploitation is eroding middle-class America as well. As working people take on substantial amounts of debt to buy their small house plots, the wealth gap that exists in this country is further widened.

We are on the threshold of the second American revolution. Either we will be in bondage, or we will build an economic democracy based firmly on the most basic principle—that the Earth belongs equally to everyone as a birthright. We must find the way and quickly using the non-violent approach taught by Thoreau, Gandhi and King. And we need to proceed towards this goal now. The forces benefiting from concentration of wealth and power have nearly overpowered us.

These are not new ideas or concerns. At the time of the first American Revolution, Thomas Jefferson gave us a first principle ethic when he said, "The earth is given as a common stock for men to labor and live on." Tom Paine also gave us a policy approach to the problem of escalating land values when he said, "Men did not make the earth. . . . It is the value of the improvement only, and not the earth itself, that is individual property. . . . Every proprietor owes to the community a ground rent for the land which he holds."

Early political economists had also begun to grasp the problem and the solution. John Stuart Mill was aware that "Landlords grow richer in their sleep without working, risking, or economizing. The increase in the value of land, arising as it does from the efforts of an entire community, should belong to the community and not to the individual who might hold title."[6]

More than a century ago Henry George had this insight: "Our primary social adjustment is a denial of justice. In allowing one man to own the land on which and from which other men must live, we have made him a bondsmen in a degree which increases as material progress goes on. It is this that turns the blessings of material progress into a curse."[7]

During the past one hundred years, governments have been destabilized and wars have been fought over land and natural resources in Indonesia, Viet Nam, Iran, Iraq, Nigeria, Chile, El Salvador, Nicaragua, Guatemala and many other small countries. We have seen oil conflicts in the Persian Gulf, the Caspian Sea Basin, Nigeria and the South China Sea and water conflicts in the Nile Basin, the Jordan, Tigris-Euphrates and Indus River Basins. Internal wars have been or are being fought over minerals and timber in Angola, Sierra Leone, Liberia, the Congo, Bougainville/Papua New Guinea, Borneo, Brazil and Indonesia. Hostilities over valuable gems, minerals and timber are under way in Angola, Brazil, Burma, Cambodia, Columbia, Congo, Indonesia, Liberia and the Philippines.

In his book, *Resource Wars*, Michael Klare astutely observes: "What we are seeing is the emergence of a new geography of conflict—a global landscape in which competition over vital resources is becoming the governing principle behind the disposition and use of military power.... The result is a new strategic geography in which resource concentrations rather than political boundaries are the major defining features."[8]

To remedy this injustice we must first understand the land problem. What if, instead of concentrated ownership, we were to find a way to share the Earth? What if we, instead, were to find a way to end tax tyranny and align our visions and values with how we finance government?

One possible way to do this is being developed by ecological economists who are attempting to cost the Earth—to put a dollar value on the services the planet provides. The value of services provided by the Earth is, as we might suspect, in the multi-trillions of dollars. Geonomic economists are calculating resource rents—the market value of surface land and natural resources—and are finding that for the U.S. the amount could be as much as half of GDP. Visionary philosophers say these sums represent our common heritage and should profit the many, not the few. A prophet once said, as recorded in Ecclesiastes (5:9), "The profit of the earth is for all."

In 1996, the United Nations Center for Human Settlements (UNCHS) issued a global agenda for ensuring access to land which weaves together person/planet concerns. This document, adopted by consensus of all UN member states, states in part that "Access to land and legal security of tenure are strategic prerequisites for the provision of adequate shelter for all and for the development of sustainable human settlements affecting both urban and rural areas. . . . The failure to adopt, at all levels, appropriate rural and urban land policies . . . remains a primary cause of inequity and poverty. It is also the cause of increased living costs, the occupation of hazard-prone land, environmental degradation and the increased vulnerability of urban and rural habitats, affecting all people...."[9]

Among many policies, the UNCHS document recommends the following three:

- Apply transparent, comprehensive and equitable fiscal incentive mechanisms, as appropriate, to stimulate the efficient, accessible and environmentally sound use of land

- Consider the adoption of innovative instruments that capture gains in land value and recover public investments

- Develop land codes and legal framework that define the nature of land and real property and the rights that are formally recognized[10]

Decades earlier, another international conference produced a document which provided such a land code and framework that defined land rights. "The International Declaration on Individual and Common Rights to Land" states that the Earth is the common heritage of all and that all people have natural and equal rights to the land of the planet. The term "land" encompasses all natural resources.

An economic rent placed on all natural resources can be collected for the use of the community by methods similar to those by which real estate taxes are now collected. This is what is meant by Land Value Taxation—the collection of taxes on community-created land value would result in the abolishment of the many taxes which impede the production of wealth and limit purchasing power.

The exercise of both common and individual rights in land is essential to a society based on justice. But the rights of individuals in natural resources are limited by the just rights of the community. Denying the existence of common rights in land creates a condition of society wherein the exercise of individual rights becomes impossible for the great mass of the people.

These two important international documents lay out how we can build economic democracy based on the equal right of all to the land and resources of the planet. They give us both the ethics and the policies whereby the Earth can be secured as the birthright of all people. They carry forward the previously quoted democratic Earth Rights ideas of Paine, Mill, and George. Several progressive think tanks[11] are developing public finance frameworks—sometimes called "green taxation policy"—which are fundamentally based on the ethic and policies of these two important international documents.

Green tax reform makes a clear distinction between private property and common property. Private property is that which is created by labor. Common property is that which is provided by nature. Green tax policy removes taxes from wages and other private property and increases taxes and user fees on common property. Reducing taxes on labor increases purchasing capacity, reducing taxes on capital encourages efficiency. Shifting taxes to land and resources curbs speculation and private profiteering in our common property and is a practical way to conserve and fairly share the earth. Captured in brief sound bites, you could hear: "Tax waste, not work; tax bads, not goods; pay for what you take, not what you make; and the polluter pays." These become tax shift principles readily translated into voter-friendly policy recommendations which could win broad-based political support.

Green tax policy seeks to eliminate subsidies that are environmentally or socially harmful, unnecessary, or inequitable. Proposed for drastic reduction or complete removal by tax cut campaigns are subsidies for:

- Energy production
- Resource extraction
- Commerce and industry
- Agriculture and forestry
- Weapons of mass destruction

Green tax policy aims to eliminate taxes on:

- Wages and earned income
- Productive and sustainable capital
- Sales, especially for basic necessities
- Homes and other buildings

Green tax policy would increase taxes and fees, thus capturing resource rents, on:

- Emissions into air, water, or soil
- Land sites according to land value
- Lands used for timber, grazing, mining
- Ocean and freshwater resources
- Electromagnetic spectrum
- Satellite orbital zones
- Oil and minerals

These tax policies both enhance the power of the people as a whole and trigger environmental improvements. One of the first examples of environmental tax reform as a two-pronged incentive strategy—raising taxes on the use of resources while decreasing taxes on income—was in 1991 when Sweden began levying a carbon dioxide tax and, in conjunction with it, cut the income tax. Other countries followed Sweden's lead, as Denmark, Spain, the Netherlands, the United Kingdom, and Finland cut taxes on personal income and wages and raised taxes on motor fuel, coal, electricity, water, waste, carbon emissions, pesticide, natural gas, and other energy sales. These were small shifts to be sure, with the largest being Denmark, which eco-shifted 2.5 percent of total tax revenues.

In the U.S., J. Andrew Hoerner, a senior research scholar with the Center for a Sustainable Economy, a nonprofit public interest research organization based in Washington, DC, has compiled a "Survey of State Initiatives" detailing 462 environmental tax provisions currently in place at the state level. "We are still learning how to design environmental taxes and tax incentives, and many current approaches to environmental taxation will surely be found wanting," says Hoerner. "But there is a danger in a rush to judgment, in trying to impose a single theoretical paradigm on the immense diversity of emerging instruments."

Movements are underway in several countries to collect increasing amounts of resource rents for public benefits. The Alaska Permanent Fund is an excellent example of a transparent, public institution which collects and distributes resource rents for the people as a whole. Under the Alaska Constitution, all the natural resources of Alaska belong to the state to be used, developed and conserved for the maximum benefit of the people. The Alaska Permanent Fund was established in 1976 as a state institution with the task of responsibly administering and conserving oil royalties and other resource royalties for the citizenry. The principal of the Fund is invested permanently and cannot be spent without a vote of the people.

In 1980, the Alaskan Legislature created the Permanent Fund Dividend Program to distribute each year a portion of the income from the Permanent Fund to eligible Alaskans as direct personal dividend payments. Individuals who received the annual dividends each year from 1982 to 2003 have received a total of more than $20,000. Alaska is the only state where the wealth gap decreased during the past decade. There is strong citizen interest in the Fund's operation and activities. The Alaska Permanent Fund website (www.apfc.org) tracks all of its investment and distribution activities and posts stories, puzzles and games for teachers to use in their classes to educate their students about the Fund.

The Alaska Permanent Fund is a well managed and transparent Earth Rights institution. It is a remarkable pioneering model for a fair and effective way of securing common heritage wealth benefits for the people as a whole. However, the challenges of global warming and non-renewable resource depletion dictates that oil and other non-renewable resource rents should be invested in socially and environmentally responsible ways—primarily in the needed transition to renewable energy technologies.

The handful of non-renewable resource rent funds in the world should be citizen empowered to both increase their resource rents and royalties and should transition towards capturing from surface land site values substantial resource rents, called ground rent, and other permanent and sustainable sources of rent, such as hydropower points, electromagnetic spectrum and satellite orbital zones. Resource rent funds should be established worldwide from the local to the global level.

Cities in Pennsylvania have been pioneering ways and means of capturing the value of land for public benefits. Civic officials in 20 municipalities are decreasing taxes on buildings, which encourages improvements and renovations, and increasing taxes on land values, which discourages land speculation, encourages good site use, and expands access to more affordable land. Shifting the tax burden from buildings to land values promotes a more efficient use of urban infrastructure and recaptures the values that society creates. The benefits of development can be broadly shared when housing maintains affordability and public coffers are solvent.

Pennsylvania's capitol city of Harrisburg was near insolvency in 1980 when it began to shift to land value tax; now this city of about 55,000 people taxes land values six times more than buildings. Harrisburg's mayor, Stephen Reed, writes, "The City of Harrisburg continues in the view that a land value taxation system, which places a much higher tax rate on land than on improvements, is an important incentive for the highest and best use of land.... With over 90 percent of the property owners in the City of Harrisburg, (this) tax system actually saves money over what would otherwise be a single tax system that is currently in use in nearly all municipalities in Pennsylvania.... Harrisburg was considered the second most distressed in the United States twelve years ago under Federal "distressed city" criteria. Since then, over $1.2 billion in new investment has occurred here, reversing nearly three decades of very serious decline. None of this happened by accident and a variety of economic development initiatives and policies were created and utilized. The (land value tax) system has been and continues to be one of the key local policies that has been factored into this initial economic success here."

There are many more examples of the successful implementation of resource rent and green tax policy approaches than can be mentioned in this paper. Movements for land value taxation and resource rent for revenue are now underway in other states and in England, Scotland, South Korea, Russia, Nigeria, Namibia, Australia and Venezuela. Historically, versions of this public finance approach have resulted in substantial land reforms in Taiwan, Japan and the central valley of California.

Green tax reform is a comprehensive, holistic framework and could become a universally accepted approach to public finance policy. The policies and principles of green tax reform can provide the underpinnings for worldwide economic democracy. Freedom to live or work in any part of the globe would also further equality of entitlement to the planet.

Green tax policy provides a basis for the resolution of resource wars and territorial conflicts. There would be no more private profit as unearned income from Earth's resources. Instead, transparent and accountable resource agencies would collect resource rents and distribute those funds in public services or as direct citizen dividends. With fundamental democracy in rights to the Earth firmly established through legal means and mandates, basic needs would be secured for all and the militarized national security state and its bloated budgets could wither away.

Full resource rents from surface land would eliminate the need for land mortgages as land could be secured on the basis of a simple annual fee according to land value. No other charges would fall on the backs of labor and thus wages and purchasing capacity would increase. Secure private home ownership would be the rule. Labor with access to affordable land would produce quality affordable housing for all.

It has been calculated that nearly half of corporate profits comes from real estate related activities. A tax on land would thus fall heavily on corporate-held lands which cannot escape from taxation via offshore accounts and other tax shelters. With the power of the people focused laser-like on the task of taxing monopolistic land holdings, corporate rule would erode. Labor would gain affordable access to land resources and capital. The products of labor on land would increasingly be owned and controlled by voluntary cooperative organizations. The removal of federal subsidies for agribusiness combined with affordable land access will give a great impetus to organic, sustainable agriculture.

Green tax policy is a mechanism for full cost recovery of environmental damages. Permission to extract the community's resources or to use water or air would be the advanced payment of environmental security deposits. While heavy pollution taxes would drastically increase incentives for clean technologies, the environmental security deposits would only be returned if the land resource was left in an acceptably healthy condition.[12]

There is a huge task ahead of us. The incentives inherent in the world's taxation systems currently promote waste, war, environmental damage, and the concentration of wealth. Approximating the composition of the world's $7.5-trillion tax pie reveals that 93 percent of taxes fall on work while only 3 percent is collected from environmentally damaging activities. A mere 4 percent of global tax revenues is captured from natural resource use and access fees. A modest global tax shift scenario proposed by David Roodman at Worldwatch would collect 15 percent from environmental damage and 12 percent from land use and resource royalties, a total of $900 billion each year, while cutting environmentally harmful subsidies by 90 percent. This would free up an additional 8 percent of current revenues, $600 billion, and permit a nearly one-third reduction in taxes on wages and capital to 65 percent of total global taxes.[13]

Public finance legislation is underway in several states based on green tax shift calculations done by Northwest Environment Watch for the Pacific Northwest. [14]

The planet and all its resources of land, water, forests, minerals, the atmosphere, electro-magnetic frequencies, and even satellite orbits are the common heritage of all and must no longer be appropriated for the private profit of a few to the exclusion of the many. As we place this fundamentally just Earth Rights ethic within a fully established green tax agenda, the profits of the Earth will benefit the people and the planet and secure an age of peace and plenty for all.

Endnotes

[1]   E.G. Vallianatos, "Why Small Farmers Are Essential to Democracy," *The Progressive Populist*, August 1-15, 2002, p. 6.

[2]   J. W. Smith, *Economic Democracy: The Political Struggle of the Twenty-First Century*, 3rd edition, p. 309.

[3]   United States Senator Jesse Helms read these facts and figures into the *Congressional Record* in 1981 as his way of "proving" that there was no need for land reform in the U.S. as land is more concentrated in ownership in the U.S. than in Central America where the U.S. was waging wars against those seeking land reform.

[4]   Urban Land Institute, *America's Real Estate*, 1997, p. 14.

[5]   John Mohawk," The Problem of the Modern World," *CREATION*, May/June, p. 18.

[6]   Eli Siegel, essay on Ownership: Some Moments in *The Right of Aesthetic Realism to be Known*, a periodical of the Aesthetic Realism Foundation, May 5, 1999.

[7]   Henry George, *Social Problems*, Robert Schalkenbach Foundation, p. 202.

8   Michael T. Klare, *Resource Wars: The New Landscape of Global Conflict* (New York, Henry Holt, 2001), p. 214.

9   For the UNCHS document go to United Nations website www.uno.org or to www.earth-rights.net

10 Originally composed and declared at a conference of the International Union for Land Value Taxation held in 1949.

11 For instance, books, papers and studies published by Worldwatch Institute, Northwest Environment Watch, Robert Schalkenbach Foundation, Center for Economic Studies, Institute for Land Policy, Land and Labor Campaign, Land Reform Scotland, Earth Rights Institute, New Economics Foundation. For others see Council of Georgist Organizations and International Union for Land Value Taxation websites.

12 For these and additional examples, references and details on green tax policies see several articles by Alanna Hartzok posted on Earth Rights Institute: www.earthrights.net.

13 David Malin Roodman, *The Natural Wealth of Nations: Harnessing the Market for the Environment* (New York, W. W. Norton & Company/World Watch, 1998).

14 Alan Thein Durning and Yoram Bauman, *Tax Shift* (Seattle, Northwest Environment Watch, 1998).

PARTICIPATORY DEMOCRACY
AND PORTO ALEGRE

Dave Lewitt

A few days ago I heard Episcopal Archbishop Desmond Tutu of South Africa speak in Boston. His sermon was all about inclusion—that we must relate to everyone as brothers and sisters, and not sideline or demonize anyone. Before he started this sermon he greeted everyone present with a warm "thank you" for helping to free South Africa—particularly black South Africans—from the agony of the apartheid system. Because he repeated "freedom" several times without going on to give us an update on that freedom, I shook my head in disbelief. The American press and television haven't featured this, but the hope for freedom with the withdrawal of a chastened apartheid government has for several years soured and turned to bitterness as the new government with Nelson Mandela and then Thabo Mbeki adopted the dogma of neoliberalism—the dogma of free trade, deregulation, and privatization of state enterprises like airlines and services like electricity, clinics, drinking water, and mail delivery.

Poor South Africans, who are most South Africans, have had their water and electricity shut off, their hopes for housing and schools frustrated, their urgent need for HIV/AIDS medicine frustrated, and so on. These services for which poor people look to the state have been denied to those who cannot pay unwelcome bills, even though unemployment grows and the state seems to be reluctant to generate jobs or to ensure basic income. The state's actions are consistent with the neoliberal requirements of the World Bank and the International Monetary Fund in order to obtain big loans—a dynamic which has devastated Thailand, Indonesia, Brazil, Russia, and Argentina and threatens India, Mexico, and so on. For trade in crops, minerals, and manufactured goods the World Trade Organization demands the same policies which in the end benefit stock-holders in North America, Europe, Japan, and other wealthy countries while putting "the two-thirds world" on an economic treadmill. In other words, neoliberalism—adopted by the South African government in the absence of effective opposition—is a policy of exclusion, not the inclusion which Bishop Tutu extols. It is this policy of growth, with prof-its for the few, which has been promoted so blithely by the so-called World Economic Forum, an annual winter gathering of elites from around the world in Davos, Switzerland, moved this year to the Waldorf-Astoria in New York City.

Two years ago certain people in Brazil and France realized that they'd had enough of that latter-day colonialism and decided to stage a World Social Forum (WSF) at the same time as the World Economic Forum. They were spearheaded by ATTAC—a French organization dedicated to a world-wide tax on all international money transactions in order to dampen speculation and to fund human services or debt retirement—and PT, the Partido dos Trabalhadores or Workers Party of Brazil, particularly the PT people in the city of Porto Alegre in the south of that vast country, near Uruguay and Argentina. Since the fall of Brazil's 20-year dictatorship in the mid 1980s, the people of Porto Alegre have elected and re-elected PT mayors, while the PT has also triumphed in many other cities including São Paolo, one of the world's largest. So Porto Alegre sponsored and helped to underwrite the WSF in its first year and again this year.

The motto of the World Social Forum is "Another World Is Possible." This appeals to a lot of people. Last year the organizers expected 2,000 and 12,000 came. This year they expected 20,000 and more than 60,000 came. Next year the WSF will again be in Porto Alegre, and in 2004 it may be in Kerala, India, though will Kerala be able to lodge 100,000 eager delegates? However that may be, Porto Alegre received this multitude of delegates with open arms. The few police in evidence were mounted and ceremonial, and there were no soldiers. The march through the city to the parade grounds, with red banners fluttering, was more like a pleasant stroll than a demon-stration. At the mildly warm parade ground, a determined group had a hard time inflating a giant hot air balloon bearing the words—in Portuguese and English: "Your mouth, fundamental." Speak up, folks, no matter what clown is in the White House. Our social concerns are paramount.

Another World Is Possible

Did the World Social Forum II come up with viable alternatives to the near-global overlay we refer to as the neoliberal agenda? Actually, the World Social Forum did not act as one body, did not generate a single document or endorse resolutions as one body. Instead this forum was more like the Forum in ancient Rome—a place where many views that broadly fit the motto could be heard and argued in relation to all sorts of expected and unexpected conditions. Of the 800 or 900 panels and workshops scheduled on dozens of globalization topics, only a few could be considered alternatives in the sense of a social or political blueprint.

The International Forum on Globalization, a group of advocate-experts based in San Francisco, including Vandana Shiva of India, Maude Barlow of Canada, Walden Bello of the Philippines, Colin Hines of the UK, and Martin Khor of Malaysia, offered the document "Alternatives to Economic Globalization." It recommends replacing IMF and the World bank with an Intenational Finance Organization under the United Nations, several regional Monetary Funds, an Organization for Corporate Accountability under the UN, and an International Insolvency Court. It recommends strengthening the International Labor Organization, the UN Conference on Trade and Development, and the UN Environmental Program.

The Washington-based Institute for Policy Studies, represented by John Cavanagh who is also in the International Forum on Globalization, led people-oriented organizations in Canada, Mexico, the U.S., and South America in developing "Alternatives for the Americas." Such a semi-global proposal makes sense especially in view of the FTAA—the proposed Free Trade Area of the Americas. FTAA, if it comes about, will be based on NAFTA—the North American Free Trade Agreement—which for seven years now has imposed its corporate "iron maiden" on Mexico, Canada, and the U.S., forcing the national governing bodies to alter or repeal its laws. Under NAFTA foreign corporations have sued for as much as $1 billion annually to compensate them for business lost or potentially lost to restrictions on trade on account of national concerns for health, labor rights, clean environment, or any other measure which might stand in the way of corporate profits.

Some of you may have seen the Bill Moyers show "Trading Democracy" on public TV a few weeks ago. This dealt with the enforcement features of NAFTA wherein corporations, for the first time in history, have the right to sue national governments—not their own, mind you, but governments of one of the other two countries in the Area. They can sue their own government only under the old rules where that government is sovereign and must give its permission to be sued by a private organization, and where long-standing constitutional process rules. But of course they could get one of their foreign subsidiaries to sue. Under the NAFTA rules a corporation (or conceivably an individual) could sue a foreign government in a NAFTA court or "arbitration tribunal" where the rules are different—the hearing is closed; there are no rules of evidence or limits on the otherwise narrow outlooks of the three-man arbitration panel of trade specialists. (After all, what does "arbitrary" mean?) Like public relations or propaganda, the plaintiff corporation gets to decide what evidence or other information, if any, it will release to the public.

The NAFTA tribunal trumps the constitutions of the constituent countries. The ruling of its arbitration panel is binding on the country—they must pay the so-called damages or suffer an official trade boycott from all other countries in the Agreement, which would upset any or all sectors of their economy. The corporate-driven negotiators of FTAA, the Free Trade Area of the Americas, want to extend these provisions of NAFTA to the whole Hemisphere. There is a form of corruption here where, like all recent economic treaties, big business lobbyists secretly get to draft proposals and stay cozy with Treasury and State Department negotiators while union and civil society representatives are virtually excluded. When they change jobs, government negotiators like government regulators often are welcomed into corporate headquarters.

Anyway, the "Alternatives for the Americas" document, driven by worries over NAFTA and the proposed FTAA, reorients FTAA's economic concerns with investment, finance, agriculture, and so on, and adds human rights, environment, labor, immigration, gender, and the role of the state—which are, after all, emphasized by long-sidetracked United Nations agreements. This document elaborates objectives of a democratic hemispheric economic system, but does not design institutions or specify their functional relationships which would enable the system to operate.

[At the UN Millennium Forum of Civil Society which met in New York in May of 2000, a group of 37 citizens from many countries produced from scratch a plan called "Facing the Challenges of Globalization," in three days of intensive meetings. (If you search for it on the web, look under TheAllianceForDemocracy.org so as not to mistake it for another, more conservative document of the same name.) Quite comprehensive, it says many things that the UN should do, that governments should do, and that organizations of civil society should do. It often specifies roles for such institutions as the UN Economic and Social Council, the UN Conference on Trade and Development, and a UN International Local Employment and Trading System (UNILETS). I don't think that the group's able coordinator, Felicity Hill, made it to Porto Alegre, so I don't think it was represented there.]

Over a period of three years I led a diverse group of 14 citizens in debating and constructing "A Common Agreement on Investment and Society" as an Alliance for Democracy project, but in the welter of presentations at Porto Alegre I was unable to squeeze in a workshop on time. This proposal is the most specific of these four, describing six new international institutions and how they may complement one another and interact with corporations, governments, and civil society. The focus of this system is a network of eventually thousands of Local System Organizations, locally and democratically controlled and cooperating with one another and with international agencies including the UN. The general idea is that "localization" is the answer to overbearing globalization. The various alternatives above share this idea, more or less.

Keep in mind that all these documents are for discussion—they are offered as models or spring-boards to help local or regional groups get insights into new ways of organizing people and resources and ideas about systems to benefit all people in a region. No powerhouse of a Congress is going to take one of these plans intact and spring it on a large population in any democracy. The ANC in South Africa did that, but their neoliberal plan was backed by some of the most powerful governments in the world, while plans coming from alternative philosophies are not widely known and have only potential support.

Well, the main reason I went to Porto Alegre was to hear more about a local alternative to corporate-driven globalization—an alternative which looks very powerful, very fair, and engages huge numbers of citizens—a hot-house of democracy. It's called participatory budgeting. "Participatory what? Give me a break—I'm not an accountant," you may say. Well suppose I put it this way—How would you like to distribute $200 million to your fellow citizens? That's the amount of money the city of Porto Alegre spends in an average year for housing, public transport, street paving, garbage collection, clinics, hospitals, sewage, environment, social housing, literacy, schooling, culture, law and order, et cetera. What is to be done, and exactly for whom? It seemed to me—here is a Local System Organization already working. Here is a local alternative to top-down, back-scratching, back-room, police-backed elite business as usual. So in four conference days I went to two large panel sessions, one workshop, and one informal consultation on participatory budgeting, and one large panel on participatory democracy more generally. I was not disappointed. In the consultation I also got some key references— you can read three very good research and theoretical articles about PB in *Politics & Society*, for March 2001.

Before I go into exactly how it works on the ground, let me say that this social experiment has been very successful, and has spread to more than 100 cities in Brazil and other places like Montevideo, Uruguay and Córdoba, Argentina. Something like 50,000 residents of Porto Alegre—poor and middle class, women and men, leftist and centrist—now participate in the budgeting cycle of this city of a million and a half people—and the numbers of participants have grown each year since its start 12 years ago. Each year the bulk of new street-paving has gone to the poorer, outlying districts. When PB started, only 75 percent of homes had running water, while today 99 percent have treated water and 85 percent have piped sewerage. In seven years housing assistance jumped from 1,700 families to 29,000. In 12 years of participatory budgeting the number of public schools jumped from 29 to 86, and literacy has reached 98 percent.

Apart from such concrete achievements in addressing inequality and exclusion, corruption—which before was the rule—has disappeared. Democracy has thrived not merely in numbers participating in various discussion or deliberative bodies, but has included competence in talking effectively and sympathetically with the mayor, specialists in agencies, and fellow citizens of different means. Locally, it has been proven that "another world is possible."

Here are the words of Luis Carlos Pereira, who has participated in "theme" conferences on education and on sports and recreation, "In the 'Partenon' region [of the city] there was no sewerage, school, health clinic, or transportation. Since PB, a reservoir has been built with six million liters of water, the streets have been paved, and a school opened."

Eloah dos Santos Alves, a white-haired woman from the "Leste" region of the city, says, "I have participated in the PB process since 1989 as a community and party militant, today representing PPB. In my region we have done many good things. In general, 85 percent of the needs have been met. We have a recycling warehouse, schools, day cares, and medical clinics. And I would like to let everyone know that I have never been treated differently for not being part of the PT" (the leading party).

The Participatory Budgeting process has been quickly and flexibly institutionalized. The cycle starts in January of each year with dozens of assemblies across the city to review the system and discuss the by-laws, and to become familiar with how the meetings are facilitated for maximum participation and friendly interaction as well as accomplishment of meeting purposes. One study of participatory budgeting shows that poor people, less well educated people, and black people are not inhibited in attending and speaking up, even though racial discrimination is strong in Brazil despite the myth of one big happy family. The major impediments to participation are a person's time and schedule, such as when the children must be fed. This has to do with the dynamic of the assemblies as a cultural institution, almost like a church which has sprung up in a few short years. One experienced participant described the dynamic as follows:

"The most important thing is that more and more persons come. Those who come for the first time are welcome; we have a lot of patience for them, there is no problem, we let them make demands during technical meetings, they can speak their mind and their anxieties. We have patience for it because we were like that once. And if he has an issue, we set up a meeting for him, and create a commission to accompany him. You have the responsibility of not abandoning him. That is the most important thing."

Sérgio Baierle, director of the civic organization CIDADE, believes that civil society can indeed rise above the apathy and distraction fostered by the mass media. "Boycotted for years by the main newspapers, radio stations, and television networks," he says, "the Participatory Budgeting [process] has itself become a popular media form."

During February there is instruction from city specialists in technical and system aspects of city budgeting. Regular folks learn fast because what they are learning empowers them to change conditions which limit or extend their lives, on a level with their professional or vocational learning. This is, perhaps, an extension of the teachings of Paolo Freire, the Brazilian priest who enabled peasants to learn to read fast through materials about power, landlords and politicians, and by a learning process of liberation as much as deliberation.

In March, there are "plenary" assemblies in each of the city's 16 districts or "regions." There is also a series of "thematic" assemblies, each dealing with a different theme like government, transportation, health, education, sports, culture, or economic development. These large meetings, with occasional participation of upward of 1,000 persons, elect delegates to represent specific neighborhoods and to review the previous year's projects and budgets. The mayor and staff attend these meetings to reply to the concerns of citizens about projects in the district. In subsequent months these 40 or 60 delegates meet in each district on a weekly or biweekly basis to acquaint themselves with the technical criteria involved in demanding a project as well as to deliberate about the district's needs. Representatives from each of the city's departments participate according to their specialties. These smaller "intermediary meetings" come to a close when, at a second "regional plenary" a vote among regional delegates serves to prioritize the district's demands and elect councilors to serve on the Municipal Council of the Budget, beginning in May or June, as I recall.

This Council is a 42-member forum of representatives of all the districts and thematic meetings. Its main function is to reconcile the demands of each district with available resources, and propose and approve an overall municipal budget in conjunction with members of the administration, detailing what each district gets. An essential aspect of this work is making sure that each district gets city funds according to their needs as the local assemblies see them. The Council has worked out a matrix or spreadsheet of weights according to absolute need and also priority among the several needs a district votes, balancing across the city's 16 regions, and they do the necessary arithmetic.

The budget resulting from this discussion, deliberation, and arithmetic is binding in that the regular City Council, presently with a rather conservative majority, can suggest changes but not require them. The budget is submitted to the mayor who may veto it and remand it to the Municipal Council of the Budget, but this has never happened. The mayor puts the staffs of the city's departments to work to implement the budget. If there are residual problems the Council works out changes in the rules of the whole process, returning to their neighborhoods for feedback. For instance, in recent years some of the changes have broadened the powers of the Council to cover city personnel expenditures, and changed the criteria for assessing how resources are to be allocated to each of the districts.

I should add that the Internet provides an on-going vehicle of involvement in participatory budgeting, now extended by Porto Alegre to city planning features like land use and long-term major investments. The city posts progress reports on all city projects along with budget figures and expenditures, and a calendar of all meetings. Some 200,000 residents have access to the Internet, allowing them to interact with city officials and district participants as well as to follow the process through Internet links with each project.

Okay, that's the process. It's inclusive, well-structured, and responsive as a start to a more democratic and dominant civil society—in the face of old class divisions and the corporate-driven institutions and practices of neoliberalism. It has begun to overcome the message I saw on a union-sponsored billboard along the parade route in Porto Alegre: "NEOLIBERALISM IS MASS PRODUCTION (and they show a cemetery full of little stone crosses)—IN BRAZIL, 30,000 CHILDREN DIE ANNUALLY BEFORE THE AGE OF 5. ANOTHER WORLD IS POSSIBLE."

An important by-product of the participatory budgeting process is a burgeoning of civic activity. As PB developed the numbers of political, cultural, and neighborhood groups has doubled, especially in poorer districts where results of self-generated new city expenditures are remarkable. People in wealthier districts also like what's going on. The value of their properties in poorer districts is rising. The new city "energy of effectance," we might call it, spawned a campaign to get property owners to pay their taxes, and it worked.

Porto Alegre is one of the best cities in Brazil in which to live. It will be interesting to see how this plays out in comparison with Curitiba, about 400 miles to the north, much touted by Hawken, Lovins & Lovins in their book *Natural Capitalism*. Curitiba is a top-down model city, an architect's dream made real. Perhaps we will have here a test of democracy versus meritocracy. Curitiba's beauty and efficiency is already compromised by its builder's toleration of right-wing death squads. Jaime Lerner is already governor of that state.

The concern and comparison are real. A strong ally of the Workers Party, the dominant party in Porto Alegre and the state of Rio Grande do Sul to which participatory budgeting has spread (with 320,000 participants!) is the MST, the landless farmers movement. Often, when these displaced people have formed communities and have occupied idle farmland, they have been murdered by *pistoleros* hired by wealthy landholders, just as shop owners in Rio de Janeiro have hired paramilitary groups to shoot and kill 5,000 street kids. Workers Party candidates may not be immune from bullets paid for by privileged political rivals, especially as the party's perennial presidential candidate, Luiz Inácio Lula da Silva, may have a good chance of winning this fall in view of what happened in Argentina as well as the success of Participatory Budgeting.

So, can Brazil's participatory democracy experience help the Democracy Movement in the United States and around the world? There are some major differences which will make difficult any direct translation. The principal issues may be popular mobilization and engagement in local governmental processes. We have plenty of grounds to criticize traditional representative democracy. Mobilization may be easy once some popular process gets results—consistent results. One thing which has made substantial results possible in Brazilian municipalities is a provision of their 1987 constitution requiring a certain percentage of national revenues to be turned over to the municipalities. We used to have "revenue sharing," but today's North American cities and towns are more on their own for resources. As in Montevideo, citizens may lose interest in participation in city budgeting unless substantial allocations can be made to projects they decide.

Another major obstacle is our lack of popular progressive political parties. The success of participatory budgeting in Brazil has been exclusively in those cities which have elected labor or progressive popular front governments. It hasn't hurt that southern Brazil has been home to Italian anarchist immigrants and German socialist immigrants. The so-called "Republicrat" monopoly in Washington would not necessarily preclude independent party activity at the local level here, but only a few cities like Milwaukee have elected such governments. Also, the distance and language barriers against interaction with Brazil are formidable in building a party, though Sister Cities might present an opportunity. Local church-based organizations like GBIO—the Greater Boston Interfaith Organization founded by Saul Alinsky's Industrial Areas Foundation—have had success on sectoral issues like housing, and might be expanded.

Perhaps the best connection would be in the development of the struggling international labor solidarity movement, though North American unions—a small minority of them—are only now beginning to reach out. If they would partner with the likes of GBIO they might achieve working momentum as a multi-issue group capable of gaining a city hall. Until then the smartness of participatory budgeting remains to be demonstrated in the U.S. Perhaps civil society in a few cities might organize a "shadow PB" to unofficially develop a city budget similar to Porto Alegre's, and hope to gain credibility by phantom allocations to a number of key municipal districts, using some of Porto Alegre's methods.

We have a tradition of the New England Town Meeting. We have many energetic anarchist youth to whom PB may appeal. We are often democratic as parents. We are a nation of local problem-solvers. We widely accept the "win-win" strategic approach. It took Brazil years of organizing under the dictatorship before the PT and its coalition partners could succeed. Brazilian and North American conditions may be converging. The income gap is widening here and we are experiencing the development of a Big Oil and Big Media dictatorship. When we admit to widespread corruption, albeit a "legal" variety where candidates and media support corporate influence and where corporations essentially buy regulatory agencies, the US public may begin to experiment with local populist parties.

If civic politics is chemistry, then what or who is the catalyst to start the action?

CREATING SUSTAINABLE AGRICULTURE AND RELOCALIZING FOOD SYSTEMS

Joan Dye Gussow

I am going to talk about a subject that may seem quite strange. I am going to talk to you not as a nutritionist, which I am, because, as I once said to someone, "I don't really care as much about what you eat as I care about where it comes from." I am going to talk to you about changing your diet, but not changing your diet for your own health or to lose weight. I am going to talk to you about changing your diet so that you can contribute to the survival of farmers, and to the planet on which they have to grow food for us. I am going to urge you to move out of what a farmer that I recently met called "homogoscene era"—where everyone's eating the same across the planet—and begin to choose your diets from foods that are grown closer to where you live. I am going to talk in short about eating locally, which means accepting the notion of self-maintenance.

When you talk about eating locally as long as I have, you naturally hope that by this time everyone knows why they should do it. I understand, however, that most people don't—most people have never even thought about it, particularly people from the last few generations who have had the advantage (if that's what it is!) of having available almost anything they want almost anytime they want it, with no reference to seasons or places. People are very used to shopping without reference to the season or location. People are mostly shopping happily—although a little overwhelmed by choice in a marketplace that seems to offer them everything. But I am convinced that the system that presently offers you everything is totally unsustainable, and I am going to begin my talk by giving you three reasons why I think that is true.

After I have gone over the principal reasons for my concern about how we are presently eating, I will talk some about my own experiences as what my publishers have incautiously called a "suburban homesteader." I got a book recently from a woman who really was a homesteader and it embarrassed me. She heard of my book and she thought I should see hers. Her book is called

Carrying Water as a Way of Life. I am not a homesteader. I have never carried water from the well to my house, but I do try to grow my own food. And my reasons for doing that, which are what I am going to talk about tonight, are probably a lot more important than my minor successes as a min-farmer.

And finally, I want to talk about what all this would mean to consumers. What would it mean if we tried to eat locally? What would it mean if we tried to un-homogenize our diets and eat diets more in keeping with the unique foods of our own regions?

So let me start with the three reasons why I think we need to worry about the future of our food supply. And they are in the order in which I identified them myself. They are: global hunger, saving local farmers, and food safety.

Let's begin with global hunger—how does that fit in? When I concluded about 30 years ago that we needed to relocalize our eating, my reasons were entirely theoretical. I had gone into the field of nutrition late in life, worrying about the fact that the food supply seemed to be very frivolous—increasingly frivolous—in the face of the world in which many people were hungry. And a year or so after I began studying nutrition, I came to the conclusion that much of what we were doing around the world that was supposed to be increasing the food supply was in fact threatening in the long term to decrease it. And the solutions that we in the U.S. were supporting were a large part of the problem. We were contaminating the planet. We were polluting local water systems. We were destroying local soils, local crops, local communities and, critically, we were undercutting people who knew how to grow food in a very, very efficient way in those different places where we were introducing what were for them exotic varieties.

Food is unique as a consumer item. If we can afford it—we can have several cars, 300 pairs of shoes, a closet full of bottled water—we can have great numbers of most things. But there is only a limit to what we can eat in the way of food—about 1,500 lbs. a year. And if we just buy more, it will just sit in a corner and rot. So food is a commodity that is limited in its consumption, in a country which believes in unlimited consumption.

And of equal importance, nature is essential to the production of food. If we need to eat, we need to keep local ecosystems functioning to provide all those free services that nature provides—from pollination to the cycling of nitrogen and oxygen and phosphorous, to the maintenance of all the intricate biological systems, from bacteria all the way up—to keep everything running. But we don't anymore eat food that comes from our local ecosystem as we did when we were much more "undeveloped." We have a global food system that takes food from all over the world and ships it around, and ends up pitting our farmers against the poorest farmers in the world.

In order to produce food, you have to have three things. You have to have land, you have to have labor, and you have to have some form of capital to put in. The first two cannot move—you can't move land and labor. Although labor tries to move, we try to stop it when it tries to move to our country. But capital can move easily, and capital is moving. Corporations are moving all around the world, setting up systems sometimes where things have never been grown before, setting up systems to produce certain products. They set up systems to produce chickens and shrimp and soybeans and fruits and vegetables wherever land and labor are cheapest, and they pay no attention to the sustainability of what they are doing in the place where they are doing it. So they are using pesticides, they are using herbicides, they are letting the soil erode. And their shrimp farms become so contaminated after a certain length of time that they have to be abandoned. And the corporations move on, leaving devastation in their wake.

The earth is not at all happy about this. We are surrounded by signs that what humans are doing on the planet is unsustainable. And the only places where we might be able to act to get the system right are in local ecosystems. And although local ecosystems are in danger around the world—I mean in each area—altogether as the great planetary ecosystem they continue to support us. We don't know that we need to worry about all this because we don't know local ecosystems are feeding us. We don't know that our food is coming from there.

For years, I have asked people when I go out to lecture, and I have asked my classes, to write down what they ate the day before, and then pick any one item and tell me where it came from . . . usually nobody knows where any single item came from. They can't even guess the continent. Our food is so separated from the land that produces it that we have no idea where it's coming from. Ultimately I realized as an educator how hard it was going to be to get anyone to worry about those farmers out there who are trying—often under terrible circumstances—to produce food for us. I realized that we couldn't even attract the attention of people here, to the farm crisis in California . . . and even if we could, we couldn't do anything about Californians losing their farmland, because we live here, and can't vote there.

And I certainly wasn't going to be able to get people to worry about farmers in Ethiopia or South Africa or Haiti who send us beef. We—who produce much more meat than we can eat—are importing beef and pork from Haiti! But I feared I wasn't going to be able to get people to worry about that. So I decided that what we had to do was bring food production closer to home.

And so I started going out and talking to my colleagues in nutrition education about the fact that we needed to change what we were doing. We ought to be promoting local diets as a way of saying "no" to the global food system enterprise. That was my goal, that people would understand where food came from. But very quickly after I hit on this idea, I realized it was another equally powerful reason for having local food systems; namely that we are losing all our farmers. We need to save our farmers if we are going to have any capacity to feed ourselves in this region or any region.

Looking at it as a northeasterner, I argued that if those of us who lived here didn't start helping local farmers survive, we are going to become totally dependent on the long-distance transport of food. As you have probably heard, the average molecule of food travels something like 1,300 miles. Lots of us have tried to figure out where those statistics come from, so the number varies from 1,000 to 2,000, but basically it is a long distance. We are shipping food around all the time, so it's very energy intensive, and it's ridiculous. Sending all that truck and airplane exhaust and CO_2 into the air adds to greenhouse warming. Most of the trucks you are seeing on the highways are carrying food, and those trucks are breaking down our highways. There is an astonishingly large movement of food into and out of and around the country which we have become very dependent on. If petroleum prices rose, we would have increasingly expensive food and we would find our diets changing inescapably.

In fact, there was a time in the '70s when gasoline prices went really high, and very briefly California produce—straight, ordinary, non-organic produce—sold for more money in New York than local organic produce. That is, you could literally buy organic produce cheaper than you could buy produce brought in from California. Alas, that didn't last long. The minute we were convinced that it was a false crisis and fuel prices went down, then food prices changed.

Even after prices went down, however, we thought organic might be able to save local agriculture simply because customers would pay a premium to get organic produce. And that meant that local farmers who grew organically could get enough money for it to stay on their farms. On the whole, farming in our part of the country is in a great deal of trouble because there is so much development pressure. The land can be sold for multiples of what a farmer could ever make from growing food. So farmers are under tremendous pressure to sell their land, and when they can't make a living, they sell out and we lose more farms.

So we thought that organic might save these farmers, and then of course organic got to be very popular. And when things get to be very popular, they become a niche market and the big guys move in and they did, and they began producing organic crops on a large scale. And we now have a federal standard for organic food, which has made things even worse for the small grower. It's reached the point where organic produce grown in California or Mexico can undersell local organic produce despite all the transportation costs. And what that means is that the local organic farmer is out of business. A couple of years ago there was a time when in New York City you could buy organic tomatoes from California, while across the river in New Jersey there were organic tomatoes that the farmers couldn't sell! It's a totally distorted system.

So just buying organic is not going to help local farmers unless it is the local farmer selling it. Just organic doesn't do the trick. I talk in my book about the time I was served juice by a neighbor of mine who thought she was pleasing me because she served me this organic juice. I looked at the can and saw that it came from Patagonia. I don't know if many of you know where Patagonia is, but it's at the foot of Latin America, just up from Antarctica. I said to her, "Oh my God, this is from Patagonia!" and she was sort of offended, as well she should have been—I was being rude—but I was really appalled to be served juice from Patagonia!

Everywhere in the world farms and farmland are hemorrhaging. We are losing them so fast that there is almost no blood left to lose. The U.S. census doesn't even count farmers anymore. They don't have a "category" for farmers anymore, because so few people are in farming in this country. The latest figures show that for every farmer under 35, there are 4.5 farmers over 65, which means of course there is no new generation of farmers. The fastest growing category is farmers over 70. And, as someone who is at that age, I can assure you that I wouldn't want to farm much longer if I had a full-sized farm to manage. If I were a farmer over 70 I would be thinking of retiring soon. I am a farmer over 70, but my farm is very small.

Not too long ago an economist named Blank, Steven Blank, wrote a book called *The End of Agriculture in the American Portfolio*. His thesis was that capital was not going to be invested in U.S. agriculture because there wasn't enough return on investment (as I told you before, capital moves around). It wasn't going to be cost-effective to invest in U.S.agriculture, he said, and he thought that all our agriculture would move overseas because it didn't pay, and of course it doesn't. Farmers are going broke. The cranberry growers in the northeast last June were told to cut down production because there were so many cranberries and the price they could get for a barrel of cranberries was 20 cents less than it cost them to produce it.

Two years ago I visited a New York State dairy farm that had made more money from growing one acre of gourmet potatoes than they had made in a whole year of dairying. Looking at his success, the neighboring farmers all took up growing gourmet potatoes, and the result was the over-supply knocked the price down, and that little stream of hope was dead. I also visited an upstate apple orchard with a friend of mine who is a landscape architect. He was not there to buy apples, he went up there to buy apple trees. The big new "McMansions" that they are building like to have ready-made apple orchards in their back yards that look like they've been there forever. These giant machines simply cut around aging apple trees full of bent branches, take them up and move them to some new home. And the farmer who sold these antiques probably made more money from selling four trees than he made from selling apples all year!

So you can see it is a totally dysfunctional system. The loss of local farmers and farmland is one of the most frightening and dangerous crises we face across the planet, because somebody has to grow food. Almost everyone in the world—developed, underdeveloped, developing countries—is behaving as if there were a giant food production machine just over the horizon and we could always buy what we want to eat from somewhere else. But everyone can't import food—it has to be grown somewhere. And the only security we have is to retain the capacity to grow food near where we live. So that is the second reason why I think we have to eat locally.

My third reason is food safety. This is a pretty recent issue, although I have been concerned about food safety for a long time because the way we are growing our food and raising our animals introduces so many bacteria into the food system. In fact, I once said to someone that if we suffered a bioterrorist attack, it would come from our own food supply, because things were so bad. And here's a snapshot of where farming is, I recently heard on national public radio a story about a government conference on preventing bioterrorism on the farm, and one of the Washington state apple farmers in attendance said: "You know, I really wouldn't mind if somebody terrorized my crops, because the government payments would be better than what I could make selling the apples." That's the state the farmers are in. I said earlier that I didn't think that people had responded in any significant way to 9/11 in regard to food. I think people have responded in many other ways to that event, but there was a story in the paper some time ago about upgrading our security, and the person being quoted, who was from the Office of Homeland Security, said we had to be on guard at all the places our nation touches the rest of the world. And I couldn't help asking myself if he had been to a supermarket lately. I mean, our supermarkets are full of foods from all over the world, and they are coming in across our borders by the ton.

Several years ago, I wrote an article for *Mother Earth News* in which I quoted a message that a neighbor of mine had left on my phone machine while I was away on a trip. This is what she said: "This may be the only time in history when humans have had complete strangers—strangers who are badly treated or ignored—growing and preparing all of our food." She is essentially right. We are being fed by strangers from everywhere in the world, many of whom do not have our well-being at heart. As we now know, not everyone is crazy about us! That is something I think we should be concerned about. You will say: "Obviously we cannot trust everyone in the world, but surely we have some sort of regulations. We have the FDA (Food and Drug Administration). We have the USDA. We all have all kinds of regulations."

A few years ago I spoke to a woman at the FDA about an article I was writing. I wanted to be sure I had my figures right, and I had heard that there were 700 inspectors inspecting 50,000 food plants in the U.S. along with all the food that was imported, so I called to confirm that. And I got to this lady and she told me that I was wrong. This was 1998—by the way.

At that time there were 1,417 people in the inspection team, of which 805 were in what they call "operations." Of those, 350 worked in laboratories, not in the field. That is, when inspectors got the samples and brought them in, they had to take them to laboratories. And 337 people actually went out and inspected those 50,000 factories, which left 118 people responsible for inspecting all the food that was imported. All the trucks across the Mexican and Canadian borders. All the ships that land in our ports. All the airplanes that carry produce. I don't know how secure that makes you feel, but I know at the time there were 150,000 trucks coming across just the Mexican border every year.

I have tried to update these figures and nobody would call me back, and I have a feeling I never would have gotten an answer anyway, because there is a lot of suppression of information for fear that terrorists will get it. So I doubt very much that the FDA is being public about the kind of inspection they now have for imported foods. But this is what I found out in 1998 when we already had concerns about such issues as unlicensed pesticides on produce. You will have to extrapolate from there. I myself seriously doubt we can be confident that food coming into the U.S. from outside the country is carefully inspected.

And border inspection is entirely in the hands of the FDA. In case that doesn't bother you, let me read you an email I got from a friend of mine in Wisconsin—a dairy farmer—to tell you how the Department of Agriculture is doing with the food issues it is in charge of regulating. This is what my friend says: "Joan, I just came across a potentially frightening bit of news. Apparently the USDA is holding public comment hearings on March 20th on changing the manufacturing standards for cheese. This would include cheddar, mozzarella, provolone, and others. The change would allow the use of milk protein concentrate (MPC), which is like powdered milk really, a product that is all imported." (We have much too much milk in this country, but we import cheap powdered milk for reasons which you will understand in a minute.) "It is all imported in the manufacture of standardized cheeses." I should remind you that we have a glut of milk in this country, and that the large cheese producers want to keep the price of materials low.

"We have been concerned about MPC for a long time," my friend goes on, "because it is really keeping domestic milk prices down. The really bad part of this proposal is that the MPC would be allowed to contain the milk from water buffalo, and the product would not have to be pasteurized. I am trying to find an FAO (UN Food and Agriculture Organization) document that contains an email conference at which someone from India was describing the milking procedure for water buffalo. Apparently they are rather difficult to milk by hand, and since almost 100 percent of them are milked by hand, farmers use a wet-handed milking technique. The moisture gets supplied by using water, milk, or even saliva. It would indeed be appetizing to know that the cheese one eats may contain unpasteurized water buffalo milk that was collected by a farmer who may have been spitting on his hands. USDA will do almost anything to keep the cost of the raw materials low for the processors." And then he adds, "Safest food supply in the world, Jim."

So, while losing the ability to grow food may be the most serious long-term threat we face in looking at our food future, I think the most dramatic immediate reason to eat locally is because it is one way of being relatively certain that your food is free of unpasteurized spit, or a number of the other contaminants that have entered our food since we started moving it from countries where people are poor and sanitary standards are low, to our country where we can afford to pay for what these poor people produce.

Things were pretty risky even before 9/11. We had a number of serious food poisoning outbreaks in this country—salmonella contaminated raspberries, E. coli-tainted strawberries, poisoned melons, toxic mesclun, and other fallouts from our habit of bringing perishable foods from poor countries where they can be cheaply grown to rich ones where people like us can afford to buy them. I know how fragile raspberries are. I can barely get them intact to the breakfast table. I wouldn't dream of eating a raspberry that had been grown in a country where I wouldn't drink the water. But that's what we are doing.

So those are my reasons for believing we need to eat locally, the reasons I use when someone tells me it's silly or pointless or too complicated to give up eating blindly from the supermarket. Which brings me to the part of my talk on which I am actually an expert: my own experience in trying to become a local eater.

In the 1980s, when I had reached the point I talked about earlier and decided that we had to relocalize the food supply, I finally worked up the nerve to go out and suggest to my nutrition colleagues that we ought to move people toward more local diets. I told them that we needed to change not just our methods, but our message. My colleagues at the time were almost inevitably horrified and astonished at the idea that we should move away from the bounteous global supermarket that we had all been taught was the goal toward which we were aiming.

More than 20 years ago, I mentioned the idea of relocalization during a talk I gave at the University of California at Davis, and one of the professors asked, with withering sarcasm, what did I think the people in Iowa were going to do for Vitamin C in the winter? Now both my parents came from Iowa long before there was a citrus commission in either California or Florida, and they survived, and they didn't either of them get scurvy. So obviously there were ways that people got Vitamin C before we were told that we had to have citrus for breakfast every morning.

My response to that kind of criticism wasn't to shut up, however. I couldn't unlearn what I had learned. I needed to try to walk my talk. Because when I first talked about eating locally, I didn't really have a clue what it would mean where I lived. To find local produce at that time, 25 or 30 years ago, wasn't possible—there were almost no authentic farmers' markets, so if you wanted to be sure it was local, you had to grow it yourself. So my husband and I set out to see what we could grow and live on.

I think the way we said it was that we intended to grow our own food, which was very naive because we don't grow our own food and never did. We could grow fruits and vegetables, but we also ate grains and eat animal products. However, when you talk about eating locally, the thing that seems to disturb people the most is the produce, is the fruits and vegetables. "What will I do for salad in February?" they want to know.

Now my goal in all this was not to prove that everyone could grow their own if they wanted to, which would have been silly—I mean after all, I live 20 minutes north of Manhattan. My goal was to create a model of what local farmers could make available if we set out to create a market for what they could produce. I was trying to model the fact that you could eat locally without suffering, without living on old cabbage and sprouting potatoes, from the cold cellar by this time of year. I was trying to show that you could live by the seasons without sacrifice and pain. So I began trying to grow my own as a way of showing that we could support local farmers by buying what they could grow year around. The ultimate goal was to make people more willing to take chances on that kind of diet.

I have now thoroughly demonstrated how tasty local eating can be, and would obviously help farmers more by buying their food than by growing my own, assuming I could find a year-round source. But by now I am thoroughly addicted to growing what I eat and eating what I grow. And in order to assure myself that this obsession is rational, I tell myself that I am growing now because it keeps reminding me of lessons that we all need to keep in mind about farmers. It is very easy to forget what farmers are going through. So I am going to end this talk by just giving a couple of illustrations from my book—two of the lessons that I have learned in all these years. And the first of them is that if we eat locally, weather will matter a lot more.

Two summers ago we had a drought in my region, and it got so dry that rats were biting into every single tomato that I grew. If one ripened, the rat would discover it before I did and take the back out of the tomato. I live on the Hudson, which is a tidal river with a wedge of salt flowing upriver under its surface. When there is no rain going into the river, it gets increasingly salty. It is salty right now because of the drought we are having this month.

Well into my rat crisis, I learned from a fisherman that the rats couldn't handle the salt, so what they were doing was coming up to my land in order to get liquid. I called Roger, the exterminator, the person in charge of keeping my community free from rats. He scouts the waterfront for the village. He does the community garden which is next door to me, just as a favor, and because I am right next door he also tucks me in. So he came and we talked and, after he left, I shared my frustration and his diagnosis by email with the community gardeners. I am going to read you my email, because it says it all.

"Fellow gardeners, just thought you would like to know I haven't harvested a ripe tomato yet. The rats have gotten them all. Roger came, announced that there were no rat burrows on either my property or in the community garden, so he couldn't put poison down the den. He said he'd put out bait stations, then he said 'Joan, vegetables and fruits are rats' favorite food. They are going to stand there (and he looked back and forth between the bait station and the tomatoes) and they are going to say 'chicken or sirloin, chicken or sirloin?' and they are going to choose sirloin. So if you find chomped tomatoes, don't, DON'T, throw them on the ground, but remove them from the compost pails. Pick up the compost, all dropped tomatoes, surround your plants with netting if you can, stake them high, get a little rag doll and stick pins in it, and hope that Roger's bait is more attractive than he thinks! And if you ever wonder why rats will outlast us on the planet, just remember they don't contribute to global warming by driving to the store in a Humvee, and they love fruits and vegetables!

Most of this was probably hysterically bad advice, because if we left the tomatoes lying there, the rats might have finished off the ones they already started instead of starting a new one every night. But the rat crisis ended with a flood. I got six inches of rain in a couple of hours, and it put my entire yard under water. My yard is lower than anything else around it, so it's a bathtub. This killed off the tomato plants and a number of other weather-sensitive crops. The sweet potatoes, which are a mainstay of my winter diet, looked fine at the time, but when I dug them later in the year I found that the sudden water had swelled them and cracked them open, and 1/3 of the crop had rotted, leaving the rest of them looking like "Frankenfoods"—sort of crude lumpy things.

A couple of years earlier I had also lost some of my crops—mostly potatoes and onions—after the wettest year in history. I found myself then in a kind of unexplained panic about the crop loss and I had to ask myself what was bothering me. I wasn't going to go hungry. After all, I could afford to buy food. And then I realized that I was suffering from symbolic angst, because it really didn't matter if my crop failed, but the trouble was that it did matter to the farmers. And if I was having trouble, they were probably also having trouble. I assumed nothing protected their crops from the kinds of troubles that I had. And it turned out that I was right. The upstate onion growers had one of the worst years ever, and the potato blight that had caused the Irish famine had returned to New York State and was causing the same kind of havoc upstate. So my garden tells me what's going on out where our food is grown.

Now I know that no sensible farmer would choose my land, which is very flood-prone, and they are certainly better than I am at what we both do, but the problems that farmers have with weather are true of what I see in my own garden. I bought peaches at our local farmers' market in the September after the flood, and I remarked to the local farmer on the fact that he still had peaches. And he said "Yes," and I said, "I lost all my tomatoes," and he said, "Me too," and I (being totally obsessed) said "Oh, I am so glad."

Then I caught myself, and I apologized, and told him I had thought it was me, and he smiled and he said, "No, no. When a full-grown plant is hit by stress, it just dies." So I was reassured that it wasn't me or my soil or my lack of skill, or whatever, but it was the weather. And by restricting myself to the vegetables I grow, I am constantly being reminded that food is the generous outcome of a collaboration between our species and the rest of nature, and not simply another product of industrial civilization.

(I read about a product recently called "No Fat Cheddar Slices," and I asked myself what it was. It is a product of industrial civilization. It is not cheese. It is not a food. Not in my opinion.)

And understanding that both my crops and the farmers' crops will sometimes fail has not convinced me that we can't eat locally. It's just that we are going to have to be more flexible. It's just that we are going to have to decide that sometimes we will have less of certain things than we are used to, and we will have to go by what nature decides to give us. But climate dependence is not a lesson that will be easy to learn in this country, because the current marketplace doesn't provide us with any hint about when weather has battered our local farmers.

I remember once going to the market looking for local tomatoes—I wasn't trying to buy them, I was with a reporter who was surveying the local food scene. We looked at the tomatoes, and the only tomatoes in the market in August when the fruits are falling off the vines in this part of the country . . . the only ones were from Holland! And I asked the store manager, "Don't you have any local tomatoes?" and he said, "Well, we did get New Jersey tomatoes, but there was a hail storm and they had little dents in them and we didn't want them because they weren't perfect." So that is where we are. It's going to be very, very hard to teach people about climate dependence because we have all forgotten it.

This summer may help. We are now in the midst of one of the worst droughts we have ever experienced in this part of the country. I myself am deeply disturbed because they are going to bar outdoor watering, and that means that my food—not just my garden—my food will be eliminated. I am going to try to plead that I am a farmer, which I am. I have after all, written a whole book about growing my own food. But the approach is very disturbing. I think we need to ask ourselves whether we are going to try to save water indoors and out and be as conserving as we can so that farmers can continue to grow food. Are we capable of that or are we just going to go on pretending that what happens to local farmers is less urgent than our morning shower or the family lawn. That's where we are now. We really don't know how dependent we are. When water is short it's the farmers that ought to have first place.

The second major lesson I learned from growing my own is that if we really want to live by the seasons we will have to change what we eat a lot. Because I restrict myself to what I grow, I recognize that I narrow my winter choices more than I would have to if a much better farmer than I were growing everything he or she could grow. But some things would affect everyone. Fresh tomatoes are only available for a short period during the year. I put some green ones in my cold cellar and the last one ripens maybe in December, and then there is nothing until maybe July or August. Asparagus comes for about a month in the spring almost anywhere north of the equator, and I never have a lettuce salad in the winter unless I have been farsighted enough to plant in my cold frame, which I did this year and I have had salads. I had a salad yesterday.

Some inventive organic farmers have found ways of extending the seasons; even in Maine there is somebody growing carrots and greens in an unheated greenhouse in the middle of winter. So there are a lot of inventive people out there who may be able to broaden our choices. But in the northeast we would have to get used to a lot more winter vegetables and dried or frozen fruits, than we are used to. In fact, fruits and vegetables make much better salads than iceberg lettuce, I can assure you.

And I would like to say that if you want to know the practicalities of going local, you should read my book. You can get it from the library, you don't have to buy it. It has recipes in it. And there is another book . . . Deborah Madison, one of the great recipe writers in the country to my mind, has just written a new book called *Local Flavors: Cooking and Eating from America's Farmers' Markets*, which is more enticingly seasonal than any other cookbook I've ever seen. So there are ways you can learn to be local.

I have found out for myself in my region, 20 minutes north of New York City, what a seasonal local diet would taste like, and I can tell you it's delicious. But if you don't believe me, you will just have to try to get me to ask you to dinner. I cook very well. I grow enough vegetables in a relatively small area—with enough space left for mistakes and for beds planted to green manure crops and flowers—to keep myself in fresh and preserved vegetables and most of my fruits through the whole year.

We are going to have to make a lot of decisions about what local really means, what we should produce, what we should import, because we now import so much. And we are unaware of what is or could be available locally. Should we be allowed—if this were a rational system—would we ship between the regions? We just need to do a lot of serious thinking about what eating locally would mean.

I have concluded that here in the Northeast we probably would import grains and dry beans for reasons that I explain in my book. Spices would probably continue to be shipped around the world since they are light and of very high value. They are a wonderful crop in poor countries because they make a lot of money for a very small amount of product.

As for meat, we should obviously stop importing animals and their products because we produce a surplus. And we should, of course, eat much less of animal products. Our present animal slums (which is what they are) are an absolute horror. They are unsustainable. And when the animals get to the slaughterhouses, the situation there is such that it endangers both us and the people working there. And because meat, like eggs and milk, has to be kept cold when it's shipped, all these foods should be as local as possible. I now get my meat directly from an upstate farmer who raises all his animals and poultry on grass.

And then there is produce which is, overall, about 90 percent water, and will rot if it isn't kept cold. So we are spending a hell of a lot of money and wasting a lot of energy shipping cold water around the world. I see no reason, however, why people who live in colder climates can't occasionally have an orange. Ever since I started talking about local eating, a quarter of a century ago, citrus has been the deprivation symbol of choice for my critics. The minute you talk about eating locally, somebody says "You're telling me that I can't ever have an orange again!" and I have to say "No, that's not what I am saying." I'm not saying you can't ever have an orange again. The reality is that citrus is a very familiar dietary item that most people like a lot that just does-n't grow where most of us live.

There is no need to abandon hope, however, because moderation is the key—it's where most of our food comes from that matters. If we had a more rational diet so that most of what we got came from close to home, then we could decide what we could afford to ship without warming the planet beyond what it can handle.

I have found it a lot of fun to try to eat from what my region will provide, entirely avoiding out-of-season produce. When I see someone buying out-of-season now, I want to grab her arm and say "Don't you know those vegetables and fruits aren't going to taste like anything?" But I restrain myself. But I'm right, nonetheless. We have forgotten what real produce tastes like.

So now, in closing, let me give you a starting way in. When my book was coming out and I worried that I was going to have to be the local eating guru, I decided I would write up five things people can do to start eating locally. So here are my five recommended actions on how to start to be a local here.

Find out what is grown within 15 miles of where you live. Who is growing what? You can do that by calling the cooperative extension. In New York it is Cornell Cooperative Extension. I suspect in New Jersey it's Rutgers Cooperative Extension. Go to local farmers' markets and ask what's in season. When you find out what's in season in what area, plan your meals around it. If you are totally de-seasoned, start with one meal a week when you try to use only seasonal local produce.

Start in the summer when it's easy, but continue it all year, and increase the number of meals as you go—2, 3, 4 meals a week. When you shop in the supermarket, ask the produce manager where the produce you are buying comes from, and keep asking—as was the case when I asked about the tomatoes that came from Holland. Try to buy local organic milk, eggs, cheese and meat if possible. Not just organic, but local. My milk comes from Pennsylvania and New York farmers; my meat—bacon, ham, chicken, lamb, turkey and eggs—comes from a farmer north of where I live. And I have a neighbor who salvages deer from the roadside, so on Friday I have a "Bambiburger." (It's roadkill, but it's quite fresh. It's very local, and it's ecologically sound. Better than letting it rot on the road.)

Most processed products, even those sold in health food stores, contain soy and corn. Not all products labeled "natural" are free of genetically modified organisms. Buy organic, which is not supposed to contain any genetically modified organisms, and check with the health food store to see whether products like "veggie burgers" are labeled as not containing GMO soy.

And finally, join the National Campaign for Sustainable Agriculture in order to influence federal policies that have an effect on whether people are able to buy local produce. If you can't buy local produce, it is not only because nobody's growing it, it's because there are a lot of policies that prevent local farmers from functioning. The campaign and its partners are making huge inroads on the issue of concentration, one of the big issues before us.

Everything about our present food supply tells you that you should just "enjoy" and pay no attention to where what you are eating comes from. But given the present threats to environmental sustainability and farmer survival, trying to shorten the chain between yourself and local farmers may in the end turn out to be one of the most important things you have ever done . . . for yourself, and for the planet.

THE 21st CENTURY TRANSITION
TO SUSTAINABLE ENERGY

William J. Makofske

Introduction

As we enter the 21st century, American society is ill-prepared to deal with the realities of the evolving energy situation. U.S. policy has been based on the concept of cheap, abundant fossil fuel energy; however, in the coming decades, much of our most used fossil fuel supplies will no longer be cheap or abundant. And the cost of "externalities," items not included in the price that we pay for energy, such as environmental degradation, damage to health, economic risk from importing oil supplies from unstable regions, the cost of war and conflict, and climate change, make the present course unsustainable in the longer run.

With our economy almost 90 percent dependent on fossil fuels and nuclear power (U.S. Energy Information Agency), we are increasingly vulnerable to an obvious fact of life: non-renewable sources of energy, in particular, petroleum and natural gas, are rapidly reaching their peaks, the curve describing the maximum rates of production first developed by geophysicist M. King Hubbert in 1956, and may be effectively depleted around mid-century (Campbell, 2001; Deffeyes, 2001; Goodstein, 2004). There is wide agreement on this eventuality, although there is still some debate about exactly when this will happen. With a 30-year projection of oil depletion at constant consumption rates, we do not have until mid-century to act on this knowledge. Once demand exceeds production, prices will rise dramatically, affecting the economies of all nations. The competition for remaining fossil fuel resources also could lead to greater conflict among nations.

Today, the U. S. uses over 20 million barrels of oil per day, about 25 percent of the petroleum produced in the world. Over 60 percent of U.S. petroleum is imported and that percentage is only expected to increase. The current U.S. response to this situation, evidenced in the futile energy plan before

Congress over the past several years, is to increase our production by drilling in Arctic National Wildlife Refuge (ANWR) and, potentially, offshore of several coastal states. The estimated 3- to 5-billion barrels in the ANWR, while a relatively large amount for new discoveries in the U.S., will provide barely one to two percent of U.S. demand over its extraction lifetime of 20 years (Hinrichs and Kleinbach, 2002). Moreover, contrary to what most Americans believe, the oil will most likely find its way to Japan, the easiest transport route, rather than being shipped to the U.S. The situation with regard to U.S. natural gas supply, while not quite as severe, also is problematical (Kopp, 2005). While some gas is imported in pipelines from adjacent countries of Canada and Mexico, continued use may well depend on substantially more expensive and potentially risky liquefied natural gas from unstable areas of the Middle East and from several Asian countries formerly part of the Soviet Union. Moreover, the addition of proposed tanker port terminals around the U.S. to facilitate natural gas imports has met with serious opposition, for good reason. An explosion of a tanker in a port, whether from accident or terrorist activity, could have catastrophic consequences.

The U.S. desperately needs to develop an effective response to the current energy situation before economic recession, caused by rising energy prices, prevents thoughtful investment into viable long-term solutions. When both the laws of science and the marketplace align and point to a powerful emerging crisis, it would be foolish for any government to ignore the inevitable. Yet the Federal government continues to fiddle as fossil fuels deplete and the earth warms, while the real solutions to the crisis are being developed by many state governments, local governments, environmental and community organizations, and individual citizens. These approaches are based on an understanding of how we use energy and involve strong conservation efforts, increasing technological efficiency, and the use of renewable energy. These efforts involve research, demonstration of effective approaches and technologies, and educational efforts so that citizens can competently select from among the many viable options open to them. The following sections provide an overview of some of these solutions.

Using Energy More Efficiently

The U.S. uses energy at roughly twice the per capita rate of almost all other industrialized countries, including Japan and Germany. One could argue that the extraordinary efficiency of these other countries is due to their destruction during WWII, and the subsequent building of a more efficient infrastructure. However, that rebuilding took place a long time ago, and the U.S. has clearly rebuilt much of its infrastructure as well. In the U.S., a transportation infrastructure built on ever larger and inefficient SUVs and trucks, poorly-designed oversized houses in ever-widening suburbs, and a heavily petroleum-dependent centralized agricultural food system, has created an infrastructure of enormous fossil fuel dependence. These systems can and must be gradually changed into efficient ones.

The transportation system in the U.S. is almost entirely dependent on petroleum and will be one of the hardest hit as oil prices rise. While Corporate Average Fuel Efficiency (CAFE) standards increased in response to the energy crisis of the 1970s and 1980s, almost doubling the average mileage of vehicles at that time, average miles per gallon has actually dropped since then. A government study (NAS, 2002) of CAFE standards indicates that using the best technologies that already exist, vehicle energy efficiency may be substantially and cost-effectively increased by 40 percent; the extra cost will be paid back as a result of improved gasoline efficiency over the life of the car. In the past few years, hybrid cars, mostly from Japan, have entered the U.S., and are being successfully marketed. In order to compete, most U.S. auto manufacturers are beginning to offer some models with hybrid technology. This pattern is familiar; in the '70s and '80s, Detroit consistently opposed increasing mileage standards, claiming they couldn't achieve them, but finally met the standards after losing market share to the more efficient imports. The current improvement in mileage efficiency is a welcome change. But given the expected market penetration of new hybrid vehicles, it will not provide a significant drop in petroleum consumption. In addition, the extra cost of the vehicles is barely compensated by the gasoline savings and existing federal tax credits, making this a marginal choice for thrifty-minded consumers. What is needed are gradually increasing mandated CAFE standards that will lift the entire vehicle fleet to around 40 mpg (UCS). The U.S. consumer will adjust to the minor tradeoffs that result: decreasing size and weight, and less powerful engines, as they did in the '70s. Even today, consumers can find standard gasoline-driven cars of similar size, capacity and performance that get twice as many miles per gallon as others.

In recent years, the idea of fuel cell cars as the new technology that will save the inefficient U.S. transportation system has become common. Indeed, most car manufacturers have research programs that are looking at the possibility of fuel cell vehicles. However, because of the many major obstacles to a large transportation fleet of fuel cell vehicles, such a complete shift may be possible in a time frame of 30-40 years, not the 10-20 year shift needed based on a response to declining petroleum supplies.

First of all, hydrogen, the "fuel" of interest for fuel cells, is not a fuel at all. It is an energy carrier, like electricity, and must be made from a real energy source such as methane, coal, solar or wind energy. The manufacture of hydrogen, from any source, involves another step in the energy conversion scheme, and will have significant energy losses and added costs for the conversion devices. Second, the storage of hydrogen in vehicles, as either compressed gas, liquefied hydrogen, or as a metal hydride, is likely to pose difficulties of weight, cost and, perhaps, safety. Third, not only must the hydrogen be produced, it must be stored and distributed. Since vehicles are naturally decentralized in their operation, the equivalent capacity of all of our current gasoline stations must be developed. And finally, the fuel cell itself needs to be improved significantly in terms of its cost, performance, and lifetime. The technical inadequacy or high cost of any one of these will likely prevent the development of a widespread and viable transportation system based on fuel cell technology. The viability of the hydrogen alternative is an increasingly studied and hotly debated issue (see for example, *Solar Today*, May/June 2004; Newell, 2005).

For consumers today, the most viable options are to choose a vehicle based on its energy efficiency, and to put as much pressure as possible on car manufacturers and the government to develop vehicles that are much more efficient and sustainable than our present choices. For others in cities and high-density areas, increased mass transportation in the form of light rail and buses may provide some possible alternatives. However, in many parts of the country, widening suburban sprawl increases the dependence on individually-owned vehicles, expands the miles that must be traveled, and increasingly leads to greater congestion. There is no sign that sprawl is lessening; without good development planning, such as clustering of suburban towns as practiced in Europe, cost-effective mass transportation will be an illusion for most suburban communities in the U.S. Other less energy dependent options such as walking and biking also need good planning to be effective and efficient.

Buildings, which directly consume some 40 percent of the total energy use in this country, can be cost-effectively designed and, in most cases, retrofitted to use much less energy. New construction offers the most cost-effective options. An integrated design approach that uses simple design features for providing daylighting, solar heating, and natural ventilation can have dramatic savings in energy use (Chiras, 2004a, 2004b). Couple design with attention to the building's thermal envelope, the barrier of insulation and air tightness that separates the interior conditioned space from the environment; the efficiency of lighting, HVAC, and appliances; and current average levels of energy use can be dropped dramatically. At the same time, such attention to energy use, if done properly, offers other benefits such as improved indoor air quality and more comfortable indoor spaces. Surprisingly, this can be generally achieved with little extra monetary investment and with excellent pay-back times.

Although improved car efficiency may take several years to achieve, the knowledge and technology needed to build very efficient, cost-effective hous-es is available today, but not widely used. This is shameful, given that over a million new homes are built each year. Among the most effective approach-es to new housing is to provide higher levels of insulation (termed superin-sulation), together with enhanced air tightness offset by controlled ventila-tion. While this may add a few percent to the cost of a house, it often is immediately cost-effective because of the downsized heating and cooling sys-tems that need to be installed. In any case, energy savings quickly pay for any remaining investment.

Attention to room and window placement, and house orientation with regard to the surrounding external environment, can have large benefits as well. For example, placing daytime living spaces on the south side of the house with adequate windows provides daylighting, thus avoiding unneces-sary electricity use in the daytime. Reduced expanses of windows facing east or, especially, west drops unwanted solar gain in the summer, thus minimiz-ing air conditioning costs. Providing adequate overhangs on the south side of the house also avoids unwanted summer gain, while allowing desirable win-ter solar radiation to enter and heat the house. Use of landscaping, especial-ly deciduous trees on the east and west, can block summer sun, while the appropriate use of evergreen species on the windward side can reduce air infiltration in the winter (Moffat and Schiler, 1991; Olgyay, 1963).

A focus on appliance efficiency is another area where all households can achieve significant energy savings. Because of continuing upgrades to appli-ance efficiency standards, newer appliances usually offer major energy sav-ings. For example, the most efficient refrigerators on the market today may use half or less of the electricity of 10- to 15-year-old refrigerators. Refrigerators, freezers and air conditioners are among the most energy-intensive appliances. Since people generally do not discard working appli-ances, the opportunity for major savings occurs when replacing an old appliance. Information on energy efficiency is readily available (NCEEE, EPA). Unfortunately, bad habits abound, like putting the old refrigerator in the basement with a single can of soda in it. Much more education is need-ed so people have a realistic understanding of where their energy comes from, where it's primarily used in their households, and what the true costs of energy consumption are for people's health and the environment.

There is also room for significant savings in energy at the household level based on simple lifestyle changes. These include reducing thermostat tem-peratures at night or when not at home, turning out the lights when the space is not in use, lowering the hot water temperature if above 120 degrees, hanging out the wash to dry in the sun, and taking shorter showers. These actions can have substantial savings if practiced regularly. For those with families not inclined to pay attention to house operating conditions, there is an increasing number of excellent programmable setback thermostats for controlling temperature, and heat and motion sensors for turning out lights.

While energy efficiency and energy conservation are essential for cost-effective energy savings, these strategies can and should be augmented by using sustainable energy sources. Energy efficiency should be done first, as it is normally the most cost-effective approach. Renewable energy is typically more expensive than conservation and efficiency, and thus should be applied after the efficiency gains have been maximized. Today, there is increasing emphasis on renewable energy technologies that can be implemented depending upon specific location and form of energy desired. On a small scale, some of these technologies include passive solar heating, active solar heating, solar hot water, solar electricity from photovoltaics or wind, small-scale hydro, geothermal heat pumps, and biomass in various forms. More centralized and larger scale renewable technologies include concentrating solar power for electricity production, hydropower, tidal and wave power, geothermal power, wind farms, and grid-integrated photovoltaics.

Luckily, the amount of renewable energy in these various forms available from the sun is enormous (all of the fossil fuels represent only a tiny amount of stored sunlight); its lifetime is some 6 billion years, the remaining life of the sun. Nor do we need to get all of our energy from one source; the diversity represented by the full range of solar-related energy sources provides for reliability and resilience. Some regions have greater potential for certain energy sources, and these will dominate their economies. However, the widespread nature and magnitude of direct solar energy make it one of the most important sources. Using local renewable energy resources in an environmentally responsible way can provide an effective road to development for many countries, eliminating the need for importing scarce and increasingly expensive fossil fuels. While many renewable technologies such as passive solar, solar hot water, and wind power are cost-effective today, others such as photovoltaics and centralized solar thermal power require additional research and development to reach maturity. In some cases, policies have been developed to drive the technology into the mass production stage, leading to price reductions that will allow the technology to compete with existing subsidized technologies (Starrs, 2001).

The Transition to Renewable Energy

Renewable energy in various forms can be harnessed to provide a significant amount of energy used in buildings. Major energy loads in buildings come from space heating and cooling and the use of hot water. Electricity is used to run some heating and cooling equipment, but it is also used for lighting and many types of appliances. Each of these uses may be addressed by specific applications of renewable energy.

Passive solar heating is one of the most cost-effective and simple approaches to providing heat for buildings. This approach was known and developed by ancient Greek and Roman societies after they depleted their supplies of wood. Its efficient application to houses today requires initial planning when a house is built. By choosing to place lived-in spaces on the south side, and by putting a greater proportion of the windows on the south side of the house, heating needs may be greatly diminished. All house design is climate dependent, so the discussion below will focus on the temperate and cooler parts of the U.S.; the same principles apply but will have to be modified somewhat in warmer climates.

In the winter, the sun path is low in the southern sky over the entire day, providing direct sunshine into south windows. In most locales in the U.S., one square foot of south facing window will save about a gallon of oil over the heating season (Anderson and Riorden, 1996). However, south windows need overhangs to prevent unwanted solar gain in the warmer weather. More window area is not necessarily better; the area must be sized to the heat loss and thermal characteristics of the house, otherwise overheating or under-heating may occur. As the window area is increased beyond a certain level, thermal performance may be enhanced by adding thermal mass in the house in order to absorb and store the sun's energy for nighttime use. Insulated slabs covered with tile so that the sun's rays are absorbed over the day are one excellent way to provide thermal storage.

Done right, passive solar heating requires little or no extra cost. The number of windows used is about the same as a regular house; they are just distributed differently. Typical south window areas are equivalent to 7 to 12 percent of the total house floor area, and at the lower percentages require no additional thermal mass (DOE). A typical house at 2,400 square feet with 10 percent south window area could save the equivalent of 240 gallons of oil a year. The solar energy is seamlessly integrated into the regular heating system; when the solar gain is inadequate the thermostat automatically turns on the backup heater. There are other savings as well. Daylighting from the windows reduces electrical lighting use. And properly shaded south windows, with reduced window areas on the east and west, will reduce cooling costs.

In addition to south windows, there are a number of other methods of enhancing direct gain into a structure (Mazria, 1979). These include: the Trombe wall, a south-facing mass wall that is glazed and absorbs and stores the sun's energy; solar greenhouses and sunspaces, where excess energy is directed into the larger dwelling; clerestories and skylights, other ways of getting direct sunlight into the living space; and convective approaches, where the wall itself acts as a solar collector. Adding a greenhouse or sunspace, and convective air collectors are relatively easy to do for a retrofit to an existing house.

Solar hot water is another renewable energy technology that offers cost-effective energy savings to households (Gillet and Pine, 2004; Gillet and Vandermark, 2000). Used mostly for pool and domestic hot water heating, there are many designs for such systems (Sklar, 2004). These include batch solar heaters, which are simple enough to be built by most people, as well as fairly complex evacuated tube collectors. However, the most common solar system is based on a flat plate solar collector, where typically antifreeze is circulated through tubes in the collector, and the heat collected by the antifreeze is transferred to water in an insulated tank. This tank then feeds automatically into the regular hot water heater. For non-freezing climates, the design can be simpler, without the need for antifreeze or heat exchangers.

Solar water heaters are not meant to provide all of a family's hot water. However, in most climates, two or three collectors, each 32 square feet in size, will provide most families with 50 to 75 percent of their hot water over the year. Households that use electricity to heat their water will find that solar water heaters are quite cost effective. And as the price of oil, natural gas and propane continue to rise, the demand for these relatively simple devices should continue to grow. In California, Hawaii, and in parts of the Southwest, there is currently a viable solar hot water industry. Solar hot water is also used extensively in other parts of the world, including Japan, Israel, Germany, Turkey, Austria and Greece. With proper incentives, consumer education and some government regulation, solar hot water could make a greater contribution in the U.S. as well.

Another solar technology that has been growing rapidly worldwide at 20 to 30 percent per year is photovoltaics (PV) or solar cells. Similar to the technology for producing computer chips, silicon is processed into a sandwich of positive and negative layers, with the physical boundary between them, called a PN junction, producing electricity whenever sunlight hits it. The technology is long-lived, noiseless, with no moving parts, and currently produces electricity with efficiencies between 7 to 15 percent. From its start in the space program, the technology has taken over various electricity production markets, starting with remote applications for communications and lighting, off-grid housing, and now moving into the grid-connected house and direct grid supply applications.

Placed on the roof, or incorporated into shingles, or as the roof itself, a 4 to 5 peak kilowatt PV system can provide essentially all of a typical home's electrical consumption in most areas of the country. Good electrical conservation measures might reduce the needed size by a factor of two. The key to its recent growth in residences is the concept of net metering (Starrs, Wenger, 1998). In many states, the law requires that utilities connect residential PV producers to the grid, and pay them the retail price for the electricity produced and sent to the grid. When consumers are not producing their own electricity, or not enough of it for their needs, the meter runs forward in the usual way. But when they are producing more than they use, the excess is sent to the grid and the meter runs backward. In essence, the grid becomes the storage vehicle for excess electricity that can be delivered back to the consumer whenever they need it. By eliminating the need for and expense of battery storage, net metering has made PV installations more acceptable and cheaper for consumers. But this by itself has not made the technology viable. The cost of PV, today around $8 to $11 per peak watt installed, is still rather difficult for the homeowner to justify economically. However, many states offer rebates and tax credits that make the homeowner cost acceptable (see below). In addition, the development of a renewable energy credit (REC) market system has spawned companies which provide consumers with a PV system at no up front cost, and guarantees them a monthly payment 10 to 15 percent lower than their current monthly electrical bill over a 15-year payback period. Progressive governments have had little difficulty in providing support mechanisms for PV technology. This is because many of the benefits of the technology do not accrue to the individual using it, but to the society as a whole. Looked at from a larger perspective, it is easier to understand the clear benefits of PV technology, and to justify government involvement in its deployment.

The benefits of PV derive partly from its green environmental characteristics. Providing no air pollution during operation, PV offers areas with significant air pollution a considerable drop in peak pollution concentrations. This is because peak electrical production occurs in the summer during sunny hot afternoons when air conditioning is maximized. Meeting peak demand usually means bringing on-line many smaller peaking generators at considerable extra expense; in many cases, diesel fuel is used which aggravates the air pollution problem and associated health impacts. However, PV offers its own peak production under these same conditions, and can reduce both the extra cost of producing peak power and the extra pollution. In addition, because of its decentralized production, PV can protect the grid from over-loads that occur from peaking, thus reducing the potential of brownouts and blackouts. In other cases, added PV capacity at select locations can delay or reduce the need to expand grid capacity, saving investment capital. As a distributed electrical generation system, PV improves both the reliability and resilience of the transmission system.

In addition to all the above-mentioned benefits, the PV industry brings good paying jobs to the local community, in the form of module production and the installation and maintenance of systems. By producing its own energy, a community recycles its dollars into the local economy, not to faraway states or countries. There is little worry about disruption of supply and price increases. Once they are installed, PV offers lifetimes that are typically 25-30 years, and perhaps even 40 years, without the worry of inflation. For all of these reasons, there is an increasing number of states (now numbering about 20) that offer rebates and sometimes tax incentives to homeowners who install PV on their houses. In New Jersey, the Clean Energy Program is run by the utilities but regulated by the Board of Public Utilities (McGarry, 2004). The program offers a buy down of approximately 60 percent on the total installed price of a PV system. The incentive money is paid directly to installers so homeowners pay only their portion of the installed cost. The program is offered to homeowners, businesses and public entities like schools. In New York State, a similar program offered through NYSERDA provides buy down and state tax credits. California also provides substantial financial incentives (Asmus, 2002), and is in the process of approving a Three Million Solar Roofs Bill, one of the most ambitious efforts in the country. Overall, state and local efforts in this area have far surpassed any federal actions. Subsidized PV and green design are making inroads even among production builders (Gourley, 2002). The web site www.dsireusa.org provides a nationwide listing of renewable energy incentives at the state level.

While solar energy offers many options for producing power, it is by no means the only option. Decentralized wind power, that is, electricity generated by the wind on the customers' side of the meter, just like PV, offers similar benefits and is increasingly subsidized by various states. (Both NJ and NY offer net metering and buy downs similar to PV for small-scale wind energy). Just as PV technology has improved, small wind systems have become dependable and reasonably cost-effective, depending upon the local wind regime.

Wind is classified according to its average speed into seven distinct classes, with 1 being the least and 7 being the highest. Certain areas of the country have excellent winds, while other parts, particularly the Southeast and

Southwest, have less. However, it is difficult to generalize in many regions since wind resources vary considerably, even within a small locale (NREL, AWEA). Areas with class 3 or greater winds have the potential to be very cost-effective, and with subsidies, many class 2 wind sites may be quite good.

There are some hindrances to the development of small wind power. The chief drawback is the need to get local town approval to put towers up that might be 80 to 120 feet high. In rural areas with larger land properties, such as farms and ranches, this is not difficult, but in more densely populated areas, this can be a problem. There is a need to develop uniform siting laws that would simplify the procedure, and set standards for what is aesthetically acceptable.

The siting of large-scale wind farms, sometimes consisting of hundreds of turbines in very visible locations, magnifies these aesthetic concerns for some people and sometimes raises significant controversy (Houlihan, 2003). There are currently proposals for offshore wind farms in Massachusetts, New York and New Jersey that are being debated. While there is little doubt that there should be limitations to the number and location of wind towers, many large-scale wind installations in Germany and the U.S. are, in my opinion, attractive and appropriate to the setting. On the other hand, opponents to wind siting need to weigh the costs of the alternatives to wind, and to realize that coal and nuclear power have numerous impacts on their lives as well, even if they are not immediately visible.

The Transition

There is clearly worldwide movement towards a more efficient and sustainable energy production and consumption system (Sawin, 2004). This is driven in part by concern about depleting fossil fuel reserves, and in part, by the need to reduce carbon dioxide emissions from fossil fuel burning due to global climate change. With the Kyoto Treaty now in effect in almost all of the industrialized countries (with the exception of the U.S. and three other countries), many developed countries are striving to reduce their greenhouse gas emissions. However, in order to stabilize the climate, many scientists estimate that global greenhouse gas emissions will need to drop 60 percent or so, considerably more than the current goals set by the Kyoto Protocol.

It is difficult to predict exactly how and when, but it is clear that the U.S. will be pushed and pulled more directly into the emerging sustainable energy economy. The impetus may come as a shock, a sudden price surge to $100 a barrel for oil or, perhaps, as a severe climate surprise that forces a national response. However, there is a real danger that sudden increases in fuel prices will cause world recession, making it less likely that new investments in energy efficiency and renewable energy will be made. And continued current investments in the wrong energy sources might lock us into an undesirable, and likely bankrupt, energy future. While the transition to renewable energy is inevitable, its smoothness is not. It is clear that other major industrialized countries are taking the transition seriously, developing a competitive advantage in renewable energy technologies (Aitken, 2005; Bihn, 2005).

In the meantime, communities and some states are responding with an array of programs and policies to move us in the right direction. As individuals and communities, we have the responsibility to try to shape federal and state policies that enhance efficient infrastructure and sustainable energy choices. This is most often effectively accomplished by acting collectively as members of groups that educate and lobby elected officials, that try to set new standards and goals for organizations that we participate in, and that encourage our schools to take leadership positions in the coming energy transformation.

As individuals, we are responsible for our own energy use and the choices that we make. This involves the responsibility to become educated about the possible alternatives, and to actually see that they are implemented in our own lives. Applying the approaches and technologies described in this article to our houses and our society, using integrated systems design methods and common sense, can substantially reduce our energy footprint. From my own experience, with attention to design details, a new home in the New York metropolitan region can be designed and constructed that incorporates energy efficiency and tested solar technologies for little extra cost of a house not so fitted. Coupled with life-style changes that address conservation, it is possible to reduce fossil fuel energy consumption in a home by 90 percent compared to average household consumption, savings that have been successfully achieved today. Widespread implementation of similar approaches to houses, and innovative applications of efficiency and renewable energy to transportation, food production and industry, may succeed in making the significant greenhouse gas reductions needed to stabilize the climate. We owe no less to the future.

References

Aitken, D. W., "Germany Launches its Transition," *Solar Today*, American Solar Energy Society, March/April 2005, pp. 26-29.

Anderson, B., Riorden, M., *The New Solar Home Book*, 2nd edition (Brick House Publishing, Andover, MA, 1996).

Asmus, P., "California Governments Go Solar," *Solar Today*, American Solar Energy Society, November/December 2002, pp. 42-45.

AWEA, American Wind Energy Association: www.awea.org

Bihn, D., "Japan Takes the Lead," *Solar Today*, American Solar Energy Society, January/February 2005, pp. 20-23.

Campbell, C. J., "The Oil Peak: A Turning Point," *Solar Today*, American Solar Energy Society, July/August 2001, pp. 40-43.

Chiras, D., *The New Ecological Home* (Chelsea Green Publishing Company, White River Junction, VT, 2004a).

Chiras, D., "The Energy Efficient Home," *Solar Today*, American Solar Energy Society, September/October 2004b, pp. 22-27.

Deffeyes, Kenneth, S., *Hubbert's Peak: The Impending World Oil Shortage* (Princeton University Press, Princeton, NJ, 2001).

DOE, Department of Energy: www.eere.energy.gov

EPA, Environmental Protection Agency: www.epa.gov. Energy Star Program.

Gillett, D., Pine, N., "Turn Up the Heat," *Solar Today*, American Solar Energy Society, Nov/Dec 2004, pp. 36-39.

Gillett, D., Vandermark, H., "Solar Hot Water," *Northeast Sun*, Northeast Sustainable Energy Association, Vol. 18, No. 3, Fall 2000.

Goodstein, David, *Out of Gas: The End of the Age of Oil* (W. W. Norton & Company, New York, 1974).

Gourley, C., "Production Builders Go Solar," *Solar Today*, American Solar Energy Society, January/February 2002, pp. 24-27.

Hinrichs, R. A., Kleinbach, M., *Energy: Its Use and the Environment* (Harcourt College Publishers, Orlando, FL, 2002).

Houlihan, M., "Controversy on the Cape," *Northeast Sun*, Vol. 21, No. 2, Northeast Sustainable Energy Association, Spring 2003, p. 11.

Kopp, R. J., "Natural Gas: Supply Problems Are Key," *Resources*, No. 156, Resources for the Future, Washington, DC, Winter 2005.

Mazria, E., *The Passive Solar Energy Book* (Rodale Press, Emmaus, PA, 1979).

McGarry, J., "New Jersey Charges Ahead with Renewables," *Northeast Sun*, Northeast Sustainable Energy Association, Spring 2004, pp. 27-29. See also www.njcleanenergy.com

Moffat, A. S., Schiler, M., *Landscape Design That Saves Energy* (William Morrow and Company, Inc., New York, 1991).

NAS, National Academy of Sciences, *Effectiveness and Impact of Corporate Average Fuel Economy (CAFE) Standards* (National Academy Press, Washington, DC, 2002).

National Council for an Energy Efficient Economy: www.nceee.org

Newell, R. G., "The Hydrogen Economy: Laying Out the Groundwork," *Resources*, No. 156, Resources for the Future, Washington, DC, Winter 2005.

NREL, National Renewable Energy Laboratory: www.nrel.gov

NYSERDA, New York State Energy Research and Development Authority: www.nyserda.gov. See also www.powernaturally.org

Olgyay, V., *Design with Climate: Bioclimatic Approach to Architectural Regionalism* (Princeton Univ. Press, Princeton, NJ, 1963).

Sawin, J. L., "Mainstreaming Renewable Energy in the 21st Century," Worldwatch Paper 169, Worldwatch Institute, Washington, DC, May 2004, pp. 1-76.

Sklar, S., "Selecting a Solar Heating System," *Solar Today*, American Solar Energy Society, September/October 2004, pp. 42-45.

Solar Today, May/June 2004 issue, published by the American Solar Energy Society. Hydrogen articles include: "The Right Future," Larson, R. W., pp. 20-23; "Can We Get There?" Hock, S., Elam, C., Sandor, D., pp. 24-27; "Can We Afford It?" Mann, M. K., Ivy, J. S., pp. 28-31; "Hydrogen?" West, R., Kreith, F., p. 46.

Starrs, T., "Green Tags: A New Way to Support Renewable Energy," *Solar Today*, American Solar Energy Society, July/August 2001, pp. 24-27.

Starrs, T. J., Wenger, H. J., "Net Metering and Small-Scale Renewables," *Solar Today*, American Solar Energy Society, May/June 1998, pp. 32-35.

UCS, Union of Concerned Scientists: www.ucsusa.org

U.S. Energy Information Agency: www.eia.doe.gov

Epilogue

SELF REFLECTIONS OF
SUSTAINABILITY WORKERS

Introduction to the Epilogue

SELF REFLECTIONS
OF SUSTAINABILITY WORKERS

Trent Schroyer

THOSE WHO WORK EVERYDAY on the problems of sustaining communities and ecologies have strong reactions to their work. Here are two very different responses to this vocational calling. The first, by Michael Edelstein, signals realism as the appropriate virtue, while Gene Bazan's reflections are a deconstruction of the entire project of sustainability and an affirmation of a self-activated subsistence.

Edelstein records his experience as the head of a county non-profit environmental organization and what he calls a dystopian of actual sustainability practice. This is a record of the realities confronting an on-the-ground sustainability worker.

Edelstein's practice is especially concerned with the problems of contaminated communities. The inertia of institutions and other constraints that surround these poisoned communities amount to a reality check of the constraints confronting sustainability enthusiasts. He recalls a range of horrendous situations he has faced in the U.S. and Russia.

Describing in detail his sustainability work in Orange County, New York as the head of Orange Environment (OE), he tells the story of dealing with the attempted expansion of a local landfill and reflects that leadership is central to sustainability processes. A plan to expand the landfill required the organizing of expert witnesses over a two-year period who provided evidence that even a minor expansion would have physical and psychological health impacts. Despite the testimony, the county prevailed and planning for an expansion began. However, a chance discovery uncovered information that showed the expansion was illegal. Later litigations resulted in a victory for OE, and the county's ecology, because the landfill planners had presumed an illegal usurpation of wetlands.

What Edelstein is suggesting is that the maintenance of the status quo is dominant and the possibility of participatory learning is difficult to achieve, even when it makes obvious environmental sense.

Gene Bazan's essay also records the experience of an on-the-ground sustainability worker, although his conclusions are quite different than

Edelstein's. He discusses his startling realization that the unsustainable lifestyle is not new—in fact there is evidence this has been human practice for the past 12,000 years. What we are actually doing is summed up by Daniel Quinn as totalitarian agriculture, messianic expansionism, and the "Great Forgetting"—or the extirpating of cultures that could subsist on their own, absent the outside pressures of Western civilization.

This leads Bazan to reexamine the sustainability mind-frames he now believes are flawed and holistically deficient. For example, he argues that much of the justification for sustainable development is made in terms solely bounded by efficiency—without ever incorporating into the equation the concept of "savings." What good are sustainable development initiatives, if not tied to some larger goal of reducing overall consumption? Bazan's analysis is a sharp critique of professional sustainability experts' illusion that they are designing for sustainability and he shows systematic ambiguities in their analytic frameworks.

For Bazan, sustainability arguments assume the core of the neo-liberals' economic justifications for their policies—the self-justifying response to all criticism that "There Is No Alternative," or TINA. Sustainable development is a new use of TINA, one which, with zeal and righteousness, turns away from other possible approaches. This systematic misunderstanding is illustrated in the 'sustainability' story of a brand of ice cream created so rainforest tribes "can earn a living." This ignores the fact that these people's relationship with the Earth is a subsistence one, they are integrated with their environments in ways the Western mind, obviously, cannot apprehend. They are not "earning a living." The West sees these as people in need of saving, Bazan says, but without ever examining the basis of that response. It assumes a context that allows no other frame than that provided by Western civilization.

He concludes that sustainability is the name moderns give to what we have destroyed. It is the name for our disease! It looks to him that what we are trying to mean by "sustainability" is actually something more like subsistence, the art of living within the realm of local ecological necessity. The answer for Bazan is not so much the imposition of sustainable development as a new framework for life for everyone—including indigenous peoples. Rather, the West's salvation may lie in the adaptation of not the sustainable model, but the subsistence model, in which economy and business fall wholly within the larger circle of community, rather than the other way around. The environment, rather than being an issue tagged onto our lifestyle, subsumes all.

THE REALITIES OF
SUSTAINABLE PRACTICE:
CONSTRAINTS AND OPPORTUNITIES
IN ORANGE COUNTY, NEW YORK

Michael R. Edelstein, Ph.D.

IT WAS NO ACCIDENT that most of the environmental faculty at Ramapo College of New Jersey ended up living to the north in Orange County, New York. Stretching along the New Jersey Highlands region on its southern border to meet the Skunymunks and Hudson Highlands and then the Hudson River fjord, in the opposite direction the county stretches west to the Delaware and Neversink Rivers just beyond the majestic old Shawangunk Ridge. The center of the county is the broad Wallkill River Valley with its scenic rolling hills and filled primordial sea. The Ramapo River arises in Orange County and makes a southern run to the college, bonding the two. Beyond its diverse scenery, Orange County had maintained its integrity of place in a way lost by much of northern New Jersey. It was a beautiful and affordable place to live.

Against this variegated green pallet was set the realities of human occupation. Already by the time I moved there in 1975, there were evident threats to this landscape. They came in the many forms of unsustainable human land use practice, themselves reflections of the inherent unsustainability of the social and economic foundations of the county and its forty-some communities.

Constrained versus Utopian Sustainability

Over most of my thirty years in the environmental program at Ramapo College, I have served as a community environmental leader in Orange County, for the past twenty five years as President of a non-profit, tax exempt organization, Orange Environment, Inc. (OE). OE was never a conventional environmental organization, having a deeper mission focused upon a vision for a sustainable county. We have created an important model for local action, the intermediate scale organization—regional enough to see the big picture but close enough to the ground to understand the importance and integrity of place. Much of our work has been at the grass roots, organizing and training local action groups. OE is similar to other sustainability organizations in seizing available opportunities to create successful models for sustainable practice. At the other end of the scale, we take on the big environmental issues that many sustainability groups pretend don't exist, challenging government, industry and organized crime.

To us, these concerns are complexly linked; how can we create sustainable communities without confronting contamination of our air, water and soil?

As a result, we have less followed what I call the "utopian model" of sustainability—the perfection of our world through adopting better (i.e., sustainable) ways of doing things—than what can be termed the "constraints model." The latter rather more dystopian approach recognizes that all communities are constrained from achieving sustainability by their past (and current) mistakes, embedded often invisibly in the state of the local environment. These constraints represent "collateral damage" from the ways that we have sought to solve our problems of life, particularly under an ideology of growth and progress. They are sins of past practice. Thus, we have dotted our landscapes with ecological landmines (incubating disasters waiting to explode) in the form of landfills and dumping sites, underground pipes and tanks, industrial lagoons, polluted areas, and other wastes both concentrated and dispersed. Many of our ecosystems have become places of biomagnified contaminants that affect life all the way up the food chain, often reaching humans as well. These are legacy issues that strike to the heart of sustainability rhetoric. Unless and until these toxic legacies and degraded ecosystems are addressed, no truly sustainable future can be achieved. At a minimum, an effort must be made to stop continuing practices that add to this adverse legacy.

The broad adoption of sustainability as a goal stems from the influential 1987 report of the U.N. Commission on Environment and Development, referred to often under the name of the commission's chairwoman, Gro Harlem Brundtland. The most cited framework for defining sustainability stems from the portion of the Brundtland report that addressed intragenerational equity, our bequeath to future generations. The formulation is simple and seemingly irrefutable—namely our obligation to leave to future generations the same possibilities for a good life that we ourselves have enjoyed. My work has given me an unhappy perspective on this legacy. For the prospects for creating a sustainable society, even at the community level, are unbelievably constrained by the toxic legacy that we have already released. Even as we focus increasingly on the horrendous prospects for a terrorist release of some toxic substances in a populated place, our reality is that we have already done just this on a massive scale worldwide.

I tend to think of Brundtland's challenge as one of three equity issues demanded by a move toward sustainability. Beyond this "intergenerational equity," we must also attend to "intragenerational equity" by solving issues of inequity in consumption and addressing environmental injustice. And we also must address "interspecies equity" by ending our wholesale slaughter of biota and loss of diversity through contamination, changed conditions that exceed adaptive range and habitat destruction. To address these three inequities of sustainability requires a fundamental shift in social and economic relationships expressed in dramatically different ways of relating to the natural world we live in. Environmental legacy issues are constraints to equity across these three frames.

Nevertheless, sustainability is easily rationalized as a utopian ideal. In my own field of environmental psychology, for example, my colleagues routinely consider how to create more livable and supportive environments without taking into account environmental legacy constraints. Therefore, when I was asked to write a chapter on contamination for a recent review of the field, I entitled it "Contamination: the Invisible Built Environment" (Edelstein 2002). It is human to focus on the positive artifice that we construct; contaminants are invisible both physically and psychologically. We prefer not to deal with them. Even good practitioners are easily swayed to look at the prospects for sustainable change without taking into account the legacy problems. Given my experience, I do not have that luxury.

My work as an environmental psychologist centers on environmental contamination as an impediment to sustainability and is summarized in my book *Contaminated Communities*, now out in its second edition (Edelstein 2004b). I am interested in how people cope with life in contaminated environments.

I have witnessed some unbelievable constraints in my work. I have visited people living in regions having every stripe of contamination problem. In many cases, the groundwater was polluted, erasing a key resource that is becoming ever scarcer. In other cases, I have seen the soil poisoned in ways that made it infertile or unavailable for planting. Many times my body has ached with the air pollution that people live with on a daily basis. I have visited with populations exposed on a regular basis to dangerous levels of radiation. These problems have rendered homes and communities marginal as places to live.

Sometimes entire ecosystems are contaminated. For example, the scenic Middle Fork of Little Beaver Creek in Ohio is contaminated for a thirty mile stretch with the pesticide Myrex. Flooding in the river has assured that all the floodplains are contaminated, meaning that gardens, farms, and farm animals are off limits. Every fish and every animal and bird in this system is exposed to Myrex over the course of its life. The chemical bioaccumulates up the food chain to make local foods off limits for consumption. Some residents themselves revealed body burdens of Myrex. Such contaminated ecosystems are found across America and the globe. I have seen them in Triana, Alabama, a classic environmental injustice site, in the pristine Skagit River Valley in Washington, and in the plutonium-contaminated areas of the Ural Mountains in Russia. When I return home from my travels, I find the PCB-contaminated Hudson River and DDT in the Wallkill River that I have long championed.

We do not usually have the luxury to erase places and to start over. I wrote the original draft of this chapter sitting in an apartment in Volgograd, Russia. As the former Stalingrad, this city was completely destroyed in World War II. When Stalingrad was erased from the face of the earth, Stalin's vision of the perfect city was constructed by German prisoners of war. The resulting long narrow city stretched along the western shore of the Volga, creating in perfect scale close relationships between the river on one side and farmland on the other and between workers' neighborhoods and the major industries spaced periodically along the shoreline.

Stalin may not have been thinking about how quickly a toxic legacy can be created. Volgograd combines a large population with chemical and industrial plants that have long bathed the population in high amounts of air pollution. Until fairly recently, it was a center for the production of chemical weapons. And, Volgograd illustrates another type of historical legacy based upon massive environmental change. The erection here of the huge hydroelectric dam on the Volga River caused major ecological and hydrological disasters. And just to the south another huge public works project connected the Volga and Don Rivers, mingling two very different biotic reservoirs.

It is both a large world and a small one. Long before "globalization," we had globalized environmental contamination. In some form, every problem found in one place is mirrored in another. To a remarkable degree, virtually every problem I witness somewhere else exists back home in Orange County. Suggested is a basic rule—if specific mistakes are unique, the type of mistake is remarkably universal. As a result, a concentrated local effort to create sustainable communities must address serious constraints even as it seeks sustainable opportunities. To speak now of charting a sustainable future without having a clean slate means that we must pick our way (sometimes literally) between already armed and dispersed environmental land mines.

Orange County

The story of my sustainability work in Orange County, New York reveals many attempts, some successes and much unfinished business. Much of the effort has been directed at erasing old constraints to sustainability while trying to prevent new ones. The addition of new sustainable practices is a luxury that has taken a long time to reach. Through OE, I have worked on scores of issues—environmental health, industrial pollution, water, prehistoric resources, sewage—to name a few. Rather than ramble over a long list, I will focus on one sample issue—waste.

In 1979, I observed my first Administrative Hearing as the representative of the Town of Goshen's Environmental Review Board. This occurred in the neighboring Town of Wawayanda, where shady proponents sought to create a state permitted facility for using human wastes as agricultural fertilizer (specifically to fertilize sod). In the next six months, I learned the administrative law process and came to understand how citizens are disadvantaged in technocratic decision making. I also witnessed the efforts of the citizens to organize within and outside the process to protect their community. In the end, the facility was permitted and went on to quickly fulfill every fear that the supposedly irrational citizens had expressed about the allegedly rational plan. It was eventually closed and made into a State Superfund Site. The Wawayanda experience offered me a basic foundation in regulatory and community dynamics surrounding the siting and impact of hazardous facilities (see Edelstein 1986/87). The same summer, I visited the Love Canal contamination site in Niagara Falls and interviewed residents engaged in a battle for relocation. Love Canal was a primer on toxic victimization.

Waste issues have been central to my life ever since, and as a key focus of OE, a key area for transformation toward sustainable alternatives. At the heart of this transformation is the shift from waste disposal to materials cycling. In the former instance, the focus is on hidden entropy, spent materials that must be removed from view. In the latter case, the focus has shifted to an ongoing stream of materials cycling through different stages of use and recovery.

The Case of Solid Waste

In 1980, Al Turi Landfill, Inc., which operated a landfill in Goshen, sought a permit from New York State to dramatically expand. The original landfill had begun as a small town-scale dump in the late 1960s. Acquired by the Genevese-Tieri crime family in the early 1970s, the facility grew in scope, taking garbage from across the New York region. Now it wanted to grow more. As Goshen's liaison to the community, it was my job to work with our attorney and consulting geologist to stop the project. In the resulting administrative hearing, I found myself conducting research and then taking the stand as an expert witness to testify about the psycho-social impacts of the landfill expansion. Although Goshen lost and the landfill expanded, the hearings proved a major learning experience. Moreover, my organizing effort ended with my becoming the president of a local grass roots group in Goshen that, within a few years, led to my co-founding and assuming the presidency of OE, a countywide non-profit, tax exempt organization. My experience underscores a second principle of sustainability. Leadership is necessary to launch and maintain community sustainability efforts. They do not happen on their own.

Turi landfill and the adjacent Orange County landfill remained key issues for OE through the new millennium. These landfills received massive amounts of solid waste from across the region, including some toxic industrial wastes (both would become New York State Superfund sites). They grew to massive heights along the banks of the Wallkill River, where leachate (contaminated liquid) polluted the river and its sole source aquifer, the Southern Wallkill Valley Aquifer. Turi, in particular, emitted large amounts of methane gas. Orange County Landfill was visibly bulging out as too much weight was placed on slippery soils; it threatened to block the entire Wallkill river. Over time, despite improved technology, I saw little improvement in the state of these landfills. They needed to go. They were the antithesis of sustainable.

More generically, the concept of waste also needed to go. In the early 1980s, I floated a plan for Orange County to begin a massive recycling effort to ease its demand for landfilling. Monthly meetings of interested parties attempted to advance this effort, but county officials gave only lip service. When they instead wheeled out plans for a massive expansion, it became necessary to stop speaking softly and to pull out the big stick. In 1986-87, OE intervened in an administrative hearing for the landfill expansion before the New York State Department of Environmental Conservation (NYDEC). Our intervention asserted that the county did not need the expansion because it could instead rely upon a combination of waste avoidance, reuse and recycling. The administrative law judge accepted this issue for adjudication. Now I had to figure out how to prove our case. We brought two superb expert witnesses to the hearing. Trish Ferrand, then the head of the New Jersey Organization of Recyclers, and Brenda Platt, a young waste process engineer from the Institute for Local Self Reliance. The Institute was responsive to my request for support to cover the expenses for both witnesses.

I got to cross examine all the witnesses in the lengthy hearing that stretched over two years. But the most exciting point was when I put our witnesses on the stand and proved two points. First, with Trish's help, I showed the success of New Jersey's contemporary court-mandate that some communities reach fifty percent recycling within one year. My point was that it is feasible on short notice to reach recycling of half the waste stream using existing methods of separation and marketing. Second, with Brenda's help, I showed that emerging innovations promised a variety of technologies that could move from 50 percent to 90 percent and maybe beyond. In sum, if Orange County were willing to spend on recycling a portion of the approximately $50 million it was willing to spend on a landfill expansion, it would not need to expand the landfill. In 1987, the administrative judge concurred; the permit was denied by the Commissioner. It appeared, for the moment at least, as though recycling and waste reduction had prevailed. In a white paper based upon our testimony, OE established the concept of a 90 percent waste recycling goal for Orange County.

However, the state heeded the county's claim that at least a smaller landfill expansion was required immediately. Citing an "emergency," the state circumvented its procedures and prepared to grant a permit. OE, at this point had enough clout to enter the negotiations. With the help of community data we collected, showing adverse physical and psychological health impacts, we forced a series of concessions in the permit, making it perhaps the most community-friendly permit in the state's history. Among the concessions, Orange County had to pass and enforce a mandatory recycling law under the guidance of a new recycling coordinator. Steve Preiser, a graduate of our Ramapo Environmental Program, was hired for this position and began a serious effort to establish a working program.

Despite continuing parties-of-interest meetings under the permit, the County and OE never established a common path. The County spent $52 million to hastily build a modest facility that was doomed to failure. In our thinking, this facility should only be used to accept materials under the transition to our 90 percent goal and thereafter only the 10 percent of the waste stream that could not be recovered. The County instead had every intention to use this facility to keep up garbage business as usual rather than to shift toward waste cycling.

It was only by serendipity that OE's Attorney Scott Thornton and I learned an unsettling piece of information. OE had intervened in state hearings to block yet another project, the Orange County Water Loop. The water loop would have been the largest new water project in the country. Our opposition was primarily based on the grounds that the water loop would induce growth beyond our carrying capacity. I had testified against permits for filling wetlands sought by Orange County from the U.S. Army Corps of Engineers. After the hearing, Scott and I stayed chatting with the administrator and counsel for the Corps region. Scott asked why the county had been granted the permits it needed to fill wetlands in order to build the expansion landfill. The response from the officials was startling. They asked, "What landfill expansion?"

It was thus that we learned that Orange County never applied for permits required to build the expanded landfill atop regulated wetlands. Instead, they gambled that no one would learn that the $52-million landfill project had filled federally-protected wetlands illegally. Or, more accurately, they had feared that their request for permits would attract our attention and we would block the project. But now that the landfill was built and the money spent, they were apparently sure no one would call their bluff. Had Scott not asked the right question when he did, we might never have known.

In 1990, we captured everyone's attention when our notice of intent to sue the county under the Clean Water Act became public. As we proceeded to mobilize to bring this action, reasoning that the contamination of the aquifer and river occasioned by the landfill created a public interest that we must serve, the County prepared to fight us. Over the next ten years and three administrations, OE fought a sustained legal battle to prevent the landfill from ever being used and to force repair of the damage done to the wetlands. In this case, the major value of the wetlands was their serving as a screened conduit for recharge of the principle aquifer. In 1999, with OE finally on the verge of a clear court victory, Orange County settled the case, agreeing to pay our nearly million dollars in costs, to forgo any effort to ever use the landfill, and to pay for their errors by establishing a $750,000 fund to promote protection and recreational use of the Wallkill River (we selected the Orange County Land Trust to receive and manage this money). Orange County, however, refused to fix the aquifer and agreed only to a re-landscaping of the unused landfill (Thornton and Edelstein, 1999).

At the cost of nearly destroying OE, which diverted a decade of effort to fundraising for the lawsuit and was subject to sustained vilification for blocking use of the landfill, we had closed the illegal expansion and ended County landfilling efforts. It took ten years of total involvement and exhaustion. Numerous other issues fell by the wayside. But we prevailed.

Setbacks and Successes

A number of other setbacks and successes occurred over this time in our war against constraints. These are illustrative of what I have elsewhere referred to as the one step forward, two steps back nature of sustainability action (Edelstein, 2004a).

In the later 1980s, Al Turi Landfill was given a permit extension that included a backdoor expansion. The reason was that a garbage incinerator permitted in Dutchess County, New York had no place to take its ash wastes. Turi was allowed to build a special ashfill section and accept the material from Dutchess. OE challenged the state for not requiring an environmental impact statement for this project. We argued that incinerator ash is a hazardous material because it is contaminated with heavy metals, dioxin and furans. We also argued that the failure to disclose Turi as the waste site for the ash during the incinerator's permit hearings had deprived Orange County residents of the right to participate in those hearings. Dutchess County was able to burn its trash knowing that the toxic residues would come to us. Not only was this environmentally unsound, but it violated norms of environmental justice, where your dumping occurs in somebody else's backyard. OE spent all available funds to bring these arguments before the state Supreme Court only to be dismissed.

Second, even in the midst of our landfill lawsuit battle, the County realized that its landfilling days were numbered. A vacuum was created that national waste companies rushed to fill. The brother of powerful U.S. Senator Alphonse D'Amato appeared as a representative for a firm named American Refuel, which sought backing to build a garbage incinerator. Although originally promising in the late 1970s and early 1980s at a time when the problems with landfilling were just becoming understood, incineration had been successively diminished by the experiences of the 1980s. Incineration competes with materials recycling and recovery. It is very expensive. And, as we knew from our Turi experience, incineration creates hazardous materials (dioxins and furans) and concentrates toxic metals, to be either dispersed through the stack or remain in the incinerator ash, which comprises some 15 percent of the waste stream. OE successfully beat back the project before an investment was made in the application.

Third, with the cessation of the state permit to use the expansion landfill, the County fired the recycling coordinator and cut back its efforts. As a result, the County program has never saved more than 15 percent of the waste stream from landfilling, a fraction of what it can achieve. For a period of time, even this minimal achievement was at risk.

At the same time, with its existing landfill blocked from use, Orange County developed a comprehensive plan to find a new landfill site. On a Monday morning, the local paper carried a front page map showing 17 sites under consideration. County residents rose in revolt. OE worked with residents from all the threatened communities with the result that the new landfill plan was withdrawn.

The County, blocked from incineration and landfilling, next opted to practice the same unethical practice as Dutchess County. Beginning in the early 1990s, the County's trash was exported to Pennsylvania landfills that had been opened to accommodate New York and New Jersey's penchant for generating waste. The new Solid Waste Plan of the mid-1990s indicated an intent to build no more landfills. The County would now wash its hands in waste disposal and handle only shipment to other sites. While pleased that the county had abandoned landfilling and incineration, OE could not accept waste export as a permanent solution. We continued to advance our policy of 90 percent waste avoidance and cycling as an alternative. If waste export was necessary, it should occur for only materials that could not be salvaged from the waste stream.

Conclusion

This description has touched only on a few of OE's many projects and areas of work. But it illustrates that considerable energy must be devoted to addressing the toxic legacy if these constraints to sustainability are to be relaxed. OE's goal is to educate, empower, organize, and facilitate a shift toward sustainability. It seeks to promote social learning. Sustainable communities must be, above all else, mutual learning communities where a serious effort is made to gain experience, assess impacts, and share information for mutual edification. Communities must be in a perpetual state of learning if they are to become sustainable. In this regard, colleges, as well as community organizations, must serve as models (See Edelstein, 2004b).

In his classic analysis of scientific change, Kuhn argued that shared views of realities are hard to change; it takes a true anomaly that cannot be explained by the old system to support a paradigmatic revolution (Kuhn, 1962). Short of such a "crisis," the old way of explanation hangs on and the problems are dismissed. In just this way, modernity has denied problems of the environment, energy, soil and food, of the degradation of the landscape, of the drying up and pollution of the waters, of the permanent displacement of so many people, of the spread of desserts, the loss of habitats, the shrinking of biodiversity, etc.

Much has been written about the post modern era and the shift to what Beck called the "risk society," a realm in which the joys of progress become spoiled by the realization of all the ways it has sabotaged our health, security and happiness (Beck, 1992). Presumably, those living in this risk society will be relatively open to paradigmatic change.

My own work has some interesting implications for a discussion of how we create a transformation toward a sustainable society. In my studies of victims of contamination, I have confirmed Beck's thesis time and again, finding people from all walks of modern life who have come to view themselves as victims of toxic contamination and who are subsequently transformed by their situations to an orientation of fear. If my water is polluted, how do I know if water elsewhere is polluted? How do I know if my food is safe? How do I know all the exposures I have had to contaminants and what the effects might be? Will I die of cancer because of this? The paradigm, with all of its assumptions about life, quickly disintegrates.

But what strikes me most in my work is that these victims almost invariably have been forced into this transition by events not under their control. Until faced with their changed circumstances, they were engaged in modern life, not the risk society. My work clearly demonstrates how fixed people are with their high-consumption, high eco-destructive lifestyle; it is normal life for the affluent and the desired life by the poor. In short, it is vastly premature to conclude that moderns have entered into a new phase of post modernity because they fear the consequences. Just check the ratio of SUVs to hybrid vehicles in the parking lot.

How then do we create a shift toward sustainability? Do we wait for contamination and other disconfirming factors to convince and coerce people toward change? Do we educate? The answer in both cases is yes. But my work in Orange County makes clear one of Kuhn's basic rules of paradigmatic change. Even convinced that modern ways are destructive, no change will occur until the new paradigm is defined, understood and accepted. Our existing approaches to achieve this definition fail because our ways of decision making readily defeat such change. New "third paths" are required. OE illustrates such paths in our innovations in community control and decision making and in our outside the box thinking about technological development.

As an example of a third path, I developed a project eight years ago as part of my work as the head of the Mayor's Advisory Committee for the Port of Newburgh, New York. The project combined two approaches toward empowering the community to consider proposals to revitalize and rebuild the port using the profits from a temporary project to barge New York Harbor dredge spoils up the Hudson River to the port, where the wastes would be transferred to train for its journey to an eventual disposal site. To consider this proposal, we first created an open "collaborative process" that brought together diverse local residents and other stakeholders, including the owner of the project. Under the direction of this collaborative process, a Sustainability Planning and Impact Assessment was to be undertaken. This generic impact statement for the port would compare alternatives, including those informed by sustainable practices. This process takes advantage of federal, state and local impact assessment regulations to create a "sustainability forcing mechanism" by infusing mandated assessment with sustainability tools. Although the Newburgh project dissolved in community conflict, the SPIA remains as a promising third path approach (See Edelstein, 1999, 2004b).

To conclude, we must view sustainability as a descriptor for a new social paradigm that will replace modernity. As the successor paradigm, it must be fleshed out in multiple ways and paths connecting the social world we live in to this new framework must be created. An enormous amount of visionary work rests in our hands now. We are increasingly in a position to show the bankruptcy of the unsustainable modern period. We need to clarify where it is we go instead. Serious legacy problems from this period will remain a burden. These legacies are constraints, but not a reason not to move forward. Rather, they make it vital that we create ways to not enhance the problems we face even while we try to solve them.

Postscript

The lack of real progress in this sustainability context, just as in the others OE has addressed, prodded me to recently accept the nomination as the Democratic candidate for Orange County executive in the November 2005 election. As I write, I have plunged into the electoral process full force. I am testing a further issue for sustainability, namely the extent to which it can be achieved from the grassroots or requires top down assistance from government leaders. My assumption is that I will be able to smooth the transition to sustainability because of my position.

References

Beck, Ulrich, *Risk Society: Towards a New Modernity* (Newbury Park, CA, Sage. 1992).

Edelstein, Michael R., "Sustaining Sustainability," pp. 271-292 in Geoff Chase and Peggy Barlett (Eds.), *Strategies for Sustainability: Stories from the Ivory Tower* (Boston, MIT Press. 2004a).

Edelstein, Michael R., *Contaminated Communities: Coping with Residential Toxic Exposure*, Second Edition. 2004b.

Edelstein, Michael R. "Sustainable Innovation and the Siting Dilemma: Thoughts on the Stigmatization of Projects Good and Bad." *Journal of Risk Research*, Vol. 6, No. 1. 2003.

Michael R. Edelstein, "Contamination: the Invisible Built Environment." In Robert Bechtel and Arza Churchman, (Eds.) *The Handbook of Environmental Psychology* (New York, John Wiley and Sons, 2002, pp. 559-588).

Edelstein, Michael R., "The Challenge of Implementing Sustainable Planning in a Troubled American City," pp. 37-60 in Maria Tysiachniouk and George McCarthy, *Towards a Sustainable Future: Environmental Activism in Russia and the United States—Selected Readings* (St. Petersburg, Russia, Publishing Group of the Institute of Chemistry, St. Petersburg State University, 1999).

Edelstein, Michael R., "Disabling Communities: The Impact of Regulatory Proceedings." *Journal of Environmental Systems*, Vol. 16, No. 2, 1986-87, 87-110.

Kuhn, Thomas, *The Structure of Scientific Revolutions* (Chicago, University of Chicago Press, 1962).

Thornton, Scott Esq. and Michael R. Edelstein, Ph.D., "Citizen Enforcers or Bothersome Meddlers? A Plaintiff's Perspective on the Orange County Landfill Case," *Environmental Law in New York*, 10, 6, June 1999.

World Commission on Environment and Development. *Our Common Future; The World Commission on Environment and Development* (New York, Oxford University Press, 1987).

FROM SUSTAINABILITY
TO SUBSISTENCE

Gene Bazan, Ph.D.

Introduction

The topic of sustainability can cause confusion and angst. Proponents of living more lightly feel charged with righteous indignation at the low state to which humans have brought the planet. Activists among us follow one of two courses: we charge ahead with solutions, or we level charges against the enemy—corporations, government bodies.

On the other side of our wagging fingers lies the vast majority of Americans whose reactions range from open hostility to confusion. Doesn't the Bible permit us to subdue and conquer the earth? Hasn't our own President urged us not to let terrorism interfere with our lifestyles?

I've charged ahead with what I thought were solutions, and was probably equally adept at finger wagging. Having been at this for 25 years or so, a doubt of sorts has crept into my mind. At first it was vague—I wondered whether we were making any headway on things.

Sure, some indicators were improving but, on examination, I felt we "first worlders" were claiming shallow victories. Yes, we had community recycling programs, but on the global scale we were shifting the waste burden of industrial pollution to other countries—oil development to Siberia, gold mining to Papua New Guinea, cattle ranches to the Amazon rainforest.

About eight years ago, my vague unease enjoyed a brief remission on reading Mathis Wackernagel and William Rees' book, *Our Ecological Footprint*. Here, I thought, was a sturdy indicator of sustainability. In my enthusiasm, I wrote a proposal to the Environmental Protection Agency to apply Ecological Footprint Analysis (EFA) to the three instruments of city planning: the comprehensive plan, the zoning ordinance, and the building code. While the proposal didn't go anywhere, it did raise a few questions about EFA in my own mind.

My vague unease turned to vertigo during Christmas of 1999 after read-
ing Daniel Quinn's *Beyond Civilization* and Story of B. Quinn shook my
Western mindset to its roots. I had been pushing back the historical horizon
of Western development hoping to find the threshold before which
Westerners were sustainable. I pushed it back to Fernand Braudel's
Mediterranean at the outset of the 17th century, to Imperial Rome and
Ancient Greece, but could go no further back than the ecological collapse of
the Fertile Crescent, something that looks a lot like what is now happening
in places as diverse as California's San Joachin Valley, the Aral Sea area, many
parts of northern and western China, and sub-Sahel Africa.

Quinn's work pushed back the threshold of sustainability to roughly
12,000 BP. Wanting confirmation of his lay account, I investigated a few key
anthropological and archeological sources and concluded that Quinn's story
couldn't be rejected! That is, it was plausible. In short, my fellow Westerners,
we have 12,000 years of practice in living the other way. For moderns, living
sustainably is beyond our grasp. We have forgotten how.

Six Observations on Sustainability

Consequently, I have become skeptical of the sustainability framework. I
wonder whether it can deliver. I make six observations that get to the core of
my doubts.

Observation 1

In 1997, the Brundtland Commission Report, *Our Common Future*, cata-
pulted the concept of sustainability into widespread, even popular, discussion. Within a short time, intellectuals recognized its signature phrase, sustainable development, for what it was—an oxymoron. Nonetheless, an entire
intellectual and business enterprise rose up to advance its cause. The sustainable indicators movement came into being, and residents of one city after
another undertook studies on how to measure their city's sustainability.

Our language was profoundly affected. Figure 1 shows the shift in mean-
ings of the root "sustain" from before to after the Brundtland Report.
Instructive here is the elevation of definitions 5 and 6 to slots 2 and 1, respec-
tively. These two definitions capture the conflict inherent in the term "sustainable development." Environmentalists wanted to protect the basis for
providing the necessities of life. Developers wanted to keep the economic
juggernaut going. For example, sustainable agriculture has not generally been
about ecological agriculture, but about keeping industrial agriculture going.

A particular framework, the three-circle model, became dominant (top of
Figure 2). A few (some biologists and environmentalists) subscribed to the
bottom version of this framework.

Figure 1. Shift in the Meaning of the Root: Sustain

Older Dictionaries (1913-1972)	Recent Dictionaries
1. to provide with the basic necessities of life	1. to hold up or bear from below
2. to bear a burden or charge	2. to keep in existence (constant effort sustained the project)
3. to experience or suffer injury	3. to support, bankroll, underwrite (donations sustained the museum)
4. to keep a person (mind, spirit) from giving way	4. to keep up, encourage the spirits of (he sustained her through the crisis)
5. to keep going (as a conversation)	5. to endure, survive, tolerate, weather
6 to supply with food and drink, or necessaries of life	6. to suffer loss or damage (he sustained a terrible injury)

My first observation is that the framework is so muddy as to allow little progress toward its program.

For starters, consider the phrases in popular use: sustainable economy, sustainable community, and sustainable environment. What can these mean? If sustainability is a property of their collective overlap—the bulls-eye at the center—then you cannot export this property to the periphery. Therefore, using these phrases leads one to believe that the implicit model is not three intersecting circles, but rather three separate circles (and three separate paths).

Which brings us to the second problem: treating sustainability as something you arrive at after balancing one sector against another, what economists call tradeoffs. In sustainability, you do not trade off the economy against the environment. But that's what we have been doing, and we already know who wins. Sustainability is about meeting the criteria in all sectors simultaneously. This requires creative design. By contrast, tradeoffs exist in a mental model where the three circles are separate!

Having said this, I think the framework can be redeemed by rotating our attention 60 degrees—from the sectors to their intersects—and to the three questions implied by the framework: Q1, Q2, Q3.

Observation 2

My second observation is that modern western culture focuses on Q1 (efficiency, green or eco-efficiency). Q2 and Q3 are culturally invisible to us. We

Figure 2. Sustainability Framework Shift

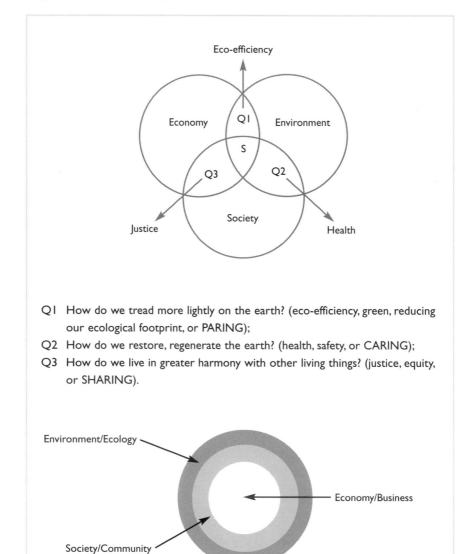

Q1 How do we tread more lightly on the earth? (eco-efficiency, green, reducing our ecological footprint, or PARING);
Q2 How do we restore, regenerate the earth? (health, safety, or CARING);
Q3 How do we live in greater harmony with other living things? (justice, equity, or SHARING).

Note: Intersection labels from a report by New Jersey Future, "Measures and Means. Background Paper: Leadership Conference on Indicators for Sustainable Development in New Jersey," May 8, 1997.

owe this analysis to C.V. Seshadri, an Asian Indian scientist, who reminds us that we in the West focus on Q1, or Carnot efficiency (after the French mathematician Nicholas Carnot [1796-1832] who sought to provide a rational basis for improving the steam engine [Watt: 1736-1819]).

We focus on Q1 because we are heirs to the invention of the heat engine. Heat engines became emblematic of progress. Cultures without these were judged to be "inefficient" or "backward."

We coupled the efficiency mantra with fossil fuels in a market that does not price non-renewables or externalities. This has the effect of removing corrective feedback loops. We've designed our economy such that every dollar we spend efficiently combusts some part of the earth.

This arrangement is perverse in a second way: we eat up our efficiency gains through the greater consumption enabled by what economists call the price effect and the income effect. What Amory Lovins calls "factor 4" or "factor 10" technology, which would reduce our impacts to one quarter or one tenth of the present, ignores the prospect that more efficient appliances alone are insufficient if we merely use our savings to consume more. For example, consider making our cars more gas efficient. We save money. We buy more gas and bigger cars and drive farther. GM is working on hybrid vehicle engines to improve overall fleet efficiency. Guess where they are starting: with SUVs.

In addition, we have unhinged energy extraction from another invention, market pricing. To this day, few economists talk with physicists. Economists still think that when the price of oil goes up, this will call forth more oil exploration. No price will call forth more oil if it takes more oil to recover the oil than the amount you get! Ditto for other forms of energy. H.T. Odum reminds us of another facet. Authentic sustainability in energy requires that you produce solar panels with solar power, not fossil fuel.

ECO-efficiency is the green version of efficiency. It does little to repair the damage, because it, too, is based on the same fallacy. You will find this in the hydrogen fuel cell propaganda. It is the modern variant of nuclear energy from the fifties: energy too cheap to meter. Folks, if it is too cheap to meter, it will not find a market producer. In addition, regardless of how cheap it is, if it produces greenhouse gases, we are back to global warming.

Note that the Ecological Footprint, as good an indicator as it is, is NOT an indicator for sustainability, but only for eco-efficiency. It remains largely in the camp of Q1.

In addition, EFA itself has one tricky implication easy to overlook that none of its enthusiasts, to my knowledge, has mentioned:

Ask yourself: What is required to reduce our Ecological Footprint? Not just green development, whatever that may mean, but development that replaces old energy consumptive dinosaurs. Thus, whenever a green shopping center, a green industrial park, or a green car fleet comes into being, to achieve a reduction in total EF, we must retire an old shopping center, an old industrial park, or our old fleet of cars. Otherwise, we cannot mathematically reduce our EF. Thus, proposals for eco-development must also contain proposals for un-development.

If you get that, do you get the following? Since every American on average adds 24 acres to our Ecological Footprint, to reduce our EF we have to reduce the number of Americans. Moreover, as soon as a Mexican crosses the border, his footprint quadruples from 6.25 to 24 acres. When an Asian Indian emigrates, her footprint climbs from 2.5 to 24 acres. Dare we think of reverse migration? Exporting Americans to Mexico and India? This is factor 4 and factor 10 eco-efficiency.

In short, resolving Q1 using EFA cannot be attained without confronting the growth mantra head-on, both economic growth and population growth. We are not doing this. Instead, we are urging *global* development. If the entire world could achieve our level of development, we would require four Planet Earths to supply our collective requirements (sustainably, of course).

Observation 3

We name places by what we have destroyed or lost. Near my house there is a street called Orchard Drive. The orchard has long been replaced by housing. Even had it survived, the farmer could not have competed with the flood of cheap apples and apple juice concentrate from China.

Likewise, I suggest that our use of the term "sustainability" reflects something of the same kind of thinking. Contrary to the marketing hype surrounding eco-friendly products and green lifestyles, I think we use the term to recall a past beyond memory—when we used to live that way. We try to remember, but we can't. We have destroyed this past. We have largely expunged it from memory.

More to the point, and this is my third observation, sustainability is the name we moderns give to what we have destroyed. It is the name for our disease. We are unable to live sustainably, and this inability, for Westerners, goes back 12,000 years. Therefore, it is not surprising to me that we have not witnessed any real movement toward sustainability during the past 15 years or so that this term has been in widespread use.

What we have done instead is "learn up our disease." We have become proficient at describing our symptoms, the causes, even possible treatments. We gather at forums, international summits, and in classrooms to talk about our disease, its gravity, and the consequences if nothing is done. But, somehow, we have managed to escape cure. Instead, we push ahead, gas pedal to the floor, maintaining our present lifestyle. We make slight changes at the margin—USDA's latest food pyramid is urging us to eat more fruit and vegetables, without condemning their importation from Chile and New Zealand, or cross-country via truck from California industrial farms.

Observation 4

The alternative to sustainability looks more and more like what Veronika Bennholdt-Thomsen and Maria Mies call *subsistence*. And that is my fourth observation: that ONE alternative to sustainability looks more and more like what we had in its multiple expressions 12,000 years ago in the West, and what we have been busily extirpating ever since: subsistence.

Not that I feel qualified to speak about subsistence. Nonetheless, I hear voices speaking from the past. I hear my grandfathers, both peasants from Europe. I hear my graduate students in Ghana whose parents were subsistence farmers. I hear the !Kung of the Kalahari, the Aborigines of Australia, the Indians and Inuits of North America, the Siberian tribes, the Mayans who melted into the forest after their civilization collapsed, the Hoplite farmers who went back to the land after the Mycenean Empire disintegrated.

Civilization, and for us, Western civilization, has extirpated subsistence cultures from the face of the earth, one after another. This practice started 12,000 years ago in what is now the Middle East, spread north and east to Asia, and north and west to Europe, and has continued to this day. For a gut-wrenching account of this extirpation in modern times, see *Late Victorian Holocausts* by Mike Davis.

In his popular accounts, principally *Story of B* and *Beyond Civilization*, Daniel Quinn posits the conjunction of three practices that came together, reinforced one another and led to the juggernaut that we now call Western civilization. These three practices were: totalitarian agriculture, messianic expansionism, and the Great Forgetting—extirpating cultures that could subsist on their own outside Western civilization.

Our modern versions of these three practices are industrial agriculture, global markets and free trade, and mass media entertainment. (For compelling archaeological and anthropological confirmation, check out Price, Douglas and Gebauer, *Last Hunters—First Farmers*.)

In embracing subsistence, it is important to recognize that subsistence is not necessarily sustainable. Polynesian islanders exterminated many species of mammals and denuded landscapes as they moved from one island to another (see Kirch, *On the Road of the Winds*). The Tikopians were one exception among this group (see Raymond Firth, *We, the Tikopia*).

Observation 5

Our hubris as Westerners has allowed us to conclude that subsistence is an unnatural state, an animal state, a less desirable state, a state that befalls peoples who are without the advantages of civilization. Our disgust for such peoples shows up in our language: barbarians, Neanderthals, heathens, lost souls, peasants, Indians, even indigenous people—in short, any who may follow some way other than the *one way* of Western civilization.

So, my fifth observation is that we have strapped our minds around the thought that "There Is No Alternative"—TINA for short. We have frozen our thinking. As a farmer friend of mine says, "We've become as dumb as stumps." Our solutions take odd forms. Ben and Jerry's created Rainforest Crunch ice cream so that rainforest tribes can "earn a living." But they had a living before Rainforest Crunch. What we really want is for them to earn a living our way, so we can rip off their trees and nuts without paying for the damage we have done and will do.

Likewise with botanical species ripped off for drugs. Earlier, oil ripped off in the Middle East by the Seven Sisters. During the Spanish conquest of South America, the ripping off of gold and silver to fuel the purchase of spices from the east. Before this, the Roman plundering of North Africa for grain to support the same cheap grain policy we follow today.

Our cheap food policy has an important secondary effect: it makes subsistence uncompetitive by flooding local markets with cheap corn and grain produced with fossil fuel. Thus, blue corn in Mexican peasant villages is undercut by cheap U.S. corn, and this pauperizes local farmers, who then migrate to the cities and across the border looking for work.

This denial of alternatives invades us where we live: try raising chickens in your urban backyard—assuming you have a back yard. Many urban and suburban zoning codes do not allow the keeping of farm animals. Try digging your own well, or composting your own waste, or keeping your own garden. Many municipalities prohibit such remainders of subsistence. In short, you have been subjected to modern enclosures—you have been denied access to land.

Observation 6

Bennholdt-Thomsen and Mies have written a challenging book titled *The Subsistence Perspective*. In it, they pose a model that, coincidentally, also has three "sectors": household economy/reciprocity, community or tribe, and commons. We can easily map these onto the three-circle sustainability model.

My sixth observation is that their subsistence model suggests three pathways out of the sustainability thicket: from economy to household economy and reciprocity, from society to community or tribe, from environment to commons. We can then look at this as a design exercise and ask ourselves how we would describe the intersect of these three pathways—the bulls-eye of subsistence cultures:

First, such cultures live lightly on the earth. These live at ambient temperature, and do not have to rely on heat engines. Examples include American Indians, Inuit, Australian aborigines, and the !Kung.

Second, such cultures would be based on decentralized and localized self-determination within the limits of necessity, not a hierarchy supported by global strip mining of the earth, as our industrial agriculture does.

Third, such cultures would share their place as a commons. Bennholdt-Thomsen and Mies assert that "Wherever commons have existed over time they were protected, cared for, used, regulated by a distinct local community of people for whom these commons constituted the basis for their livelihood" (p. 152). This stands against the present corporate practice of creating global commons for the purpose of enclosure and exploitation. It also stands against Garrett Hardin's *Tragedy of the Commons* scenario.

Fourth, to care for the commons, subsistence cultures create a moral economy. This means that production and consumption must be seen as one act. Consumption whose waste cannot be handled internally cannot be morally produced. Thus, using Yucca Mountain as a repository for nuclear waste would not be morally acceptable. Nor landfilling garbage.

Fifth, these cultures replace the ordinary economy by the Household Economy and introduce reciprocity to replace what Bennholdt-Thomsen and Mies call "mechanical mass solidarity." Mass solidarity argues that everybody has an equal share of the booty from the plunder of the environment. This is usually called social justice. By contrast, reciprocity arises out of "all members of society feeling an obligation to conduct their economic affairs in such a way that others are able to survive, drawing assurance from the knowledge that their own basis of existence will always be safe. Social behavior is thus determined not by competition but by reciprocity."

Sixth, such commons-based economies are necessarily local. Not large power plants or large waste recycling centers but small, local facilities, devices and arrangements.

Seventh, labor becomes unwaged. The trap we have gotten into is that almost all of us depend on wage work, but we cannot rely on it. We get laid off, without any alternatives. One alternative: begin to take up again as our daily activity the means and condition of our own subsistence.

Eighth, such cultures conduct their business in the taro field rather than the assembly chamber.

Ninth, we would expect such cultures to exhibit persistence and stamina in the face of change.

To give some flesh to the subsistence framework, I end with a few examples:

- Religious tribes which have walked away: the Anabaptists sects (Amish, Mennonites and Hutterites), who are largely farmers.

- Still existing indigenous tribal groups.

- The Israel kibbutz during their formative period between the 1930s and 1960s. Daniel Gavron has written an insightful account of their origins and transformation from successful subsistence-based settlements to their present atrophied condition as largely residential enclaves. Another Israeli, Yaacov Oved, an Israeli and member of a kibbutz, looked to the early commune movement in the U.S. for insight.

- Back to land groups (The Farm, in Tennessee, which still exists though in atrophied form).

- Community Supported Agriculture, originally based on an idea of Rudolf Steiner.

- Tribal groups: Ecology Action in California.

- Co-housing, following the Danish model, represented to some extent by Ecovillage Ithaca outside Ithaca, New York.

- Eco-villages, including many in Europe, Natures Spirit in South Carolina (now defunct), Cobb Hill in Vermont, Gaviotas in Columbia.

- At the "national" level, Cuba, especially since the fall of the Soviet bloc, which forced Cuba to look within for its food, fertilizers, traction power. That is, Cubans had to live within their own commons, and their own limits of necessity.

In his book, *Ecology of Commerce*, Paul Hawken defined sustainability as the midpoint between destruction and regeneration. It strikes me that the subsistence perspective is one of these regenerative strategies. For those of us who think about these matters, I raise the challenge: isn't it time to raise the bar?

Reading List

Where Has Western Civilization Gone Wrong?

Bower, Bruce, "Cultivating Revolutions: Early Farmers May Have Sown Social Upheavals from the Middle East to Europe," *Science News*, February 5, 2005, Vol. 167 No. 6.

Davis, Mike, *Late Victorian Holocausts: El Nino Famines and the Making of the Third World* (Verso. London, 2001).

Eisenberg, Evan. *The Ecology of Eden* (Alfred A. Knopf. New York, 1998). Great look at the origins of the Eden myth. Incredibly well researched. Final chapters on solutions weak.

Gimbutas, Marija, *The Civilization of the Goddess: The World of Old Europe* (Harper. San Francisco, 1991). Quinn put me onto her. An amazing, if challenged, "account" of human culture in middle Europe before agriculturalists invaded from Middle East.

Hartmann, Thom, *The Last Hours of Ancient Sunlight* (Harmony Books. New York, 1999).

Quinn, Daniel, *Story of B* (Bantam. New York, 1997).

Quinn, Daniel, *Beyond Civilization: Humanity's Next Great Adventure* (Harmony Books. New York, 1999).

Subsistence Cultures

Bennholdt-Thomsen, Veronika and Maria Mies. *The Subsistence Perspective* (Zed Books. London, 1999).

Firth, Raymond. *We, the Tikopia: A Sociological Study of Kinship in Primitive Polynesia.* (American Book Company. New York, 1936).

Gavron, Daniel. *The Kibbutz: Awakening from Utopia* (Rowman & Littlefield Publishers. Lanham, MD, 2000). Insightful look at the transformation of Kibbutz from successful, subsistence-based settlements to fragile, marginal communities today.

Jacob, Jeffrey. *New Pioneers: The Back-to-the-Land Movement and the Search for a Sustainable Future* (The Pennsylvania State University Press. University Park, PA, 1997). We don't have kibbutzim, but this is a good look at our white American history with subsistence. Jacob at least owns up to the core of sustainability: getting off fossil fuel!

Kirch, Patrick Vinton. *On the Road of the Winds: An Archeological History of the Pacific Islands Before European Contact* (University of California Press. Berkeley, 2000).

Krech, Shepard III. *The Ecological Indian: Myth and History* (W.W. Norton and Company. New York, 1999). Excellent, excellent, excellent. Well-footnoted.

Lee, Richard B. and Irven DeVore (eds.), *Kalahari Hunter-Gatherers: Studies of the !Kung and Their Neighbors* (Cambridge University Press. Cambridge, MA, 1976) (2nd printing, 1978). Wonderfully full look at the !Kung based on research going back to the 60s.

Nerburn, Kent. *The Wisdom of the Native Americans* (Novato, California. New World Library, 1999). Great quotes from the American Indians!

Price, T. Douglas and Anne Birgitte Gebauer, *Last Hunters—First Farmers: New Perspectives on the Prehistoric Transition to Agriculture* (School of American Research Press, Sante Fe, New Mexico, 1995). Supports Quinn's tale of Western descent.

Schweitzer, Peter P., Megan Biesele, and Robert K. Hitchcock (eds.), *Hunters & Gatherers in the Modern World* (Berghahn Books. New York, 2000). Proceedings of the Seventh International Conference of Hunting and Gathering Societies. This pointed out to me that the extirpation of subsistence cultures continues to this day.

Yaacov Oved, *Two Hundred Years of American Communes* (Transactions Books, 1988). Of course, the whole eco-village movement (and possibly some co-housing groups) can be seen as the heir to the utopian community experience in this country, cast in an environmentalist hue. Best web site is http://www.gaia.org. Co-housing is at http://www.cohousing.org.

On Sustainability

Bartlett, Albert A., "Reflections on Sustainability, Population Growth, and the Environment" in the journal *Population and Environment*, Vol. 16, No. 1, September 1994, pp. 5-35. Excellent.

Bowers, C.A., *Educating for an Ecologically Sustainable Culture* (SUNY Press 1995). A deeply intellectual, but difficult read. Two organizations actually doing education at the university level are University Leaders for a Sustainable Future (http://www.ulsf.org) and Second Nature (http://www.secondnature.org).

Chambers, Nicky; Craig Simmons, Mathis Wackernagel. *Sharing Nature's Interest: Ecological Footprints as an Indicator of Sustainability* (Earthscan Publications Ltd. London, 2000).

Fodor, Eben, *Better Not Bigger: How to Take Control of Urban Growth and Improve Your Community* (New Society Publishers. Gabriola Island, BC, 1999). Upbeat, can-do approach focusing on the "society" circle of sustainability pretzel. Solutions may not stand up to critical scrutiny, and the premise that cities are sustainable, ecologically, is not addressed.

Funes, Fernando; Luis Garcia, Martin Bourque, Nilda Perez, Peter Rosset (eds.), *Sustainable Agriculture and Resistance: Transforming Food Production in Cuba* (Food First Books, Oakland, CA, 2002). Distributed by LPC Group, 22 Broad St., Suite 34, Milford, CT 06460.

Hansen, Jay, www.dieoff.org for a look at prospects after the end of oil.

Hawkin, Paul and Amory Lovins, *Natural Capitalism*.

Oelschlaeger, Max, *Caring for Creation: An Ecumenical Approach to the Environmental Crisis* (Yale University Press, New Haven, 1994). Good analysis of the religious take on sustainability and the importance of religion's institutional strength. However, recommendations are not up to the analysis.

Ponting, Clive, *A Green History of the World* (Sinclair-Stevenson Ltd. London, 1991).

Seshadri, For reference, see Claude Alvares' chapter on "Science" in Wolfgang Sachs, *The Development Dictionary* (Zed Books. London, 1992).

Wackernagel, Mathis and William Rees, *Our Ecological Footprint* (New Society Publishers, Philadelphia, 1996). Focus is on the intersect of "Environment" and "Economy" in the sustainability pretzel, what I call Q1: "How do we live more lightly on the earth?" (green, eco-efficiency, or PARING). See also web sites: http://www.rprogress.org/newprojects/ecolFoot.shtml the main site. If you want to explore what your own footprint is, play around with their "Footprint Calculator for Households" by clicking on the Swedish calculator: http://www.demesta.com/ecofoot.

Wiezsacker, Ernst von; Amory Lovins; Hunter Lovins, *Factor Four: Doubling Wealth, Halving Resource Use* (Earthscan. London, 1997).

ABOUT THE AUTHORS

Frederique Appfel-Marglin received her B.A. and Ph.D. in anthropology from Brandeis University. She has done field research among subsistence agricultural communities of coastal Orissa in India and, since 1994, has begun a collaboration with indigenous non-governmental organizations in Peru and Bolivia, part of her activities as the coordinator of Centers for Mutual Learning, a project funded by a MacArthur grant. With the Peruvian NGO PRATEC, she has created a Research and Community Center in the Peruvian High Amazon where she has started a program in Biocultural Diversity. She was a research advisor at the World Institute for Development Economics Research (WIDER) in Helsinki, an affiliate of the United Nations University, from 1985 to 1991. As part of that endeavor she and Stephen A. Marglin formed an interdisciplinary and international collaborative team that has produced three books on critical approaches to development and globalization.

Kathryn Pyne Addelson, the Mary Huggins Gamble Professor of Philosophy, History of Science, is a co-founder of the Center for Mutual Learning at Smith College in Massachustetts.
The Center endeavors to connect the academic world to communities in the United States and South America. Dr. Addelson's work centers on how professional expert knowledge needs to change in order to learn with, and from, local communities. Working with Frederique Appfel-Marglin, they have developed new epistemological theories and concepts, which help to form a bridge between learning in the academy and learning in the community.

Dr. Michael R. Edelstein has been a professor of Environmental Psychology at Ramapo College of New Jersey for more than thirty years, where he has taught Environmental Studies as part of an interdisciplinary faculty. His private research has heavily focused on the social and psychological impacts of environmental contamination. In 2004, Westview Press published a second edition of Dr. Edelstein's *Contaminated Communities: Coping with Residential Toxic Exposure,* subsequently nominated for the C. Wright Mills

Award. His work on local sustainability involves his presidency of Orange Environment, a non-profit environmental organization based in Orange County, New York, whose work over the past twenty plus years runs the gamut of environmental and sustainability issues and activities. Dr. Edelstein holds a Ph.D. in Social Psychology from SUNY Buffalo.

Robert Engler is widely recognized for his interpretations of American political institutions and thought, as well as the political economy of energy resources and technology. His book, *The Politics of Oil*, has been credited with sparking Congressional investigations in the United States, probes and reports by various government agencies, the press and television and political action by consumer, labor, environmental and nationalist movements in many countries. His book *The Brotherhood of Oil* continued the analysis and appraised such counter forces as the environmental movement, OPEC, and the new economic order of the developing regions. He has won the Sidney Hillman Foundation Prize for political writing. His "Many Bhopals—Technology Out of Control" appeared as a special issue of *The Nation*. He has taught at the Graduate School of the City University of New York, Sarah Lawrence College, Princeton University and Columbia University.

Thomas Golodik has worked in the field of communications in the public and private sectors and has held appointed public office. A former teacher, newspaper reporter and editor, he currently works as a writer for a large environmental company, specializing in water and wastewater projects. He holds a master's in public administration from Kean College and is currently working on a degree in Environmental Studies at Ramapo College of New Jersey.

Joan Dye Gussow is the Mary Swartz Rose Professor Emerita and former chair of the Nutrition Education Program at Teachers College, Columbia University. She is currently chair of the board of Just Food and a member of the Board of Overseers of the Chefs' Collaborative. She has served on various public, private and governmental organizations, chairing the boards of the National Gardening Association, the Society for Nutrition Education, and the Jesse Smith Noyes Foundation, and serving on the Food and Nutrition Board of the National Academy of Sciences, the FDA's Food Advisory Committee and the National Organic Standards Board. Her books include *The Feeding Web*, *The Nutrition Debate*, and *Chicken Little, Tomato Sauce and Agriculture*. Her most recent book, based on the lessons she has learned from 40 years of growing her own, is *This Organic Life: Confessions of a Suburban Homesteader*.

Alanna Hartzok is co-director of the Earth Rights Institute, a civil society organization working for economic justice and peaceful resolution of conflicts. She presented the 2001 E.F. Schumacher Lecture, which was published as "Democracy, Earth Rights and the Next Economy." That same year she was a candidate for Congress in the Ninth District of Pennsylvania. In 1993, she initiated tax reform legislation, working with state Senator Terry Punt and his staff to guide it through Pennsylvania legislative hearings to nearly unanimous passage. She is one of several people featured in *Planet Champions: Adventures in Saving the World—New Paths to Peace, Prosperity & Human Rights*, authored by Jack Yost. She is a United Nations ECOSOC NGO Representative for the International Union for Land Value Taxation based in London and as such is working to develop land value taxation policy trainings worldwide.

Wayne Hayes, professor of City and Regional Planning at Ramapo College, holds a Ph.D. in City and Regional Planning from Cornell University. He has served a number of community and environmental organizations as an advocate planner, and was a founding trustee and member of the Jersey City Economic Development Commission for ten years. His long-term academic interests include regional and urban development that today approximate sustainable development. He also serves as president of the Ramapo College local of the AFT, which sharpens his administrative and political skills, and continues his long-term advocacy of the interests of those stakeholders often disadvantaged by existing institutional practices.

Dave Lewit is co-chair of the Alliance for Democracy's "Campaign on Corporate Globalization and Positive Alternatives," and coordinator of the citizen document "A Common Agreement on Investment and Society." A social psychologist, he conducted research and taught at the Universities of Massachusetts, Michigan, Hawaii, and New York/Stony Brook, and has consulted on organization matters with corporations, nonprofits, and public institutions. He is also co-chair of the Boston-Cambridge Alliance and edits the organization's publication, *Dispatch*, and actively seeks localization solutions in the Boston area.

William Makofske is professor of Physics at Ramapo College of New Jersey where he teaches in the environmental physics and energy areas. He has installed four wind systems with students at the college, and is currently involved in studying the potential of small wind systems in New Jersey. Dr. Makofske received a Ph.D. in physics from Rutgers University and has been a faculty member at Rutgers, the University of Minnesota, and Columbia University. He has focused on the environmental impacts of energy production, computer modeling of environmental systems, alternative energy sources, radon, and global climate change. He has been a visiting scientist at the Building Research Establishment in England and at Argonne National Laboratory in Illinois. In 1999, he received a Fulbright Fellow in alternative energy and environmental protection in Germany.

Stephen A. Marglin is the Walter S. Barker Professor of Economics at Harvard University and research adviser at the World Institute of Development Economics Research, a research and training institute of the United Nations University which began operations in1985 in Helsinki.

Peter Montague founded and publishes *Rachel's Environment and Health News*, http://www.rachel.org/home_eng.htm. Before that he published the *New Jersey Hazardous Waste News* from 1982-1985. He has also directed the Institute of Natural Resources at Princeton University and worked with Greenpeace. In 1980, he co-founded the Environmental Research Foundation in New Brunswick, where he still holds the position of Director. He has recently become the executive editor for the *Garden State EnviroNews*.

Ward Morehouse is president of the Council on International and Public Affairs, a research, education, and advocacy group working on environmental and social justice issues. He is a co-founder of the Program on Corporations, Law and Democracy and former chairman of the Intermediate Technology Development Group of North America. Morehouse has written or edited some 20 books, including *The Bhopal Tragedy, Abuse of Power: The Social Performance of Multinational Corporations, Worker Empowerment in a Changing Economy, Building Sustainable Communities*, and *The Underbelly of the US Economy*. He is a founder of the International Coalition for Justice in Bhopal and Communities Concerned about Corporations, a network of workers, community activists, victims of industrial disasters, and socially concerned investors fighting corporate power.

Wolfgang Sachs is ex-president of German Greenpeace and senior research fellow at the Wuppertal Institute for Climate, Environment and Energy. He is author of *Greening the North, Planet Dialectics, Global Ecology Editor, Development Dictionary,* and *For Love of the Automobile*. He is co-editor of the Society for International Development's journal *Development* in Rome. He is Visiting Professor of Science, Technology and Society at Penn State.

Trent Schroyer is Professor of Sociology-Philosophy in the school of Theoretical and Applied Science at Ramapo College. He attended the Earth Summit in Rio in 1992 and participated in the first three sessions of the Commission on Sustainable Development (CSD) at the United Nations as an NGO representative. He has been program coordinator for the counter G-7 summits in the United States in 1990, 1997 and 2004. He edited *A World that Works: Building Blocks for a Just and Sustainable World.*

Vandana Shiva is a physicist, ecologist, activist, editor, and author of many books. In India Dr. Shiva has established Navdanya, a movement for biodiversity conservation and farmers' rights. She directs the Research Foundation for Science, Technology and Natural Resource Policy. Her most recent books are *Biopiracy: The Plunder of Nature and Knowledge* and *Stolen Harvest: The Hijacking of the Global Food Supply.*

Michael Shuman, an attorney and economist, is vice president for Enterprise Development for the Training and Development Corporation (TDC) of Bucksport, Maine. He has written, co-written, or edited six books, including *Going Local: Creating Self-Reliant Communities in the Global Age.* He has written over a hundred articles on community economics, federalism, foreign policy, and philanthropy. In recent years Shuman has been promoting the concepts in *Going Local* through a variety of projects, including creating a small-business venture capital fund in New Mexico; launching a community-owned company in Salisbury, Maryland; and building the Business Alliance for Local Living Economies (BALLE).

Siddhartha is the founder of Fireflies Ashram and director of Pipal Tree. He writes regularly for Indian and international newspapers and journals, and lectures widely all over the world on issues related to culture, ecology, and sustainable development. His essays have been published in *Lettres du Gange* and a book, *The Birdwoman,* appeared in English in 2003. He was the international coordinator of INODEP-International Paris, a Center of alternative education founded by Paulo Freire.